Capital, Saving & Credit in Peasant Societies

Capital, Saving & Credit in Peasant Societies

Editors: Raymond Firth
& B.S. Yamey

Routledge
Taylor & Francis Group

LONDON AND NEW YORK

First published 1964 by Transaction Publishers

Published 2017 by Routledge
2 Park Square, Milton Park, Abingdon, Oxon OX14 4RN
711 Third Avenue, New York, NY 10017, USA

Routledge is an imprint of the Taylor & Francis Group, an informa business

Library of Congress Catalog Number: 2006052675

Library of Congress Cataloging-in-Publication Data

Capital, saving, and credit in peasant societies / Raymond Firth and B.S.
    Yamey, editors.
        p. cm.
    Originally published: Chicago: Aldine Pub. Co., c1964; with subtitle:
        studies from Asia, Oceania, the Caribbean and Middle America / essays
    edited with two general essays, by Raymond Firth and B. S. Yamey.
    "Preliminary drafts of most of the essays in this book served as data papers
        for a symposium on Economics and Anthropology at Burg Wartenstein,
        Austria, on August 21 to 27, 1960"—P.
    ISBN 978-0-202-30918-7 (alk. paper)
        1. Agriculture—Economic aspects. 2. Agricultural credit. 3. Developing
    countries. I. Firth, Raymond, 1901-2002. II. Yamey, Basil S.
HD1415.F5   2007
338.109172'4—dc22   2006052675

ISBN 13: 978-0-202-30918-7 (pbk)

PREFACE

With the exception of an historical sociologist to whom economics is no novelty, the authors of all the descriptive essays in this volume are social anthropologists, some with and some without formal training in economics. All have been impressed by the significance of a knowledge of economic processes and relationships for the understanding of the social relationships with which they are primarily concerned. Conversely, they have been impressed by the necessity of an understanding of social relationships for the interpretation of observed economic situations and behaviour. This book has been planned to present detailed studies, drawn from a variety of peasant societies, to illustrate this theme of the inter-action between social and economic factors, and the nature of the contribution of social anthropology to its study. It is also planned to show the interest and significance of such anthropological studies for students of the economics of 'under-developed' countries.

To delimit the scope of the individual essays, it was decided to confine them within an area of some specific, though broad, group of related topics. Since the formation and management of capital are central to the economic functioning and growth of all but the simplest societies, we have chosen 'capital, saving and credit' as the appropriate band of topics, leaving it largely to the individual authors to decide where, within this band, to place the major emphasis in their essays. We have not tried, that is, to impose a common pattern of content on all the essays; their authors have written about those phenomena or problems, within this broad field, which interested them most.

The essays cover a wide field geographically. They omit Africa, which in recent years has tended to take the lion's share of scientific publication in this socio-economic field. But they provide examples from two other continents and various oceanic areas; with two exceptions, all deal with communities in the tropical zone (see map). Culturally, the range also is wide, from small communities of fairly simple structure—Pacific islanders, Persian nomads, tribal villagers in Eastern Indian highlands—to sectors of more massive traditional farming societies of more elaborate structure, in south-east Asia and in Meso-America; and to the relatively sophisticated and complex societies of Mauritius, the Caribbean and the Maori of New Zealand.

As chapters in this volume the essays are not grouped either regionally or in any very strict thematic order. They are, however, arranged with general reference to the main problems and types of economic situation dealt with in each. An essay by one of the editors begins the volume with an extended outline discussion of the main problems and issues. An essay by the other editor ends the volume with some comments and questions from an economist's point of view. The volume on its descriptive side begins with the examination of a credit system in a non-monetary stationary economy of apparently primitive type, and of operations in a more advanced system which still uses both monetary and non-monetary media side by side. Capital and investment problems among a money-using folk who still practise pastoral nomadism as a way of life are then considered. Then follow studies of capital and its management among traditional Asian peasantry in four countries—farmers for most of whom rice is a staple crop but who have other significant forms of production as well and who have a fairly wide range of economic choice. Aspects of rural savings and credit associations appear in many of the essays, but are specifically considered in further material from the south Pacific. Another two essays focus especially on questions of capital in market trading. In several of the preceding essays comparison is significant. But comparative economic performance between communities is studied specifically for Middle American examples, and is to the fore in the consideration of the position of some communities of Asian origin and plantation background, in situations of much ethnic diversity. Finally, an essay of much broader character summarizes and comments on relevant data for a major agricultural area, rural India. Though overtly it is very different in its statistical survey materials from the other essays, this essay belongs to the volume by reason of its complementary approach and its insistence on the need for a combination of economic and anthropological techniques of enquiry into these problems of capital and credit in peasant societies.

Preliminary drafts of most of the essays in this book served as data papers for a symposium on Economics and Anthropology at Burg Wartenstein, Austria, on August 21 to 27, 1960. The symposium was organized by Raymond Firth and Bert Hoselitz, under the auspices of the Wenner-Gren Foundation for Anthropological Research. The discussion of the data papers at the symposium has been of great help to the editors in the preparation of this volume, as has been the unpublished report of the proceedings by Mrs Lorraine Lancaster. The editors wish to acknowledge the generous help of the Foundation, and its late President, Dr Paul Fejos, in making possible the symposium and their participation in it. Finally, the editors acknowledge the co-operation and forbearance of the contributors to this book, in what has been inevitably a protracted task.

R.F.
B.S.Y.

April 1963.

8

CONTENTS

THE AUTHORS

F. G. Bailey   Reader in Asian Anthropology,
University of London.

Lorraine Barić   (formerly Lecturer in Anthropology, London School
of Economics and Political Science),
Chief Assistant Planning Officer (Sociology),
Liverpool City Planning Department,
Liverpool.

Fredrik Barth   Professor of Social Anthorpology,
University of Bergen.

C. S. Belshaw   Professor of Anthropology,
University of British Columbia.

Burton Benedict   Lecturer in Anthropology,
London School of Economics and Political Science.

Alice Dewey   Assistant Professor of Anthropology,
University of Hawaii.

Scarlett Epstein   Senior Lecturer, Department of Liberal Studies,
Royal College of Advanced Technology,
Salford.

Raymond Firth   Professor of Anthropology,
University of London.

Joel M. Halpern   Associate Professor of Anthropology,
Brandeis University.

Bert F. Hoselitz   Professor of Social Science and Economics,
University of Chicago.

Sidney W. Mintz   Associate Professor of Anthropology,
Yale University.

Joan Metge   Tutor, Adult Education Department,
University of Auckland.

Manning Nash   Associate Professor of Anthropology,
University of Chicago.

Raymond T. Smith   Senior Lecturer in Social Anthropology,
University of the West Indies.

M. G. Swift   Lecturer in Anthropology,
University of Sydney.

Marjorie Topley   Occasional Lecturer, Chung Chi College,
and Department of Extra Mural Studies,
Hong Kong.

B. S. Yamey   Professor of Economics,
University of London.

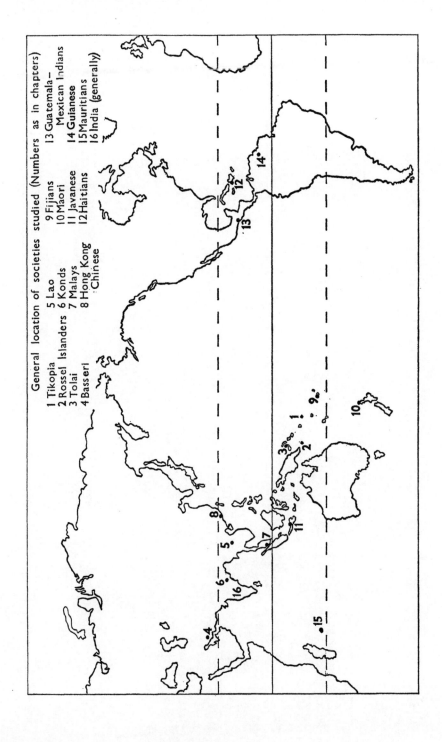

General location of societies studied (Numbers as in chapters)

1 Tikopia 5 Lao 9 Fijians 13 Guatemala–
2 Rossel Islanders 6 Konds 10 Maori Mexican Indians
3 Tolai 7 Malays 11 Javanese 14 Guianese
4 Basseri 8 Hong Kong 12 Haitians 15 Mauritians
  Chinese 16 India (generally)

1

Capital, Saving and Credit in Peasant Societies: A Viewpoint from Economic Anthropology

BY RAYMOND FIRTH

Contributions by anthropologists to the analysis of the diverse range of economic institutions they have observed have not yet been very impressive. This is partly because of their lack of training in formal economic theory and partly because much analysis by economists which might have been a stimulus may seem remote from the conditions studied by anthropologists. But as time has gone on the bearing of economic conditions on the character of a social system has become more apparent. Moreover, a more marked interest in problems of economic growth in the 'under-developed' countries, and an increasing realization that such growth depends as much on social as on economic conditions, have helped many economists to see more clearly the relevance of social factors to economic decisions. So the way is now open for closer co-operation in the empirical study of economic data, and for a more significant use of their knowledge by anthropologists for the clearer formulation of theory in the socio-economic field.

Some work has already been done in this direction. The contributions of anthropologists in this field lie primarily in their knowledge of the working of socio-economic systems different from, though not now outside the orbit of, developed commercial and industrial economies. From this point of view anthropological study has shown, over a variety of systems ranging from those of very simple technology to those of what may be termed peasant character, a number of significant relationships.

These include: the ways in which different types of right-holding in land affect its use; what kinds of choices are involved in the assembly of a labour force; what sanctions maintain it in operation; how far magical and other ritual procedures affect the allocation of productive effort; what kinds of social factors provide the basis for

15

and give meaning to the scheme of distribution of the product of labour; what local media of exchange there are and how they operate; what the major incentives, individual and communal, are in inter-community trade. More generally, anthropologists have been able to answer in some detail for many societies the three fundamental questions posed by economists as, for instance, by Samuelson (1948, pp. 12–13): what commodities shall be produced and in what quantities; by whom and with what resources of technology; how is the total product to be distributed among individuals and families? The *what, how* and *by whom* of economic effort have received examination by anthropologists in, one might estimate, some fifty different societies at least. Yet such examination is still apt to be selective, not systematic.[1]

To the anthropologist economic relationships are part of an overall system of social relationships (however weakly this system be structured and integrated). The economic system (or sub-system) is therefore to be fully understood only in a context of social, political, ritual, moral and even aesthetic activities and values, and in turn affects these. Studies on the more strictly anthropological side have benefited from this economic orientation. The social implications of alternative uses of labour power by individuals and by groups have been examined for their effects on family organization and authority structures—an important set of materials here has come from studies of the flow of labour from tribal economic conditions to industrial employment. Data on the complexities of land tenure, including the recognition of rights of a mystical order over land, have been correlated with the political structure and kinship structure of the societies concerned. For some spectacular and classic cases, such as the Trobrianders and the Rossel islanders (Malinowski, 1922, with critique by Firth, 1957; Armstrong, 1928, with critique by Lorraine Lancaster, *infra*, chapter 2), there are illuminating analyses of the relation between the accumulation and disbursement of capital and the status structure in the society. Similar analyses have multiplied in recent years. But anthropologists need much more systematic study of many phases of these and other problems. What are the actual processes of decision-making at various levels of economic enterprise and for various categories of groups and individuals, and what is their relation to political power? How far is the distribution process likely to facilitate the social aims of the community or the factional or individual aims of certain sectors of it only? Is the economy under scrutiny a stationary one or is it a progressive one with increase of net assets, and what are the effects in either case upon

---

[1] For a recent sophisticated analysis dealing with such matters in a relatively primitive society, see Salisbury, 1962.

the structure of the society? What framework of ideas is required in order to tackle such questions?

STUDIES IN THE PEASANT 'CAPITAL' SECTOR

These and other problems can usefully be taken up in connection with the formation and use of capital since this constitutes one of the least developed aspects of socio-economic study. This introductory essay attempts merely to outline some of the major questions involved.

It is convenient for anthropologists to consider capital problems in the sphere of 'peasant' societies for two reasons. The 'peasant' concept emphasizes that the range of data is wider than the 'primitive', to include monetary economic systems and specifically allow of the inclusion of the work of modern anthropologists from relatively advanced countries such as China, India or Mexico. It also allows of more direct co-operation with economists, economic historians and rural sociologists, who have had little or no experience with non-monetary economic systems but who, among them, have a vast historical and contemporary knowledge of European or Oriental peasantry.

Definition of the term 'peasant' has been the subject of some argument in recent years. It can be held that this is not a critical term, capable of much theoretical handling, but it is a broad descriptive term of an empirical kind, suitable only for demarcating rough boundaries in categorization.[1] From this point of view, 'peasant' refers to a socio-economic category. It describes a socio-economic system of small-scale producers with a relatively simple, non-industrial technology. The system is a rural one, though as Robert Redfield has shown, it depends on a rural-urban antinomy and interrelationship, particularly upon the existence of a market. Definition of a system as 'peasant' implies that it has its own particular local character, partly because of intricate community interrelationships and partly because, in economic and social affairs, it both contributes to and draws upon a town in trade, cultural exchange and general ideology. The term 'peasant' is commonly restricted to agricultural producers, even to those who retain effective control of the land and are not tenants. But such distinctions are difficult to maintain when owners and tenants, as in a Malay rice-growing area, are mingled together and may be related by kinship or live in the same village.

In my opinion it is not necessary then to restrict the term 'peasant'

[1] v. Firth, 1946, pp. 22–5; 1951b, pp. 87–90. One of the most effective discussions on the concept from an anthropological point of view is by Eric R. Wolf. His statement that 'the peasant aims at subsistence not at reinvestment' (1955, p. 454), however, is too sweeping.

only to those people who cultivate the soil, and as owners. It can usefully include other 'countrymen' also, who share the social life and values of the cultivators, so that we can speak not only of peasant agriculturalists but also of peasant fishermen, peasant craftsmen and peasant marketers, if they are part of the same social system. In any case, such people are often in fact part-time cultivators as well. If the concept of 'peasant' be viewed as indicating a set of structural or social relationships rather than a technological category of persons engaged in the same employment, then this unconventional inclusive usage seems justified.

IDENTIFICATION OF PEASANT CAPITAL

The definition of capital for economic and anthropological analysis is of a different, much more precise, order. Capital is a critical term, capable of much theoretical exploration, as the history of economic thought has shown. In the course of time the major elements in the definition of what is to be understood by capital have crystallized out. So while economists may differ among themselves as to precisely what elements should be included in the concept, especially for empirical measurement, the alternative implications of such inclusion or exclusion (e.g. stocks of consumer goods in the hands of consumers) are clearly recognized. The main delimiting elements in the concept of capital may be very briefly summarized as follows. Capital represents a stock of goods and services not devoted to immediate consumption but operated to increase the volume of consumption in future periods, either directly or indirectly, through production. A primary criterion of capital is thus its capacity to assist future consumption, and it is oriented towards the future, not merely held back in the present. Put another way, the stock of capital at any moment of time is the sum of the existing assets, i.e. resources capable of yielding goods and services in a future period. These resources are largely material. But there are also immaterial assets such as technical knowledge and skill. The difficulty here is to assign magnitudes to such assets, especially to make them comparable with other more material forms of assets. The value of assets derives from the expected value of the goods and services which may be obtained from them in the future, allowing by discounting for the fact that people normally prefer a less distant to a more distant benefit of otherwise equivalent value. This may raise difficulties of valuation in practice unless there is a continuing active market for the assets in question. One of the major problems in measurement of capital in peasant societies (especially for comparative purposes) often is the absence of regular markets for important types of asset, including perhaps productive equipment.

18

A Viewpoint from Economic Anthropology

From this characterization emerge several critical questions which the anthropologist, if not the economist, must try to answer in any particular economic system. Why are goods withheld from consumption; what kinds of *reasons* determine people to save now and consume later rather than do what many consider to be a natural human action—consume now while they have the goods and take the future as it comes? If certain goods are withheld from present consumption, what *type* of goods—what principles of selection are involved? What kind of *estimate* is given to the future—long-term or short-term? If the value of assets derives from their expected value in the future, what is the nature of these *expectations*—by reference to what considerations? These questions about reasons, principles, estimates and expectations immediately suggest to an anthropologist that we are concerned here with factors of a social kind, involving on the one hand considerations of family interest or personal association and on the other the general pressures of social norms.

In relating it 'functionally' to the economic process, capital may be regarded, according to circumstance, from three major points of view: capital as productive assets; capital as affording control over purchasing power; and capital as a fund for investment. Anthropological studies have shown that in even the simplest economic systems, these three functions can usefully be identified. In Tikopia, for instance, an economy in which until recently the use of Western money was not understood, the productive equipment involved a capital of canoes, paddles, digging sticks, nets, etc., which in use yielded crops and fish. There was also considerable fixed capital, especially in land improved by generations of labour. The control over purchasing power was given by food, lengths of bark-cloth, pandanus mats, coconut sinnet cord and wooden bowls, which were used as 'gifts' to secure or repay various kinds of articles and services. Such goods were also used as a fund for investment by accumulating them over a period and then disbursing them *en masse*. They might be used to pay for having a new canoe built, which represented an addition to productive equipment providing a future yield; or they might be transferred at an initiation or funeral ceremony, thus laying upon the recipient an obligation to reciprocate with goods and services at a later period.[1] Much of the food, bark-cloth, etc., was produced and accumulated a year or more in advance, with such aims in mind and consciously expressed.

Special problems about the valuation of such assets arise in a non-monetary economy of this kind, where no general medium of exchange allows of direct comparison of all types of goods and

---

[1] The question of whether such investment, to be ranked as capital, should yield an increment, interest, over and above the original outlay, does not seem particularly significant here.

Capital, Saving and Credit in Peasant Societies

services. But the significant point to note is that consumer goods, even food, can perform an important capital role, and that liquidity, or ease of conversion into goods or services of another kind, is not necessarily confined to a monetary economy, or to the monetary sectors of an economy. The anthropologist then can look for capital functions in unexpected places. Moreover, even in non-monetary economic systems he can usually make some assessment of capital magnitudes by counting various types of goods and services, and by making quantitative estimates he can also note changes in the economic position over time without any monetary evaluation.

Can conceptions of the role of capital exist without any specific terms to refer to them? It would appear so. In Tikopia, for instance, no words can be directly translated as 'capital' or 'income'. But these ideas are subsumed under terms connoting 'valuable goods', 'reciprocity', etc., combined with terms indicating more or less than equivalence in return. The notions of value, of durable stock, of increment over initial expenditure are there, though not arranged in the conventional economic form, and some capital accounting takes place. In most peasant communities it appears that such conceptions can be very directly expressed—as in Malaya, where capital (*modal*) is very clearly differentiated from its yield (*untong*). (Firth, 1939, pp. 237–78, 305; 1946, p. 128.)

FORMATION AND MANAGEMENT OF PEASANT CAPITAL

In general, all over the world it would seem that the level of peasant capital is low. On the whole, peasants are poor, and their low income level, their poverty, is one of the prime factors in creating such un-favourable conditions for saving and capital formation. One of the most significant practical problems of peasant economics at the present time is, then, how can their level of income and of capital operations be improved? This problem of economic growth raises some general questions for economic anthropology. What social and economic conditions are associated with a low income level and a small capital equipment? What possibilities of modification seem open, in view of the nature of the social structure, which sometimes seems to offer few possibilities of variation? What may be the effects on social relationships of capital improvement, for individuals and for the community?

These problems are important to economic anthropology because from an analytical point of view it does not seem to be always clear to administrators or even to economists just what are the factors in the peasant evaluation of resources which are most relevant to capital formation and operation. In consequence, well-meant practical efforts to improve the capital position of the peasant may fail in their

20

aim or produce unintended effects (cf. Firth, 1951a). For an anthropologist, then, there are scientific jobs of both theoretical and practical value to be done, in investigation and interpretation both in relatively stationary and in developing economic conditions.

Few will expect that the level of peasant economies will be raised effectively by some dramatic increase in capital formation by peasants in their traditional or customary activities. The scale of individual operations is too small and income levels are too low for that. (The title of *Penny Capitalism* which Tax (1953) gave to his analysis of the economy of a Guatemalan peasantry is an apt illustration of this.) Improvements are to be expected, rather, where new types of superior market opportunity become available—for crops, as with rubber or cocoa, or for labour, as with factory development in the vicinity—or where external capital is provided, possibly with the imposition of a new overall administrative frame, as with the Gezira or other irrigation schemes. But if peasant saving be not the key to reasonably rapid economic advance, more general peasant economic attitudes may be the key to efficient capital maintenance and management.

A first point to discuss is whether indeed peasants in general are *interested* in capital formation, or indeed in the economical management of capital generally. This is necessary because among the reasons sometimes given for lack of success in a programme to develop peasant saving, or provide peasants with improved equipment, is that they seem not to have any wish to improve their position, and often no sustained interest in maintaining any advance. It is alleged that they are not interested in saving but only in maintaining their current level of consumption; that they have no concern for a better tool, especially a piece of machinery, but let it rust in the fields or run unserviced until it breaks down. There may be misconceptions here. Peasants are usually careful about the maintenance of their traditional equipment. They clean their tools and put them away in the house or shed after use. A Malay fisherman is careful to re-dye his nets and re-paint his boat periodically; a Malay cultivator will carry home his wooden plough on his shoulder after work and not let it lie in the fields. Failure to maintain new types of equipment properly is usually due to lack of proper technical training, including lack of general education in the basic principles involved; to lack of full employment for the equipment, which can lead to neglect; or to lack of cash to pay for running repairs. There is also a broader issue—the competing claims of other interests. When outlay is required, social demands—such as the requirements of a marriage or funeral of a kinsman—may make to the peasant a more imperative call upon his resources of cash or time than attention to a machine or to a savings programme. As Tax (1953, p. 204) and others have pointed out, simple disinterest can hardly ever be assumed as a

reason for lack of response in a situation of potential capital accumulation. Patterns of consumption do not operate as a simple negative
to the propensity to save; they have strong positive sanctions, and
these sanctions are of a social as well as an individual order.

It is sometimes thought that obedience to the social dictates of
'custom' inhibits rational calculation. This is not at all the case. In
some of the most primitive societies known, as in the Highlands of
New Guinea or aboriginal Australia, there is the keenest discussion
of alternatives in any proposal for the use of resources, of the
relative economic advantages of exchange with one party as against
another, and the closest scrutiny of the quality of goods which
change hands and of services performed. Again, some men emerge
as entrepreneurs by controlling the flow of capital goods in
exchanges between groups and taking a profit thereby either in
material items or in that intangible good, reputation. (v. e.g.
Stanner, 1933–34; Reay, 1959, pp. 96–9, 110–11; Salisbury, 1962,
pp. 52–60, 158.)

That there can still be misunderstandings in this field can be seen
from a reference by Samuelson to the economics of the Northwest
Coast Indians. He states (1948, *loc. cit.*) ' . . . some tribes consider it
desirable not to accumulate wealth but to give it away in the *potlatch*
—a riotous celebration'. Such behaviour, described as a 'deviation
from the acquisitive behaviour of competition', it is said, 'will not
surprise anthropologists', used to the eccentricities of custom. But in
fact such a description of the *potlatch is* likely to surprise anthropologists, especially coming from an economist noted for his
subtlety of interpretation. The Haida, Kwakiutl, etc. *do* consider it
desirable to accumulate wealth—they must in order to be able to
give it away; the hundreds or thousands of blankets, the 'coppers'
and other goods disbursed are patiently accumulated over a considerable period. Again, the goods are certainly given away—though
some are destroyed—but the action takes place *within* the socio-
economic system, and those who receive them, members of the same
or allied tribe, certainly are eager to have them. This may be as
recognition of social bonds but probably also means a recognized
increase to their capital stock. There is no absence of acquisitive
competition *at some level*. But the major competition is not for material goods but for immaterial resources—prestige and social status.
In effect, what takes place is a set of transfer payments, whereby one
man or set of people hand over blankets and other goods and
receive in return social advantages. For these there is the fiercest
struggle, and men try to build up their stocks to be able to compete.
Moreover, the handing over of the material goods is not necessarily
the end; it may constitute an item in a complex series of credit transactions by which at some future time other material goods may have

22

to be returned, perhaps with increment.[1] These transfers may well be a stimulus to further production. Hence, to call the *potlatch* a 'riotous celebration' may miss the point of its importance in the whole scheme of capital formation of the peoples concerned. It is not 'giving away' but essentially a type of exchange. It may in fact be a powerful element in the incentive pattern of capital accumulation. Some writers indeed stress the economic aspects of the *potlatch*, and its use as an equilibrating mechanism, allowing goods to flow where there is temporary scarcity.

SAVING AND INVESTMENT

Normally, as one might expect, peasant saving is not a purely individual affair. It is guided, as all saving is, by the general set of ideas and values current about capital accumulation in the particular society. Moreover, as anthropological field research has shown, the actual decisions about saving are often shared. In some communities, by convention, the earner of the income does not have the prime decision in the domestic circle about the saving of it. In parts of rural Malaya, e.g. in coastal Kelantan, it is the husband who earns the major income from fishing, and the wife who acts as custodian of the husband's earnings. A decision about saving, or expenditure of part of the income upon a new boat or net, may depend to a significant degree upon her view of how prudent such outlay is (Firth, Raymond, 1946, pp. 133, 144; Firth, Rosemary, 1943, pp. 17–19). The existence of money promotes saving, if only because it helps to solve the problems of storage. In a community such as Tikopia, where fish, root crops, breadfruit and coconuts are the staple foods, only the coconuts can be stored for any length of time without special preparations of an elaborate kind, involving much labour. Even bark-cloth and pandanus mats—which have sometimes been described as 'currency' —need special care and periodic unwrapping for exposure to sunlight to preserve them from mould and pests. Storage of money avoids most of these difficulties.

In a monetary economy, a peasant has the alternative of saving in the form of cash or of goods. Grain, the holding of which may avoid deleterious changes in the value of money, may be favoured especially since it can be used as a direct contribution to the feasts of neighbours and kinsfolk. Different preferences may operate here, depending, e.g., on the adequacy of storage facilities, the possibility of exchanging goods for cash, attitudes regarding the forms of currency as such, and competing demands in the consumer field for items such as jewellery,

[1] There appear to be two types of incremental transaction. One is lending with stipulated interest, regularly enforced. The other has no such stipulation but an increment is irregularly given.

which can serve as easily realizable assets and also for display. Among the reasons for these different preferences and decisions, social elements such as possible demands for loans by kinsfolk and neighbours may be significant.

Examination of what are held as assets in a peasant economy may reveal a range of goods which a sophisticated Western observer might not be inclined at first sight to include in the capital category. Mention has been made of the blankets used in enormous quantity by the Northwest Coast Indians. Originally made of cedar-bark or furs sewn together, the blankets in later times were Hudson Bay trade blankets priced at 60 cents for a single one or 1 dollar 50 cents for a double one. Hundreds or even thousands of these items were accumulated and disbursed in a single *potlatch*—200, 400, up to as much as 14,500 blankets have been mentioned as having changed hands (Codere, 1950, pp. 73, 78, 79, 126). Other consumer goods were also handed over in numbers, such as hundreds of silver bracelets, dozens of zinc wash-boilers and yards of calico. Accumulated far in excess of the practical needs of the holders, these goods were put into a system of circulation by lending and distribution, and had important capital functions, including the production of interest. In other peasant societies, food either in the form of raw grain or as cooked meals has been used as working capital, for the payment of workers engaged in capital formation in agriculture, housebuilding or other craft enterprises. In many of these systems, especially those associated with the simpler technologies, the distinction between consumers' goods and producers' goods cannot be at all clearly maintained. Items may move into or out of one or the other category without difficulty as occasion demands. What is particularly significant is that preparations are made a long way ahead—perhaps months in advance—to mobilize food resources for such an act of production. In effect this is a form of saving—a storing up of energy in labour rather than expending it in leisure.

The liquidity of assets in a peasant economy is very varied. In some economic systems, land assets are almost completely illiquid. Rights to land spring essentially from the position of a person as a member of a specific descent group. They are either non-transferable or transferable only within very narrow limits, as to a daughter on her marriage (sometimes only for her lifetime and that of her children). Other restrictions on liquidity not only of land but also of other assets may exist through group rights of various kinds—for example, a boat may be held by a set of brothers who have inherited it from their father, and none of them may dispose of his share. But there is a difference between these two types of example. In the second case the restriction on liquidity arises from rights which are specific to the individuals concerned and which may not be the same for other

24

individuals with other assets of the same type. In the first example, the general system of property conventions or values in the society is such that it is not regarded as conceivable that the particular kind of asset is transmutable into any other kind. In the more primitive economic systems such restrictions on liquidity through social convention are not infrequent, and in turn may have an important bearing on the liquidity preferences of individuals in that society. Hence one of the tasks of economic anthropology is to contribute towards an understanding of what Postan (1939, p. 23) has termed the 'social forces that lurk behind liquidity preferences'.

Primitive and sometimes even peasant assets may be divided into several categories, the items in each being regarded as not mutually exchangeable or substitutable. Such non-substitutable categories of exchange have been described as spheres or circuits of exchange (Firth, 1939, pp. 340–4; cf. Bohannan, 1955, and the analysis by Salisbury in terms of 'nexuses of activity', 1962, pp. 187 *et seq.*). Commonly food and some other simple subsistence goods such as household equipment are in the first and lowest category, regular capital goods such as cattle, cloth or metal objects are in the second category, and the most prized possessions such as rare ornaments, canoes or rights over land (or over human beings) are in the third category. In some systems, as with the Tikopia, no effective conversion of assets from one category into the other directly is possible; in others, such as the Tiv of Eastern Nigeria, this conversion can be done (Bohannan, 1955, pp. 60–70). Tiv endeavour to convert assets from a lower to a higher category and, according to Bohannan, regard it as unprofitable and lacking in dignity to convert assets downwards.[1] Bohannan uses the term 'conveyance' for transfers within the same category and 'conversion' for transfers between categories. Commonly also the different categories of goods correspond to different types of social action, ranging from everyday exchange to highly ceremonial 'presentations'.

This leads to some questions regarding the concept of 'investment' in the primitive and peasant capital spheres which seem to be of basic relevance. What flow of goods and services deriving from current transactions should be included in capital formation? How shall they be valued? By what criteria are capital transactions judged? In many primitive and even some peasant economic systems the transfers between persons seem to be mere reshuffling of control over wealth. Yet in the estimation of the people concerned they do add to immaterial possessions such as status, or strengthen symbolic ties between individuals and groups. Here seems to be a fundamental

---

[1] But for the system to work there must be either some Tiv who buy these lesser assets as well as some who sell them; or alien traders who, not being interested in the Tiv status system, are willing to convert higher to lower category goods.

problem in evaluation. No increase in physical productivity may necessarily follow these transactions—though they frequently involve heavy input of labour in food production, etc., to accompany them and give them appropriate dignity. Yet unless one is to disregard all immaterial assets, significant forms of net investment for those individuals who are entrepreneurs do seem to be engaged in by such employment of capital. An important criterion would seem to be convertibility. If an individual acquired a shell arm-ring which has been highly sought after, having given other prized valuables to obtain it, he may be thought to have made an investment if his possession of the arm-ring not only gives him added status but later on enables him to command a fresh set of services previously not under his control. This may be considered as private capital formation. Whether there has been net community capital formation depends partly on whether his status increment can be reckoned as part of the community advantage, and partly on what is done with the valuables he has relinquished.

It is possible to conceive of an economic system in which the items of productivity, of concern in maximization, are status tokens and symbolic ties. Whether it is worth while trying to operate an economic analysis wholly within such a field of concepts I am doubtful, especially in view of the difficulty of their measurement or comparability—although Lorraine Barić, following Armstrong, has shown some of the possibilities of such an approach. But whether this be so or not, I am sure that such a system should be distinguished from one in which investment of wealth leads to increase of material output. I am not saying that the latter is any more a 'real' economic system than the former—but they are different. This difference, seen in the different requirements for the estimation of economic growth, is significant for the future structure of the economy and society. Moreover, since elements of both status increment and physical increment in assets appear often side by side in the same economy, it is relevant to examine why decisions are taken to invest in the one rather than in the other. Such decisions can be shown to change in accordance with changes in external circumstances—as when a new market for goods arises.

In many works of economic anthropology it is difficult to see whether the multiple transactions involving transfers of goods and services do involve forms of physical capital formation or not. Admittedly it is difficult for practical reasons to distinguish expenditure on capital account from expenditure on income account in many of the economies studied. Admittedly, too, there would seem to be some theoretical difficulty here. In a Western economy 'conspicuous expenditure' in accumulation for disbursals of a *potlatch* type would be classified as consumption, irrespective of any reciprocities and

26

complications in status increment which would seem to be involved. If a captain of industry invites some hundreds of guests to his daughter's wedding and gives them lavish entertainment, this is not regarded as investment, nor even can it presumably be entered on his 'expense account'. Yet in status and even in commerce his benefits may be considerable. This distinction exists because in a Western industrial system there are other alternative ways of great magnitude of utilizing capital—ways which initiate productivity in an obvious and measurable sense. In primitive systems, and even in some peasant systems which are partly monetized, it is possible that there may be no other ways of capital utilization of any magnitude at the given time which will further physical productivity. But this is unlikely. Even in an economy such as that of Rossel Island there would appear to be some alternative to the circulation of shell 'money' as by investment in technological activities. Moreover, when brought in contact with economic systems of a Western type, the 'primitive' system soon seems to recognize the possibility of using capital for physical productivity.

In their preoccupation with the immediate relevance of some economic factors for social group structure and operations, anthropologists often seem to have ignored the possibility of such alternative uses of resources. Another weakness allied to this has been their tendency to discuss problems of capital expenditure without relating it effectively to the magnitudes involved. In Mauss's analysis (1925) there are hardly any references to the quantities of goods which change hands, and where there are such references they are not related in any way to the total quantities of goods and services available to the community or to individual members. Even such an admirable treatment of the problems of investment among the Tiv as that of Bohannan seems to have ignored completely the rates at which goods and services were exchanged and the magnitudes of such goods and services involved. Without such rates and magnitudes, his examination of the processes of conversion of one type of resource into another, and the bases of decision, loses much of its significance.

How far in a peasant economic system does one find the separation between saver and investor characteristic of a Western industrial system? The situation would seem to vary considerably, not merely according to the character of the economic system, but also according to the character of the institutional mechanisms in which capital uses are embedded. In many circumstances where savings are made by household decision and abstention, investment of them lies primarily at the discretion of the household head. In essence, decisions about saving and decisions about investment are taken by the same persons. But where descent groups of some magnitude are traditionally a characteristic feature of the social system, investment decisions

27

may be taken by a senior person in the descent group with only tacit assent of the other members of the group, including household heads. As the economic system becomes more affected by monetary relationships, some differentiation of practice may occur. Frequently decisions are arrived at on a more individual basis, and there is some loss of collective action. Whereas formerly the head of the descent group was able to mobilize the saved resources of his group to produce, say, a new boat or a net, when these resources come to be expressed in money form the men who have saved the money tend to reserve to themselves the expenditure of it. Large-scale investment then may suffer. On the other hand, in some conditions the system of descent groups is still fairly firmly maintained by social and moral bonds, and significant collective operations are performed. The leaders of the descent groups are then still able to mobilize effectively the saved resources of their kin, even when these are in a highly liquid form, and apply them to major capital investment. The rise of a new class of entrepreneurs in some economic systems which are now being radically transformed by contact with the West seems in part to be due to the ability of these entrepreneurs to utilize and aggregate the savings of their kinsfolk for profitable investment (see Belshaw, 1955a, pp. 19, 59–61). Even where descent groups are less clear-cut, there may still be corporate groups of a modern legally sanctioned type, with administrators appointed by the members to act for them and take effective working decisions in regard to the use of the collective assets. This is the case among the Maori of New Zealand (Firth, 1959b, p. 470).

Considerable variation, however, is possible in this sphere since the social definition of the role of an entrepreneur does not necessarily link his functions so specifically with increase of productivity as in a Western system. The whole Western set of institutions for capital investment in many cases is specifically and legally prescribed. In a peasant system the social prescriptions may have no legal backing in a direction of productive investment and may leave the accumulator of other people's savings a fairly free hand in what he does with them. One example of this is the North-Eastern Malay peasant institution of a ceremonial feast. The organizer of this, normally having a marriage or other social event as prime reason, receives payment from his guests, which is in part a mobilization of his credit with them, and in part a contraction of new credit obligations. If he makes a profit he can use this either for expenditure on consumers' goods for his own pleasure or for investment in some item of producers' equipment such as a fishing boat. The circumstances in which he has mobilized the savings of his friends and kin are socially regulated only to the degree that the possibility of investment or non-investment decision remains with him. (He may of course also lose on the transaction.)

28

A Viewpoint from Economic Anthropology

One of the most important ways obviously in which peasant savings are drained off and made available for possible investment may be through government taxation. Large-scale public works and 'social capital' of various kinds are increased by such means. As the economy becomes modernized the role of government in this respect seems almost certain to develop. The question then arises whether such taxation affects capital formation by the peasants themselves.

CREDIT IN THE PEASANT ECONOMY

Even in the most primitive non-monetary economic system the concept of credit exists—the lending of goods or services without immediate return against the promise of a future repayment. It involves an obligation by the borrower to make a return and confidence by the lender in the borrower's good faith and ability to repay. The return may be the same article or service as lent, or a different one. It may be equivalent in value to the loan or augmented in value above the loan (i.e. with interest). The augmentation may be voluntary or prescribed, and it may be proportionate or not to the amount of time for which the object lent has been held. The repayment may be contractual and enforceable at law, or it may have no legal backing but be socially binding. Such a list of alternative elements indicates not only the possible variations in the structure of credit transactions in an economy, but also various points at which such variation may be conditioned by social forces.

Some attention has been given by economic anthropologists to the incentives for seeking credit, the conditions in which it is obtained and the incentives to repay it. As a rule, borrowing for consumption can be distinguished from borrowing for investment, the latter being for productive purposes and hence normally more easily repaid. Borrowing on consumer account includes normal consumption borrowing—to tide over seasonal shortages—and special consumption borrowing of a social order—to meet the expense of a marriage or a funeral. Borrowing of an exceptional kind to meet litigation expenses may be in theory classified as having a productive aim, but in practice often seems to have failed to get the hoped-for yield, and to land the parties with a heavy burden of indebtedness (e.g. Havers, 1945). Yet the division between these forms of credit is by no means clearcut, since some forms which appear at first sight to be of a consumption kind do tend ultimately to strengthen the borrower's position as producer. But what it is essential to realize is that borrowing for defraying the expenses involved in, say, a wedding, a circumcision or a funeral, is not simply an individual whim. Such events are part of the way of life in that particular phase of

29

the economy and society, and strong sanctions are brought to bear on a person who does not conform.

The range of practice in peasant credit systems often seems to include 'social' loans as much as primarily economic loans. In the former the accent is on the pattern of service as much as on the specific articles handed over. The credit relationship between the parties is indicative of a social tie and also may establish some degree of relative status between them. But such a form of credit can result in promoting the circulation of goods and to some degree increasing the production of them in order to fulfil credit demands. In primarily economic loans the accent is on the need for the actual good or overt service borrowed. Such loans may be of various kinds. Household loans of implements and utensils are common. They are normally not interest-bearing since the frequency and duration of service between the same sets of persons obviates the need for any incremental attitude. The services in the long run tend to cancel out. The security is personal knowledge plus the potential need for reciprocal borrowing. Short-term loans of liquid capital are often also required. The borrowing both of grain and of cash is often practised by poorer households to tide them over a short supply period before harvest, or in the case of a fishing community during the bad weather season. Such borrowing may allow them to carry on with productive activities such as manufacture of tools, or net-making, which give no immediate yield.

Such loans may not incur interest, though frequently they do. In a peasant economy, commodity rates of interest—ordinarily of little direct importance to an economist (Hicks, 1940, p. 142)—may be of considerable significance. Among the Hausa, as reported some two decades ago (Forde & Scott, 1946, pp. 166 *et seq.*), non-interest bearing loans took place only from wife to husband or between close kin. But between all other people two bundles of guinea corn had to be repaid at harvest for every one lent in the early farming season or, if the lender was generous, three bundles for every two lent. There was a general preference for such borrowing rather than for working on other men's farms, which was regarded as degrading, apart from being poorly paid.

Some repayment which appears to be interest may not in fact be so. Among the Hausa, increments in repayment were about cancelled out as far as value was concerned by a fall in the price of grain after harvest. It is interesting to note that according to the local commercial ethic bundle for bundle was regarded as the correct equivalent and the excess was thought to be illicit. Something similar used to occur among the Ifugao of the Philippines, where a loan of rice during a growing season was repaid by double the quantity after harvest. Here again, owing to the fall in the price of grain at harvest, no interest was really exacted. It is not clear whether in such situations the zero rate of interest was maintained in times of short supply of grain. Here differentiation between would-be borrowers by lenders might be their way of seeking maximal advantage—choosing closer kinsmen or others from whom most future benefit might be expected.

Various other forms of short-term credit may occur in a peasant economy. In Kelantan, Malay fishmarket dealers who make a settlement weekly operate in fact on the capital of the sellers—the fishermen—for an average period of three days. In some other cases dealers operate on the capital of the buyers.

Long-term loans in the peasant economy are a common phenomenon. The general difficulties in their repayment—including the role of the moneylender—have been the subject of much study, and need not be examined further here. (Moneylenders in such cases are often thought to exact unreasonably high interest. As Wilmington has shown (1955), much of the high interest rate may be risk-premium.) Something may be said, however, about the general character of such credit. One way of coping with pressures for repayment is to fragment the debt, borrowing further from several lenders on a relatively short-term basis in smaller amounts, and handing these over to pacify the initial creditor at least temporarily. The smaller debts are then dealt with *seriatim* more easily, and some postponements arranged where necessary (see Firth, 1946, pp. 173–5). As with shorter-term loans, the security is often of a personal character, resting on the knowledge of the parties and their respect for social sanctions. Sometimes land may be taken as security for a cash loan, with the right to the usufruct going to the creditor so long as the loan is not repaid. Documentary instruments tend to be rare, but where they do exist, as in India or Malaya—often with a thumbprint as substitute for signature—they are usually not regarded as negotiable instruments. In other words, long-term loans in a peasant economic system, even when they are made to producers, are not apt to serve as a vehicle for further transactions in a capital market.

An interesting example of the way in which peasant credit institutions are embedded in the social matrix is given by such institutions as temporary loan clubs which operate in many Asian and some African peasant societies. As described for the Esusu among the Yoruba, these have elements of a credit union, an insurance scheme and a savings club. The essential point is that there is a fund to which a group of individuals make fixed contributions of money at fixed intervals, and the total amount contributed by the entire group is assigned to each of the members in rotation on a competitive auction basis. Such institutions provide a useful alternative channel for credit that is more impersonal than in the case of relatives or friends. Because of the considerable sums of money they

31

supply, and the limitations of other forms of saving and investment—and the high interest rates charged by moneylenders—such institutions often play an important role in the peasant economy (see e.g. Bascom, 1952; Nguyen Van Vinh, 1949; Freedman, 1958, p. 93). But it is very doubtful if such credit associations can contribute very substantially to capital formation to promote economic growth significantly. Moreover, by no means every African or Oriental peasant society uses these institutions, nor if they do occur are they employed to the same degree. The Negri Sembilan Malays have a type of temporary loan association known as *kutu*, but do not use it extensively. (See M. G. Swift in Chapter 7, *infra*.)

It may be difficult, however, to relate the amount of credit in existence at a given time to the productive organization of the community. Observers of credit operations in primitive or peasant economic systems have sometimes been struck by the great proliferation of credit relationships. It has been fairly clear that, as in our own system, it would be quite impracticable to call in all credit simultaneously. But not only this—it has also been pointed out, in one case at least, that having regard to the total community income it may not be possible for *all* the credit obligations existing in a community *ever* to be fully serviced (Booker, 1949). In a community such as this, where more than half the private debt is internal, credit situations are interpreted socially as well as economically. One has to distinguish therefore specific returns from diffuse returns. In a narrow economic or material sense the debt cannot all be serviced, but some forms of social service or recognition may be taken into consideration. Economically, in a wider sense some social benefits may be regarded as providing a measure of equivalence to the original loan.

In considering incentives to repayment of credit obligations in a peasant economy, one expects to find prominently figuring the economic sanction—that failure to repay will lead to a cutting-off of all future sources of credit. In addition, there may well be some legal sanctions through resort to the courts. But the whole question of seeking of credit and repayment involves a theory of obligation not comprised merely in terms of economic and legal sanctions. In the simpler economic systems sanctions of a social, moral and even ritual order may be invoked. Appeals are made to the debtor's pride and reputation with his fellows, even to his conscience and fear of retaliation by supernatural forces. The operation of social sanctions in more complex societies may be illustrated by variations in conceptions about the nature of interest in a credit transaction. To Western ideas the notion of interest is that of a 'natural' return for the use of money or other capital during a period. When the capital is used for productive purposes it seems even more obvious that the user should allow the supplier of capital some share in the increment which he

32

has been able to obtain. Such a Western conception, however, is not universal. In the classical Muslim view, for example, the notion of return for the use of capital as such is separated from the notion of sharing in any increment which that use may have secured. Increment sharing is regarded as legitimate; use-payment for loans is not. Hence, the widespread stigmatization of interest in Muslim economic life. This has found expression in some interesting forms as, for example, the conjuring up of the spirit of Keynes by a Muslim economist, who seems to regard Keynes's economic view of the tendency of interest to a minimum as backing up—or anticipated by—the Muslim moral concept of zero interest (Qureshi, 1945; cf. Firth, 1951b, pp. 148–53). The need to bring the Muslim concept more directly into relation with modern economic institutions has led in turn to various reinterpretations of the Muslim idea on the one hand and to some tendency to discard the strict letter of the Muslim law on the other. Elizabeth Monroe records that an agreement by the Shaik of Kuwait to establish an investment board for some of his annual oil revenues was a novel plunge for a religious man. The idea of making interest-bearing investments other than in real property or goods completely within personal control had long been repellant to him as to other Muslims (Monroe, Elizabeth, 1954, p. 281). But, in general, the more interest-bearing can be regarded as removed from association with personal loans, the more it seems to be tolerated in modern times.

SOCIAL CONDITIONS AND CAPITAL DEVELOPMENT

It seems generally held that prospects for any large-scale capital development and increase of investment from a peasant economic system must rest upon some changes in social as well as economic conditions. Lewis (1955, pp. 225 *et seq.*) has argued that it is particularly important to stimulate saving among the peasantry because of the role which agriculture has to play in economic development, but he has also stressed that what is required for large-scale changes is the emergence of a new class in the society, a class of profit-making entrepreneurs, who will think in terms of reinvesting income productively.

There are two points to make about this position, with which in general one may agree. The first is that entrepreneurs may not necessarily have to subscribe completely to all the conventions of a Western economic system. Arab economic history has very many examples of successful entrepreneurship conducted with due regard to the prohibition of the Koran upon taking of interest. The economic manipulations of Arab business men have been carried out with a high degree of success by their operations being couched in the form of profit-sharing, i.e. sharing of a productive increment, while excluding the taking of usury. The second point is that budding entrepreneurs may forge ahead not merely by borrowing resources from other members of their community but also by being given administrative charge of such resources, perhaps because they are genealogically the leaders of appropriate descent groups. Entrepreneurs can emerge even in relatively simple economic systems, but in understanding their development it is necessary to place the activity of the entrepreneur in an extremely wide cultural and institutional framework. As Belshaw has expressed it, credit and debit must be assigned in the ledger of social accounting, in which many factors of a collective kind must be taken into consideration.

2

Some Aspects of Credit, Saving and Investment in a 'Non-Monetary' Economy (Rossel Island)[1]

BY LORRAINE BARIĆ

SOCIOLOGICAL AND PSYCHOLOGICAL EXPLANATION
IN ECONOMIC DEVELOPMENT

Among some economists who are concerned with the analysis of economic growth in underdeveloped societies, there has grown up a set of ideas that Myint (1960) has called the 'orthodoxy' of development.[2] One might borrow this notion and say that there is also, among some economists, an orthodoxy of the relevant background factors in development. When the tools of economic analysis appear inadequate fully to deal with specific instances of economic change or economic stagnation, the psychology and attitudes of the people concerned are invoked, as is the inertia of indigenous institutions.

Frequently, background factors in economic change are so imprecisely incorporated into the total picture that it is difficult to do more than assent in a general way to their significance. Sometimes they are couched wholly in psychological terms, perhaps implying that in the process of change some posited characteristic—the 'will to economize', for instance—can be identified, abstracted from a situation and used to account for movements in economic relations. The risk of circularity in explanation here is evident. Sometimes it is assumed that in attempts to initiate or encourage development in a society or community, by channelling existing indigenous forms of

[1] I have been greatly helped in writing this paper by discussion with Professor W. E. Armstrong. I am also indebted to Dr Lucy Mair for detailed comments. Another version (in French) of this study has been published: Lancaster (1962).
[2] Briefly, this set of ideas includes these notions: in underdeveloped countries, since they lack a sufficiency of private entrepreneurship, it is the government that should undertake the encouragement of growth; outside capital should be injected into these countries to jerk them out of their underdeveloped equilibrium; and investment programmes should aim at balanced growth.

accumulation and investment, or by investment programmes and institutional changes originating from without, an attack must first be made on attitudes. Baumol (1959, p. 87), for example, writing on the possibility of introducing corporate enterprise characteristic of Western society into underdeveloped countries, says: 'We simply do not know enough about the *working of men's minds* and the mores which are rooted in them to be sure how to go about creating the appropriate *psychological* climate.' (My italics.)

Furthermore, it is sometimes taken for granted that if people show a wish to accumulate goods, to maximize individual advantage, to become entrepreneurs, and to plan in economic terms, then the institutions and social organization of the society will change in such a way as to tend towards economic growth. W. A. Lewis (1955, p. 57) has said that the association between the willingness of people to make the effort required for economic growth and the appropriateness of social institutions in promoting growth is such that an increase in willingness will lead to an increase in appropriateness. Certainly, attitudes, values and personality structure may be linked with institutions. But apart from the difficulty of identifying psychological predisposition, the argument over-simplifies matters. It is at most half of the explanation in organizational terms of a society's support for, or opposition to, movements of economic change, however generated. It is possible to have a situation in which members of a society have an approach to economic matters which one would expect to meet with in an active and developing economy, and yet the autonomy of the self-supporting system of social relationships in the society is such that it damps down any tendencies towards economic change and material improvement. Anthropologists and others have found many examples of such situations (some of which have been termed by Polanyi (1957, p. 13)—rather inaccurately—'pseudo-economies') in which people show a strong preference for 'investing' in social relationships and in the ceremonial reinforcement of social ties.

One of the most useful contributions an anthropologist or a sociologist can make to the analysis of the nature of economic systems lies in the study of such preferences and their association with the network of relationships arising from transactions (such as customary gifts, borrowing and lending) in small-scale societies. From the intensive study of such societies it is possible to discover the inter-relationships of factors in the microcosm more precisely than is likely in a more complex society. It is possible to see, in intensified form, certain principles of social organization common to technologically primitive and to peasant societies, which are among the most significant factors in questions of development. Here a sort of continuum 'primitive/tribal—peasant—industrial' is a useful way of looking at some of the elements involved. Many factors suggest themselves as characteristics to distinguish the poles on this continuum. Participation in a monetary economy is an evident one. The separateness of the community is also significant: primitive and tribal societies usually do not find themselves sharing the same cultural orbit with urban communities, while peasant societies have many links with towns and markets. Primitive and tribal societies tend towards being self sufficient in terms of production and consumption. Peasant societies may be less centripetal and closed as social and cultural systems than are tribal societies, but they are more so than are those agricultural communities which are part of industrial societies.

Most important of all, in primitive and tribal societies social roles are multiplex: a kinsman may be a neighbour, a workmate and an exchange partner all at the same time. The overlapping of social roles affects behaviour in different contexts, particularly in the economic sphere. Elements of such multiplex role structures may be more evident in peasant societies than in industrialized societies. The claims of kin, for instance, and of fulfilment of ritual obligations frequently override considerations of economic efficiency. One can examine many underdeveloped societies with a view to assessing the 'cost' of social relationships and the 'cost' of ritual and ceremony.

In this framework of multiplex social roles, economic transactions (borrowing and lending, exchange of goods and services) may have wide implications in non-economic spheres. Reciprocity, as a general principle of balancing out transactions of all varieties and of actively promoting the recognition of a nexus between participants in transactions, is important in any closely knit community where people tend to be born, marry and die, work and play, regulate conduct and support common values within a single unit.

The internal prestige system of such units is important, since it has repercussions on accumulation of material goods and the way in which they may be allocated for different purposes. Wealth is often highly valued, but it may include non-productive assets, or it may be immediately turned to social display or destroyed to enhance prestige, as in the famous challenge of the *potlatch* (ceremonial destruction or dispersal of goods) of the Indian of the north-west coast of North America. Some types of prestige system have the effect of ensuring that the aggregate level of wealth in a community shall not rise but that increases merely make some individuals better off *vis-à-vis* others.

The purpose of this essay is to describe and analyse as a case study the situation in a small-scale society in which the will to economize, the desire to maximize advantage individually, and economic calculation can be directed willy-nilly into a complicated and largely stagnant economic system. This case study is provided by Rossel Island,

37

a little community in the south-western Pacific, in which elements mentioned above as being relevant to the study of social factors in economic development appear in clear but striking—one might almost say peculiar—form.

ROSSEL ISLAND—A 'NON-MONETARY' ECONOMY

The growth of interest in underdeveloped and primitive economies, and of concepts useful for analysing them, has occurred at the same time as a decrease in the number of societies in which indigenous economic systems are not as yet appreciably influenced by Western money and trading. Evidence about traditional societies is not merely of antiquarian interest; it provides a means of understanding some of the social processes by which relatively unchanging or 'repetitive' economies can maintain themselves (not purposively, of course) at traditional levels and in customary forms. Among the all too few studies in which important detail is provided is W. E. Armstrong's *Rossel Island*, published in 1928. This pioneer work, from which I draw most of my ethnographic data, describes two months' research in Rossel Island carried out in 1921 by Professor W. E. Armstrong, then Assistant Government Anthropologist, Territory of Papua. No full scale published study of Rossel Island has been based on field work done later than 1921; in the ethnographic record, the society remains frozen at a point in time about forty years ago. The interesting material contained in *Rossel Island* deserves to be better known than it is, although it has been referred to in various places.[1]

The most distinctive cultural feature of the society was its indigenous currency sustem. It may seem strange that I insist on qualifying the Rossel Island economy as 'non-monetary', when it is best known for its remarkably elaborate system of native currency and when Armstrong himself accepted the media of exchange in Rossel Island as being money. To understand why, it is necessary to examine its economy and social relationships.

Rossel Island lies to the south-east of Papua, in the Louisiade group of islands, in the south-west Pacific Ocean. The society and culture of its inhabitants were largely unknown before Armstrong carried out his research. Up till this time it had been remarkably isolated and enclosed, and particularly known to Europeans in the

[1] P. Métais, who has made important contributions to the comparative study of shell currency, has, in the course of his analyses, briefly summarized some of Armstrong's points (e.g. in 1949–50). His concern is largely with the general question of 'archaic currency' rather than with Rossel Island as a stationary economy. See also Raymond Firth, 1938, pp. 94–6; 1958, pp. 79–80; P. Einzig, 1949, *passim*. The latest example that has come to my notice is an almost completely inaccurate few sentences in Robert L. Heilbroner (1958, p. 32).

Pacific for the allegation that its cannibal inhabitants had, in the middle of the nineteenth century, killed and eaten some 300 Chinese labourers, shipwrecked on a Rossel reef on their way to Australia. On the whole the island was, not unexpectedly, regarded with disfavour and had few European residents; missionary influence was negligible. It was also insulated, by the treacherous seas and by its lack of voyaging tradition, from neighbouring islands, with the exception of Sudest. Native voyagers from other islands avoided Rossel, which seems to have appeared as sinister to them as it did to Europeans. The result of all these factors was that Rossel was to a large extent (though not entirely) unaffected by the economy and culture of surrounding areas. Armstrong[1] is inclined to think that the elaborate exchange and currency system represents a degeneration of an earlier, less stylized and more 'monetary' system that had diffused from some other, higher centre. But since there is no evidence bearing on the point, at best one can only speculate as to diffusion and the relationship between Rossel currency and that of other Pacific island communities, some of which have currency with certain similarities.[2]

Rossel Island was therefore almost entirely a self-sufficient economy, segregated from other native economies and from Western monetary systems and wider spheres of trade of a Western type. In terms of productivity and income per head, the Rossel Island economy can probably be placed below that of any fully or partly monetized economy (although specific figures cannot be arrived at). Certainly, from the point of view of relevant aspects of money in Western societies—medium of exchange, unit of account, store of wealth, liquid asset—Rossel currency was more like money than was the native currency of many primitive societies. But it was not geared to any widespread monetary or trading system. Furthermore, purchase by means of currency was involved with social relationships; some sorts of currency were intrinsically preferable to others; arrangements were more complicated than would be necessary for the currency to operate like money in a Western economy. If, in the interests of clarification, one were willing to risk a statement suggesting purpose in a society, one might say that the complications of the currency operated as if they were intended to increase the necessity for doubling and redoubling social links and knitting the society into a web of lenders and borrowers, buyers and sellers, gift-givers and gift-receivers. It is consequently preferable to think of Rossel as a 'non-monetary' economy, with the connotation that it was not a

---

[1] Personal communication.

[2] Rossel Island was one of the sources of the necklaces for the traditional Trobriand *kula* exchange, according to B. Malinowski (1922, p. 207). He does not say how or with what the necklaces were 'bought' from the Rossel Islanders.

39

peasant society, and hardly incorporated at all in economic relations outside its immediate vicinity.

CURRENCY IN ECONOMIC TRANSACTIONS AND SOCIAL RELATIONSHIPS

The population of Rossel in 1921 was about 1,500; the density about fifteen persons to the square mile. The staple of subsistence was sago, as the palms grew prolifically. Bananas, plantains, coconut and bread-fruit were also cultivated. Taro, yams and sweet potato, as well as other vegetables, were grown in gardens, cultivated on the slash-and-burn or swidden method. Pigs and dogs were eaten at rituals, as were human beings. Nets, spears and poison were used to obtain turtle, dugong and fish. Several types of canoes existed, comprising those which were used for fishing and sailing to the surrounding reefs, together with a ceremonial canoe not used for ordinary sailing.

There were specialists and their products could be bought. Many small necessaries of daily life as well as minor privileges and services were purchased. Food, baskets, lime pots, lime sticks, the privilege of sailing in certain restricted areas of reefs, the services of certain specialists (including those of prostitutes and 'financiers' or 'brokers') were available, and labourers for gardens could be hired. There was no widespread barter. Currency was therefore needed for straight-forward buying and selling. But by far the largest proportion of transactions involved not only the buyer and seller, but a variety of persons linked by kinship and mutual solidarity with the principals, and the purchase price of the goods being bought was increased by the cost of feasting and ceremony, which accompanied the transfer. Such were the purchase of a piece of village ground, a big house, a prepared garden for coconut, taro or sago, a sailing or a ceremonial canoe, a large fish net, a man for a ritual feast, a pig or dog for a feast, or a case of tobacco. These transactions had wide repercussions in the sphere of social relations.

It will be seen from this list of some of the things that could be bought and sold that currency could be used for straightforward productive investment—in, for instance, a coconut, taro or sago garden, or a large fishing net. Here we have some interesting questions about the nature of the currency as capital. The currency covered a range of 'values' (I quote this for reasons explained later). Currency of low 'value' and, in some circumstances, currency of high 'value' could be considered liquid capital which could be turned into pro-ducers' capital in the ways mentioned. But some high 'value' currency was not liquid and, in view of the fact that the mere possession of some high 'value' shell coins conferred prestige, one might consider coins as durable consumers' goods.

40

Some Aspects of a 'Non-Monetary' Economy (Rossel Island)

It has been said that Rossel currency was used only in ceremonial exchanges.[1] This would detach Rossel currency, rather like the *Kula* valuables of the Trobriand Islands, from circulation in spheres of exchange other than the ceremonial one. I think it is important to recognize that the option of investment, as distinct from the purchase of consumers' assets for personal or ceremonial use or from hoarding, was open to Rossel Islanders and traditionally acceptable, even though the large bulk of transactions may have been to increase prestige and non-productive wealth. There is a distinction to be drawn here between the spheres of exchange in which currency could operate and the relative proportions of transactions of different such types which actually took place.

The most important of the transactions to increase prestige were the feasts that accompanied pig purchases or that were held on other occasions. These were conducted with ceremony. A pig feast could be held as a sort of challenge, as Armstrong points out. He writes (1928, p. 88): 'The challenge starts by one man, A, making insulting remarks about the pig of another man, B; whereupon B retorts by suggesting that A buy the pig and make a feast; and A probably accepts and states his willingness to pay. My informant emphasized these points, but I do not understand them.' The work that has been done by anthropologists on competitive display and destruction of goods in primitive societies since the publication of *Rossel Island* now provides analogies to this form of behaviour in Rossel and a framework of explanation. As in the *potlatch* mentioned earlier, fighting with property is a way of validating status. This is confirmed in Rossel by the fact that such challenge feasts often took place between potential heirs to a man's property, who were usually his son and his sister's son.

Marriage demanded payment of currency; in fact, this was the chief element of the ritual of marriage. The handing over of one particular type of coin (No. 18 *ndap*, see later) by the groom to the bride's father was the centre-piece of the transaction, but a large amount of other currency had to be distributed by the groom to the bride's kin—half to the girl's father and members of his clan and half to her mother's brother and members of her clan. (Clan descent was matrilineal.[2]) Later payments of currency had also to be made.

Mortuary feasts were held for commoners, but those for chiefs

---

[1] This mistake of simplifying the picture of the operation of Rossel currency has been made by Ruth Bunzel (1938, p. 399) and quoted approvingly by Leslie White (1959, p. 259). But though restriction to ceremonial exchange may be characteristic of many primitive societies with currency, it was not true of Rossel.

[2] Armstrong says (1928, p. 94) that half goes to 'the girl's father, and to members of her clan' and half to 'the girl's mother's brother and to members of his clan'. With matrilineal descent, this would bring in the girl's clan twice. It is probably a slip.

41

were more elaborate and included ritual cannibalism. The kin of the victim chosen for the rite were indemnified with certain specified amounts of currency. This could not always be considered a purchase since the kinsmen usually did not willingly hand over the victim, who was taken by surprise and killed by the presumed sorcerer who had 'caused' the chief's death. It was the sorcerer's task to find a victim, as the price of being left alone. In addition, he was actually paid for this task.[1]

The picture I have built up is a mosaic of scattered pieces of information given in various contexts. There is no record, in *Rossel Island*, of any actual transactions or series of transactions made by any individual. It would have needed a much longer time than Armstrong had at his disposal to gather adequate data for an analysis of buying and selling, barter, gift exchange and general patterns of reciprocity.

Even from this abbreviated account, it will be seen that in Rossel life there was a constant paying and receiving of indigenous currency (and of lending and borrowing, which will be discussed later), increased by the necessity to meet a variety of social commitments. Furthermore, the frequency of transactions must have been increased by the nature of the currency itself, which must now be discussed in more detail.

THE PECULIARITIES OF ROSSEL CURRENCY

Rossel currency was made up of shell coins of two varieties, called *ndap* and *nkö* (or *dap* and *kö*). The stock of *ndap* and *nkö* coins was internally differentiated in several ways. The two categories of coins were not interchangeable, nor could they be substituted for one another indifferently in any transaction. Armstrong does indeed provide apparent equivalences between them (1928, p. 69), but this is based merely on similarities of certain names in the two series, although the names were 'not etymologically descriptive of the values', as Armstrong had pointed out earlier (1928, p. 61). Each of the series was divided into coins of different categories, ordered and named. In his analysis of these, Armstrong decided for convenience to number each category: the *ndap* series ran from No. 1 to No. 22, and the *nkö* series from No. 7 to No. 22, No. 22 being the highest category. Not only were the twenty-two categories of *ndap* ranked, they were divided into coins of high rank and coins of low rank. The former, aristocrats among coins, were out of the ordinary field of transactions and were handled with care and ritual: the four highest ranking categories were supposed to be kept from the light of day. The highest ranking coins tended to remain in the hands of chiefs, and the highest of all hardly ever circulated and were said to be

[1] The details of this procedure are by no means clear, as Armstrong points out.

inherited patrilineally by the most powerful chiefly family on the island. The minor coin series—*nkö*—was not so divided, nor were the upper categories treated with particular respect, although the islanders were careful of them. Armstrong obtained a *nkö* coin with much difficulty, and the seller of it was fearful of being found out.

It would be interesting to know exactly how different denominations were recognized. Armstrong concluded that the *ndap* coins, which were made of spondylus shell, were individually recognized through idiosyncrasies of shape and colour. If this was so, then *ndap* categories were sets of coin 'individuals', customarily agreed to. The *nkö* consisted of a set of ten (giant clam?) shell discs strung together. No disc was individually recognized, and the strings of discs could be restrung in various ways in multiples of ten. The sixteen ranks of *nkö* 'coins' (if one can call the ten-disc strings 'coins') were recognized by the increasing diameter of the discs from lowest to highest.

Another peculiarity of the system was that the stock of coins was permanently limited, at least as far as the coins of high denomination were concerned. Possibly some coins of low denomination were being added to the stock, but these additions were effectively controlled by the fact that only ceremonial canoes (mentioned earlier) could be used to transport the shell raw material, and these canoes were owned by chiefs. In any case, new coins, which were only in the *ndap* series, were not as acceptable as the traditional ones. The myth backing this limitation was that the chief deity among the gods made all the money before man came to Rossel. One might expect the stock to dwindle over time, but there is no record of attempted replacement. The islanders did not appear to know the precise extent of the total stock, and Armstrong arrived at a total by estimation, in the vicinity of some 1,000 *ndap* coins and of some 800 *nkö* coins. The free circulation of the coins was further restricted by the fact that women alone tended to handle *nkö* coins in transactions. In view of the population level mentioned earlier, of about 1,500 persons, it seems that the total stock was frozen at a very low level, and that many people must have been completely without liquid wealth of this type. Below is a list of the ranks and estimated totals of some of the *ndap* categories (there is no complete list):

No. 22	7
No. 21	10
No. 20	10
No. 19	10
No. 18	20
No. 17	7
No. 16	7
No. 15	10

No. 14	..	30
No. 13	..	30–40
No. 4	..	200+

One might imagine that there would be a close association between the rank of a coin and the number of coins in the set with that rank. Very broadly, an association held: nevertheless, No. 4 rank contained most members (not 3, 2 or 1) and No. 21, the highest normally used, was not proportionately scarce. Numbers of coins in each rank did not regularly increase from the high to low.

As the characteristics of the currency system emerge from Armstrong's account, it becomes evident that this was a very unusual one. There are many gaps in the account that incite one to speculation as to the precise method in which islanders carried out their arithmetical operations. The most difficult concept to grasp is that islanders saw every operation that occurred in different contexts as distinctive, involving certain customary transfers of coins. There was no common denominator in terms of values. For this reason I earlier put the word 'value' between quotes. On the one hand, there was a ranked system of coins; but, on the other hand, the fact that one rank stood higher than another did not indicate *how much* higher it stood. In other words, rank No. 2 was not accepted as being twice (or three times or *n* times) as great in value as rank No. 1. No coin was expressible as a multiple of another in the series. One might think this strange, since the natives could count, up to 10,000 or further, in multiples of ten. Nevertheless, it is not unusual to find inconsistencies of this sort, which are not questioned in the day-to-day working of a system, since they are never explicitly laid out and examined. Armstrong was so disturbed by the inconsistencies that he thought that an explanation could be sought in the notion that the system was, once, more perfect, and that there were constant relationships between coins, as well as between each coin and the interest demanded on it as a loan. In the course of time, 'accidents of the environment or shortcomings on the part of the performers' (1928, p. 76) led to degeneration of this invented system. Although the Rossel way of reckoning was recalcitrant to Western logic, it is not possible to describe it as an imperfect version of something else without further information.

As corollaries of the separateness of transactions, one might expect that what was defined as being suitable payment or exchange in one context could not do for another context. This was so. If a coin of a particular 'value' or rank was needed, a number of others could not be aggregated to make it up—neither conceptually nor actually. I have mentioned the need to have a No. 18 *ndap* to conduct a valid marriage. This could not be made up of any other coins of lower rank: when a No. 18 was needed by a man who did not have it he could not use, say, six No. 3 coins, but had to borrow. Similarly,

44

if he wanted to buy something that cost a coin of a rank lower than what he had, he could not get 'change': again he had to borrow what he wanted.

The only way to relate ranks of coins was indirectly, through the credit system. I discuss this in more detail in the next section. Here it is necessary to point out that even though interest on a loan took the form of a collection of small coins or, in other circumstances, the form of the difference between the borrowed coin and the higher ranking one that was returned, this does not, strictly speaking, give any clue to relative values unless one knows that there is a constant rate of interest and what the rate is. This interest represents the cost of borrowing a particular coin for a particular length of time. The natives seemed to be clear as to the customarily defined cost in specific cases, and the hypothesis that there was this segregation of operations appears to fit the facts at least as well as the assumption that Rossel contained a degenerated monetary and credit system of a Western type.

The peculiarities and complications—one feels inclined to say unnecessary complications—of the system had social repercussions: the island was covered with a network of debtor and creditor relationships of great complexity, in which loans were manipulated so as to provide the greatest individual advantage that was possible under the circumstances. In the course of this, as will be shown, a great deal of calculation, discounting and careful allocation of resources was exercised.

THE CREDIT SYSTEM

It would greatly facilitate our understanding of the credit system if we had an actual record of any individual's transactions as debtor and creditor; unfortunately, the examples given by Armstrong turn out to be analogies or constructions aimed at elucidating principles, and it is not possible to extract from them more than Armstrong has put into them. A sifting through of the ethnographic data provides only fragmentary information on loan and repayment procedure. But, thanks to Armstrong's ability to put forward his elegant model of the credit system, its general lines are clear.

Borrowing was a constant necessity, as we have seen. After a time, the loan had to be repaid, but not with a coin of the same category as the original one. There were two ways of repaying a loan: either with a coin of the original rank plus a number of coins of lower rank, or with a coin of a higher rank than the one borrowed. It would be nice if in any transaction there was the choice of returning either a higher ranking coin *or* a series of low ones as interest. Then one could equate the series of small coins with the difference between the borrowed coin and the returned coin. There is no record of such equivalences: the two procedures were appropriate to different contexts, although the commonest form was to return a higher ranking coin. Examples of types of loans in the *ndap* series are as follows: a coin of the rank fifth from the highest, when borrowed for three weeks, could be returned with the addition of ten small coins, one from each of the ten lowest ranks; coins of the sixteenth rank from the lowest could, after a loan for an interval of time, be repaid by a coin of the seventeenth rank from the lowest; and the loan of a run of small coins of the lowest ranks could be repaid after a short period by a single coin two or more ranks higher than the series lent. In the *nkö* series, the system of borrowing and lending was the same, with the exception that loans of the high-ranking *nkö* were repaid with the accompaniment of low coins of both *ndap* and *nkö*, and not by dis-charging the debt with a higher-ranking *nkö* coin. There was an institutionalized way to stop the system of ever-increasing loans from seizing up. A particular high-ranking coin usually held by a chief could be borrowed interest-free by the debtor in difficulties and judiciously lent to his creditors. Apparently they accepted the prestige of merely having this coin in their possession as cancelling the debt.

Sometimes in the borrowing of the higher ranking coins, security was required. The usual security for *nkö* was a stone axe; for *ndap* the security was generally a higher-ranking coin than the one borrowed, although for a short-term loan a lower-ranking *ndap* might be accepted. The apparent anomaly of offering security in the form of a higher-ranking coin resulted from the fact that change could not be given and from the necessity of having a particular coin for a particular need.

It is evident that the notion of a return of capital with increase after a period of time connotes that of interest. In the case of loans that were repaid by the return of a higher-ranking coin, the difference between the two ranks was the interest; in the case of loans that were repaid by the original coin with the addition of small coins, the latter represented the interest. The general idea of the relationship between use over time and interest seems to have been quite clear to Rossel informants. But, as I have said, there were certain unexpected characteristics of the system.

The ranked categories of coins made it possible to think of the difference between ranks as the time taken to turn a lower ranking coin on loan into a higher one. Armstrong has made this point very clearly both in *Rossel Island* and in his articles (1921–22, 1924a, 1924b). But although there was a general idea of rates, they could not be expressed as any numerical ratio of the principal. Armstrong says 'there was no conception of a definite unit of time within which a value passes into the next above it in the series' (1928, p. 65). The amount of disagreement that there could be about interest is revealed by the fact that there was an accepted institution for haggling over interest—the *dong*. This was a central feature of the ceremony of borrowing or paying back a loan, in which a number of men sat facing one another in a circle and argued over the actual interest payment to be made. This was particularly so when the interest was concealed in the totality of the item to be returned, in the case of difference between ranks. There was a sort of judgment to be made about the point at which, for example, a loan crossed the threshold between requiring the next coin up, or the next coin but one up, as a return. An analogous problem exists in Malekula, which has a currency system rivalling that of Rossel in intricacy.[1] Pigs with abnormal, specially cultivated, spiral tusks are used as payment for many services as well as for bridewealth and compensation for adultery and murder. The pigs are ranked in order of the degree of the development of their tusks. When a pig is lent, it has to be repaid with interest, that is, the creditor demands the amount the tusks would have grown during the period of the loan, plus an increment. A debtor might not have a pig at this stage of development and might have to borrow. Although in many ways this system is different in operation from that of Rossel, it provides a similar basis for judgment, manoeuvre and accommodation over interest. So much was manoeuvre the rule in Rossel that there even existed a sort of specialist financier (mentioned earlier) whose aim was to accommodate clients and to borrow at a lower rate of interest and lend at a higher.

The uncertainty of interest, the impossibility of expressing interest as an exact ratio of the principal, the impossibility of aggregating coins of different categories as equivalent to one of a higher rank, the impossibility of saying that one category of coins was in any way a multiple or proportion of any other category—all these characteristics suggest that it is impossible to speak of Rossel currency in terms of 'values'. In earlier discussions of this point I have referred to 'ranks' rather than 'values', as this seems to represent the picture of relationships more accurately. There is no way of discovering the extent of intervals between ranks except vaguely, in terms of the two variables, interest and time. Armstrong, unjustifiably, in my opinion, attempts (1928, p. 63) to use the idea of values and to derive the value of coins in a series from the following equation:

$$\text{Value of No. } n = \text{Value of No. } m\,(1+k)^{n-m}.$$

In this equation m and n are two integers representing the number of the value in a series, and k is a constant. $n-m$ is taken to represent the value interval, which is proportional to the time interval taken to turn an m coin into an n. It is impossible to evaluate k to give any result; furthermore, to know the relationship between the interval of

[1] See B. Deacon, 1934; J. Layard, 1942; J. Guiart, 1952.

values and the length of time of the loan (the only certain, measurable quantity) is to presuppose that one knows something already about the values that one is attempting to find out. It appears to me that this unduly sophisticates the situation as it emerges from the ethnography, and makes Rossel currency seem to approach Western money value relationships. Possibly this arises from the fact that, having assigned numerical values to the categories of coins, which should have been ordinal rather than cardinal, Armstrong attempted to extract from these numbers, which expressed no more than that one coin category could be ranked above or below another, a more precise mathematical statement than the data warranted. It seems to be more in line with the evidence to substitute ranks for values, rather as if one had a ranked series of ace, king, queen, knave in cards, but no convention that knave equalled 1, queen equalled 2 and so on, and no situations in which two knaves could be exchanged for, or used instead of, a queen. Interest throughout the whole series was defined by custom and not by any discoverable consistent mathematical ratio.[1]

PROFITING FROM THE CREDIT SYSTEM

Profiting from the credit system was a major occupation of Rossel Islanders. There were several ways of profiting in different areas of economic and social relationships. If the system had been completely confined to gaining prestige through accumulation of currency by manipulation of the credit and interest system, with no productive investment, then it would have been very like the zero-sum game familiar to economists, in which one man's losses equal another man's gains. In fact, this does represent some elements that were very important in preserving the circular and repetitive nature of this technologically primitive economy. The largest proportion of choices were for the alternative of lending accumulated currency rather than investing in capital equipment (nets, land, canoes, etc.). Furthermore, loans were not made with an eye to having a stake in some productive enterprise, since borrowers, as we have seen, were frequently borrowing to fulfil social commitments such as wedding payments or often ceremonial feasts. This provides one of the most important lessons of the case of Rossel Island, which concerns the mechanism by which, despite great activity in the economic sphere, *aggregate* capital is largely maintained at the same level although *individuals* may become wealthy.

[1] Professor Armstrong disagrees, since he feels in any case that all ranked categories—perhaps even ranks in a social organizational sense—can be given numerical expression. *Wergild* payments as injury compensation for different ranks of persons in Anglo-Saxon England would be evidence in favour of this theory. (Personal communication.)

Some Aspects of a 'Non-Monetary' Economy (Rossel Island)

There were several routes to prestige and power. The sheer accumulation of liquid capital was one way; at the same time reckless expenditure could purchase prestige by financing ceremonial activities —in the form of feasts or the purchase of ceremonial canoes. The ceremonial canoes were a capstone of the edifice of wealth. They were the monopoly of chiefs, in effect, since those who could get them— by purchase or inheritance—became chiefs. Heirs of chiefs could inherit ceremonial canoes, while rich men with a desire to be accepted as of chiefly rank could buy ceremonial canoes. The mere possession of these then provided validation of their status. The points related to the association between wealth and power in Rossel are obscure, as Armstrong, in his short stay, was not able to examine the political structure. But there were wide differences in wealth throughout the community, which were in turn a source of greater differentiation of wealth, and still more, of prestige. There were circumstances in which chiefs would rather gain prestige through generosity than accumulate more currency through interest on loans. An example of this lies in the situation mentioned, in which a chief could save (financially) a borrower, who had gone higher and higher up the coin ranks in an attempt to cover his loans and losses and saw disaster facing him.

It is possible to see, from the nature of the currency system itself and from the commitments of social life, why there was a constant necessity to borrow. But was the incentive to lend based only on the wish to gain by interest? It was certainly not usually an investment in someone's productive enterprise. A man might similarly gain by investment in producer's capital, yet, as I have mentioned, there was proportionately little of this kind of investment. Some aspects of the absence of movement towards entrepreneurship need closer examination.

BORROWING, LENDING AND RECIPROCITY

It is not necessary to suggest that a community such as Rossel Island would inevitably move towards entrepreneurship unless something were positively stopping it: that would be making many assumptions. But there are certain forms of social interaction that are associated with circularity in economic relations. A relevant principle in such forms of interaction has been analysed by anthropologists under the general title of reciprocity. In many primitive economies, a proportion of goods and services is distributed not on the basis of purchase, or even of barter with haggling, but on the basis of a sort of reciprocity of gift exchange. This is an exchange, since somewhere in the continuing process of the transaction will come the necessity to return an object or service roughly equivalent to the one initially given. But, most important, it is a gift, with all that this implies in the

49

social sphere. These ideas were first explicitly put forward in a general context and as a general theory by Marcel Mauss (1925, 1954), and have been subsequently applied to many societies.[1]

Mauss's elucidation of gift exchange shows it to be a transfer of something (material or not) that is apparently disinterested and generous, with no strings attached, but which in fact constrains the recipient to act in a certain way. The gift is usually formally offered, without haggling, and received with dignity. The offering of the gift connotes three things: the duty to give (to maintain authority, prestige); the duty to receive (or to cut off social relations); and the duty to repay (or remain perpetually under a social obligation to the giver). In economic terms, the effect is not very different from an ordinary exchange of commodities, but in social terms the exchange is made to do a great deal of work in other spheres of relationships. The multiplex roles of tribal, and to a lesser extent peasant, societies may be drawn into the transaction; it has a meaning greater than the mere offering of something one has too much of for something one lacks and would rather have.

Now, there are many similarities between the social concomitants of gift exchange and the social concomitants of credit in societies with multiplex social relationships. Mauss (1954, pp. 34–5) went so fas as to say they were identical. At least one can say that in such societies, whoever as a result of a transaction with delayed return is actually at any moment in possession of the goods concerned is under an obligation as recipient. This applies to both gift exchange and credit relations. The debtor is in a socially dependent situation and the creditor in a socially superior situation. The cycle of the transaction is concluded by the return of the principal with interest (representing rent for use over time). But in the interval a relationship exists, which may be of much wider social dimensions than the debtor/creditor relationship in a Western economy.[2] This does not merely mean that the creditor can exercise control over the debtor's actions by calling in or threatening to call in a loan; this is well documented in peasant societies. But the creditor may prefer to maintain the status superiority that lending gives him. In societies in which roles are multiplex it may be an insult to your creditor to wish to repay him. Arensberg's work on Ireland (1937) has shown this to be true in the case of credit (of a slightly different sort from a straight loan) extended by shopkeepers to their customers, who are largely relatives. If a complete settling-up occurs, this means good relations are being broken off. It becomes a delicate task to steer between financial profit and kin solidarity.

[1] Much of Mauss's analysis was suggested by B. Malinowski (1922), already mentioned.
[2] See, for example, M. W. Wilmington (1955).

Some Aspects of a 'Non-Monetary' Economy (Rossel Island)

In Rossel, a really enviable position to be in was to hold many investments in the form of loans, although not necessarily long-term ones. One of the functions of the specialist 'financier', the *ndeb*, was to keep a client's capital circulating, and to get a less profitable loan repaid (supposedly by magic) so that more lucrative or socially advantageous loans could be made. Economic and social institutions were such as to make constant lending in the traditional system easy and desirable, financially and socially rewarding. Thus, there was a technological aid to exchange of some ingenuity, as well as pressures to increase the velocity of circulation which, in the indigenous system, failed to lead to accelerated economic growth. And, at the same time, almost all economic calculation was channelled into traditional directions, in what seems to an outside observer to have been a frenzy of financial activity in a self-supporting circular system of socio-economic relationships.

ROSSEL ISLAND ECONOMIC DEVELOPMENT TODAY

Throughout this account of the mechanics of an indigenous economic system, I have tended to treat it as a completely closed economy. One may be suspicious of this picture of *any* actual economy, although Rossel seems to have been more isolated than most, as well as to have possessed in a striking form a self-supporting circular system of economic relationships. But I did mention at the beginning of the paper the fact that Rossel was not completely cut off, and outside the orbit of Western monetary economy. When Armstrong did his field work, there were a few coconut plantations run by Europeans, and labour was employed here as well as in Queensland (through 'blackbirding'). A few Western articles (saucepans, trade tobacco) were used by the islanders. One might predict from the evidence of the foregoing analysis of the indigenous economy that it would *not* be through a development of the internal system, despite all the riches of economic calculation and activity that went into it, that a growth of the real wealth of Rossel would occur. That is not to say that the indigenous system might not contribute to growth in a dual economy, once a movement had started. This has happened elsewhere.[1] But one might imagine that it would be only by breaking into the elaborate socially supported mode of internal circulation and traditional satisfactions that an initial transformation of a non-monetary economy such as Rossel Island's might occur.

As far as one can tell, this has been the case. There has not as yet been any follow-up study of comparable detail to *Rossel Island*. From general information, one may infer that this minute Pacific island is still under-developed on any criterion, but that it has been drawn

[1] See C. S. Belshaw (1955a).

51

into the sphere of Western monetary influence by the gradual develop-ment of Papua, and of the Louisiade Islands in particular. Copra and shell are produced from Rossel, and gold production at Sudest on Tagula Island provides opportunities for wage earning. Rossel Island has been deliberately linked to Western enterprise. The question remains as to whether the indigenous credit and currency have contributed to development, become incorporated in external monetary and trading systems, or tended to become concentrated in the ceremonial and ritual sphere.

3

Personal Capital Formation among the Tolai of New Britain[1]

BY SCARLETT EPSTEIN

In this essay I set out to analyse the factors responsible for the growth of entrepreneurship in a traditional setting, where the ownership of land and capital assets is vested in a group rather than in the individual. I shall also discuss the operation as well as the reasons for the persistence of a dual shell money and money economy. Furthermore, I shall show that if economic differentiation is not displayed in everyday consumption, while income is growing, this will facilitate a high rate of savings and investment; though some money may still be hoarded due to the limited investment opportunities within the native's economic horizon. I discuss these problems on the basis of field research data from the Tolai of New Britain.

New Britain is as isolated, sparsely populated and underdeveloped as much of the rest of New Guinea, except for its north-eastern portion, the Gazelle Peninsula, which comprises only about 300 square miles. This is not only a major centre of European plantations but also the chief seat of native enterprise. The Tolai of the Gazelle Peninsula have undergone rapid economic development since the last war. Their wealth stems from cocoa and copra. Many of them own trucks, jeeps or landrovers, operate their own copra driers and live in neatly designed European-style houses. Their recent progress has been assisted by a concatenation of factors: a fertile volcanic soil with favourable rainfall; a long and close contact with Europeans, who have made use of the excellent harbour facilities and built a large network of roads; a linguistically homogeneous population with a flexible social structure; and a welfare policy by the Australian Administration.

[1] I carried out the field work on which this paper is based as a Research Fellow of the Australian National University, Canberra, in a Tolai parish, between October 1959 and October 1960, and again from April to July 1961.

Capital, Saving and Credit in Peasant Societies

The Tolai number about 40,000 and occupy an area of approximately 180 square miles. The area of Tolai settlement is traditionally divided into a number of districts (*paparagunan*), in which lie the parishes[1] (*gunan*) and hamlets (*iklik na gunan*). A hamlet usually consists of two or three households made up of a set of brothers with their wives and children, or a married man, his maternal nephews and their families, or, according to more recent tendencies, a married couple with their married sons and families. The number and size of hamlets per parish varies greatly according to the density of settlement.[2] Each hamlet, in fact each piece of land cultivated within memory, has a name, usually of a tree or other plant; rights of cultivation are tied up with knowledge of land names.

The Tolai are a matrilineal people who settle avunculo-virilocally or patri-virilocally. In cases of inter-parish marriage, the former means that sons, who grow up in their father's hamlet, have to move on his death to their mother's brother's parish, where they have rights in land. The introduction of cash crops has emphasized the ties between father and sons, because sons help their father in planting and growing cocoa and copra. A Tolai father today wants to leave his perennial crops to his own, rather than to his sisters', sons, who normally grow up in another hamlet and often in another parish and do not help him with gardening. Indeed, there is now a widespread desire to see the change from a system of landholding vested in the matrilineage to one of individual rights of ownership and disposal. However, few probably realize the full implications of such a change, which would undermine the very basis of their social system.

The tendency of sons to settle in their father's parish has been recently enhanced,[3] but such patri-virilocal settlement existed even before European contact. According to informants, it presented little problem in the past, because there was ample land, there was no perennial cash crop and the matrilineage of the father was obliged to provide land for the sons' food gardens. These cultivation rights also served to keep alive matrilineage claims in the land, since rights in land tend to lapse where the land itself is not cultivated. Moreover, the practice of leasing and selling land was quite common even in the traditional Tolai economic system.

[1] Parish denotes the largest local group forming a political unit; see H. I. Hogbin and Camilla Wedgwood, 1953.

[2] For instance Rapitok, a group of three linked parishes, consists of a total population of 651 living in 141 households distributed over sixty-three hamlets. There are no comparative figures available for other parishes.

[3] Of Rapitok's 63 hamlets, 28 have more than one household. Of these 28 hamlets, 14 consist of parental and married sons' households, 12 of a set of brothers with their families, and 2 of a married couple and the man's maternal nephew with his family.

54

The settlement of sons with their father increases the number of matrilineages in each parish and facilitates intra-parish marriage.[1] A system of moieties provides the exogamous units. These moieties cover the entire Tolai area, though moiety names differ from one part to another. All members of a moiety are conceived of as sharing common descent, but the moiety itself is not internally differentiated, and has no corporate functions. In addition, there are also restrictions on marriage between certain categories of close kin.

Members of one matrilineage (*vunatarai*) live in several parishes. A number of matrilineage sections[2] (*apiktarai*) are centred in one parish. The matrilineage section is the important unit for the purpose of landholding. Individual rights in land are established by cultivation, but residuary rights remain vested in the matrilineage section. Each matrilineage section has a leader (*lualua*), who is usually the man in the most senior genealogical position; if he is unfit to lead, he will be succeeded by a younger real or classificatory brother, or by an eldest sister's eldest son. *Lualuas* are important not only in the political but also in the economic sphere. They speak at parish meetings and help to settle disputes within the parish. They also control the land vested in their matrilineage section; a man who wants to cultivate a certain piece of land belonging to his own matrilineage can do so only with his *lualua's* permission. Similarly, if the matrilineage leases or sells some of its land the *lualua* pockets the rent or the price paid for it. He often also stores the wealth of some or all the members of his matrilineage section as well as the bride-price received for its women. The strategic political and economic importance of the *lualua* leads to a struggle for power between the *lualua* and men in junior positions, who try to break away and form their own section under their own control. At the same time the opposite process is taking place, whereby small sections try to graft themselves on to more powerful matrilineage sections.

Prior to European contact, about a century ago, Tolai society was highly segmented. Each parish was sometimes at war with its neighbours, while at other times combined with them against a common enemy. There do not appear to have been any permanent alliances between parishes. Wars were frequent and Tolai were cannibals. Today they have all been converted to Christianity and refer to their cannibal past as the 'time of darkness'.

However, despite the hostility between local settlements there was a highly developed system of trade and exchange, facilitated by an

---

[1] Seventy per cent of the extant marriages in Rapitok are intra-parish.
[2] A matrilineage section denotes the section of a matrilineage settled in one parish. A matrilineage section consists of one or more minimal lineages.

indigenous shell currency (*tambu*).[1] The coastal Tolai used to go by canoe to Nakanai, a journey of about 200 miles along the north coast of New Britain, where they traded taro, yams, coconuts and other food items for shells or for the right to fish for the shells themselves. Frequently the Tolai simply overpowered the Nakanai natives and then gathered the precious shells and took them back to their homes. On their return to the Gazelle Peninsula they made the shells into *tambu* and bought food from the inland Tolai with it. Ecological factors, which included a high degree of local variation, provided the basis for regular trade between coastal and inland natives; the latter would offer their taro and other food crops for the fish, egg of the megapode, slaked lime and other produce peculiar to the coast.

Since hostilities between parishes made long travel unsafe there was a chain of markets, at which intermediaries bought and sold goods for *tambu*. According to Schneider (1905, p. 29) there existed the institution of the 'peace of the market' which meant that even sworn enemies had to refrain from fighting while at the market.

As far as can be known, the Tolai have always attached great importance to *tambu*. Parkinson wrote in 1887 (p. 105) that to acquire *tambu* in large quantities was the serious endeavour of every native, because with it he could get anything he wanted. 'With *tambu* he bought his ornaments, his food and his wives; it also helped him to get out of any scrape. He paid *tambu* to smooth out difficulties with his worst enemies, even if he had killed their nearest relative. The man who had most *tambu* enjoyed also the highest respect and greatest influence. Each man carried about half to four fathoms of *tambu* with him to meet his daily expenses while he stored the remainder in a special hut belonging to the *lualua* of his matrilineage. The hut was always guarded by several men, who sounded the alarm if danger arose. In case of emergency all people hurried to the treasure hut and each took a load of *tambu* to carry it to safety. It is said by natives that a woman, pursued by her enemies, would rather leave her child behind than lose her *tambu*.'

Tambu possesses most of the qualities of a good currency; it is durable, can be easily stored and is divisible into small amounts. But to the Tolai *tambu* is much more than just a good currency; it is the pillar which supports their whole social system. Social ties are forged through the medium of *tambu*, while every ceremonial is accompanied by its distribution and/or exchange. Mortuary rites play a very important part in Tolai social life. In pre-contact days they believed that by cutting up and distributing a dead man's *tambu*

---

[1] *Tambu* consists of small shells (*nassa camelus*) about one third of an inch in diameter. The shells, after a hole is bored in each, are threaded on rattan string. *Tambu* is measured in fathoms or fractions thereof and stored by making large coils winding about 500 fathoms round a circle of bamboo.

they helped to secure his soul's entry to some sort of heaven. If little or no *tambu* was distributed, his spirit would haunt his descendants and never rest. Though this belief has disappeared, the practice of *tambu* distribution has remained. At a mortuary rite I attended in 1960, seven coils were distributed which belonged to the deceased, as well as a further fifteen belonging to his brothers, maternal nephews and sons. A man stakes a claim in the inheritance of a deceased by distribuing *tambu* at his mortuary rite. Thus the accumulated wealth of *tambu* is periodically re-distributed. The Tolai still cling to their traditional shell currency, despite their need for cash to purchase European goods. This is due to the fact that *tambu* is so closely interlinked with their whole social system.

The Tolai economic system consists of three sectors: the subsistence, the *tambu* and the cash sector. *Tambu* forms the connecting link between them. Food can be bought with *tambu* and sold for money. Thus *tambu* is a highly liquid asset. Tolai say that one fathom of *tambu* is worth two Australian shillings. This exchange rate was established in German times at the turn of the century, when one fathom equalled two German marks, the price paid for a fathom at Nakanai. But while the purchasing power of money has fallen much more than that of *tambu* during the last sixty years and the price has more than doubled at Nakanai in the same period, Tolai still refer to the customary exchange rate, which is a purely theoretical concept. This indicates that in practice they are not interested in a conversion from *tambu* into money or vice versa. In fact on the Gazelle Peninsula it is impossible to buy *tambu* with money. Both money and *tambu* act as media of exchange, but whereas money fulfils a purely economic function only, *tambu* acts also as an element in Tolai social cohesion. Though *tambu* is a highly liquid asset Tolai show little interest in its liquidity. Therefore the price for each food item sold both for *tambu* and money is fixed by supply and demand operating independently in the *tambu* and in the cash sectors. For instance, at Rabaul market during the first half of 1961 a chicken could be bought for one fathom of *tambu* or ten to twelve Australian shillings while six taro cost half a fathom or two Australian shillings. In the one case, one fathom equals ten, in the other it equals only four Australian shillings. This means that the cash demand for chickens was greater in relation to its supply, than that for taro, while the reverse held true for the *tambu* sector. Though the Tolai have the theoretical concept of a uniform exchange rate, in practice *tambu* prices for food items are not generally equated at a uniform rate with their cash prices.

In theory, this varying exchange rate would appear to give enterprising men the opportunity to manipulate the two sectors of the economy in such a way that they could accumulate *tambu* or money,

57

as they wished. If, for instance, a man wanted to accumulate money, he might be tempted to convert £1 into £3 by buying taro with money, selling the taro for *tambu*, then buying chickens with the *tambu* and selling them for money. Such arbitrage on a large scale would eventually bring about a uniform exchange rate. However, there are a number of considerations which militate against the actual development of such a practice. There is in fact a large surplus of unsold goods at the market so that the excess of supply over demand helps to perpetuate the varying exchange rates.[1] Then the range of transactions conducted in *tambu* is limited in relation to the total range of the market.[2] Since *tambu* is restricted to intra-Tolai trade[3] and very few Tolai ever want to buy chickens, it is unlikely that sufficient *tambu* would be offered for chickens to increase their *tambu* price and reduce the money price. Most of the demand for chickens comes from the Chinese who have to pay in money because they have no means to acquire *tambu*. Similarly, since the major part of demand for taro comes from the Tolai, who are the only buyers to have *tambu* at their disposal, it is unlikely that many of them would want to purchase taro with money in preference to *tambu*, so as to reduce the *tambu* and increase the money price. With an ever declining *tambu* sector of the Tolai economy, it is unlikely that an equalization in the exchange rate between *tambu* and money will ever occur. *Tambu* as a medium in economic transactions will persist as long as the system of trade between inland and coastal Tolai continues. It will be threatened only when the pattern of Tolai wants changes to such an extent that they will want to purchase goods only obtainable with cash. But even then *tambu* might still persist as currency in ceremonial exchanges.

It is against this background that I want now to discuss the case history of one Tolai entrepreneur, because I think it will throw into relief many of the features of Tolai capital management and rural economic development. To Dungan is a man of about fifty years, who lives in Rapitok, a parish on the frontier of Tolai settlement, some sixteen miles inland from Rabaul. His father belonged to Rapitok, whereas his mother came from Napapar, a parish about four miles away. Thus while he grew up at Rapitok his own matri-lineage was centred at Napapar. He had spent his youth in Rapitok and he had no desire to move to Napapar on his father's death. The

---

[1] A survey of Rabaul market conducted during June 1961 showed that 33 per cent of all goods brought to the market remained unsold.

[2] *Tambu* transactions form only about 10 per cent of total transactions at Rabaul market.

[3] In 1902 the German authorities passed a law prohibiting trade transactions between indigenous and non-indigenous population to be conducted in *tambu*. Although there is no such restriction under the Australian Administration, none of the non-indigenous population has since tried to enter the *tambu* trade.

attachment to locality is very strong among the Tolai and often overrides allegiance to their own kinship group. To Dungan's father had been *lualua* of his matrilineage section as well as *luluai* (Government appointed parish headman). Thus he was in a privileged position to leave some land to his son. He arranged with his matrilineage section to allocate land to To Dungan for food gardens.

Before the last war Rapitok natives had little money, since cash crops were rare. To Dungan, an enterprising young man, was soon attracted to Rabaul, where he could earn some money and enjoy life in the town. He quickly picked up driving and became a driver. His wages were fifteen shillings a month plus rations. Pre-war all natives were paid wages in silver and received cash in silver for the sale of their crops. The practice of the day was that any native with paper money was apt to be suspected of having stolen it.[1] Thus natives were at the mercy of Chinese traders, who charged them twenty-two Australian shillings for a one-pound note. Savings in silver are cumbersome and native incomes were low. Few natives therefore were able to save much money at that time, and most of their savings were still in the form of *tambu*. To Dungan saved about £A25 during his seven years' work in Rabaul. He returned to Rapitok in 1937 to take up the post of *luluai*, which his father had held before him. He planted food on the land of his father's matrilineage. However, his drive for power led him to gather a following of men and women of his matrilineage, who came from Napapar to live in Rapitok. His position was still very tenuous since he had no control over land and the members of his matrilineage section still had to lease or buy land from their respective father's matrilineage section. Nevertheless, he strengthened his political position as *lualua* through his success in the economic sphere. He managed to acquire two large coils of *tambu* from his father, which he used cleverly to accumulate more *tambu* as well as to purchase brides for the young men of his own matrilineage section. Furthermore, a distant line of his own matrilineage was settled in Rapitok and so he took over the leadership of this matrilineage section as well. However, this lasted for only a short time, for as soon as the recognized *lualua* of this section came of age and achieved married status he broke away from To Dungan, and began himself to supervise his own matrilineage affairs. To Dungan handed over some of the *tambu* he had stored on their behalf from the bride-price received for their women; but he did not deduct the *tambu* he had paid for brides on behalf of their young men, thus keeping them under obligation to him.

During the last war, the Japanese authorities demanded the surrender of all Australian currency held by natives. They searched

[1] This information was confirmed by Administration Officers and bank officials who worked in Rabaul before the last war.

59

native homes and killed anyone found to have hidden money. To Dungan was one of many Tolai who had faith in the return of the Australian Administration, and who hld his savings during the war. Immediately after the war, when ex-army vehicles were being offered cheaply, he was quick to seize the opportunity. He set about accumulating sufficient cash by converting *tambu* into money: he bought pigs for five fathoms each from other Tolai and sold them for about £20 each to some Chinese in Rabaul, who were then starved for pigs and prepared to pay high prices. After a few months of this trading To Dungan went into partnership with one of his classificatory brothers. They bought a truck for £125 of which To Dungan contributed £80 and his partner the remainder. Since To Dungan alone could drive and understood the mechanics of the car, he was in fact doing all the work, while his sleeping partner clamoured for a share in the profits. After a year To Dungan finally decided to withdraw personally from the enterprise, but left his money invested in it. He bought another vehicle with £200 he had accumulated during the year's working of the jointly owned truck. He worked this truck for ten years on his own account until it became too costly because it needed too many repairs. He decided to buy a new truck for £1,800. Since natives are restricted by law from purchasing goods on credit or hire purchase, he faced the problem of raising the capital. The usual practice amongst modern Tolai is for a number of men belonging to one matrilineage to pool their savings and buy the asset jointly. Only few intra-Tolai loans take place. They distrust interpersonal loans, because they suspect that the borrower will rely on kinship obligations when the creditor wants repayment of the loan. Therefore, joint enterprise is the only practicable means available to Tolai to raise sufficient funds to acquire a large and costly capital asset. However, joint ownership raises a number of problems. In the first place, natives have no concept of dividends as the reward for invested capital; usually, they have no arrangement whereby a man gets a share of the profits according to the amount he has invested in the joint enterprise. In many cases, natives keep separate savings accounts for a jointly owned asset into which they put all its income and out of which they pay all its expenses. Very few natives have any idea of depreciation and frequently they re-invest the income from one asset in some other enterprise, leaving no ready cash available for repairs or renewals. Consequently, many a vehicle is stranded waiting until the owners can pool more money to pay for necessary repairs. Secondly, the *lualua* is normally entrusted with the management of the vehicle and the keeping of accounts. This is a consequence of the customary practice whereby members of a matrilineage section stored *tambu* with their *lualua* and it further strengthens his position. But the actual running of the truck or car is normally in the hands of younger men, who know how to drive and look after it. The driver of the vehicle is usually a part owner and only rarely is provision made for his wages. This often causes discontent among the drivers and raises disputes between them and the *lualua,* who manages the vehicle's accounts. Thirdly, some jointly owned trucks are run on the agreement that each major co-partner, who has invested at least £100, can have the use of the vehicle for a limited period of time, say three months, during which time he is responsible for its running expenses, while he can pocket the income derived from it. This arrangement works satisfactorily until the vehicle breaks down and needs some costly repairs, when the parties now dispute amongst themselves as to who should foot the bill.

Difficulties of this kind led To Dungan to think of acquiring a vehicle on his own account. He decided to take loans of £100 each from four of his classificatory brothers and two friends. In this respect he is still one of the few Tolai to have succeeded in establishing individual ownership of capital assets through the use of loans. His success with the first truck, as well as his strong personality, was adequate guarantee to his creditors that he would repay his debt.

If a truck is well looked after it can yield substantial profits, because there are always many Tolai who want to take their produce to Rabaul or go on trips. (During one month To Dungan made a net profit of £42 making allowance for cost of petrol, repairs and depreciation.) To Dungan was able to repay his debt in about one and a half years; he paid 5 per cent interest per annum. Interest is no new concept to the Tolai, but was part of their traditional *tambu* economy. If a man wanted to borrow, say, ten fathoms of *tambu* he took one fathom to the lender and then collected his ten fathoms. However, such interest was not related to the amount borrowed nor was it confined to any particular period, but was for the duration of the loan. Such a payment served, indeed, as a form of confirmation of the contract rather than as an interest payment. But the idea itself that one has to pay for a loan of money or *tambu* is not new to the Tolai. Nor is thrift a new concept, because the Tolai attached high value to the accumulation of *tambu* even in pre-contact days.

To Dungan kept a separate savings account for his truck. At the end of 1960 he took stock and saw that he had accumulated over £1,400 while the monthly cost of repairs to the vehicle was rapidly increasing. So he decided to trade in his truck and get a new one. At the same time he calculated that he could make even better profits if he operated the truck from another parish about eight miles away, where there are fewer vehicles than in Rapitok. To Dungan has thus learned that it does not pay to operate a truck after its repairs become excessive. He also appreciates that it pays to spread one's enterprise over unexplored fields.

Immediately after the war, when the Administration began to encourage natives to sell copra and grow cocoa, To Dungan was the first in Rapitok to start a copra drier. He got the idea from a Chinese in Rabaul that he could cheaply and easily prepare a copra drier with old Japanese corrugated iron and drums, which he did quite successfully. However, he soon realized that the copra dried in such makeshift driers was much inferior to the product of a hot-air drier and fetched lower prices. A few years later he invested £400 in building a copra drier with European materials, good trays and heating arrangement. Here again To Dungan insisted on individual ownership whereas most other copra driers built subsequently in Rapitok[1] are jointly owned by members of matrilineage sections. On his instigation a co-operative store was started right opposite To Dungan's copra drier, where copra was purchased from natives. This brought more business to his copra drier until the co-operative went bankrupt a few years later. Recently, To Dungan has been trying his best to revive the co-operative again. Competition from other copra driers caused his own to stand idle many a day, so he was keen to have the co-operative working again, which would place his drier in a favoured position and bring more trade.

Tolai are very fortunate in regard to their requirements of tools and equipment for garden work. All they need is an axe for chopping down trees, a few large bush knives, spades and shovels, but no ploughs or draught animals. Thus the total investment in tools and equipment per household amounts to no more than about £5. However, To Dungan is outstanding in this respect as well. He has bought a mechanical wood-saw for about £175, which enables him to have his timber cut up quickly and evenly. Thus when his New Guinea labourers clear bush on his lands, he has the timber cut up and sells it as firewood to Europeans or Chinese in Rabaul. While in the case of the wood-saw the asset is a substitute for labour, most other assets acquired by Tolai supplement rather than substitute for labour.

To Dungan was also the first in Rapitok to heed the advice of the agricultural officers and embark on growing cocoa. He had to overcome opposition from the elders of his father's matrilineage section, who objected to his using his father's land for any other purpose than growing food. Coconuts constitute an important item in Tolai diet, and therefore people planted coconuts, their only perennial crop. To plant cocoa, a perennial crop not for consumption, was an entirely new venture. It meant investing land and labour in an enterprise which was supposedly going to yield money after about four years.

To Dungan started by planting about 200 cocoa trees; by 1960

[1] By July 1961 there were six hot-air and eight makeshift copra driers in Rapitok.

he had a total of about 2,300 trees. He proudly relates how after about four years, when he harvested his first cocoa and sold it at Rabaul for £3, he bought rice and tinned meat with the money and gave a feast for the elders of his father's matrilineage, who by that time had already become convinced of the advantages of growing cocoa. When To Dungan saw the steady profit from cocoa and copra, without much labour involved, he wanted to plant more cocoa and coconut trees. However, he is still regarded as an outsider in Rapitok and therefore has no right to land. Accordingly, he bought about ten acres of land from another matrilineage section in the name of his sons. At the same time he called a meeting of all the members of his matrilineage section and they decided that each man and woman should contribute £5 to a common fund which was to be used for a joint enterprise. Some people suggested that they should buy a truck or open a store. But To Dungan pointed out to them that none of them had any land in Rapitok and said that land was the only really productive asset. He then went on to suggest that they should pool their money and buy jointly a large tract of land, which they could then use as other matrilineage sections used theirs. It is significant to note that in the question of land To Dungan adhered to the customary system of group ownership while he preferred individual ownership of his commercial assets. He could have quite easily bought a large area of land for himself and ignored the needs of the other members of his matrilineage section. However, the powers of a *lualua* are based on his ability to control land and To Dungan is keen on being a leader. To Dungan's matrilineage section pooled £450, part of which they invested in 375 acres of land. Control of the land is vested in To Dungan to whom each member of the matrilineage section has to apply for rights of cultivation. Unfortunately for To Dungan, he bought land on the border between Rapitok and Taulil from the Taulils, but the Rapitok people questioned the right of the Taulils to this land and claimed it for themselves. It took about four years before the dispute was finally settled. In the meantime, To Dungan cleared some of the land and planted food and coconuts on it, while other members of his matrilineage planted food there but did not dare to plant perennial crops lest the case were settled in favour of the Rapitok people. To Dungan himself had bought material worth £300 to build a new permanent European-style house on the land he had purchased, but he suspended the work on it until the land dispute was settled. Early in 1961 the Native Lands Commissioner arranged a meeting between Taulil and Rapitok elders at which it was decided that the major part of the 375 acres under dispute actually belonged to Rapitok. The elders who claimed that land agreed to let To Dungan have fifty acres of it and they marked out the boundary of the land. To

63

Dungan had to accept this decision. He complained bitterly that the
Rapitok people did not like him despite all he had done for them.
The fact is that they are ambivalent towards him. On the one hand
they admire his thrift and enterprise as well as his forceful person
ality; on the other, they are envious of his economic success and
criticize his purely materialistic outlook. 'He cares more for money
than for his people,' is a constant complaint levelled against him. Yet
he is well versed in most traditional activities, such as the *Tubuan*
cult, the *Tabaran* dances, the making of *garamuts* (large drums),
kundus (small drums) and so on.

In April 1960 To Dungan had an accumulation of about 3,500
fathom of *tambu* of which he acquired 1,500 from his father; 1,000
belonged to members of his matrilineage section who stored their
tambu with him, and 1,000 he accumulated himself. In spite of his
enterprise in the money economy, he still continues to accumulate
tambu. He financed the trip of his classificatory sister's son to
Nakanai to purchase *tambu* there. The latter brought back 100
fathom which he had purchased for £20 and he spent £6 on the
journey. To Dungan was very happy when his maternal nephew
handed him the *tambu* and he gave a feast for him.

By early 1961 To Dungan's stock of *tambu* had been reduced to
3,200 fathoms. He cut up and distributed about 300 fathoms at the
mortuary rite for one of his classificatory brothers, who had died in
the meantime; he also paid 100 fathoms fine for committing moiety
incest with his classificatory sister's daughter. During the same
period he accumulated another 100 fathom *tambu* through selling
taro and pigs for *tambu* as well as attending mortuary rites at which
he received *tambu* as his share in the distribution.

To Dungan's wife, like most Tolai women, has her own store of
tambu. At the beginning of 1960 she had 500 fathoms *tambu*, which
she had accumulated, since she got married twenty-five years ago,
by the sale of taro, peanuts, chickens and pigs. A year later she had
fifty fathoms more. The drive to collect *tambu* is so great among
women that they are prepared to spend £1 on transport charges to
take a few dozen taro to Rabaul market, where they can sell them
for about six fathoms of *tambu*. Some of them are most dissatisfied
if they do not manage to sell their taro for *tambu* and have to sell for
money. They promptly purchase tobacco with the money and sell
the tobacco in their own parish for tambu. Since Tolai women's
demand for cash goods is even smaller than that of men, they are
still keener to accumulate *tambu* than money.

Early in 1960 To Dungan had a total of about £2,000 personal
cash savings as well as £900 in his truck account. A year later he had
£2,200, a new truck worth £2,150 and £100 in his truck account.
During the year he had invested another £300 in finishing his new

house and £100 in starting a shop among the neighbouring Baining people. To Dungan distributes his cash savings over three different banks. Most natives put their savings into several banks. They regard this as giving them greater security. The reason for this belief can be found in their traditional *tambu* economy. If a man wanted to accumulate a lot of shell money at any one time for himself or on behalf of his son or daughter, he announced to his relatives and friends that he was going to kill a pig and distribute taro, rice and pork. On the day arranged for the food distribution many people arrived at his hamlet. Each brought between two to ten fathoms of *tambu* and in turn collected his food parcel. A careful record was kept of how much each person gave, for eventually it would have to be returned when the donor himself organized a food distribution. Thus at any one time most Tolai had credits with some people and debts with others. Today many men hold such food distributions in the name of their small children and many again present *tambu* in the name of their small sons or daughters. Thus children grow up into a network of credits and debts from which they will find it very difficult to disentangle themselves. Probably the main reason for this system of *tambu* indebtedness is the greater security on distributing one's treasure over a large number of people. It also enables a man to collect a large amount of *tambu* at any one time, while he saves it over a long period in small amounts. Furthermore, the ties of indebtedness strengthen other social and political relations. About 90 per cent of all the *tambu* collected at such food distributions in Rapitok is donated by people from the host's own parish, while about 80 per cent comes from men and women belonging to his own moiety. Thus the links of indebtedness support intra-parish and intra-moiety ties. To Dungan, like most other Tolai, is involved in this network of credits and debts.

To Dungan has successfully managed to develop a stake in the new cash sector while still maintaining his interest in the traditional subsistence and *tambu* sectors of the economy. In this respect he is representative of most Tolai entrepreneurs. This balance between the modern and the traditional economy seems to be part of the selective approach of the Tolai to European ways. For instance, the Tolai reject European type of dress. Altogether their pattern of wants for cash goods has not widened in line with their increased income. Although in Tolai settlements near Rabaul one can find many new permanent homes, furnished and equipped with modern household goods, such houses are still rare among inland Tolai. Most of them still live in native style houses, and sleep on the floor on mats woven with coconut leaves; they continue to use earth-ovens for cooking, and eat not from plates but from leaves, and usually with their hands. On the whole, there is little differentiation noticeable in the everyday

c

standard of living of inland Tolai. Economic differentiation is mainly apparent in the ownership of capital assets, in the accumulation of *tambu* and cash savings. The incentive to investing labour in planting cocoa and coconuts is less the desire for a higher standard of living, than the prestige associated with having a share in a truck or shop. Ownership of capital assets has been adopted into the Tolai prestige pattern: it is a matter of prestige to own a lot of *tambu*; similarly, it is a matter of prestige to have a share in a capital asset. The time lag between the increase in income and the expansion of consumer demand allows for a high rate of capital formation. It enables Tolai to purchase expensive trucks, build copra driers and so on.

Thrift is no newly discovered virtue among the Tolai. However, savings never meant, and still do not mean, the forgoing of present consumption.[1] Rather they involved the sacrifice of leisure. In order to accumulate *tambu* a Tolai had to grow a surplus of food for sale; to accumulate money he has to grow cocoa and coconuts. This means a large investment of time in clearing bush and planting crops, while the yield of cocoa materializes only after four years and that of coconuts only after ten years. Thus a man has to invest his labour and forgo leisure in order to receive a cash reward in the distant future. Since most of the food consumed by inland Tolai is self-produced, except for the occasional meal of rice with tinned meat or fish, they can save most of their cash income. A large proportion of their savings is hoarded, but a considerable portion is invested in various types of assets or put into the savings bank. However, the acquisition of fixed assets on a larger scale is hampered by a number of factors: firstly, there is the restriction on natives buying goods on credit—no native in New Guinea may receive credit for more than £50 from any non-indigenous person without the consent of the Administration,[2] even where the European or Chinese firm is prepared to run the risk of lending the money. Secondly, Tolai are reluctant to lend each other money; each fears that the other will call on kinship obligations when it comes to returning the loan; furthermore, traditional Tolai thrift in terms of *tambu* finds expression in the hoarding of money. Banks in Rabaul complain about the continuous outflow of silver without any proportionate return. Indeed, the pre-war silver money in New Guinea lent itself to the practice of storing, for it had holes in the middle and could thus be threaded like shell money. Even now some Tolai regard it as a matter of prestige to have a large store of silver in their homes. Thirdly, investment opportunities are limited. The Tolai have as yet too little

---

[1] This applies only to those Tolai who have still ample land to grow their food as well as cash crops.

[2] Trading with Natives Ordinance No. 1 of 1959.

know-how to invest in manufacturing enterprises; therefore they are restricted in their investment to service industries, which, by their very nature, are protected from foreign competition. The smallness of the home market strictly limits investment openings.

In this paper I have attempted to describe and analyse the personal accumulation of one entrepreneur set against the background of the Tolai economic and social system. To Dungan is typical of Tolai entrepreneurs in his attitude towards landholding. He bought land in his sons' names and planted it with cocoa and coconuts so that they alone will inherit his perennial crops. At the same time he continues to support matrilineage interests by associating in the purchase of joint matrilineal land. Tolai these days want to leave their cash crops to their sons, while still retaining the political structure provided by the system of land rights vested in the matrilineage section.

To Dungan is also representative of most Tolai in his desire to accumulate both *tambu* and money. The decision as to how much of his liquid assets a Tolai wants to hold in the form of *tambu* or money usually depends on his immediate requirements. If he has a son or maternal nephew of marriageable age for whom he will have to pay the bride price, or if he has an aged parent or other old maternal relative who is expected to die soon, he will try to accumulate as much *tambu* as he possibly can. On the other hand, if he wants to build a new European-style house, or if he wants to have a share in a capital asset, he will try to collect money, in preference to *tambu*.

To Dungan is one of a number of outstanding men in Tolai society. Each parish has at least two or three men of his calibre. Their pioneering entrepreneurship acts as stimulus to others. For instance, To Dungan was the first in Rapitok who bought a truck immediately after the war; by 1960 there were five trucks and twelve jeeps in the parish. Similarly, he was the first to grow cocoa and sell copra; by 1961 there were about 66,000 cocoa and 25,000 coconut trees in Rapitok. Thus in Rapitok there were 102 cocoa trees and thirty-six coconut trees per head of population; the respective Tolai figures overall are 104 coconut trees and seventy-four cocoa trees.[1] To Dungan with a family membership of eight has a *per capita* holding of 287 cocoa and fifty-eight coconut trees. These figures indicate that although To Dungan has a much larger than average holding of cocoa and coconut trees as far as Rapitok is concerned, he is but one of many Tolai who cultivate cash crops on a comparatively large scale.

Most Tolai still operate their capital assets on the basis of joint ownership by matrilineage without any rules regarding the distribution of profits according to the individual member's share. In 1960

[1] New Britain Agricultural Extension, Annual Report 1959–60, dated July 30, 1960.

there was one Tolai-owned vehicle for every 130 Tolai in Rabaul district. Of these 229 vehicles at least 50 per cent are still jointly owned. At the same time there were 204 licensed Tolai trade stores and many a store operated without a licence.

In this sphere, as in others, To Dungan and other Tolai entrepreneurs like him set an example. They are not satisfied with a nebulous share of joint profits, but want maximum returns on their investment. There are signs of growth of the co-operative movement among the Tolai. In 1960 there were twelve co-operative societies with a membership of 6,827 Tolai and an annual turnover in general trade of £79,694.[1]

Most Tolai appreciate the advantages of education and want their children to be well educated. Some Tolai are already considering sending their children to England for education. As soon as this will materialize the level of consumption demand among the Tolai will rise rapidly and may leave only little for capital growth. Thus now is the time when Tolai entrepreneurs ought to be encouraged and advised to invest in profitable enterprises.

Following the example of entrepreneurs like To Dungan, younger Tolai, who have shares in vehicles or other assets owned by a matrilineage and who also operate these assets (such as drive the trucks), borrow money from their friends to buy the shares of their co-partners. Thus while capital formation was at first facilitated by the traditional Tolai system of group ownership, capital formation in turn has undermined the very system which helped to create it.

---

[1] Information received from the District Co-operative Officer, Rabaul.

4

Capital, Investment and the Social Structure of a Pastoral Nomad Group in South Persia

BY FREDRIK BARTH

In this essay, I shall present a summary analysis of some aspects of the pastoral nomad economy of the Basseri tribe of Fars, South Persia. I shall discuss the nature of pastoral capital and its implications for the social structure of the nomads, granted certain cultural premises current among the Basseri. In this discussion I shall draw on material collected in the field during the winter and spring of 1958.

The Basseri are a tribe of 15,000–20,000 pastoral nomads, divided residentially into camps of ten to fifty tents, who migrate between winter pastures in the steppes and deserts of southern Fars and summer pastures in the high mountains 300 miles forther north. A general picture of this tribe has been presented elsewhere (Barth, 1961), and certain aspects of the prevailing system of land use and migration have been analysed (Barth, 1960). In general, the following description may be taken as representative of conditions among the pastoral nomads of the whole South Persian area, a population of about half-a-million nomads.

A pastoral nomadic subsistence is based on assets of two main kinds: domesticated animals, and grazing rights. The recognition by the sedentary authorities of traditional grazing rights vested in distinct tribes is basic to the pastoral adaptation in Fars. Such tribes mostly have centralized political organizations based on chiefs, as do the Basseri, and are further united into large confederacies, which were formerly integrated into the semi-feudal traditional organization of Persia, and which are still recognized by the authorities. The association of every tribe with a corporate estate in the form of shared grazing rights has important implications for the political forms developed in the area. But in this essay I shall concentrate on the internal organization of the tribe, particularly the structure of local camp units. Within camps, all members share equal access to

69

pastures; so for my present purposes I shall concentrate my analysis on the other main form of asset, the *herds*, and try to show the connection between features of this form of capital, and the internal structure of camps and of the tribe.

CAPITAL FORM

Animals are individually owned private property, and a Basseri household makes its livelihood from the production of the animals owned by its members. A certain minimum of additional property is necessary in a nomadic adaptation, mainly a tent, bedding, saddle-bags, ropes, and leather sacks for milk and water, all produced by household members, and clothes, shoes, cooking and eating utensils, obtained from the towns. The total value of such equipment is slight compared to that represented by the animals. Of them the most important producers are sheep, subsidiarily goats, while donkeys are necessary for transport. Every household also has a watchdog.

In South Persia in 1958, the market value of a live adult female sheep was around 80 Tomans (£4). Its product per annum was estimated at:

clarified butter	..	*c.* 25 T.	
wool ..	..	..	20 T.
lamb: skin ..	..	15 T.	
total ..	..	..	60 T. or £3.

In addition, there were the lambs' meat, buttermilk and curds, to which the nomads could not give a money value of any meaning since these products are not regularly marketed. The corresponding values for goats are somewhat lower, and there is no market for their hides. On the other hand, twinning is much more frequent among them. The main reason why some goats are kept in every herd, however, is to provide goathair for the production of tent cloth.

The productive capital on which the pastoral adaptation is based is thus a large herd of sheep and goats. Of these a 10 per cent population of rams and he-goats is sufficient to ensure the fertility of the ewes and she-goats.

Certain features of this form of capital appear to have fundamental implications for the economic and social organization of the nomads:

(a) *Essentially all productive capital is in consumable form.* The livestock may at any time be slaughtered and eaten; and thus the main productive asset of a household may be consumed without the necessity of conversion through a market.

(b) *A significant fraction of the income is in the form of capital gains.*

70

Lambs reach maturity in two years, and a female sheep is estimated by the Basseri to have a productive period of about seven years. To maintain the full capital value of the herd, about 15 per cent of the lambs must thus be set aside each year to ensure replacement of stock; the remaining female lambs and a proportionate fraction of male lambs may be regarded as capital gains and give a possible capital increase rate of nearly 40 per cent per annum. As in the case of point (a), no market mechanism is necessary to effect a conversion from consumable product to productive capital.

(c) *There is a continual risk of total or partial loss of capital.* Since all nomadic property is movable, total loss through robbery or warfare is a continual and real danger in the weakly administered areas frequented by the nomads. Furthermore various other disasters may strike the herd: accidents and predatory animals threaten the sheep, particularly when they stray from the main flock, so constant vigilance is required to keep the animals together and protect them; and at times epidemic disease, drought or famine may strike the herds, reducing the total animal population by as much as 50 per cent.

(d) *The rate of income decreases with increased capital.* This is mainly a consequence of the herding and management techniques known to the Basseri. Unassisted by dogs, a shepherd cannot control a flock larger than about 400 head; the man who owns more animals is forced to divide his flock and entrust other persons with shepherding duties. In fact, since shepherding is a strenuous and exacting occupation, owners of herds larger than about 200 animals already tend to hire a shepherd. A recognized consequence of this is somewhat less careful herding and more frequent losses, as well as a continual pilfering of the produce. The larger the total number of animals, the less effective is the owner's supervision of his shepherds, and the greater is the decrease in the rate of income. Standard shepherding contracts, especially the long-term ones in which there is no supervision, reflect these expectations in their stipulations:

(i) *dandune* contract: the shepherd pays 10–15 Tomans per animal per year and takes all produce. At the expiration of the contract period, he returns a flock of the same number and age composition as he originally received;

(ii) *nimei* contract: the shepherd pays 30 Tomans per animal per year for a period of 3–5 years. He takes all produce, and at the expiration of the contract returns half the herd as it stands, and keeps the other half (cf. Lambton 1953, pp. 351 ff., Barth, 1961).

In addition to these characteristics of the pastoral form of capital, certain other aspects of the economic situation of the Basseri should be described before discussing social implications, namely consumption patterns, borrowing, and investment.

A striking feature of the consumption patterns is the importance of agricultural produce to a nomad household. Wheat is the main staple; rice, dates, sugar and tea are also consumed in large quantities. Together with the considerable needs for cloth and clothing, various equipment, and luxuries, this implies a strong productive specialization and a dependence on market exchanges. A few family budgets in the nomad camp best known to me suggest an average rate of consumption in agricultural and industrial products to a value of more than 3,000 Tomans, or nearly £200, per annum per household of about six persons.

These products are paid for by the marketing of pastoral products, which only among the very poor is augmented by seasonal labour. Marketing and purchases usually take place through the medium of 'village friends'—small peddlers who live in predominantly agricultural villages where they sell industrial goods to the peasants, while supplying nomads with both agricultural and industrial produce. A nomad householder establishes a relation with such a village friend in every area where he spends a long period; during his time there he is provisioned by the peddler, and before his departure he usually settles the accumulated debt by delivery of butter, wool and hides. Though money is rarely used in these transactions, all values are estimated in terms of fluctuating current market prices.

Where the nomad does not have accumulated stores to cover his purchases, he is usually granted a half-year's or one year's credit. While such debts are usually paid for by villagers at a rate of 5 per cent per month, nomads are rarely charged more than 20–30 per cent per annum, and this is often waived when payment is made. Some nomads' debts run up to 4,000 to 5,000 Tomans.

Though this would appear to represent borrowing for current consumption, such credit serves in fact to conserve the productive asset represented by the herd: payment could be made by delivery of livestock, but by obtaining credit with security in the flock, this loss of productive animals is prevented. With a rate of income on mature sheep of nearly 100 per cent per annum (value: 80 T., product: 60 T. plus various foodstuffs), such borrowing is clearly advantageous for the nomad even when full interest is charged; and nomads often succeed in recouping in the course of a year or two in spite of heavy indebtedness.

There are thus outside sources of credit available to members of a nomadic group; likewise, outside investments are open to them. There is, in Fars, an open market in land, and standard land tenancy contracts secure a considerable income for the absentee landowner (one sixth to two-thirds of the crop, according to the quality of the

72

land). However, there are difficulties in converting capital in herds into capital in land which partially prevent such investments. Animals may be freely sold, but the market for livestock is severely restricted. The strains of sheep owned by the nomads, though larger and more productive than those of the villagers, are less robust, and experience shows that only some 30 per cent survive if kept in one locality through the whole year. Old sheep are of course sold for slaughter to the villages, but they fetch only a small price; animals for breeding and use can only be sold to other nomads. But since fellow nomads have very few sources of income other than their own herds, those who wish to increase their flocks by purchase have relatively limited means and represent only a very small market. The marketing of livestock is thus inevitably a rather slow process.

On the other hand, income from the sale of wool, butter and hides beyond what is required to pay for the household's consumption may freely be accumulated in the form of money, and can be invested in land. The advantages offered by this investment are security, in that the land cannot be lost through epidemics or the negligence of herdsmen, and the fact that income from land is in the form of the very agricultural products which a nomad household requires.

SOCIAL IMPLICATIONS

The above sketch of some relatively simple features of the economic situation of the Basseri pastoral nomads highlights factors of relevance to the economic choices faced by nomadic householders. I shall now try to show the social implications which they have for (a) the family development cycle, (b) processes which maintain social homogeneity within the nomad camp, and (c) attitudes and practices with respect to saving and investment.

(a) *Family development cycle.* A pastoral household requires flocks to subsist as an independent productive unit; among the Basseri at the time of my visit the nomads estimated that a herd of sixty adult sheep/goats was about the minimum required by an elementary family, while the average size of flock was at that time nearly 100 head. But a pastoral adaptation also implies certain labour requirements, and the tasks that are necessary are among the Basseri traditionally divided in such a way as to require the co-operation of at least three persons: a male head of the household, who loads the pack animals and directs the migration, erects the tent, fetches water and wood, and keeps most equipment in repair; a woman who does the cooking and housework, assists in packing and camping, and milks the flock; and a man who herds the animals, driving them to camp to be milked at about 12 a.m. and 5 p.m.

These capital and labour requirements define conditions which a family must satisfy if it is to live as an independent household. It is immediately apparent that an elementary family can only expect to satisfy these conditions with regard to labour force for a limited period of its natural development cycle, i.e. from the time the first son reaches the age of about eight to ten years, till the last son marries; and that it can obtain the necessary capital, if not on credit, then only through inheritance, i.e. normally at the dissolution of the parental household(s). Yet the value placed in Basseri culture on the elementary family as an independent household has called forth certain standardized adjustments, the forms and wider consequences of which may be analysed as social implications of pastoral capital forms and uses, granted the ideal of elementary family households.

The labour requirements of such small households are safeguarded among the Basseri by the formation of co-operative herding units of two to five tents. Since a single shepherd, as noted above, can control a herd of up to 400 head, several households can usually combine their flocks and still remain below this critical number, thus together requiring only one shepherd. Families which are short on personnel establish herding co-operation with families with several adolescent sons, thereby securing the additional labour assistance they need. The increased work involved in shepherding a flock say of 300 instead of 100 is negligible, and so the payments for this service are small: a household which supplies no herdsman for the flock of its co-operative herding unit generally gives the boys from the other tents who perform this duty one or two lambs a year and occasional small presents.

The capital requirements of a newly established family, on the other hand, are obtained by a different pattern, essentially a pattern of anticipatory inheritance. Only sons, subsidiarily collateral agnates or adopted sons, receive a share of their father's flock. This share they are given at the time of their marriage, thereby losing further claims on the estate. Each son receives at the time of his marriage the share which he would have received if his father had died at that moment, with no subsequent adjustments. An example will illustrate this: A man had 200 sheep when the eldest of his three sons married. He first paid the brideprice of 20 sheep, leaving 180; of this estate the groom received his rightful third, or 60 head, leaving 120 for the father and remaining two sons. If the father's flock subsequently increases to 200 again before the next son marries, that son will, assuming the same brideprice, receive 90 sheep at his marriage; and there is no attempt to correct the disparity between the 60 and the 90 sheep received respectively by the first and second son—because, the Basseri argue, his 60 sheep may meanwhile have grown to 600, or have been lost. The marriage of the last son is usually delayed until

74

the parents are old, or one parent dies, so the son can become head of the new household in which the old parent(s) are permitted to live. If the son or only son reaches maturity while the father is still in his prime, the two often divide the flock 'as brothers' and separate.

In a culture where elementary families should live apart in separate tents, the capital forms and management patterns described above thus have clear social implications: certain technical patterns of herding co-operation and inheritance rules are developed, and these again have wider implications. Since the establishment of a household unit depends on the allocation to it of independent productive capital, the separation of men from their fathers and brothers is already completed when they marry—no vested economic or managerial interest ties them to their parental household. They are free to join whichever co-operative herding unit they wish, for personal or economic reasons—the practices prevent the formation of minimal or potential patrilineal nuclei on the basis of shared economic interests.

(b) *Social homogeneity*. The Basseri constitute a population of striking social homogeneity—apart from the unique position occupied by the quite small chiefly dynasty, which is based on a number of unique features such as private title to lands, political functions, and taxation rights. Nearly all Basseri commoners are independent small herd owners, and this homogeneity of the population has extensive implications for the political organization of the tribe. There is no effective hierarchy of authority in camps or sections, and groups of every size experience great difficulties when trying to reach corporate decisions, unless these are dictated by the tribal chief (cf. Barth, 1960a). This basic social homogeneity may be analysed as the result of a number of processes, to a large extent implicit in the economic features I have outlined. I shall try to show (i) that these features are such as to inhibit the concentration of wealth, and thus the emergence of status differences based on wealth, and furthermore (ii) that they tend to encourage the elimination from the group of persons who deviate significantly in wealth from the average.

(i) A number of different factors tend to inhibit the accumulation of capital in the form of large herds. The continual risk of capital losses has been noted: epidemics, famines, and losses of young animals in case of late frost may all strike as sudden disasters and reduce the herd in a fashion which is unpredictable, and which thus the herd owner cannot anticipate in his stock management. All herds will thus experience intermittent setbacks, sometimes gross reductions.

While this control on herd growth strikes large and small flocks alike, other controls, implicit in Basseri consumption patterns, have increased effects with growing herds. The household with larger herds not only increases its consumption of luxuries and of foodstuffs—that is lambs, as well as tea, sugar, rice, etc. With greater capital in herds, an increasing amount of the wealthy household's labour is also diverted from pastoral production and management to other pursuits: the men require greater leisure, and their efforts are taken up by training and tending horses, hunting, and political activity; the women weave and tie rugs (which are never marketed); and the increased weight of household belongings and larger tents requires more beasts of burden, including camels, which again means a need for a separate camel herder. All these activities and persons depend on the herd without significantly contributing to its care and production; their presence will serve as a brake on the rate of herd increase.

Greater wealth also generally leads to an earlier fragmentation of the household. The pattern of anticipatory inheritance noted above means that the marriage of sons effects a dispersal of the household's capital; furthermore, such a marriage is only possible if the son can be equipped with a share of animals sufficient to support his wife and himself—i.e. about fifty animals or more. The expected marriage age of men is in their twenties; among poor people it may be postponed till the man is as much as thirty-five to permit the necessary accumulation of capital. Wealthy people, on the other hand, have no reason for such delay; and pressure from the boy and the community at large assure a marriage age of eighteen to twenty for the sons of the large herd owners. In other words, within about twenty years of his own marriage, the dispersal of the successful herder's flock commences, giving only a brief period of accumulation for the wealthy, and nearly twice that time for the poorer and less successful. For the wealthy this means also an early loss of the cheap and dependable labour represented by adult, unmarried sons.

Finally, it is common for wealthy herd owners to contract plural marriages; they may after some years take a second, younger wife, and sometimes even a third and fourth. This means a significant increase in the size of household which must be supported by the flock, and the increased consumption will represent a drain on that flock. Furthermore, since plural marriage extends the herd owner's fertile period, it affects the distribution of wealth by inheritance. The elder sons will wish to be married at a time when their father's younger wife is still bearing children—this means that they will receive unduly large shares of their father's estate, since the shares of as-yet unborn half-brothers will not be deducted. In short, the effects of all these different and partly interconnected factors—accidental capital losses, differential consumption rates and the diversion of labour from pastoral production, accelerated division of household and capital, polygyny and increased family size without corresponding reduction of the inheritance shares of elder sons—these all act together to

76

inhibit the concentration of wealth in the form of large herds.

(ii) These factors are not, however, completely effective checks on the accumulation of wealth. Even less are they an effective guarantee against impoverishment, though reduced consumption, postponement of the fragmentation caused by the marriage of sons, etc., will facilitate cases of rehabilitation, just as their obverse hampers accumulation. The homogeneity of the tribe with respect to wealth will not result from these processes alone. But there are other features of the economic situation which also tend to produce homogeneity, though by a different process: there is a distinct tendency and clearly observable frequency of elimination from the tribe of households with unusually great and unusually small capital. This is possible because the Basseri, like other Persian nomads, are but a segment of a larger population where assimilation by sedentarization into peasant villages and urban centres is possible and frequent, and for different reasons sedentarization is the normal result of great capital accumulation, or capital losses.

Firstly in the case of accumulation: factors which tend to reduce the rate of income with increased size of herd have been noted. This means that while the risk of capital losses remains or increases, the increment to a large herd owner's income which results from the addition of further animals to his flocks decreases significantly. Consider, then, the possibilities of alternative investment. In nomadic activities they are nil; but the possibility of investment in agricultural land is always present. I should emphasize that sedentarization is never regarded as an ideal among the nomads; they value their way of life more highly than life in a village. But the economic advantages of land purchase are palpable: the risk of capital loss is eliminated, the profits to an absentee landowner are large, and they are in the form of products useful in a nomadic household. There is thus no feeling that land purchase implies sedentarization—a small plot of land can be let out on tenancy contracts and is merely a source of economic security and useful products. The difficulty in such investment is to convert the capital in animals to money capital by which land may be purchased. As noted, this is a relatively slow process, unless the owner is willing to take a considerable loss; none the less, with some patience it may be done, and banking facilities are available in the towns for accumulating savings, though no credit is available to nomads for investment in land.

Once a piece of land has been bought, the wealthy herd owner's money income increases rapidly, since production in marketable goods such as wool, butter and hides continues while expenses for the purchase of agricultural produce are reduced or eliminated. If a herd owner continues to be successful, he will thus accumulate wealth more rapidly, with little promise of profit through further investment

77

in herds, but increasingly in a form which may be directly invested in land. Furthermore, title to land is held in a sedentary legal system where sons upon their marriage have no rights to anticipatory inheritance—which makes it an attractive form of capital from the owner's point of view and prevents a premature dispersal of the wealth.

This gradual process of land accumulation was observed in the field in its various stages. Only towards the very end do informants see sedentarization as its natural end result: they have a house built on their property and become increasingly concerned with the need for management of house and land, they develop a taste for many comforts that can only be satisfied by sedentary residence, etc. Sudden stock losses at this stage seem to be a common precipitating factor which drives them into the village; and even when they are well established as petty landowners they generally erect their old tent in their compound, and reside in it in the summer months.

Cases of sedentarization through capital accumulation and land purchase are by the nature of things relatively rare, and my material for the above description consists mainly of a handful of life histories. Sedentarization through impoverishment, on the other hand, is a constant threat for many and has a high empirical frequency, of the order of one person in every three in the groups of my censuses. Here the process is very simple: accident, sickness or poor management of a small herd leads to losses, and thus to an annual production below what is required for the purchase of food and clothing. But the herd itself is a large food store, and hunger easily drives the nomad to invade this his only productive capital, reducing the pastoral output further, in a vicious circle. The only alternative is to seek additional sources of income. Since shepherding contracts are relatively few (because they are, as we have seen, unprofitable for the herd owner), such sources are mainly found in sedentary society: as seasonal labourer, shepherd for the village flocks, doing local transport with donkeys, etc. To be successful, these activities must give the nomad income both to support his household *and* to increase his flock (thereby constituting a market for rich herd owners who wish to buy land). But frequently such work for a village community disturbs the nomad's migratory cycle, and thus leads only to reduced pastoral production and further animal losses, which makes him all the more dependent on sedentary sources of income. The Basseri feel that once a household's flock falls significantly below the minimal level of sixty adult head, this downward spiral is pretty inevitable and quite rapid; and there is a steady flow of impoverished settlers from every South Persian tribe to the villages and towns of their area.

These features of capital form and management thus tend, in the wider economic situation of the Basseri, to maintain a general

78

economic homogeneity among the nomads, both by inhibiting the concentration of pastoral wealth, and by a constant elimination through sedentarization of the top and the bottom of the economic spectrum. As a consequence, social differentiation based on, or accompanied by, economic differences becomes impossible; and the nomad population becomes characterized by a striking social homogeneity, consisting of independent, economically self-sufficient small herd owners.

(c) *Saving and investment.* A final implication of these features may be seen in attitudes and practices relating to saving, thrift, and capital accumulation. I have noted the fact that pastoral capital is in a directly consumable form and consists of animals with a short life span. This creates a situation where a certain minimum of thrift is necessary in capital management—the capital can only be maintained through a systematic policy of reserving lambs for the replacement of stock. Whereas in agriculture the distinction between produce and land is clearly apparent, among pastoralists nearly every instance of consumption threatens the productive capital itself, and must be considered and evaluated by the nomad. What is more, many of the factors involved are unknown. Disease may strike so that even a conservative policy of slaughter of lambs and yearlings still results in a reduction of stock. Milking practice is also a field of continual economic choice: not only the question of how many sheep should be left with lambs, but also how much sheep with lambs should be milked, and how much should be left to those lambs. In a good year, near-starvation of lambs gives a greater yield in butter to the nomad and does not appear to have great ill effects; on the other hand, if such lambs are subject to special strain or mild disease, they are lost in much higher frequency than are well-fed, robust lambs. In short, the management of pastoral capital requires a constant awareness of savings and investment policy; it breeds an attitude of continual and thrifty concern for the herd in its practitioners.

The Basseri are very aware of the economics involved in these choices, and discuss such policy at length within the household, though rarely in public, except in the form of gossip about third persons. The basic guiding principle which they adopt comes out in an almost obsessive desire to postpone every incident of consumption— to let each lamb gain weight one more day, or week, or season, to have one more lamb from an old sheep, to make a worn-out pair of shoes last till the next market town, or till arrival in the summer area, or till next spring equinox (the Persian New Year, when it is customary to put on new clothes).

Yet—or perhaps precisely as a correlate of these interests— hospitality is a highly valued virtue. The hospitable man is admired

79

and people speak highly of him whether he is present or absent. Men seek his company and flock to his tent, though without importunity. By their own standards, then, most Basseri are miserly; and a few glaring examples are held up for public ridicule. Thus one of the largest herd owners in the group is popularly known as D.D.T. Khan because, they say, he is such a miser he eats his own lice.

But this failure in good manners (by Basseri canons) caricatured by some and prevalent in most need not be explained only in terms of the special habits of thrift developed as a result of pastoral life. There are also clear social reasons why a pattern of conspicuous consumption and hospitality is not only economically unwise, but also socially and politically unprofitable—in contrast to most of the local societies in the Middle East. These are found in the very features of social structure described in the previous section: the great economic and social homogeneity within Basseri camps. Where wealth differences are small, a policy of social aggrandizement through public consumption of wealth is bound to bring very limited returns. Nearly all the tents of a camp remain independent and self-supporting units; a hospitable man may gain influence in his camp through hospitality, but never to the extent of being able to dominate his camp fellows, or to expect economic support or advantage from them at a later date. On the contrary, the homogeneity itself is valued, and lampoons are sung about anyone who puts on airs and assumes an authoritative manner. For the Basseri commoner, there is little to gain by spendthriftness, and thus few inducements, but many controls, on the practice of hospitality.

CONCLUSION

The material presented in this brief paper can hardly be drawn together further, since the paper itself is already a summary of select features of the economic and social organization of a pastoral tribe which show a clear relation to certain features of sheep and goat herds as a form of capital. As noted in the introduction, other economic features (e.g. relating to pasture rights and the organization of migrations) have not been discussed, though they appear to have methodologically analogous implications for centralized authority and other features of the political organization of the tribe. In the present essay I have merely attempted to show how certain elementary characteristics of capital in the form of herds are related to a limited range of features of family organization, social homogeneity within camps, and common saving and consumption patterns—granted certain cultural values and conceptions held by the Basseri people. The characteristics of pastoral capital which I have discussed are, I believe, of a type familiar in conventional economic analysis, though here admittedly in a very elementary and rough form. What is interesting, and perhaps surprising, to a social anthropologist is the fact that it should be possible at all to show their social implications by a discussion involving relatively few 'cultural' facts—that the processes by which they are made relevant to social action and features of a local social system seem to implicate few of the other basic premises of Basseri culture. Admittedly, some of these premises are contained in the specific economic definitions and characterizations used; and it would seem a hopeless, and perhaps fundamentally impossible, task to state them all in a manner so that their implications would have the form of a deductive system. But it does seem possible to show how specific social forms are related as a product to simple constellations of determining factors, and thus how partial features of Basseri social structure are directly related to specific characteristics of pastoral capital and other economic facts.

5

Capital, Savings and Credit among Lao Peasants[1]

BY JOEL M. HALPERN

The Lao, who in language and culture closely resemble the neighbouring Thai, inhabit north-east Thailand as well as the Kingdom of Laos.
The political entity of Laos thus includes only part of the Lao people.
In Laos the Vientiane Plain is an important agricultural area, and
almost all of the significant settlements in southern Laos are located
there and elsewhere on the Mekong.[2] This discussion has reference
to the Buddhist, valley-dwelling cultivators of irrigated rice in the
Vientiane region and in the area of Luang Prabang in north central
Laos. For the most part their villages are situated along the Mekong
River or its tributaries. Most villages are composed of several dozen
houses, and some have as many as several hundred people. Households are generally nuclear families, although the ideal pattern is one
of matrilocal residence. In addition to the cultivation of glutinous
rice, they raise some vegetables along the river banks, do a little
fishing and grow fruits such as mangoes, bananas and coconuts. A
few chickens and pigs are kept. In the Luang Prabang area numbers
of Lao farmers engage in trade with the surrounding groups such as
the Meo (Sinicized hill people of northern Laos) and Khmu (indigenous tribal group). A few villages are reached by jeepable roads,

[1] This essay has primary reference to the situation in Laos as it existed in the
late 1950s. By 1962 the Communists and their allies had obtained effective
control of all of the country beyond the regions bordering on the Mekong. It is to
be presumed that they have made vigorous efforts to change or at least modify
existing administrative and land tenure patterns. Significant migration also
occurred during and after the fighting.

[2] Data for the Vientiane region derive principally from the monograph by
Howard K. Kaufman (1961) supplemented by material from a community near
Vientiane town studied by Tsuneo Ayabe (1961). Georges Condominas subsequently prepared a detailed socio-economic study of the Vientiane Plain which
was not available at the time of this writing.

82

and jeep buses provide a means of taking goods to market. Others are accessible by dugout canoe occasionally powered by outboard motor. Walking is still the most common means of travel.

Significantly, Laos remains one of the least urbanized areas in the world. Only about 3 per cent to 4 per cent of the population live in urban areas, compared with about 8 per cent in Thailand and Vietnam, and 10 per cent and upwards in Burma and India.

Prior to French rule the Lao were organized in a series of petty kingdoms with small towns as their ritual and market centres. These kingdoms had elaborate gradations of rank and an inherited royalty, but the consumption patterns of all social grades were fairly uniform. There was not enough of an economic surplus to permit widely varying standards of living, although status distinctions were strongly marked.

The traditional hierarchical status system in Laos is similar to a pattern widespread throughout south-east Asia. Traditionally the King is the military and political leader, possessing great power. One of his titles implies the power of life and death. Extreme manifestations of outward respect were required, and this has been the case up to present times. Villagers squat down before a high-ranking government official and reply to his questions in a polite and formal manner. A special honorific language is reserved for conversations with the King. Conversations of peasants with high-ranking officials in most cases must be conducted through an intermediary. But the marginal geographic position of Laos in Asia, the lack of large irrigation systems and the scattered pattern of settlement have prevented a significant feudal arrangement from coming into existence. (An exception is the immediate vicinity of the royal capital of Luang Prabang, limited to a few villages where the royal family continues to have extensive holdings.)

It is not surprising that in Laos the villagers regard the government as an exterior force over which they have no influence. The Lao peasant is not particularly interested in the outside world and is, generally speaking, quite content with the economic aspects of his life. He does not value improvement of his position sufficiently strongly to justify continued hard work. Closely connected to these attitudes are two key characteristics of Laos: first, its relatively sparse population and lack of competition for land or for livelihood in general; and second, Buddhism as a state religion. The Constitution of Laos specifies that the King must be a fervent Buddhist, and he and the members of the royal family participate extensively in all Buddhist ceremonies which are closely linked to state occasions. Yet with its emphasis on individual responsibility and forms of reincarnation dependent upon accumulated merit, this religion does not lend itself easily to purposes of secular government.

The Lao villager then views himself as existing in a traditional hierarchy in which he accepts his place and in which prestige is obtained through birth and proper behaviour defined in the religious sense. In rural Laos material wealth is not of primary significance; being a devout Buddhist and having a pleasant manner are often considered more important. Colonial rule, subsequent Western aid and Communist political activities have tended to modify these attitudes, but have by no means obliterated them.

In contemporary Laos, in form a constitutional monarchy, the idea of a royal patron is still strong. During a rural tour made by the late Viceroy of the Kingdom, he was besieged with requests from the villagers. They asked him to do something for them, to build roads and irrigation canals, to provide school and medical services. He did promise to help, but he stressed emphatically that they must begin to make their own contributions as well. Thus formally even the traditional leaders have begun a reversal in manner. In addition government officials and even members of the royal family have begun to lose some of their sacred qualities as they have tended to mingle more directly with the people in efforts to implement various programmes. Here too technicians are beginning to play a role. The children of many Lao villagers want to go to live in the towns and become government workers or obtain skilled jobs. This has begun to affect the status of agriculture as being a valued way of life.

LAND AND AGRICULTURAL INCOME

Basic capital of the Lao peasant, as in other simple agricultural communities, consists primarily of land in which there has been great investment of human resources. Traditionally the state is the ultimate proprietor of all land. But it has been estimated for Vientiane Province that over 80 per cent of the rural households own their own rice fields. The remaining families rent land from wealthier farmers in the community, paying from 20 to 50 per cent of the rice yield to the landowner, or they work on the land of others for payment in rice. The actual rental fee is based on the kin relationship of the parties involved and also on the degree of fertility of the soil. Absentee landlordism in rural areas is virtually non-existent.

A somewhat different situation appears in the area near Luang Prabang town. Here the royal family, others of noble rank and some merchants, are absentee landlords. In a number of villages in the immediate vicinity of the royal capital only a small minority of the villagers own land; in others about half the villagers possess land. As far as can be determined, this situation is not general throughout the province, but is limited to Lao villages in Luang Prabang District. In addition to this absentee landownership there exists, as in

84

Vientiane Province, the renting of land by more prosperous villagers. A villager may also own one piece of land and rent another. A chief advantage of renting land in the Luang Prabang area is that the parcel is probably well irrigated by systems maintained by the royal family or other owner. Rental for land-use alone here is from 15 to 35 per cent of the crop. If the landlord supplies buffalo, provides the seed and maintains the irrigation system, the tenant must turn over 50 per cent of his crop as rent.

Laos is under-populated. Even in the river valleys and particularly in northern Laos, extra rice land is usually available to those who can clear the land. This takes considerable time and labour, especially in terracing and irrigation works. A poor Lao farmer with a small family cannot clear land by himself, and to invite others to help necessitates incurring the expense of their labour, or at least a feast. Thus, even though absentee landlords may not exist, some Lao will hire themselves out to work as agricultural labourers for others. These are exceptions, however, the general pattern being for the Lao to work primarily on their own or rented land in areas removed from the towns.

The land is divided into several categories. For the Lao farmer it consists of gardens around the household compound, irrigated rice fields (*na*) and often some *hai* areas, swidden plots cleared by slash-and-burn cultivation, in which are grown corn, vegetables and occasionally rice. (The *hai* are used for only a limited number of years. A Lao swidden farmer said he used a cleared field for about five years before preparing another site; three years appears to be a more common figure.) Some land may also be devoted to orchards. Farms are highly fragmented and a land-use map resembles a fantastic jigsaw puzzle. The fragmentation of land through inheritance makes it difficult to attain maximum productivity even within existing technologies. A key point in this regard is often the great geographical separation of irrigated land, the rice fields in the valleys, from *hai* fields, the corn and vegetable fields on the hillsides.

The price of land has risen in the past decade due to general inflation and increase in the rural population, plus new and improved roads combined with better transport facilities which enable the peasants to market their produce more easily, and have consequently made land near the towns more valuable. Land deeds are kept in the district office, but disputes over land rights and division of land are quite common. The system of squatters' rights was practised until very recently in Vientiane and still exists essentially in most of the outlying areas, particularly with regard to *hai* land.

In most parts of Laos the approval of the traditional leader of a district may be required for land transfers. For example, the members of the hereditary princely family performed this function in Muong

Sing. In many areas the Government is now trying to establish exactly which land belongs to whom. This has created many problems, and in areas where the Government has taken action to reclaim land there has been much bitterness on the part of uprooted farmers. Also the resettlement of peoples such as groups of Meo on the plains in Xieng Khouang has created conflicts about land ownership and water rights.

There is little reliable statistical information concerning the size of landholdings. The average holdings in one village surveyed in northern Laos remote from Luang Prabang town range from six-tenths of a hectare to almost three hectares (of *na* land) although the latter is unusual. In the Vientiane area, a Lao agriculturalist estimated that there is ordinarily a 1–5 hectare variation in the size of peasant land holdings. The largest holding he could recall was one of thirty hectares. He thought that perhaps a hundred people had land holdings of this size, while 10 to 20 per cent were estimated to be without rice lands. (It is these landless peasants who appear most eager to work in the towns. But the north-east Thai appear to be more mobile than the Lao. In Vientiane, the capital, which has tripled in population in the past twenty years, much if not most of the unskilled labour has come from the Thai side of the river and not the Vientiane hinterland.)

Most villages are only semi-permanent, and forest land is still available. The irrigated rice fields, or *na*, have become fragmented because their yields are more reliable than those of the *hai*. However, the creation of new *na* involves the extension of irrigation ditches and a major investment of labour. This labour, if not hired, must be supplied by the family itself, and this implies existing fluid capital or a large extended family containing a number of able-bodied workers. Neither of these situations commonly occurs among Lao peasants. Therefore they tend to resort to the progressive division of existing *na* land and to the cultivation of *hai*, which requires less initial labour. But from the point of view of rice cultivation, given an adequate amount of capital or labour, an irrigated rice field is a much better investment: its yields are continuous and require much less maintenance than the *hai*. Moreover, the Lao feel that swidden cultivation carries less prestige than does wet-rice farming.

In Vientiane Province, a densely populated area, approximately 20 per cent of the Lao farmers rely on *hai* (swidden) farming. The villages surveyed were located mainly along river banks and near roads in the flat plain surrounding the town of Vientiane. The percentage of swidden cultivators is expected to be higher in the mountainous north of the province. Estimates obtained within Luang Prabang Province ranged from villages in which there were no swiddens, the population depending entirely on *na* cultivation, to settlements in which only one house in thirty had a permanent rice field. Other villages yielded estimates of a tenth of the households having a *na* paddy field while in an equal number of villlages about a third used swiddens. If to the Lao who practise swidden cultivation, either principally or as a supplement to wet rice cultivation, are added the tribal peoples of Laos, most of whom are swidden farmers, then swidden farming can be seen to be of great significance to the majority of the people of Laos.

A basic distinction between *na* and *hai* is, of course, the great difference in the population each can support. To cite an extreme example, the carrying capacity of irrigated land may be ten or more times as high as the maximum obtainable under swidden cultivation. But there appears to be a great deal of variation in yields from swidden farming (*v.* Izikowitz, 1951, p. 38; cf. Jin-Bee, 1958, p. 114). In Laos generally the swidden yields per household often seem to be comparable with those from the irrigated paddy fields. In many cases in Luang Prabang Province, Khmu swiddens supply the Lao traders in the valleys with a significant portion of their rice needs. According to available data, the Khmu yields from swiddens have a higher maximum than those of the Lao swiddens, a natural consequence of the fact that swidden farming is the primary Khmu technique, while *hai* cultivation is at best a second choice for those poorer Lao who practise it. An important point here also is that swidden land is free for the cultivating while *na* land must sometimes be rented. There are formal Government regulations to control this usage but little effective attempt has been made to enforce them.

But the idea that *hai* cultivation is a labour-extensive method of cultivation as opposed to the labour-intensive features of *na* cultivation is not true in the absolute sense. Among *hai* cultivators, clearing the field at the outset is certainly a labour-intensive process, and labour is required to guard the fields from marauders in both *hai* and *na* farming. It appears, however, that *hai* cultivators are less concerned about weeds and they do not have to go through the laborious transplanting process, nor do they have to worry about the maintenance of dykes and irrigation systems. Moreover, fertilizer is provided from the burnt wood in their fields, while *na* cultivators must use both green and animal manure. Again, the use of the plough and buffalo in *na* cultivation implies a greater capital investment, and so more associated labour, than does the hoe and digging stick of *hai* cultivation.

Despite the lack of precision of Lao agricultural statistics, they are specific enough to point up the problem that at present, generally speaking, the Lao farmer produces barely enough to feed himself and has relatively little if any rice to market. This makes it necessary for Vientiane, and even a smaller town of less than 10,000 population, such as Luang Prabang, to rely on imports from Thailand. The case of Vientiane might be easily explained since Thai towns with good transport facilities are just across the river, but in Luang Prabang the rice must be brought in by river barge over a distance of several hundred miles. The shortage is particularly acute in extreme northern areas where even local government employees have difficulty buying enough to eat.

The most important source of income is, of course, rice, but there are other agricultural sources in subsidiary crops. The Lao of the Vientiane area generally do not plant a second crop in the idle rice fields, primarily because of lack of sufficient water and of implements for irrigation. Where adequate water is available, cucumbers and sometimes manioc and corn are grown in the paddy fields. Individual household compounds may have some peppers, cucumbers, sugar cane, betel and a few fruit trees. No compost or other fertilizer is used in either vegetable field or garden. Some villagers of the Luang Prabang area, in addition, grow egg plant and chili in their paddy fields. Gardens on the river banks are cultivated during the dry season. These are particularly important in the vicinity of the town, since they supply the market. In some villages where people have been forced for one reason or another to give up their rice fields (drought, breakdown of irrigation system, army confiscation) increasing emphasis has been placed on gardens.

In villages in central and northern Laos bananas are grown in nearby fenced-off areas. (Prosperous villages near towns have barbed-wire fences which are designed to keep buffalo out of the cultivated areas.) Pineapple, cassava, mangoes, gourds, pomelo, papaya, yams, betel nut, sugar cane and some coffee are also culti-vated in small amounts. In every Lao village there are innumerable coconut trees surrounding the houses. There are also quite often a few fruit trees within the pagoda compound.

An important item of Laos peasant capital is livestock. All Lao groups keep poultry. About 40 per cent of the households in Vientiane keep two or three pigs apiece. The villagers claim that there is never enough food for these animals and that during the rainy season the muddy ground makes it difficult for the animals to forage for themselves. More than half the households possess one buffalo; 20 per cent have two, and a few wealthier farmers have three or more. The buffalo are used primarily for rice cultivation, and occasionally are sold for slaughter in the capital. Farmers owning buffalo gain income from renting out their animals during the ploughing and harrowing season. Payment is in rice, the amount being determined by the number of days the animal is used and by the consanguineal relationship of the two individuals. Those households with wagons also possess a pair of oxen as draught animals. (Prior to 1938

88

these ox-wagons were the sole means of land transportation.)

Buffalo are definitely a wealth symbol among the Lao villagers. In some of the more prosperous lowland areas of Laos, cattle are also important as symbolic prestige items. No use is made of the milk[1] or blood, nor are they raised primarily for food. In the capital city itself, these prestige symbols can be seen grazing in front of the National Assembly building.

PATTERNS OF CASH INCOME

We have been examining the economy of Laos mostly in the context of what has been called a natural or subsistence economy, that is, a non-cash economy. Exchange in kind is very common among the valley Lao. When rice is milled or other services are sought, such as those of the traditional healer, these services are usually paid for in rice or other products rather than in cash. But every group, even in northern Laos, no matter how 'simple' their economic or cultural state, nevertheless participates to some degree in a cash economy. At some point in their economic life they are affected by cash transactions involving the use of paper money or the exchange of silver. The latter is more prevalent in the marginal areas of the north.

Market Gardening and Craftwork
Among the ways a Lao villager obtains a cash income are sales of rice, fruits and vegetables, forest products, domestic animals and home-prepared foods. Most towns in Laos are sites of military camps, as are a number of villages, and soldiers and their families provide an important market for nearby villagers. In certain areas, as near Luang Prabang, a number of farmers have abandoned their fields and set up stores and built houses to provide for the military and their families, and Khmu coolies come in great numbers to work for brief periods. Both Khmu and Meo come to trade in much greater numbers than was the case earlier. Some villages distant from Luang Prabang provide special food products such as oranges for market. One village in the valley of the Nam Ou cultivates large areas in pineapples, and it has been estimated by an FAO investigator that the fifty households each year produced 85,000 pineapples and also raised 1,500–2,000 coffee plants. Much progress has been made in the Vientiane area in the production of vegetables such as cucumbers, eggplant, pumpkins and beans. Previously these products were either raised by local Vietnamese truck farmers or imported from Thailand. A bus service linking Vientiane with surrounding villages

[1] Fresh animal milk is traditionally not used by people east of India. But both evaporated and powdered milk, imported under the US aid programme, are bought by Lao villagers for their small children.

has stimulated vegetable production for market. The line between village and town dweller is not always sharply drawn in this respect. Many of the inhabitants of Luang Prabang town raise vegetables in riverside gardens and others do considerable fishing.

At present crafts in Laos are for the most part not well developed, although they may have flourished in the past. Generally they are derived from Thailand and are usually inferior to those of the Thai. They may, however, provide a possible base for the expansion and development of local industry. In the Luang Prabang area are villages devoted to specialities such as blacksmithing, pottery-making and weaving. (These villages are said to be unique in Laos, and are thought to have developed for the purpose of serving the King.) In southern Laos skills traditionally transmitted in families include boat-building, healing, goldsmithing and the making of musical instruments and agricultural tools.

Inseparable from a description of the crafts themselves are the attitudes and values which the Lao place on their manufactures. Some craftwork, e.g. in silver, is of durable kind. But the Lao do not value permanence in much of their art work. A special art-form practised today is that of decorating coffins with elaborate geometric designs fashioned from gold-coloured paper. This takes long hours of work by groups of men, and the product is then consumed in the funeral pyre the following day. Equally painstaking are the floral offerings of minute concentric rings of vari-coloured buds and blossoms, skewered by bamboo splints to a core of banana stalk, surmounted by a crown of frangipani and set in a silver bowl, prepared by the women to be brought to the temple. What all these art forms share, however, is religious motivation. The many temples in Luang Prabang and Vientiane display a high degree of skill, from the graceful lines of the architecture to the painting of wall frescoes, carving of balustrades and casting of bronze Buddhas.

Trade, Commercial Enterprises and Wage Labour

Many rural Lao run small shops. There is no strict sex division of labour in this, although women tend to do most of the petty trading. In the larger settlements almost all the shops and commercial activities are run by the Chinese, and in a few cases cloth stores are run by Pakistanis. Lao women in both town and village indulge in small-scale business with roadside snacks, fresh fruit and vegetable sales, or prepared-food stands in the market. They raise the produce themselves and do the actual selling. (Their income from such enterprises is usually around 150 *kip*[1] on a good day.) All over rural Laos at the various temple festivals, young marriageable girls of the village set up small tables within the temple compound where they sell fruit,

[1] In 1959, 80 *kip* were equivalent to one US dollar.

90

candy, soft drinks, cigarettes and beer to the young men. A girl may net as much as 200 *kip* in an evening, or as little as 25 *kip*, depending on her popularity.

Of great significance as a part-time occupation in northern Laos is trade with the mountain people. Formerly contact between the Lao and the other ethnic groups of Laos was more difficult than it is today, due in part to language and transportation problems. This gave rise in northern Laos to *lam*, still in use to some extent today. (The term *lam*, meaning literally 'interpreter', designates the institution as well as the individual carrying out its functions.) The *lam* is a person who acts as an intermediary between traders, and occasionally the Government, on the one hand, and the tribal peoples, usually the Khmu and sometimes the Meo, on the other hand. The *lam* himself is a Lao, usually inhabiting a village that has relatively easy access to the market town.[1]

The position of *lam* is relative to the power-political position of the various ethnic groups in a given area. The late Viceroy of the Kingdom acted as *lam* to a group of Lu living in northern Luang Prabang, a position he inherited. Here is clearly seen the hereditary and governmental aspects of the position of *lam*, which has certain feudal overtones. In this case he purchased certain Lu products and helped them attempt improved agricultural practices; in return, some of them acted as his retainers. By the late 1950s, however, only fragments of the pattern remained.

The institution of *lam* has been given an orthodox Marxist interpretation by a Communist observer (Burchett, 1957, 236–7). Among the mountain people, he holds—except the Lao Xung [Meo]—almost every village has a 'professional' Lao Lum [Lao] who settles in as a doctor or a lawyer might into a village community in Europe. Because he has learned to read and write in the pagoda and has a higher social status, he sets up as 'general adviser'. He arbitrates in quarrels between villagers, and offers to settle inter-village disputes by collecting a fee from both sides. He provokes disputes in order to settle them. He lends money at exorbitant interest rates. On holidays he makes some insignificant present to each household and collects an important contribution of rice, meat or alcohol in return. The principle was imposed that the mountain villagers 'owed' a living to any Lao Lum who condescended to live with them. 'As a tree has leaves, so a Lao Thenh must have the Lao Lum,' says a Lao Thenh proverb. This author then goes on to describe the ways in which the French increased inequalities and exploited the mountain peoples.

[1] This is the pattern in Luang Prabang Province. In some parts of northern Laos where there are no Lao the function of the *lam* may be assumed by tribal Tai. For example, in Muong Sing in northern Nam Tha a descendant of the hereditary 'Prince' of the Tai Lu acts as *lam* for the Kha Ko of the area.

But although some Lao may have lived in mountain villages, the function of the *lam* was more expediently served when the mountain people brought their trade goods to him. There is no question that the Lao and others often exploited the less culturally developed tribal peoples, but to ignore the very real symbiotic functions of the inter-relationships does violence to the facts. Traditionally the Khmu came to the *lam* whenever they had some forest products to sell or wanted to buy salt or clothing. Then the *lam* would arrange the trade with a merchant, or sometimes the *lam* himself engaged in commerce directly with the tribal people. *Lam* is distinctly a reciprocal relation-ship. Head taxes levied by the French were often paid by the *lam*, and in return the Khmu worked in the fields of their *lam* when necessary, supplying him with game and forest products. In those cases where the *lam* was also a merchant he enjoyed a complete monopoly, with all the tribal trade funnelled through his hands. The relationship between a *lam* and his clients was not formalized and depended largely on individual personalities. A man might act as the *lam* for a few tribal families or for an entire tribal village. He might be the *lam* to these people by virtue of inheriting the position, or, if the Khmu found him to be dishonest in his dealings, the latter could seek another. One of the chief reasons why this institution is beginning to break down is that the Khmu are beginning to market their own products directly.

It might seem from this description of the *lam* and the fact that it has started to disintegrate, that trade with the tribal peoples involves only a small number of the Lao valley farmers. This is not so. Almost every Lao village of any size, located along the Mekong or one of its major tributaries, is a centre of trade with tribal peoples. All house-holds participate in this trade, even if they do not act as *lam*. Barter trade is very important, the Lao supplying such goods as cotton or woven cloth produced in their own fields or homes, fish or fish pro-ducts, pottery, sugar and salt; while the mountain peoples offer opium, woven bamboo mats and baskets, betel, sticklac, forest game and other products. Both groups exchange rice, depending on which has the surplus. In addition, the Lao villagers act as a channel for the distribution of goods derived from urban markets. This includes silver for jewellery and currency, iron bars, rifles, tools, blankets, soap, matches, thread and needles. During the dry season when there is little work in the fields, many Lao farmers buy a small stock of these goods and take them into the hills to trade. This is especially true in those areas of northern Laos where the hill peoples equal or outnumber the Lao, who are confined to the narrow river valleys. Barter is perhaps the most common type of transaction there, since paper currency is not valued and silver is relatively scarce, being reserved largely for transactions involving opium.

Large villages in Vientiane Province often have one or two tailors, male or female, who earn their livelihood making pants, shirts, mosquito nets and sheets. They have purchased their foot-pedalled sewing machines in Vientiane. Profits range from 60 to 80 per cent, and in villages with several sewing machines, tailoring costs tend to be uniform. One or two members of a community may supplement their income by being herb doctors or midwives. There is also usually a barber in each village, who works from house to house. Every village has a few skilled carpenters. When not employed in construction they saw lumber to sell for 10–15 *kip* a board-foot. In larger villages there is usually one villager who owns and operates a rice mill.

As to wage labour, in Vientiane Province most landless villagers hire out their labour during the busy transplanting and harvest seasons. They work on either a daily or seasonal basis and receive their wages in rice (thirty-six pounds per day or 1,500 pounds per season from May to October). While some Lao may work for others in the village and receive payment in cash or kind, others will go to work as labourers in town. They dislike being designated by the term coolie, which they feel should be properly applied only to various Kha groups. These Lao work for local merchants, the army and the various Government offices, doing menial chores. Sometimes they work for only a month or so and then return to their villages. Recently an increasing number of people from villages near Luang Prabang have tended to give up agriculture for permanent jobs, a trend accelerated by poor rains and army confiscation of some rice lands on the town's outskirts. Yet although it is true that larger numbers of Lao peasants and tribal people have gone to work in the expanding towns since the end of World War II, their periods of work are usually short and their objective has most often been to accumulate a small sum in order to purchase some consumer goods such as clothing, and then to return home. Clear evidence of their limited participation in a cash economy has been the chronic shortages of food in the towns, forcing the importation of rice and other foods from Thailand. It is an indication of the scarcity of cash in rural areas that the Government of Laos has thought it not feasible to levy any taxes on the rural population.

CONSUMPTION PATTERNS

To the average villager real wealth is determined not by his secondary sources of income or even by size and number of fields under cultivation, but by the amount of rice harvested. In Vientiane Province a man harvesting under 200 *myn* (5,300 lb.) is poor, while a comfortably situated farmer harvests over 300 *myn*. A man obtaining 400 *myn* (10,600 lb.) or more, is considered wealthy. (In contrast, in the Thai village of Bang Chan near Bangkok more than half the households produced over 25,000 lb. of rice each.)

The ways in which the rice crop is disposed of provide significant insights into the meaning of capital and the importance of investment. Production for home consumption is the primary factor; although this is true, barter and sales for cash are also practised. There are certain types of purchases that can be defined as essential. Metal farm implements, cooking utensils, some items of clothing, salt, sugar, supplementary purchases of vegetables, fruit, meat and sometimes even grain are all felt to be required. But the Lao is not consumer-oriented; even today the peasants produce enough to satisfy most of their own needs themselves. It should be stressed that this is becoming progressively less true, however. Once immediate personal needs have been satisfied, more complex decisions are necessary.

It has been estimated that a typical rural Lao family in central Laos spends in cash about US $150 a year (data from 1957), or approximately US $35 per family member. Of this sum, about half goes for supplementary food purchases and perhaps another 20 per cent is spent on clothing. The remainder is divided among expenses for tools, entertainment in the form of gambling at holiday festivals, and gifts to the temple and priests. Although the Lao villager is not poor, in that he usually has ample food to avoid starvation and frequently has small luxuries as well, still this figure is not very high even by Asian standards. A prosperous villager in Vientiane Province may have the equivalent of US $250 a year to spend (in contrast to a prosperous Bang Chan (Thailand) farmer who spends as much as about US $500 a year). A rural household budget for the Luang Prabang area would be approximately the same, since fewer commodities are purchased while the cost of living is somewhat higher due to transportation costs. In most cases cash income would be proportionately less in areas away from the vicinity of the town.

In the Laotian context a minimum with regard to food involves getting enough rice to avoid hunger and to carry on one's daily activities. Although actual starvation is rare or non-existent in Laos, and people do not have to struggle to survive in an inhospitable environment, they often know hunger, particularly in the period before the rice harvest when the previous year's stocks near depletion. Rice forms the basis of every meal and is reflected linguistically in that the verb 'to eat'—*kin khao*—means 'to eat rice'. The Lao often mentions his preference for glutinous rice as a means of asserting cultural identity, differentiating himself from the Chinese and Vietnamese.

It is difficult to say which groups have enough only for themselves,

94

have a surplus to sell, or are forced to buy rice. There is a good deal of variation among ethnic groups, villages and even households in addition to yearly differences due to fluctuating climatic conditions. There are some general patterns, however. The Khmu and the Lamet often produce in their *hai* surpluses to sell to the valley Lao. But this is not universally the case, particularly in the area surrounding the royal capital, where the impoverished Khmu frequently must purchase rice from the Lao. The Meo appear for the most part to be self-sufficient. Poor crops due to lack of adequate rainfall in recent years have compelled more Khmu and Lao to buy rice to a greater degree than was previously the case.

To sum up, rice is the basic food of Lao, supplemented by vegetables and meat, fish and forest products. Fish is of varying importance among the Lao and meat is consumed sparingly or on special occasions by all groups. With the exceptions of rice, salt, certain vegetables, forest products and possibly crude sugar and tobacco, all other items of food for personal consumption are considered luxuries consumed on special occasions.

Housing is an important item of peasant Lao investment. There are a number of essential features which all Lao dwellings have in common. They are rectangular and are adjacent to paths and rivers, and avoid facing the west, the direction said to be travelled by the dead. They are built elevated on wooden piles about six feet off the ground, a form of construction with many advantages: it separates the living quarters from the rainy season mud, keeps out the village dogs and chickens and, in the space underneath, provides storage place for a loom, firewood, livestock and sometimes the rice bin. A house of minimum standard has a split bamboo floor and woven bamboo walls, with one main room. The thatch roof slopes over a bamboo veranda running along one length of the house, and at the rear of this porch is usually a wooden frame filled with sand, which is used as the base for the charcoal or wood fire over which cooking is done. Bamboo is usually available locally, as is hardwood (usually teak) for the house posts. The woven bamboo walls allow for relatively free circulation of air, and the floor has enough spring to make sleeping on it on mats extremely comfortable. Windows are found only in the more prosperous homes.

An average bamboo dwelling can be constructed rapidly, with a minimum of expense, at a cost of about 10,000 *kip* (US $125), when a group of villagers pool their labour in customary fashion. The builder supplies food and rice wine for the workers, who usually contribute their labour on the same reciprocal basis as in transplanting and harvesting rice. Often a celebration is held in connection with construction and dedication of a new dwelling, in which the women of the neighbourhood share the cooking, and in the evening the village youth participate in a traditional love court.

A bamboo house does not carry much prestige, nor is it adequate for a large household. Where possible it is improved upon. This means first of all a larger layout. A larger house is constructed of wooden planks although in many cases thatch continues to be the roofing material. In some of the more developed areas, such as among the Lao around Vientiane, wooden plank floors are a regular feature in house construction. These floors imply a higher standard of living, since they are usually accompanied by the use of kapok-stuffed sleeping pads instead of woven fibre mats. In more prosperous homes the walls are also of wood. The cost of materials for an all-wood house with thatch roof is approximately 16,000 *kip* (us $200). In some cases the traditional roof is replaced with corrugated iron, or more customarily, tile. A further development is the use of a sort of wattle-and-daub cementing over a bamboo framework. Sometimes there are separate sheds for cooking and storage. A small granary is often mounted on piles adjacent to the house, and occasionally there are seed beds on platforms out of reach of the animals. Larger compounds include a vegetable garden; clumps of bamboo and banana trees often serve as boundary markers.

Although wooden houses doubtless offer more protection during chilly winter nights, many of them lack sufficient ventilation. Windows, if constructed, are frequently small and ineffective, so that for most of the year these more elaborate dwellings are actually less comfortable than the simpler bamboo houses.

Only the major towns of Laos are electrified. Some rural homes use crude kerosene lamps made from tin cans, and a very few have pressure lamps with incandescent mantles; flashlights are also used. General speaking, because of the constant draughts, candles are not employed as a source of light, and the villagers retire when it gets dark.

Rural Lao consider their homes sacred places, presided over by a resident spirit (*phi huan*) for whom an altar is built near one of the posts. This spirit is frequently consulted and offerings of balls of rice, flowers and candles are left for it. Several small images of Buddha may also be kept here.

Since the Lao live and eat on the floor, home furnishings are at a minimum. There are a few low, round stools and tables, and perhaps a cradle made of plaited bamboo is suspended from the rafters. Sleeping mats are rolled up along the wall during the day. The home of a village headman might have a table and chair for conducting official business, plus a few cheap suitcases for storing clothes, and some enamel dishes and other utensils including the omnipresent spittoon. The use of mosquito nets is a conspicuous status symbol in the homes of teachers, headmen and some of the wealthier farmers.

For most, however, the cost of the netting combined with a lack of felt need precludes its widespread use.

What constitutes basic necessaries of clothing is difficult to define, since during most of the year it is possible to survive quite well with only a negligible amount. Among the Lao, infants and small children frequently go naked. When possible, most Lao villagers have at least one set of clothes for work in the fields and another for holidays. The former is usually woven at home, while the good clothes for men, a Western-style pair of trousers and shirt, are bought in town. For men, homespun clothing is regarded as inferior, Western-style clothing being considered more attractive. A Lao male outfit consists of a hand-woven indigo dyed cotton shirt and short pants for work in the fields. Sometimes a Western-style shirt is also used. A man may work in, and also bathes in, a short cotton sarong wrapped around the waist. In addition, he may have a longer plaid silk sarong for informal use around the house. The traditional male garment, still worn on ceremonial occasions, is the *sampot*, of bright silk and like a sarong, but drawn up loosely between the legs and tucked into the rear waistband. The basic dress of the rural Lao woman is a hand-loom woven skirt of cotton or silk, embellished with a characteristic Lao border woven of coloured or precious-metal thread.

More important than clothing, particularly for children, is silver or preferably gold jewellery in the form of anklets, bracelets or small gold medals of Buddha suspended on chains or cords around the neck. Jewellery is believed to protect the wearer from harm and prevent the soul from leaving the body and so causing illness. Village people believe the soul has an affinity for gold. In terms of Lao culture, this jewellery can, because of its supposed protective and therapeutic value, be considered an essential item. Much gold jewellery is worn by women and to a limited extent by men. This is said to be because the soul of a woman is weaker than that of a man and so requires more protection. Among wealthier Lao, investments in gold are quite significant, amounting to several thousand *kip* just for hair ornaments, a characteristic feature of the female Lao dress, consisting of strands of small gold beads arranged around the traditional chignon surmounted by an ornate gold hairpin. Bracelets, necklaces, rings, earrings and silver or gold belts are also worn. The Lao say, 'A chicken is pretty because of its feathers, and a woman is beautiful because of her dress.' The villager considers jewellery a sound investment, and sometimes he uses it as security for a loan when he is in need of cash. Wrist-watches are worn by some men, but can also be included in the category of jewellery, since the need for accurate time-telling cannot be called necessary or even desirable in rural Laos. Certainly a strong supporting reason for the investment in jewellery is the pronounced lack of faith among villagers in paper currency, a feeling no doubt intensified by current political changes.

In the last fifteen years, and particularly within the last five years, a whole range of new consumer items has become more easily available to the Lao villager. Bicycles, manufactured cloth, kerosene lamps, flashlights, vacuum flasks, tinned condensed milk and suitcases for storing clothes, are only a few of the items that have begun to attract the rural Lao consumer. In a village near Vientiane there were (in 1959) eighty-one bicycles, or almost one per household, two motorcycles and two cars. The latter were owned by wealthy villagers and used as taxis. This situation represented perhaps the ultimate in mechanization in a Lao village.

While the disparity between urban and rural standards of living has been a cause of social conflict, it appears that the standard of living of people in rural areas has improved somewhat over the past decade and that they now have access to many more types of goods. Here too the change has been disproportionate, with those who live along the main road benefiting most, and the mountain peoples affected to a much lesser degree. These developments are hardly surprising in view of the abundant external aid Laos has received during the past five years. Most of the consumer goods in rural areas have been a direct result of the American aid programme. Per capita, Laos received in the latter 1950s more foreign economic assistance than any other country in the world. This has been an artificial situation and has already begun to change.

Taxation does not constitute an important demand on the village economy. The head tax which existed under the French was abolished with independence. As far as the writer is aware, no effective land tax exists. The government derives its chief revenues from customs duties, levies on urban merchants and foreign aid. There are theoretically certain types of taxes levied on farmers, as on goods shipped from one village to another, store sales and on forest products. But exemptions are liberal; if a farmer breaks an arm or leg he is exempt for one year. Even more to the point is that for all practical purposes the Government, largely for political reasons, makes almost no effort to collect taxes. (In recent years, however, some Government ministers have thought about reinstating a tax of about 100 *kip* to be paid by the head of each household.)

ATTITUDES TOWARDS CONSUMPTION AND INVESTMENT

It is easy to draw an idyllic picture of the Lao peasant as a charming loafer in the midst of tropical plenty. This is definitely not true. If the rains do not come soon enough or in sufficient quantity, the Lao farmer may know real privation. Also, farming in a semi-tropical climate, the productivity of which is more mythical than real, can be very hard work. Ploughing a paddy field under a hot sun, spending hours stooped over transplanting rice seedlings, hacking a clearing from the jungle, are all tasks that require hard labour. Work for its own sake is not valued in Lao society, nor is an extremely high value placed on the acquisition of land or capital. In fact, an individual who is overly aggressive in the pursuit of these things is looked upon with disfavour, if not open hostility, by his fellow villagers. This is not to say that the Lao are not interested in material goods or their accumulation, for they can see the advantages of possessing more land, livestock, tools, better house, personal clothing and ornaments. Yet a stronger attitude in Laos is the credo *'Bo peng yang'* (it doesn't matter, i.e. I cannot determine my own destiny). Success is not felt to be capable of achievement through hard work, but rather by forces present in the individual at birth as well as those acting upon him from outside. Formal status by birth remains an important factor.

One cannot discuss rural Lao economy without detailed reference to the local pagoda. The primary objective of the villagers is to produce enough from their land and animals to feed themselves and reinvest enough in the form of seed and livestock feed to continue the production at the same level. Once this has been accomplished, it must be decided whether to work harder to increase production and how to dispose of any surplus above and beyond the family's immediate consumption needs. In Lao culture the purchase of additional consumer goods has secondary priority. Rather, first priority is the allocation of resources for religious purposes.

Every morning the Lao villager makes a religious contribution, when the Buddhist monks make their rounds with their begging bowls for their daily ration of rice. Every Lao village, even if it has only a few hundred people, possesses at least one pagoda with several monks and/or novices. They are completely supported by the local population, not only in terms of food but also with clothing and many miscellaneous gifts. A contemporary Buddhist monk requires more than a yellow robe and a begging bowl. He needs cigarettes, betel-chewing equipment, writing materials, cooking utensils, mosquito net, vacuum flask, parasol, all small items in themselves but important in their total value since they represent cash purchases made by the villagers. Unlike Christian monks in some countries, Buddhist monks do not cultivate any of their food themselves, although they do engage in physical labour necessary for the upkeep of the pagoda compound. However, the purchase of cement and other materials is the responsibility of the villagers. Almost universally the local pagoda is by far the most substantial structure in the Lao village and expenses to maintain it are not resented by the population. The monks may do some of the work of keeping the pagoda in repair, but it is the laity who provide whatever tools and materials are needed and who often contribute labour as well. Various sums are also spent in decorating the interior and particularly for gold leaf for the statues of Buddha. Villagers bring candles and elaborate floral offerings on their frequent visits to the pagoda. In a modest village of fifty houses near Vientiane the headman estimated that over 30,000 *kip* (US $3,750) had been raised for a new *wat*. Government aid was also solicited for this construction, although the road was poor and there was no school or first aid station in the village.

A further example of the value system with regard to the allocation of resources is provided by the programmes undertaken by the Bureau of Rural Affairs during the first half of 1959. Of 992 projects, 238 were for the repair of pagodas throughout Laos. (This was exceeded only by the 249 schools constructed and 59 repaired. In some provinces the majority of projects were for the repair of pagodas.) When the Lao Government recently began to undertake a programme of rural development and villagers were asked to indicate what they felt to be their most important needs, they replied, 'Metal roofing for the pagoda, cement for the pagoda, lumber for the pagoda.' Schools, roads or health facilities ran a poor second.

These attitudes are, of course, closely connected to the Lao system of religious beliefs, where it is a privilege to be able to contribute to the support of the pagoda and the monks. In this way an individual acquires merit and consequently assures himself a better rebirth. It should be stressed that there are also auxiliary expenditures such as seasonal religious festivals, ordination ceremonies sponsored by individual families and elaborate funeral rites.

Associated with Buddhism, but far antedating it, is the system of animistic beliefs in the *phi*, or nature spirits. To appease these resident spirits of the mountains, fields, villages and homes, animal sacrifices are often necessary. These may range from chickens to water buffalo, and their frequency is highly variable although their occurrence is widespread. Buffalo sacrifice has been practised by the Lao of both Vientiane and Luang Prabang. It has the function of both propitiating the spirits and controlling rainfall. This ceremony occurs before the beginning of the monsoon rains. In certain regions of northern Laos there is active collaboration in sacrificial ceremonies among the Lao, Kha peoples and tribal Tai, and it is possible that the cultural influence of aboriginal peoples is a factor in Lao buffalo sacrifice. It would be incorrect, however, to state that the majority of the poultry, pigs, cows and buffalo of the Lao serve only sacrificial purposes, since buffalo are important as draught animals, and the animals slaughtered for ritual purposes are eaten 'after the spirit has had his fill'.

There is no precise data available for any one group of the annual cost of these ceremonies. One Lao official, however, made these

100

estimates for sacrifices to the village spirit during the course of a year, as a result of his conversations with people in two Lao villages in Luang Prabang district. In the first village, the forty-four households each sacrificed two chickens which, at the then current market rates, amounted to an expense of about 8,000 *kip*; in the other village of approximately similar size, two buffalo were sacrificed by the village as a whole, each buffalo valued at 4,000–5,000 *kip*. These sacrifices represent only those to the spirits of the village, for which the village population shared expenses, and not those to spirits involved in individual personal matters.

Thus, although the inhabitants of central and northern Laos do eat meat and fowl as a result of their sacrifices, the occasion is not determined primarily by dietary needs—any discussion of domestic livestock in Laos cannot lack reference to its sacrificial significance. Since the Lao and other peoples of northern Laos can hardly be termed wealthy in poultry and livestock, it is not difficult to see that such sacrifices exert a considerable drain on their economy.

In rural areas among non-Lao groups such as the Khmu debt slavery is still reported to exist. One of the important reasons for this is the strongly felt necessity to obtain animals, especially buffalo, for sacrifice. Illness, failure of crops, demands of social status, may all force a family to go deeply into debt. Since cash or material goods to secure a loan are lacking a child is sometimes given to the creditor. This in effect often amounts to bonded servitude. Such practices are outlawed by the Lao Government, but they have by no means been eliminated. By contrast the rural Lao are largely free of such constraints. They do not have the standard of living of their urban compatriots, nor such a strong cultural imperative as the Khmu for providing sacrificial animals.

RURAL AND URBAN CREDIT AND INDEBTEDNESS

The Chinese play a very prominent role in Laos commerce, in both urban and rural areas. The most important Chinese business concerns are, of course, concentrated in Vientiane. A brief survey conducted in 1959 showed that the Chinese operated 749 or almost exactly 50 per cent of a total of 1,550 businesses. The other 50 per cent was divided among Lao, Vietnamese, Thai, French and others.

Most large enterprises such as banks, insurance companies, saw mills, motor truck transport firms and particularly export-import houses have Chinese capital and/or management, so that actually the Chinese community participates in more than half of the total commerce in Vientiane. This is particularly true in the case of Lao-Chinese partnerships, where the former supplies his name and Government contacts with perhaps some capital as well, and the latter manages the enterprise and provides capital. In the case of import-export concerns it is the Chinese partner who provides contacts in Hong Kong, Saigon and other trade centres. Lao-Chinese intermarriage is also an important factor here since a business may sometimes be registered in the name of the Lao wife. In certain cases the Lao and Chinese partners may be linked through marriage bonds between their children. Although formal Government regulations limit certain types of trade and commerce exclusively to Lao citizens, these requirements are met ostensibly by the Lao partners who supply their name, and such business relationships reach up to the highest levels of Lao society.

In rural areas not only do Chinese operate shops in many villages, but they also lend money. The villagers often feel they can obtain loans at lower rates from the Chinese than they can from their own kinsmen. The Chinese are willing to take their interest payment in rice at the next harvest. Psychologically speaking, a farmer would rather part with 100 pounds of rice at harvest time when he has thousands, than 100 *kip* in cash when he has practically none.

When a Lao peasant wishes to borrow money, he usually makes a contract before three witnesses and lists his house, garden, livestock or gold as security. The interest rates in urban areas vary from 4 to 10 per cent per month. The larger the amount borrowed, the smaller the interest rate. Generally speaking, there is more indebtedness among the urban Lao who may want to build a house (hired labour is usually used in town), start a business or buy a car. There is a tendency for Lao farmers to go into debt when there is a failure of the rice crop, but rural debt does not appear to be a major problem. This may be a reflection of the general undeveloped state of the total rural economy as far as cash exchanges are concerned. By contrast, indebtedness is a major problem among urban Vietnamese and Lao-Thai coolies and pedicab drivers, due in part to their enthusiasm for gambling.

A great deal of borrowing is done by Lao villagers, with sums of 500 *kip* or less borrowed from relatives. Larger amounts, for the purchase of a sewing machine, bicycle, radio, buffalo, rice seed for the planting season, lumber for a new house, and for weddings or funerals are borrowed in secrecy from merchants. Large loans must be repaid within six months and rural interest rates range from 10 to 15 per cent monthly. Rice is 'borrowed' quite freely among relatives in amounts not exceeding 20 lb., and is rarely expected to be repaid. Money for construction or major repair of a *wat* building is lent at interest rates of only 5 per cent, and on rare occasions, at no interest. The lender, in both cases, obtains merit by not charging the normal rate. Unfortunately, the credit of the majority of farmers is very poor since they have little which can be offered as collateral. Thus ambitious farmers interested in raising cash crops such as coffee or kapok, often do not do so, because they cannot obtain the funds.

The sources and availability of credit and accumulation of indebtedness are closely connected to the extent of participation in a cash economy. In the towns of Laos the elite and the Chinese and Vietnamese merchants definitely do engage in a considerable amount of lending and borrowing, usually at very high interest rates. Houses or other personal property are given as security, with the interest rate running as high as 10 per cent a month. There is a tendency to confine borrowing within one's ethnic group and if possible to one's extended family unit. However, it not infrequently happens that the Lao elite extend credit to the Chinese. (This may be a reflection of the channelling of foreign economic aid through the Lao Government.)

6

Capital Saving and Credit in Highland Orissa (India)

BY F. G. BAILEY

INTRODUCTION

I set out in this essay to look at those activities in highland Orissa falling within the sphere of capital, saving and credit. But these three concepts seemed to make intelligible only a fraction of actual behaviour, and I could only approach reality by looking at non-economic activities correlated with capital, saving and credit.

The fault may be in the material I collected and in my rudimentary knowledge of economic science. Alternatively, purely economic analysis in the type of peasant society which I studied, although possible, may be of little explanatory value. Of these two explanations I prefer the latter: but I do not rule out the former, since sharp economic tools, like other tools, may be blunt in the hands of an unskilled workman.

What social anthropology has to say to economics is that 'economic man' is also social and political man, someone's husband and brother and father, sometimes given to religious irrationality, and so forth. This is not new. But, while the proposition has been agreed across the table, this agreement does not emerge in action, at least so far as planning in India is concerned: and the instancing of it from Indian material may make clear that while inter-disciplinary thinking may or may not fertilize theory, lack of it sterilizes practice.

HIGHLAND ORISSA

Orissa, I have heard Oriyas boast, is one of the most backward states in India. Phulbani district, about which I am writing, is Orissa's poorest. It is mountainous: communications, both within and with the world outside, are poor. There are no railways. At the time of writing (1960), the district is connected with the coastal plain by a single all-weather road; it has no industries; there are no mines.

The forest provides two sources of wealth: the gathering and exporting of the leaf *kendu* (*Dyospyros menalexylon*), which is used for the outer wrapping of the Indian cigarette (*bidi*); and the sale of timber, mainly *sal* (*Shorea robusta*), to be used for railway sleepers. Both the leaf trade and the timber trade concern the State Government and well-to-do contractors and have little effect upon the peasants. Peasants neither invest in these two activities, nor do many find employment there.

Rice is grown in irrigated fields in the valleys and in dry fields on the hills, and, so far as I know, consumed within the district. Some peasants grow more than they and their families consume, and others grow less than they need: rice then becomes a cash crop and is used for internal trade.

Manufactures of various kinds are imported and to acquire these the peasant needs cash. This is earned by those who grow and those who trade in turmeric, the main export crop of the district, and by those who find employment, usually with the Government.

The Government itself is a major factor in the peasant economy. Its policies (sometimes policies not concerned with economics) have profoundly affected the distribution of land. Increasingly it is intervening directly in economic matters, regulating the transfer of land, restricting interest rates, investing in agricultural improvements, encouraging capital accumulation, providing credit facilities, and so forth.

I here distinguish three systems of economic activity: the 'peasant' sector, which concerns the growing of rice, internal trade in rice, and various traditional specialists and craftsmen; secondly the 'commercial' sector, which consists of those activities connecting the district with the world outside, and which are in the hands of private persons; and, thirdly, economic activity by Government agencies.

These three systems are historically distinct: they have grown, roughly speaking, in the order in which I have given them. The relationships exemplified in these three systems differ. In the indigenous economy a transaction is likely to bring in considerations of status—of kinship, friendship, enmity, caste relationship, village relationship, and so forth, and the transaction is only one strand in a rope of relationships connecting the buyer and seller, or the creditor and borrower. In the commercial economy transactions at the lower level may have some non-economic element in them, but, as one steps up through the various middlemen to the merchants, transactions tend to become 'single-interests'. In the third system—those transactions which involve Government agencies—the personal element is, theoretically but not always in fact, at its lowest. Again, the three systems differ in scale. A unit in the indigenous economy concerns a small number of people in a limited area and a small amount of goods. It can be analysed within a single large village and its surrounding hamlets. Some units in the commercial sector are larger, and some events and behaviour within them can only be understood by referring to the larger Indian economy, or even to world demand for the product concerned. In the case of Government agencies, many decisions are made in Delhi and apply to the whole of India: procedures are relatively inflexible and carried on with a high degree of bureaucracy: and the working of the system at its upper levels is beyond the horizon of the sociologist in a village, and its activities have largely to be taken as given, as a factor intruding from outside.

It is important to distinguish these three systems, because they are sometimes (if one may reify) in competition with one another: there are relationships in all three which contradict one another, and if one grows, then another declines. An obvious example is the conflict between the moneylender-merchant in the commercial sector and, in the Government sector, the agencies of co-operative credit and co-operative marketing. Another example is the way in which some of the status relationships of the indigenous system (for instance in the *jajmani* system—see below, p. 107) are being replaced by contractual relationships which entail no link enduring beyond the immediate transaction.

I have separated the systems conceptually, but in fact a transaction in one is likely to be influenced by relationships which the parties have in the other two systems. Any one individual may be an actor in all three systems, and in order to make a realistic analysis of the peasant economy, one must take all three into account.

With this analytical framework in mind, I shall examine the accumulation and management of capital, its investment, and the provision of credit, in two villages in the Kondmals subdivision of Phulbani district. In both, the main part of their economy is subsistence agriculture. But one, an Oriya village called Bisipara, is also a village of part-time traders and a minor centre of commercial activity: the other village, Baderi, which is within an hour's walk of Bisipara, is populated by tribal people, Konds, who grow turmeric for sale, but abhor the role of middleman.[1]

THE PEASANT ECONOMY

(a) *Land in the peasant economy*
Both in magnitude and in the prestige which attaches to its possession,

[1] Bisipara is described in *Caste and the Economic Frontier* (Bailey, 1957) and Baderi in *Tribe, Caste and Nation* (Bailey, 1960). In the latter parts of this essay, particularly those which concern the activity of Government agencies and the politicians, I have drawn upon my experience in other parts of Orissa in 1959.

land is the most important material asset in the peasant economy. Within that sector almost all economic relationships depend directly or indirectly upon the ownership of land. But in the last hundred years these relationships have been changing. Whereas in the past ritual and political relationships coincided with economic ties, at the present day there is a tendency for the purely economic relationship to become separated from other elements.

In former days economic relationships were organized within the framework of the caste system. In Bisipara, which now has a population of just under 700, all the land was owned by a single dominant caste, the WARRIORS.[1] This caste forms about a fifth, but probably in the past was a larger proportion, of the village population. The WARRIORS are cultivators with military traditions. There were two categories of dependents: agricultural labourers, most of whom belonged to an Untouchable caste; and specialists—BRAHMIN priests, BARBERS, WASHERMEN, HERDSMEN, and so forth. Both these categories derived their share in the produce of the village land through a relationship of dependence upon the land-holding WARRIORS.

Neither of these relationships were purely economic, nor were they temporary. Farm-servants were regarded as part of their master's household. They were paid in kind, receiving food for their daily meals, clothing two or three times a year, the gift of grain at harvest-time, and sometimes the grant of a field to cultivate for themselves with the use of the master's plough-cattle and possibly also his seed grain. Politically they were the master's retainers, supporting him in his disputes, being protected by him, and performing numerous customary services and having numerous customary rights not immediately connected with their work on the land. The master was (and in a few instances still is) the *raja* (king), and the farm servants were *praja* (subjects). The relationship was hereditary, and, finally, it coincided with the high ritual status of the WARRIOR and the low ritual status of the Untouchable servant.

Members of specialist castes were not employed exclusively by one WARRIOR family, but were the hereditary servants of the whole group of landholders. Like the farm-servants they received a daily allowance of food, or a payment (always in kind) when their services were called for, and a gift of grain at harvest-time. This is the *jajmani* system. Their economic dependence coincided with a political and ritual subordination to the WARRIORS (except in the case of the BRAHMIN who is the highest in the ritual hierarchy).

Such a system can be described in terms of the use of capital assets,

[1] The names of most castes have been put into English and are printed in capital letters. The caste name is not an infallible index of present occupation. DISTILLERS, for example, do not distil nor do WARRIORS fight.

and the mechanisms of credit, saving and investment. But all these activities were open only to the WARRIORS. The hereditary servants owned some productive capital—the POTTER had his wheel and his stock of clay, the WASHERMAN had his pots for boiling clothes, the WEAVER had his loom, but none of these was acquired in an open market. The farm-servants no doubt borrowed grain to meet contingent expenses, but again these loans were not taken in the market, but were part of the hereditary relationship between the master and servant. In this system apparent economic relationships were in fact of more-than-economic significance.

What I have written is not an adequate description of the working of Bisipara's economy today. In the past hundred years there have been many changes. It is also possible that the neat outline which I have given was never perfectly exemplified. But this is the form which the people say existed in the past, which is congruent with present ritual and to a lesser extent present political relationships, and which (to the WARRIORS at least) seems the normal and right kind of economic relationship within the village. Finally it is important to know about this traditional form of economic relationship, because even those who now resent it and see that under it they were underprivileged, nevertheless try to re-create multiple relationships in their essentially impersonal dealings in the commercial sector and in their relationships with Government agencies.

The situation has changed because the presence of Government and the expansion of commerce have given those who formerly had no capital an opportunity to acquire assets. Often the necessary saving has come about from income made outside the traditional landholding system. The typical example is the person who holds a job in Government service, as a schoolmaster or a peon, or a man who has made money in commerce. Those who became rich in either of these ways invested their money in land. The opportunities were not confined to the dominant caste of WARRIORS, and persons who were formerly in the dependent category acquired land of their own. Land, in other words, is bought and sold, and it is no longer a monopoly of the one dominant caste.

Other variables affect capital accumulation in land, and I have discussed them in detail elsewhere (Bailey, 1957, Part II). Briefly the system of inheritance, by which property is divided between all the sons of a man, and secondly the almost complete absence of joint families, mean that sometimes estates are broken up into small units which cannot afford the traditional management, under which a part of the income from an estate was invested in 'retainers'. A small estate cannot afford this, and the owner may do most of the work himself and require assistance only at the critical times of transplanting and harvesting paddy. The owner then rejects a permanent relationship with a *praja* (who must be supported throughout the year) and takes on casual labourers (*mulya*) who are paid by the day. This has the advantage of flexibility: other things being equal the labour force can be easily expanded or contracted. A second point is that land comes into the market often through contingent expenditure on ceremonies—for a marriage or at a death. This factor too may bring estates down to the size where they are more efficiently worked by casual labour than under the traditional system.

Labourers are not only thrust out of the traditional system by a decrease in the size of the unit of production. From their point of view a flexible relationship is preferable, since they are then free to try their luck in the commercial sector of the economy.

The change is less striking for the *jajmani* servants. Bisipara still has its hereditary servants and they are still paid in the traditional way by the majority of their clients. But they also work for cash, both in the village—particularly with the newly-rich, of relatively low caste, whose humble ritual status would make a *jajmani* relationship, with its hierarchical implications, degrading for the servant—and most of them, where possible, ply their trade or sell their wares in the marketplaces. Secondly, some persons of hereditary-specialist caste are now employees outside the village economy, or are landholders, or support themselves as casual labourers.

These changes have had a profound effect upon the political structure of the village, and are beginning to affect ritual relationships (Bailey, 1957, Part III).

Bisipara is a village of Oriyas who are part-time traders, and is not typical of all villages in the Kond hills. Five in every eight persons in the Kondmals sub-division are Konds, who play a different role in the economy of the area. As an example I will briefly describe the same problem—the connection between the nature of economic relationships and landholding—in the Kond village of Baderi.

Unlike Bisipara, which is a nucleated village, Baderi consists of nine hamlets dispersed through a two-mile valley, and the aggregate population of these hamlets is about 500 persons.

Seven out of ten people in Baderi are Konds. The rest comprise a few HERDSMEN, a family of SMITHS and some Untouchables. With the two specialist castes the Baderi Konds had, and still largely have, a *jajmani* relationship. Like the WARRIORS of Bisipara they formerly had a *raja-praja* relationship with the labouring castes, who are Untouchables, but this has been replaced almost entirely by casual day-labour. The reasons are basically the same as in Bisipara: that most Baderi estates can be adequately worked by the owner and cannot afford to support a servant and his family throughout the year: and secondly that the Untouchables have some opportunity of earning an income outside the village. But there are differences. The income which the Baderi Untouchables get from outside is not large, and none of them, unlike their fellows in Bisipara, have been able to gain large estates for themselves. Secondly, Kond lands have not passed, in Baderi at least, into the possession of other castes, but the average size of estates is growing smaller through an increase in the population relative to the land available. Thirdly, the outside income which the Konds enjoy is derived almost entirely from the sale of a cash crop, turmeric, and they have little experience in, and a great scorn for, the role of middlemen, which in former days they delegated to their Untouchable servants.

Economically these changes mean (1) that the main productive asset of the village is no longer the monopoly of a single caste (in Bisipara) and, (2) that economic relationships no longer coincide—to the same extent—with the ritual and political relationships of the caste system: to some extent they have become single-interest relationships. An economic description has become more meaningful than it was before, firstly because activities concerning goods and services today are more purely economic than they were in the past, and secondly because the behaviour of a larger number of people can be comprehended through such an analysis.

(b) *Investment in land*

In metropolitan Orissa the bigger landlords have for the last five or six years been running down their estates in an effort to avoid expropriation which would be the result of a ceiling on landholdings. They have been encouraged to do this by increases in the rates of agricultural income-tax and by difficulties arising from post-Independence legislation protecting share-croppers.

But in the Kondmals people know little or nothing of the Congress and left-wing parties' proposals about limits upon landholding, and in any case no-one there to my knowledge—and certainly no-one in the two villages under discussion—comes even remotely near the present (1959) suggested ceiling of thirty-three acres. There, investment in land is still considered the normal investment: it is apparently secure; it is productive; it brings prestige; and the land is under the close control of the investor.

But there are some disincentives. Firstly, to break new land is costly, for it has to be levelled and cleared and in a mountainous forested terrain this is expensive. Land which might be cleared is often too far away from the owner's other fields and from his home to make the investment profitable. If the field is distant then it becomes more difficult to protect the crop from animals and from thieves, and the journey to the fields will waste the time and energy both of the cultivator and of his plough-cattle. In other words, new land is to be found only on the margins, and the cost of working it may be prohibitive. Secondly, various Government regulations impede the ready transfer of land already under cultivation. Land may not be transferred from a Kond to a non-Kond without the permission of the Deputy Collector. Again, a sale of land has to be registered in the Government's Record of Rights, and for an illiterate peasant this can be a troublesome and expensive business. Thirdly, there are occasions when the peasant prefers to invest in gold and silver ornaments. Like land, these bring prestige and they have the advantage of being a more liquid form of capital than land, but less liquid than cash, which is likely to be frittered away in day-to-day expenditure.

But capital may be invested in land in other ways than through outright ownership. A few Oriyas in Bisipara owned land in Kond villages from two to seven miles away from their homes. This land was let out to share-croppers, who cultivated the land with their own plough-cattle and took a half-share in the produce. This same form of investment is used within the village by those who cannot cultivate their lands themselves—by widows, by the disabled, by the lazy but wealthy, by those who have a job outside the village, by those who have too much land to cultivate by themselves but not enough to make it worth their while hiring a full-time servant and buying more plough-cattle, and by those who have a little land but no plough-cattle. Share-cropping of land in Kond villages is now less common, firstly because Konds today are richer than they were a generation ago and have bought back land, and secondly because the Konds have grown more sophisticated and it has become more difficult for the absentee owner to ensure that he is not cheated out of a part of his share.

A third form of investment in land is by taking it in pledge. In this transaction the creditor, in return for advancing a sum of money, or in payment of an existing debt, cultivates a field belonging to the borrower. He has the use of this field until the money is paid back, and his use of the land represents the interest on the sum borrowed. This type of transaction is significant in two ways: firstly, through it the regulation prohibiting transfer of land between Kond and non-Kond can be evaded: secondly, land becomes in effect a more liquid asset, because the transaction lacks the finality of an outright sale and is therefore entered into with less reluctance by the borrowers.

There are various kinds of ancillary investment associated with the land. Some of this is trifling—an axe, a hoe, a wooden plough, a yoke, and so forth. But for some smaller cultivators the purchase of plough-cattle represents a considerable investment, and might even, measuring the value of the oxen against the value of the fields cultivated, justify describing such cultivation as capital-intensive. When their own fields are ploughed and sown, men in this category will usually hire themselves and their cattle out, on a daily wage, to larger cultivators.

(c) *Investment and credit in the peasant economy*

A common form of investment is in lending paddy (unhusked rice). The cultivation of paddy in this district begins in mid-June and the first harvest appears about the third week in September. The main harvest is reaped in the first two weeks of December. The price of paddy is lowest after the main harvest but from February until about October it rises steadily as more and more people exhaust their stock and are forced to buy or borrow. The demand is intensified in August and again during the harvest months, since it is the practice sometimes to pay labourers in paddy or cooked food. Paddy (being grain in the husk) will last, so I was told, for four years if properly stored. Those who have a surplus lend paddy between February and October, and get it back after the December harvest at 50 per cent interest. Seed paddy (paddy grown the previous year) commands 100 per cent interest.

The paddy loan is only given to those who themselves have land, and the lender has first call on the harvest after it has been threshed. I cannot remember any cases of default, or, indeed, any disputes about this kind of transaction.

Cash loans are given by wealthy landowners to other peasants, to provide the finance for petty trading. Women travel around Kond villages buying paddy, which they then husk and sell as rice, making a small profit from their labour and from the slightly lower price at which they can buy paddy in remoter hamlets. There are also a few poor people, both old men and women, who travel around the Kond villages hawking oils, salt, parched paddy, and so forth. Both these classes of trader can borrow the necessary capital. The interest rate, on a loan of eight days, is half an anna in the rupee (about 150 per cent *per annum*) and the sum involved is usually between ten and twenty rupees (a rupee is worth eighteenpence). Security—an ornament for example—is demanded only from an Untouchable. Like the paddy loans, these small cash advances entail little risk. The sum involved is small: the parties have known one another for a long time; and there is little chance of loss in the trading.

Money is also lent for other purposes and in larger amounts. It may be borrowed to meet a ceremonial expense (a death or a marriage or the cost of entertaining relatives at a festival in the village), or to replace essential equipment, most typically to buy an ox or a buffalo or, indeed, for any other purposes. For these larger sums a security is demanded unless the debt is between close relatives (for example, a man and wealthy affines or uterine kin) or, exceptionally, between close friends (usually *maitro*—a ritual friend). There are two main

112

types of security, ornaments and land. The way in which land is used for a security I have already described: the lender has the use of the field agreed upon until the debt is repaid. An alternative is to hand over an ornament as a security. The creditor may wear the ornament, if he wishes, and it is returned when the debt and its interest are paid off. In all cases which I recorded the security amply covered the principal and a year's interest. Rates of interest are limited by regulation in the Kondmals to 25 per cent *per annum* and the accumulated interest may never exceed the principal on the loan. These regulations have been in force for many years, but in fact the rate of interest is a matter for bargaining between the parties, and it seems to vary between 16 per cent and 25 per cent, and probably is a lot more for an unwary and illiterate borrower. It does not seem to be the practice, either among the money-lending shopkeepers or among the wealthy peasant-lenders, to keep monetary debts of this kind going on from year to year, or from generation to generation for the sake of the interest. If the debt is not paid back within a year or two, and the creditor judges that he is unlikely to get it back in full, then he sells the security.[1] This may be the result of Government regulations against debt-enslavement. It may also be that at the present time investors do not like to tie up their capital in the form of retainers and bond-servants.

The rates of interest, taking all forms of lending into account, vary from little or nothing (between close friends and relatives); through 8 per cent (for Government loans—see below); through a range of 16 per cent to 25 per cent or more for monetary loans; 50 per cent and 100 per cent for paddy loans; 150 per cent, which is the annual equivalent of an interest of half an anna in the rupee for an eight-day loan; to the enormous figure of 250 per cent, which I calculated to be the interest represented by the average yield of a particular field, the owner of which had struck a very bad bargain in pledging it (see Bailey, 1957, p. 59). There is an Oriya word for 'interest' (*kolontro*) and it could be used in all these cases. Nevertheless it is clear that all these different kinds of loan are kept in separate compartments, and governed by different conventions of behaviour. No-one calculates that half an anna in the rupee is equivalent to 150 per cent *per annum*: nor that seed paddy borrowed in July and returned in December carries an *annual* interest of 200 per cent. Yet to demand an interest of 200 per cent on a monetary loan would be considered outrageous. Again, while people haggle over the interest on larger monetary loans or over the price to be paid for a pledged field, I have never heard of anyone disputing about the rate of interest on paddy

---

[1] If the security is a field and not an ornament then the creditor may not and does not sell it: he continues to cultivate the field. In this case there can be no arrears of interest.

113

oans or on the rate demanded for the small weekly loans to traders.

(d) *Capital accumulation within the peasant economy*

Most of the means of capital accumulation within the peasant economy have already found mention. There may be a windfall accumulation when a man stands as heir to several men in his father's generation. Good management, luck, judicious trading and lending, either
of paddy or of money, can serve to increase the fortune. The most
spectacular gains have come either from the commercial sector or
through the activities of Government, or both, and these will be
discussed in a later section.

The very poor find it difficult to accumulate capital. The potentiality of saving is not measured by absolute standards of wealth but by
the difference between expenditure and income. There are some
estates which have many calls upon them and therefore do not grow,
and, conversely, there are poor people who have only themselves to
support and are thus able to save although their gross income may
be small. But the very poor—the landless labourer, whether on his
own or with a wife—lives at a standard which does little more than
keep him alive, and in the peasant sector has no chance whatsoever
to save.

Those hereditary servants who practise their craft or follow their
calling full-time have little chance of growing rich in normal circumstances. Their work prevents them from taking advantage of opportunities in other sectors of the economy. Their rates of pay are fixed
at an annual meeting of the village council and vary little from year
to year. There is no collective bargaining—as is found, for example,
among SWEEPERS in towns—and if one servant is sacked, the
village seldom has difficulty in finding another to take his place.
Finally the rates of pay are based on the expectation that the village
servant is a *servant* and a subordinate, and ought not to be allowed to
get rich at the expense of his clients. In one case (Bailey, 1957, p. 107)
where a WASHERMAN did become rich, the village took quite
practical steps to make him poor again.

The attitude towards the wealthy and towards the newly-rich is the
familiar one of admiration, envy, and distrust. A man who loses a
fortune is either foolish or unlucky: a man who makes one is lucky
or clever, and is necessarily a rogue. No-one believes that riches can
be gained honestly, and dishonesty, in certain forms, is even admired
when it is practised upon outsiders. There is nothing in the *mores* to
condemn the search for wealth in itself, and even those who violate
social obligations in their climb to riches are admired for their
toughness. Some lip service is paid to the ascetic tradition of
Hinduism—here meaning the refusal to enter into the competiton for
wealth—but on the few occasions when the modern emissaries of self-

denial (for instance, Bhoodan workers) have visited the area, they were regarded as humbugs and hypocrites.

On the other hand, hostility towards those who become wealthy, particularly if they are of lower caste (as in the case of the WASHER-MAN mentioned above), is shown by frequent accusations of black magic. To worship and maintain a particular kind of spirit is believed to bring wealth. But such spirits are apt to break loose and visit sickness and death indiscriminately in the village. This, perhaps, can be regarded as the ritual equivalent of the belief that there are no fair means of becoming rich quickly: it can only be done at the expense of others. The enquiry and punishment which follow upon an accusation of keeping a harmful spirit are in fact a convenient means by which the majority can penalize and impede a man who is prospering too much for their liking, but who has not yet prospered enough to make him able to defy the village.

There are also received opinions about what the wealthy should do with their savings. Further productive investment is only one, and not the most publicized, course of action. Spiritual merit, which may result in benefits even in this existence (leaving aside the prospect of a better birth in the next life), can be got by feeding BRAHMINS, by building a temple or excavating a tank, or by various other actions, some of which are socially useful. Both villages provide examples. In Baderi a wealthy man who wanted a son spent large sums on excavating a tank, and then got his much-desired son. In Bisipara a man who had risen to spectacular riches within his own lifetime built a temple and imported an image, which later was pronounced by a BRAHMIN to be unhappy there: in finding a place where the image would be happy and in paying the BRAHMINS for their services (in the end it was taken to Puri), the once-rich man became poor and is now destitute, but full of merit.

(e) *Social capital in the peasant economy*

Excavating a tank, or planting trees for shade, or (accepting local values) building a temple or feeding BRAHMINS, are investments by an individual not for himself alone but for the community. There are other means by which the community invests. These investments may be in such amenities as a meeting-house for the men, or in cleaning the village streets, or improving the village water-supply; or it may be in ritual amenities (which the people would regard as productive investments) such as a temple, or an expensive rite carried out by a renowned BRAHMIN to avert a drought; or, finally, the investment may be straightforwardly productive, as in building a diversion weir to irrigate a larger number of fields.

Work of this kind is done by means of a compulsory levy either of money or of labour. In Bisipara, during my stay, a diversion weir

115

was repaired by compulsory labour and, through labour and money contributions, an old wooden temple was demolished and a brick one was built in its place.

In both villages there are common funds used for a paddy-lending business. In the Kond village the fund is entirely secular, and represents the accumulated profits on a gift of paddy to the village by one of its wealthy residents (in gratitude for the support they gave her—a widow—in the Government courts) and since lent out at the usual 50 per cent rate of interest. In Bisipara several fields have been given to endow the temple. The greater part of these temple funds are kept in paddy and used for loans.

Finally there is a sense in which all the lands around the village and brought under cultivation may be regarded as social capital in the same way as a factory, established in a depressed area, is something more than a profit-making machine for the owner. Much of this capital was accumulated by forced saving, in the following sense. In Baderi, a generation ago, there was an unscrupulous and forceful man, who deprived many other families of their land. Some of them stayed in the village and worked as labourers or share-croppers for him. With his large resources he was able to bring under cultivation much land which none of the individuals, by themselves, could have done. Large disparities in income make possible capital accumulation and investment, and this investment brings some benefit to the community as a whole.[1] In neither village, to my knowledge, has there been any co-operative activity to bring new land under cultivation. The poor, willy-nilly, forgo present consumption and make investment possible.

(f) *The peasant economy; conclusions*

The old relationship between the dominant caste (which monopolized the capital resources of the village) and its dependent castes is being to some extent replaced by the relationship between the wealthy landowner and those who borrow from him. But there is as yet no structuring in the new system—or perhaps it is a more fluid system. The wealthy are drawn from almost all castes and, although they have interests in common, they do not act together to protect these interests. They do not form a class in conflict with the poor. If there is any grouping in this system, it is the group formed by a rich man and his dependents, and the cleavage is between individual wealthy men rather than between the wealthy and the poor.

One reason for this is the separation enjoined by caste, and this operates particularly to keep the wealthy 'untouchables' apart from

[1] There are signs that Government funds and investments in agriculture go largely to the wealthier peasants, one reason being that investment in a rich man shows better results (in terms of production) than investment through a poor man.

116

rich men of 'clean' caste. A more important reason is the instability of all those who are wealthy by village standards. Both in Bisipara and Baderi practically all the wealthy families would become poor families if four sons grew to manhood. Even within a single lifetime a run of bad luck or persistent miscalculation (especially ill-judged litigation) can make rich landowners poor. In short, there is considerable economic mobility, and it is difficult for a structural cleavage to come about between rich and poor, when people move fairly frequently from one category to the other.

The economic relationships so far described are based upon the produce of land, and the changes which have come about have followed upon a change in the ownership of land. Formerly economic relationships were a part of political and ritual relationships. Even at the present day what at first sight are economic relationships in fact still include other elements. For example, the rates of interest vary according to the social relationship of the borrower and the creditor. Uterine and affinal kinsmen are preferred as creditors, since, even if they have demanded interest, they are unlikely to press hard upon a defaulter. The same is true of the relationship of ritual friendship. Social status was again relevant when the community penalized the WASHERMAN mentioned earlier, who was becoming richer through his traditional work than they thought proper. Status is also relevant in the fact that men of clean caste, for reasons of prestige, will only borrow from a rich Untouchable if they can get money nowhere else, but Untouchables will borrow readily from higher castes.

On the other hand, the security demanded for all large loans reflects either the absence of any relationship, other than economic, between borrower and creditor, or, even where there is such a relationship, of the fact that it does not in itself constitute sufficient security.

But even where security is demanded, in the great majority of cases, the transaction is not between strangers. There is always at least the potentiality of something more than economics entering into the relationship. If, for example, the creditor feels that a little pressure may get him his payment, he is unlikely to threaten court proceedings, still less likely to resort to them, but very likely to use or establish a tie with a third person in order to put pressure on the borrower. From his side the borrower, if he is in difficulties, will search for some 'contact', who can invoke obligations (possibly non-economic) which he already has with the creditor, in order to soften his heart.[1]

---

[1] These attempts to transform single-interest economic relationships into multiple relationships also occur within the Government and commercial sectors of the economy. Much of what goes on in Government departments appears to be jobbery and a curiously involved and indirect nepotism, until one realizes that in the small world of the peasant and the equally small world of the professional

Traditional institutions allowed for none but multiple ties, and no economic activity—capital accumulation, credit arrangements, investment, and so forth—could be adequately described without invoking other kinds of relationship. Modern institutions permit single-interest relationships, but it is sometimes to the interest of one, sometimes of both parties to transform these into multiple ties. I have taken multiple relationships as one of the defining characteristics of the peasant economy, but single-interest ties are in some degree exemplified there. The difference between the peasant sector and the other two sectors is that in them it becomes more difficult to establish multiple relationships.

THE COMMERCIAL SECTOR

(a) *Introduction*
The peasant economy includes commercial activities. Rice is bought and sold: indigenous manufactures are sold in the market-places and to individual customers. These include most articles required for cultivation and many needed in the household. The iron plough-share, the axe invariably and usually the hoe blade, clay pots for cooking and storage, cloth for garments, brass vessels and iron tools used in the kitchen, mats and baskets are made by indigenous crafts-men and sold, nowadays usually for cash. Some of these products link the village with the world outside, as when the WEAVER uses syn-thetic dyes or mill-spun yarn, or when his products or the pots of the BRASS-WORKER are marketed in the towns by co-operatives or by the Khadi and Village Industries Board. But these links are not the main connections between the peasant economy and the com-mercial sector.

Besides 'cottage' manufactures, peasants buy factory-made aluminium cooking-pots, steel hoe blades, mill-cloth, a few guns, a few bicycles, proprietary brands of hair oil, soap, tea, coffee tablets, *bidis* (cigarettes), matches, mirrors, pens and combs. By 1959 more people were buying artificial manures. The cash which pays for these goods comes partly from the gains of those engaged in commerce or employed by the Government, and partly from the export of turmeric and oilseeds.

(b) *Growing turmeric*
Turmeric is a root-crop which is used in making dye and as an ingre-dient in curry powder.

To grow turmeric a man requires land, tubers, and a yoke of oxen.[1]

middle-class, purely single-interest relationships are rare and regarded with dis-favour; neither in the statistical, nor in the ethical, sense are they 'normal'.

[1] It is technically possible to hoe the land for growing turmeric. No one does so, at least in this part of the Kondmals. (See Bailey, 1960, p.98.)

The land is on the mountainside. The secondary growth of jungle is felled, the larger stumps are axed out of the ground, and later the brush is burned to clear and to fertilize the soil. Stones are gathered from the field and piled at its boundaries, and then the earth is ploughed. The tubers are planted and the field is overlaid with brushwood in order to protect the young shoots from the hot sun. A normal crop takes two years, although sometimes the roots are dug out after one year, the yield then being less. The roots are boiled and cleaned and dried, and they are then ready to be sold.

Those who have the oxen and know the techniques and are not put off by hard work can usually find land in which to grow turmeric. A small village usually has more jungle nearby, and the grower does not have to go far to cut brushwood to protect the field. Better crops can be grown in fertile garden land in or near the village, but this land can also be used to grow other crops, and its distance from the jungle increases the labour of bringing brushwood. The waste in which turmeric is usually grown is free, and the grower has a right to the site only so long as he cultivates it. This period is never more than three years, since in that time the fertility of the soil is exhausted.

In Baderi the only Konds who never grew turmeric were those who had no oxen, and many had two or three fields at different stages of cultivation and harvested a crop every year. These crops, depending on the size of the field and the price of turmeric, brought in anything from Rs. 30 (exceptionally low) to a high figure of Rs. 400, with an average (of twenty-five sales which I recorded one year) at Rs. 220. (The highest wage paid to a labourer at that time was Rs. 1 a day.)

Credit scarcely enters into the growing of turmeric. I know of no loans taken specifically for the purpose of growing turmeric. There was no regular market for seed turmeric (the unboiled tubers). There was neither the need for nor the possibility of buying land to grow turmeric. I know of no merchants financing turmeric-growers. In rare cases a Kond accepted from a middleman an advance on a growing crop, thereby binding himself not to sell it to anyone else. But most growers processed the roots before permitting the trader to approach them.

The high figure of Rs. 400 and the average of Rs. 220 in a year indicate that relatively large sums of money could be earned from growing turmeric. When this money was used productively, the usual investment was in irrigated land for growing paddy. It might also be used for lending paddy at rates of interest and under conditions similar to those already described for Bisipara. But I have the impression that Konds put a greater part of their savings than did the Oriyas into ornaments and into 'social' expenditure. The wife and daughters of a rich Kond, at holiday times, are adorned literally from head to foot, from golden hair pins to ten silver rings on their toes. Dowries

119

and bride-prices can be much larger, and expenditure on feasting at weddings and funerals can be much higher than among the Oriyas. I know of no rich Kond who used his wealth for commercial enterprises, although I heard of a few who lent money to Oriyas for the purpose.

What factors govern the amount of turmeric grown? I have the impression that there is very little communication of demand downwards to the grower. I never heard of a merchant offering incentives to growers or urging them to plant more. One assumes that a run of good prices will make some growers enlarge their fields, and that bad prices will have the reverse effect, but I made no enquiries on this point. My impression rather is that the decision to expand was made by those who needed money for specific purposes—for a funeral rite, a bride-price, or a daughter's dowry—and that an upper limit was set by the hard work involved in growing and processing the roots (see Bailey, 1960, p. 99). The profits got from growing turmeric were not so much seen as a means of accumulating capital (as an end in itself), but rather as the solution to particular financial difficulties.

(c) *Trading in turmeric*

The Oriyas from Bisipara and other mercantile villages go out in parties of two to about seven persons to search for turmeric. These are not regular trading parties but are recruited *ad hoc* for each expedition. Konds do not bring out their turmeric without persuasion, and a large party has greater collective powers of persuasion than an individual alone. The trade is highly competitive, both between the merchants for whom the middlemen work, and between the trading parties themselves, even when they come from the same village. A larger party is less likely to be intimidated by rivals than a smaller one. Individuals may be invited to join the party because they can provide finance, or because they have some special contacts through whom to get turmeric. Lastly, a large party can save money on porters by bringing home the turmeric itself.

Members of an expedition sometimes provide finance of their own but this is rather private side-trading, and the main capital is always advanced by the merchant-shopkeeper. Except in those years (rare in recent times) when the outside demand for turmeric is not good, the men of Bisipara have little difficulty in getting advances from the merchants. The merchant wants to retain their goodwill and therefore gives a lower rate to any Kond who has the temerity to bring his own turmeric to the shop. Konds themselves believe that merchants and their servants cheat more than do the peasant-middlemen who come to Kond villages. In fact there is double-dealing from one end of the line to the other.

The rewards which the middlemen get from three months' intermittent trading are far less than the Kond grower makes, and the question of what they do with the money scarcely arises. It is not a spectacular outside source of income and is not invested or spent differently from ordinary income.

The relationships which characterize the turmeric trade are, in almost all cases, single-interest. Those who form a trading party are likely to belong to one village, and are unlikely to include Untouchables: but, with that exception, there is no patterning along the lines of caste or kinship or traditional retainer-relationships: nor are the groups stable, but continually disband and reform along different lines. Between the middlemen and the Konds with whom they deal there seems to be no enduring relationship. The Kond sells to the highest bidder, or the first comer, or the most persuasive talker. There are a few exceptions: the Bisipara headman uses his special relationship with his own Konds to help in his trading (Bailey, 1960, pp. 178–9); sometimes an Oriya schoolmaster, serving in a Kond village, may act as an intelligence agent and go-between in return for being included in the trading party.

Between the middlemen and the merchant, of whom there were two largely engaged and three slightly engaged in the trade in Bisipara, there is a more enduring link. But, since the merchants are somewhat outside the village community (see below, p. 123), economic attitudes are on the whole not modified by, for example, village solidarity: Bisipara trading parties accepted advances from merchants in the headquarters village of Phulbani, and on one occasion at least took an advance from one of their own merchants and sold the turmeric to a Phulbani merchant (returning the money to their own man and telling him they had failed to find any turmeric).

Why is there a single-interest relationship in these transactions? Why do both parties not try to stabilize and secure their economic links in this field, as they do in the peasant sector? The Oriyas, both middlemen and merchants, would like to do so, for much energy and time is spent in scouting for turmeric and persuading the grower to sell it, before another middleman comes along with a higher bid. The answer is partly that demand has been rather strong in recent years (I do not know what the prices have been since 1955) and in such conditions the Konds benefit by keeping an element of flexibility in their transactions and not binding themselves to particular middlemen. Secondly, there has been a long tradition of hostility between Konds and Oriyas (Bailey, 1960, chap. VII), and a long history of Konds suffering from Oriya exploitation. Konds prefer a minimal relationship with the Oriyas, and in present economic conditions (so far as concerns turmeric trading) they have the initiative.

Larger sums are earned by growing turmeric than by trading in it, and it is surprising that Oriyas themselves do not attempt to grow it.

Oriyas say that the work is too hard; that their villages are too far from the jungle; that turmeric-growing is work for Konds; and that only Konds know how to grow it. They also say that they make their money by trading in turmeric and therefore do not need to grow it. In fact they earn less than the growers: there are no particularly difficult techniques of cultivation to be mastered: and Oriya villages are no further from the jungle than the villages of many Kond turmeric-growers. The abstention, in other words, is not so much based on economic factors, but rests on convention—on the tradition that Oriyas do not grow turmeric.

(d) *The merchant-shopkeepers*

Between 1952 and 1955 there were five well-established shops in Bisipara. Three were owned by Ganjam DISTILLERS, a caste first represented in the village about 1870, and occupied in making and selling liquor, from which they made considerable profits (see p. 127). The liquor shops were closed in 1910, and since that time the Ganjam DISTILLERS have prospered as shopkeepers and merchant-exporters of turmeric and oilseeds. Another shop was owned by a WEAVER. The fifth shop belonged to a WRITER who came to the area from the plains of Orissa about 1948. The smallest shop is the WEAVER'S and he alone of the five is not a merchant-exporter.

The shops sell those imported manufactures which I have listed above and they also have a large turnover in grain (both paddy and rice), oils and oilseeds, and lentils. They accept payment both in cash and (for small everyday purchases) in rice and paddy. They lend paddy at the usual rates and they lend money, but I had the impression that this was not their main activity. Rather it was a sideline to retail selling of consumer goods and wholesale exporting of turmeric and oilseeds.

Their relationships are managed after the pattern familiar in peasant societies. They allow customers a running debt, on which there is no declared interest. Peasant customers reduce their debt (but seldom pay it off completely unless they intend to shift their custom elsewhere) after the harvest. If the debtor pays in grain the shopkeeper allows him the price ruling at the time of harvest, which, when I was there, was Rs. 1 for ten measures of paddy. The shopkeeper can sell this grain nine months later at the scarcity rate of Rs. 1 for three measures. If the debt looks like becoming too high, then the shopkeeper might ask for a field to be given in pledge, until the debt is paid off, or occasionally a field will be sold to pay off a debt.

The shopkeeper has at least three sanctions at his disposal. He can refuse further credit, and if he judges that the customer is no longer credit-worthy, other shopkeepers are likely to do the same. Secondly, all the shopkeepers were careful to maintain good relations with the village as a whole (by making contributions generously and promptly to communal causes, and by keeping on good terms with men of influence in the village), so that the pressures could be brought upon a defaulting customer through his fellow-villagers. Finally, in the last resort, their superior sophistication, their contacts with the world outside, and most of all their wealth, make the threat of litigation in Government courts an effective sanction.

The four merchants, even the DISTILLERS who were born in the village, are to some extent outsiders. The reason lies partly in their history and their relatively recent alien origin (the plains of Orissa, from where the Ganjam DISTILLERS came, are regarded almost as a foreign land); partly in the fact that they retain ties of kinship with plains people; but mainly in their occupation, which brings them into closer contact with the world outside and at the same time limits the advantages which they would get from a very close relationship with their fellow-villagers.

I have already described the activities of the merchant-shopkeepers as financiers in the turmeric trade, and their relationships with the middlemen and agents from their own village. Whether they themselves work on credit got from bigger merchants in the coastal towns, or whether their work is financed through capital accumulated in their business or borrowed from financiers on the plains, I do not know.

All the four merchant-shopkeepers are wealthy men, and two of them, by the standards of the Kondmals, are extremely wealthy. Some of the capital they accumulate is no doubt put back into the business. In other investments the three DISTILLERS act differently from the WRITER. The DISTILLERS are big landowners: the WRITER has not invested in land in the locality, although he may have done so in his native village on the plains.

There are several reasons. The estates which the DISTILLERS own were built up a generation back and much of this land came from the profits of liquor shops. A drunken customer would be persuaded to pledge or sign over a field in return for credit at the shop. The drink trade had long since ended when the WRITER opened his business in Bisipara. Secondly, since Independence those who know what is promised for landlords no longer consider land a good investment.

The WRITER has a pattern of local investment of a different kind, which will be described in the next section, since it is closely related to politics and the Administration.

(e) *The commercial sector: summary*
The commercial sector shows little investment in productive capital. Turmeric-growing is labour-intensive. The middleman needs no

equipment besides his brass weighing-rod. The shopkeeper-merchants maintain their premises (built of cheap country materials) and they have carts and one (the WRITER) now has a lorry. Turmeric is collected from the others by transporters from the plains. Credit institutions within this sector provide working capital rather than productive capital. Between the grower of turmeric and the middle-man there are no credit arrangements. The credit supplied by the merchant to the middlemen does not finance production.

Merchant-shopkeepers belong both to the peasant and to the commercial sectors of the economy. With the exception of the WRITER they invest in the same way as a rich landowner: they buy land, they lend paddy, and they lend money. Nevertheless their position in village society is not the same as that of the wealthy culti-vator. Their links tend towards the single-interest rather than the multiplex. The ritual status of the Ganjam DISTILLERS (low in the traditional system) is kept distinct from their economic status. They try to keep themselves outside village politics. They do not use their money on retainers, and their ties with their employees do not have the ritual and political significance of the traditional relation-ship between, for example, a WARRIOR and his Untouchable retainer.

These are the people who for many years have linked the peasants with the outside economy. Their presence has caused many changes—in land-ownership and in political power within the village—but they and their work do not provide a dynamic element within the economy. They are merchants, interested in exchange but not in production. When they invest in productive capital, they buy land like an ordinary rich cultivator. This is one criterion distinguishing the commercial entrepreneur from another and increasingly typical figure on the economic stage, the contractor.

THE GOVERNMENT SECTOR

(a) *Introduction*
Since 1855, when it was fully established in the Kond Hills, the Government has taken an interest in economic activities. There have always been attempts to plan and direct, to remedy abuses and to introduce new forms of economic activity, to increase production and to alter the pattern of distribution. Government actions have sometimes had unforeseen effects.

A main aim at the present day is to enlist the co-operation of the people, and to persuade them to pay for some of the investment by giving their labour. This is uphill work: the peasants are not often co-operative and seldom grateful. Investment by Government is closely scrutinized for the hidden benefits which are supposed to

124

accrue to outsiders: and credit facilities are regarded with suspicion, even with fear, when offered by Government agencies.

(b) *Government and the provision of capital*
Some general effects upon the possession, use and distribution of capital follow everywhere the establishment of an ordered administration. Government brings security. Even a minimal Government provides some wealth which did not previously exist. Roads are built: communications improve: people are employed in service or in public works.

Before Independence (1947) a much larger proportion of local public investment was provided from internal resources than has been the case since Independence. In British days the local administrators concerned themselves with roads, schools, internal trade through the provision of markets, and with remedying inequities in the distribution of wealth. Markets required the least capital provision, and, so far as one can tell from limited information, they grew out of existing smaller markets, following the establishment of peace in the area. Roads and schools were largely the work of a single administrator, who ruled the Kondmals between 1900 and 1924. He imposed a tax on ploughs, doubled the amount from other Government sources of revenue, and used this to pay the salaries of schoolteachers. The construction of both roads and schools was done by a system of forced labour, under which the labourers received their subsistence from the Government, and skilled men got a small payment in addition. Wells in the larger villages, a few hospitals and dispensaries, a craft school, and Government buildings were provided largely by the same method. A few irrigation works were constructed and maintained. Towards the end of British rule the scope for Government activity became wider, and there were, for example, development loans for agriculturists, and a more generous provision of funds for education.

All these elements are found after Independence, but expanded in scale and of a much greater complexity. There is a road building and improvement programme, and the State runs an efficient bus service. Schools now include vocational Ashram schools (reserved for tribal children), Middle English and Middle Vernacular schools, and High schools teaching up to Matriculation. These are paid for by the State Government and are not so closely linked to local finances, as they were in the past. Loans are available for agriculture, for housebuilding, for the establishment of cottage industries and small industries, and for other purposes. The Government runs marketing co-operatives, principally for weavers. There are relatively large funds available for investment in local agriculture, mainly in improved seed, artificial fertilizers and irrigation projects.

Forced labour was abandoned immediately after Independence. The first result, before Government investment got into its stride, was a spectacular decline in the fabric of roads and buildings. Recently more funds have been available and there is an all-round improvement. Nevertheless, it is not intended that work should be financed entirely from State and Union funds. In many projects which involve building—a road, a dam, a diversion weir, a new school—those who benefit are expected to contribute a part of the cost, sometimes in money, more often in labour, the Administration providing materials and the services of skilled men. This contribution is voluntary, but not everyone realizes that it is voluntary and older people recall that under forced labour at least they were fed, and that in those days there was no contractor making a big profit. Bigger construction works, or works which cannot be immediately identified as being for the benefit of a particular community, are financed entirely by Government funds and usually entrusted to a contractor.

In this way, both before and after Independence, the Government has enforced saving and social investment, but the local contribution[1] was a large proportion of a small total before 1947, and has been a small sum in a large total after Independence.

(c) *Government and the distribution of capital*

The Administration in the Kond hills has always been conducted in Oriya, which is not the language of the Konds. Most employees of the Administration, even at the lowest level, were Oriyas, and, by and large, Konds had few opportunities to influence the Administration while the Oriyas had many. For many years some Oriyas used these advantages to exploit Konds. Kond lands drained steadily away in the possession of Oriya settlers, both those who had long been in the area and those who had come in the wake of the Administration. The British tried to control this situation. Oriyas could not buy land from Konds without the Magistrate's permission: there were regulations limiting interest rates: and court procedure was relaxed to make it easier for an illiterate Kond to use the law to protect himself against Oriya exploitations.

Since Independence the Administration has provided, besides protective legislation, opportunities for the Konds to improve their education and their economic standing. There are, for example, the Ashram schools to which only Kond children are admitted; there are scholarships to regular schools for Kond children and bursaries for higher education; and a number of places are reserved for Konds in the Administration's employ. The Harijans (Untouchables) enjoy the

[1] Land-taxes have not been significantly raised in the Kond hills since Independence. But, as elsewhere in India, a sales tax on many commodities has been imposed.

126

same opportunities. Economic opportunities, together with the encouragement provided by legislation and propaganda, have made a considerable change in the position of Harijans in the political and economic structure of Bisipara. Several of them—mostly schoolmasters—have become substantial landowners.

The Government intended the betterment of the Harijans. The Konds too are better off, but this is the result as much of improved turmeric prices as of Government tenderness. But the most spectacular shift in the pattern of landholding occurred without the intention of, and against the wishes of, the Administration. In 1870 a system of out-stills was established. Konds were forbidden to distil their own liquor (which they require for ceremonies and because they like it), and they were compelled to patronize liquor shops. Licences to manage these shops were auctioned, and all the buyers came from two DISTILLER castes, who are Oriyas. These people made high profits and invested the money in land: they acquired large estates in Kond villages and bought land from WARRIORS in Oriya villages, and they are today, forty years after prohibition was introduced, still the largest landholders in Bisipara. Indeed, it was largely as a result of their activities that legislation was introduced to protect the Konds.

There are analogous, but on the whole less spectacular, chances for capital accumulation by small entrepreneurs today. The rise and fall of individuals within the peasant sector of the economy is partly governed by their opportunities to make a second income. But at the present day it is the contractor, rather than the landowner, who becomes rich. The contractor is of an economic and social significance quite different from that of the peasant who has a side income from Government employ, or, indeed, from the merchant-entrepreneur, whose profits are largely invested in land. The contractor belongs to the future: they belong to the past.

(d) *Government and credit*

Government provides credit to individuals at a low rate of interest (about 8 per cent), to be used for productive purposes: for a craftsman to buy factory-made tools or the stock which he requires to start his enterprise; for a peasant loans to develop land, to buy oxen, to buy fertilizer or improved seed. There are also loans and grants for house-building and for many other purposes.

These loans are not always put to the purpose for which they were intended. Even when the money is taken without any wrong intentions, it sometimes happens that a crisis in the home will cause the money to be spent on ceremonies and not on productive enterprise. The borrower then has to sell one of his fields—if he has any—in order to pay off the loan and interest. If he has no fields—and the loans are not only given to propertied persons, since they are intended to help the poor more than the rich—then his house will be auctioned to pay off the debt.

Although peasants are attracted by the low rate of interest, there are other factors which make them sometimes prefer the old method of borrowing from a rich man and paying twice or three times the interest which the Government demands. Firstly, the moneylender does not insist that the money be used for a productive purpose, and the borrower does not have to go through the ordeal of scrutiny by a Government servant, who may demand a bribe for certifying work correctly done, even when it has been correctly done. Secondly, the moneylender does not operate according to rigid rules, and is more amenable to persuasion—to extending the period of the loan, for example, or he may take a field in pledge which the Government will not. Thirdly, the peasants fear all Government institutions and find difficulty in making contact with them.

The co-operative comes mid-way between the Government institutions and traditional credit organs in the village. One was set up in Bisipara in 1958 and I saw a little of its working during a brief visit in 1959. It was primarily a credit institution and closely linked to agriculture. Building materials were provided by the Government and the people gave their labour. The Government advanced money and a stock of grain and fertilizer. A salaried secretary was brought in from outside the village and the co-operative was managed by a committee of five persons, all of whom were wealthy by village standards. Many people took loans from the co-operative, partly in cash and partly in fertilizer and seed-grain. (The borrower had no choice: everyone wanted cash and no-one wanted grain or fertilizer.) Some loans were put to productive use: some were not.

At the end of 1958 the secretary absconded, allegedly with the account books, and on the day I arrived in the village I shared the bungalow with an official from the Co-operative Department who had come to investigate, no easy task since there was no record of borrowings. I did not have the chance to follow the case in detail, but from conversations I judged that neither the committee nor the members felt responsibility for what had happened (the secretary being an outsider) and thought that the most sensible course would be for the Government to write off the money as a bad debt and start again. On the other hand the readiness with which the people had come forward to take loans shows that the co-operative and its local managers had to some extent closed the gap between Government and people so far as borrowing was concerned: but not, perhaps, when it came to paying back.

(e) *The 'brokers'*
Critics of Community Development work say that credit and grants

intended to help the poor are sometimes cornered by the rich. Comunity Development makes the rich richer and the poor, relatively at least, poorer.

It is also said that some programmes fail because they are not channelled through the 'real' leaders of the village. The 'brokers' for development work—the people who come forward to mediate between the Government and the villagers—command the respect but not the confidence of the villagers. In the villages the Development programme is a battle to make people do things for themselves, both because this is considered good in itself and for the simpler reason that the officials are not numerous enough—and probably never could be—to organize and supervise thousands of small projects. Officials look for people in the village who will accept responsibility. In many instances the traditional leaders do not come forward. Their influence depends partly upon their being unambiguously identified with the village and disassociated from Government and its Administration (Bailey, 1957, p. 257). Besides this, many of the traditional leaders are not sufficiently sophisticated to handle officials and are afraid of financial responsibilities. There are no doubt cases where such men could be persuaded to undertake the work, but before they realize what is happening someone in the broker category has taken control.

Most brokers have a connection not only with the Administrators but also with local politicians, generally with the ruling Congress party. The local Member of the Legislative Assembly has some influence over the allocation of contracts for development work and of licences for buying and selling controlled consumer goods (at different times in the last ten years these have been cloth, rice and other food-grains) which offer a large and secure profit to the licence holder. In many constituencies there has come into existence a patronage organization headed by a political boss and manned by brokers of various degrees of importance down to the little fishers in the troubled waters of village politics.

Such an organization, although one instinctively condemns it, is in fact a channel of communication between the Administrator and the peasants. If the Development official wants something done in a village, then he will find that the line of least resistance is to make use of the local boss. This man comes forward and cajoles his fellow-villagers into doing what the Government wants: everyone else hangs back, indifferent or mutely hostile. Both the villagers and the official know that the volunteer is not disinterested and expects, either then or on another occasion, to be rewarded: both sides distrust him but both are forced to use him. Equally if a villager wants a favour from the Administration, then it pays him—or everyone believes it will pay him—to make his approach not only through the

E   129 official channels, but also through some knowing intermediary.

These brokers are the new men who interpret village life to the officials and officialdom to the villagers. They are one factor channelling Government investment and the allocation of Government credit to the villages, and at the same time they are a hidden cost upon these services.

Brokers and would-be brokers are people whose experience and ambitions have given them an horizon wider than the village. In Bisipara there were two such important men. One, a shopkeeper when I first knew him, by 1959 had become a contractor, a licence-holder, and merchant on a large scale, was vaguely rumoured to be the grey eminence of political finance in the area, and now resides at the district headquarters. The second was a DISTILLER (wealthy enough but not a merchant) who had begun as a clerk in a Government-organized marketing co-operative at the district headquarters, climbed the ladder of small contracts (feeding convicts, collecting tolls in the marketplace), graduated into building-contracts, and was now up to his neck in manipulation and political manoeuvre.

Neither of these persons has invested money in land. The estate owned by the DISTILLER has not grown larger since his meteoric success in the world of brokerage: the other man has not bought any local land so far as I know. I do not know how either of them in fact invests the money he earns, but clearly there is one investment which all successful brokers must make: in keeping an army of agents and retainers and sub-brokers. This is an involved and complex affair and not one to which the enquiring sociologist is readily admitted: but one might guess that it would range from a straight loan of money to a bribe judiciously placed to secure a favour for the retainer.

An analysis of Government investment and credit in the villages which does not take account of political correlates will not be realistic. For example, the irresponsible attitude of the peasant towards Government money, and the sharp cynicism with which he chews over Government offers to benefit or claims to have benefited him are quite clearly connected with his assumption that local politicians, bosses, brokers and 'touters' (this improved-English epithet is in common use), not to speak of some officials, are making enormous profits for themselves, both inside and outside the law, from development work. A Government publication (in Oriya) revealed how much money had been spent on two miles of roadway near Bisipara, where the villagers themselves had worked and been paid and therefore knew exactly the labour costs. The report was received in Bisipara with a knowing and self-satisfied disgust.

Is this not again an example of the way in which economic relationships have become entangled with relationships of another kind? A

130

loan taken from the Government is not a straight economic transaction between A and the Government, but involves also A's ties as a client with B, and B's link with the politician C, and C's relationship with the Administrator who represents the Government. Again, part of the loan is in effect used as a means of communication between the peasants on the one side and on the other side the Administration and the political parties. Not every loan, not every licence, not every contract is of this kind. I do not say that these instruments do not also serve their ostensible purpose of raising the standard of living: they do. But it would be wrong to assume that development money is used only for productive ends: some of it goes into corruption and nepotism, which I have here been viewing through the amoral glass of functionalism and calling 'communication'. It would be equally wrong to think that the borrower of Government money has nothing more to pay than the 8 per cent interest: in time, energy, and perhaps cash, it may cost him a lot more than that.

(f) Government activities: conclusion

Since its inception in the Kond hills the Government has taken an ever-expanding interest in productive activities and in the distribution of wealth. Throughout the period it has compelled investment of some sort from its subjects, and to an ever-increasing degree it has itself either used local taxes for improvements or has subsidized them by using other funds.

In the absence of statistics it is impossible to measure the increase in production in the Kondmals during the last hundred years and it is therefore impossible to state numerically what has been the success of the Government's effort to invest and to stimulate investment.

It is rather the social and political effects of economic and other kinds of policy that catch the sociologist's eye: the startling changes in the pattern of land-ownership in Bisipara and in the Kondmals generally; and, at the present day, the emergence of that category of men who are mostly known by abusive names—touters or opportunists—but whose function essentially is to bridge the gap between the people and the Administration.

CONCLUSIONS

I have tried in this essay to analyse activities categorized as capital, saving and credit in highland Orissa. There has been very little quantification. The reason for this is that very few statistics exist and the task of collecting them in the field is beyond the capacity of a single field-worker. Even when resources are available to make surveys, the figures must be suspect: the peasant does not keep accounts, and would not reveal them if he did; the moneylender and merchant are equally reticent.

In the absence of magnitude one is driven back to crude classifications: between those who accumulate capital and those who do not; those who lend money and those who borrow it; those who go in for trading and those who do not.

The enquiry is then turned not into refining these categories by magnitude and attempting to correlate different magnitudes, but into categorizing by the criteria of social status—by caste, by ethnic affiliation, by social and political position in village society. We get some understanding of economic behaviour by looking at non-economic relationships. In this way we can understand, for example, why peasants do not leap to take advantage of the low rate of interest on Government loans.

The value of this kind of explanation depends on the degree to which economic transactions are mingled with other kinds of relationships. This was most true in the peasant economy: it seems to be least true of the commercial sector of the economy: in the sector of Government economic activity there seems to be a conscious attempt to make economic transactions serve non-economic ends—or at least not the ends for which they were intended.

In peasant societies of this kind there is a general expectation that economic transactions should be secured by a more-than-economic relationship. In the absence of this relationship, economic transactions are characterized by a low degree of integrity, honesty and trust—sentiments which are apparent in the turmeric trade and in the handling of Government money.

I do not think that this analysis has much to say to economic science, since that science deals mainly with single-interest relationships in a more complex society. But it does suggest that in underdeveloped countries economic planning—at least its community development wing—should involve more than economics.

7

Capital, Saving and Credit
in a
Malay Peasant Economy

BY M. G. SWIFT

Using the principal product as the basis of classification there are five major types of Malay peasant economy.[1]

1. Rice-growing: this type of economy is typical of the large alluvial plains of Malaya; on the west coast from Tanjong Karang northwards into Perlis, and on the east coast in Kelantan. In these areas terrain, soil and the availability of water allow extensive areas to be devoted to the cultivation of irrigated rice, and this crop is almost the sole foundation of the Malay peasant economy.

2. Fishing: Malay fishermen are found all around the coasts of Malaya, but they are especially prominent in the eastern States of Pahang, Trengganu and Kelantan, and, indeed, over the border into southern Siam.[2]

3. Rubber-growing: almost exclusive dependence on rubber-growing is common in much of Johore, but can also be found in other 'developed' states such as Negri Sembilan, Selangor and Perak.

4. Mixed farming: this term is used to refer to an economic type where three major crops are grown, rubber, fruit and rice. This economic type is typical of central Malaya, broadly, the states of Negri Sembilan, Pahang, Selangor and souther Perak.

5. A strip extending along the west coast is generally devoted to small holder cultivation of a combination of coconut, banana and areca-nut.[3]

The differing nature of the major product in each of these five economic types implies differences in production technique and in

---

[1] 'Malay', not Malayan; although many Chinese in Malaya may be regarded as peasants their economy is not considered in this essay.

[2] Cf. Raymond Firth, 1946; T. F. Fraser Jr., 1960.

[3] I am grateful to my colleague Ungku A. Aziz for calling my attention to the existence of this type.

economic organization generally. Specifically, the role of capital, saving and credit will differ in each type of economy.

This essay will be solely concerned with a discussion of these issues with regard to the mixed farming type of economy as found in Jelebu, one of the districts of Negri Sembilan. While the following account cannot claim to describe an exact average of conditions within the economic type, it will serve to outline some of the general features of the economic organization. This analysis can be regarded as the presentation of an ideal type which may be used for a comparative understanding of other related examples which do not exactly correspond. The most obvious variable making for difference within the type is a range of related features connected with urban influence and the pressure of population on the land which, in turn, is connected with the development of estates and mines and the presence of alien ethnic groups.

In general the economy may be characterized as a developed monetary economy, and the number of commercial terms in the vocabulary, together with the history of the area, indicates that this character is of long standing.[1] Calculation in monetary terms is general. Even in transactions where money is not actually used, the villagers show that notions about the current market rate are a factor in their calculations. A man hired to repair a house may agree to accept payment in rice after the harvest, but both parties speak of the transaction as if it were to be in cash, and decide the quantity of rice that should change hands in terms of the expected price of rice. Or, men who have been to the forest to collect rattan for use as rope feel obliged to justify the irrationality of expending so much effort to acquire a good which can be easily and cheaply purchased. Monetary calculation forms a part of most economic decisions.

The peasantry are dependent on purchase for their commonest daily needs. Vegetables, peppers, cooking oil are usually bought, to mention only items that could easily be grown on a subsistence basis. Mats, an essential item of Malay furniture, are generally bought although the raw materials are available in the village. But the extent of dependence on the market is not fixed, as for the urban wage-earner. The peasant economy is tied to the world market for rubber, directly, through the sale of village rubber, and indirectly, through the urban demand for their fruit. Prosperity leads not only to an increased consumption of goods usually purchased, but also to the substitution of purchase for home production. At a given level of prosperity the wealthier peasant relies more on purchase than his poorer neighbour; except for the staple, rice, he buys not only more goods, but a wider variety.

[1] The developed commercial character is typical of Malay society generally, not merely the 'mixed-farming' type.

Despite this widespread reliance on purchase, traditional subsistence techniques are still known. The impact of a decline in cash income on consumption is lessened by a reversion to subsistence production. A time of severe general hardship, such as the Japanese occupation, showed that the peasantry could become almost self-sufficient.

Consideration of the relative roles of purchase and subsistence production not only serves to define the general character of the economy, but also raises a point more central to our present concern. In the creation of capital assets the peasant has a real choice between purchase and the direct investment of his own labour. Almost every feature of the productive process can, if desired, be carried out without cash investment, employing techniques and materials in common everyday use in the village.

SAVING

For the economy saving is defined as that proportion of income not spent on consumption. For the individual it is desirable to regard provision for the purchase of consumption goods as saving when resources have to be accumulated beforehand. The villager planning a feast has to 'save', even though the goods he will purchase are clearly consumption goods. Goods which the wealthy man can buy, that is consume, the poor peasant has to acquire by saving. This is not surprising where the purchase of expensive durable consumer goods is concerned, but the very poor may be obliged to buy even their clothes through hire-purchase.

Saving is refraining from consuming income as soon as it is received. Income saved may eventually be consumed, or it may be invested, but the process of refraining from consumption may be discussed without immediate consideration of the final destination of these resources.

The saving process in the village has a number of well-defined special characteristics.

Money is rarely saved directly, whether by hoarding coins and notes, or through deposits in banks. The Post Office Savings Bank is available to all, and will accept the smallest of deposits. The peasantry are familiar with, and trust, this institution. School children are encouraged to open accounts by their teachers. Nor is the Islamic abhorrence of interest-taking a serious bar to the peasantry using the bank. A saver may decline to accept the interest, and in any case, interest on Post Office accounts is regarded as in a different, really harmless, category, as compared with interest payments on personal loans.

Certain tangible assets are regarded as 'property', *harta*. The

135

possession of them gives the villager a sense of worth and security. Land is pre-eminently the most desirable form of property, but the purchase of land will not be discussed as saving here. There are other, less expensive items, and the peasant saves by acquiring these. Assets, once converted into property, tend to be immobile. Above all property should not be realized and used for ordinary consumption. Such behaviour is disapproved as profligate, and individual peasants will endure great short-term hardship rather than convert any of their property. This relates to the villagers' own perception of themselves as spendthrifts. They say that if you sell a piece of property the money will certainly all be spent, and there may never be another chance to acquire a replacement.

It cannot be maintained that no peasant saves money. Some of the wealthier keep a store of money in their houses while others have accounts with the Savings Bank. This is partly an emergency store, something over and above property. But, as will become clear later, the unsuitability of the traditional forms of saving for more than a limited quantity of savings provides an incentive for the wealthier peasants to hold some of their wealth in monetary form while awaiting an opportunity to acquire land or make some other major investment. Most of the peasants do not pass this limit, and the need does not arise for them.

Gold, in the form of simple jewellery, is a favoured means of village saving. In their estimation of jewellery the peasantry show a marked interest in the weight and quality of the gold, but regard expensive workmanship as a waste, which it is if the jewellery is destined to be converted into cash in the future. Medallions, bracelets and chains are readily liquid. Cash may be realized by one of two major methods. In Negri Sembilan, but not elsewhere in Malaya, all jewellery is sold with a guarantee from the goldsmith to buy it back at 90 per cent of the gold weight at which he sold it. (Thus, if a peasant buys a gold chain for (M)$200.00 of which $20.00 is the cost of workmanship, the shop will receive it back for $162.00, assuming that the price of gold is constant. If it has risen the peasant will get more, if it has fallen, less.) Or the jewellery may be taken to a Government licensed pawnshop. Here interest is charged at the rate of 5 per cent per month on loans of less than $10.00 and 4 per cent on loans above this figure. Choice between these two methods of getting liquidity is determined by the size of the sum required, and the likelihood of the peasant being able to redeem the valuable if pledged. Many feel that if the cash needed is very near the value of the item to be pledged it is best to return it; for pawning not only involves paying interest, but also the risk that the item will be lost anyway through failure to redeem. If only a small sum is required then the peasant will take only what he requires from the pawnshop, regardless of the value

136

of the asset, or what the pawnbroker is prepared to offer on it. To take more is foolish, the money will certainly be spent without bringing any permanent benefit. This sentiment is part of the general constellation of attitudes around the concept *harta*.

Gold is the only jewellery used in this way. Silver and pinchbeck are now regarded as only semi-precious, suitable for men's rings; indeed, Chinese shops, the major goldsmiths, no longer undertake work in these metals. Precious stones too are not appreciated. They are expensive, require skill to buy, and do not retain their value if they have to be converted into cash.

Gold jewellery is an efficient means of saving. The asset is very readily realized, and the value of gold is more certain to a peasantry that has twice seen worthless currency in a decade (the 1940s). The peasant who retains a piece of old jewellery finds it worth much more than was originally paid for it, while he sees the value of money continually declining. The peasantry are aware of these considerations, but every individual wishing to make savings does not necessarily rationally weigh all these factors. Saving in gold is a culturally defined method of saving, and so, to some extent is given for the individual. Above all, a wife expects that her husband will buy her jewellery to wear at weddings and other feasts.

Gold is a family asset, but within the family it is especially the property of the wife. A man who has given jewellery to his wife can feel that the family has something in reserve for a crisis, but he cannot expect to use the jewellery just as he pleases. To be readily available it is necessary for the wife to be convinced of the desirability of the expenditure. If hardship face the family, perhaps through sickness, a wife should allow her jewellery to be pawned or returned without demur. But she will strongly resist the use of her jewellery to pay for a feast, or to finance a purchase or economic venture by her husband. This arises from two features of the family organization. The peasantry regard the marriage tie as a fragile one. Divorce is spoken of as an ever-present possibility with any marriage. Compared with Malay society generally this is not an accurate appraisal of the situation, but it is the way the members perceive their society (cf. M. G. Swift, 1958). Accordingly, women are concerned to make provision for the economic security of themselves and their children. This they attempt to do by acquiring gold jewellery, and land registered in their own, or their children's names. A husband should be prepared to make presents of jewellery to his wife, and register some of the land he acquires in this way, as a sign that he is satisfied with the marriage.

Secondly, within the family as an economic unit there is a clear division of labour whereby provision for the cash needs of the household is the duty of the husband. Women work in the ricefields, and perform domestic duties, but they are not expected to make a cash

contribution. Indeed, where a wife does so the husband is often concerned to maintain that he does not use any of the money, and leaves
it entirely at his wife's disposal. When property is divided on inheritance it is recognized that a daughter has prior claim to ricefields and
the land used as house-site and homestead, while a son's share should
be composed of fruit and rubber land, yielding a cash income. A son
will have to provide for the cash needs of a household while his
sister may expect her husband to do so. She, however, should
possess ricefields and a house-site (marriage is matrilocal). Need to
call on a wife's jewellery is a sign of failure, and, except in an emergency, it might well be refused.

The ownership of cattle is another favoured method of holding
wealth. This might appear to be better regarded as a form of production rather than as saving. Cattle multiply, they can be eaten or
sold, and, if one owns a bull, make a contribution working in the ricefields. But pasture is scarce, and keeping cattle involves the owner in
a great deal of work. During the rice-growing season fodder may have
to be collected, and at least the beasts must be driven to the edge of
the jungle, watched while they feed, and then brought back at dusk.
Stalls must be built, and fires lit at night as a protection against
mosquitoes. The increase in value of a beast over a year is a poor
return for the work involved as compared with devoting the time to
the tapping of extra rubber trees. The peasants accept this calculation,
but argue that the cows are property, while an increase in daily
income would simply be spent as soon as it was received without
giving lasting benefit.

The cow is a poor form in which to hold wealth. The beast itself is
liable to loss in value through lack of fodder, disease or other misfortune. And it is not a readily liquid asset. Every family tries to buy
some meat for the feast ending the Fasting Month when cattle can
readily be sold, or slaughtered and sold as meat. The lesser feasts at
the beginning of the fast, and at Hari Raya Haji (Id-ul-Adhar), are
also favourable occasions for selling cattle, but at no other time can
a cattle owner be sure that he will find a buyer at a good price. If he
knows in advance that he will be needing money he can look for a
buyer, perhaps another peasant planning a feast or with money he
wishes to save, or a buyer for the urban markets, and with luck he
will get a satisfactory price. But if he needs money in a hurry he will
probably have to stand a considerable loss. If, for example, a cow is
injured on the highway, and has to be slaughtered, the beef is typically
very difficult to sell.

But in the ownership of cattle the peasant is not only seeking
rational monetary satisfaction. The very possession of wealth in the
form of cattle yields satisfactions.

Certain features of the favourite village saving methods explain

138

why the wealthy man does not keep all his liquid assets in these forms. To keep on acquiring gold would be to hand over control of his wealth to his wife, and even she, beyond the limit of satisfying her desire for display, would rather the money be invested in land. With cattle there is only a limited number that he can rear himself or with the help of his young sons. If he exceeds this number he is forced to hire help, so making a poorly paying proposition into a loss. To some extent this difficulty can be avoided by giving the cattle to the care of others to be reared on an issue-sharing basis. Such an opportunity to acquire property is welcome to the poor man whose entire income is devoted to immediate consumption needs. But it is not economically attractive to the wealthy man, who is more likely to consider giving his cattle to others in this way as a form of charity rather than an investment. An exception to this rule would be wage-earners living away from the village. For them buying stock which are left in the care of kin is a common practice. In this way the wage-earner who is not yet rich enough to start buying land can begin to acquire property. Also he can feel that he is helping his relatives who are still in the village; but apart from this, the ownership of property in the village gives a feeling of security to the man away from home.

Goats, sheep and poultry have some of the property qualities of cattle, and the villagers often speak of owning them as a shield against sudden misfortune or other need for cash. But these animals yield a larger and quicker return, and do not require so much effort to rear as cows. Rearing these types of stock is therefore better regarded simply as a form of production rather than as saving.

Even when the peasant is saving with a definite end in mind he will not usually save money. This is particularly apparent in the building and major repair of houses. Typically the villager converts surplus cash into materials for the projected undertaking, storing planks and timbers under his house until he has accumulated sufficient. The frame of the house may be raised and roofed, and then left for months, or even years, until more resources can be accumulated to carry on with the work. A familiar village joke is the house with a fine frame and rough walls of bamboo which stands with these intended-to-be-temporary walls uncompleted until the frame has worn out.

In this discussion of the way in which saving is carried out mention should be made of the acquisition of durable goods, such as radios, bicycles, sewing machines and watches, through hire purchase. In a sense hire purchase is an alternative to saving, a means of consuming income before it is earned, paying for the privilege by a price higher than the list price which is in turn more than would be paid after the usual cash discount. On the other hand, through hire purchase the peasant can acquire assets which can be converted back into cash

139

through the pawnshop, and this knowledge lies behind many decisions to buy. So it may also be said that he has acquired savings.

Socially interesting, but not of great economic importance, is the temporary loan association known as *kutu*. A number of villagers join together agreeing to pay a fixed sum at regular intervals into a common pool which will be taken by each of them in turn. A villager who wishes to use rather a large sum of cash, perhaps $50.00 to $100.00, tries to find between five and ten other men to join him. It is usually difficult to find the necessary number as these schemes are expected to break down through default before every contributor has had a chance to draw his share. This is partly due to the peasant's perennial difficulty to meet a regular cash obligation, and partly due to an attitude to debts which will be mentioned further below. The organizer therefore has to put pressure on people who 'didn't like to refuse', phrasing his invitation as a request for help, and treating refusal as a refusal of assistance and a lack of trust in his honesty.

The regular income from rubber tapping (as a share tapper, owner tapper, or owner) is usually spent as soon as it is received on the consumption needs of the household. The only savings that a peasant might make out of this income are *kutu* payments, and hire purchase instalments, if these latter are to be regarded as saving. It is mainly only the younger peasants who are able to undertake hire purchase agreements. The youth or young man who is not married or does not yet have a large family to support can earn as much as the older peasant with heavy family responsibilities. He accordingly has a greater surplus after meeting his primary obligations and can afford radio, bicycle, fountain pen or watch. Indeed, it might be said that these items are regarded as vanities of the young with which the family man is not expected to concern himself.

Nor is rice income a major source of saving. Not all villages in the area are self-sufficient in rice for the entire year, but even in villages that are, the primary purpose of rice cultivation is subsistence. This contrasts with the past when rice sales were reportedly large. Population growth has reduced the acreage available to each family, new crops, and new demands for old crops have furnished more attractive opportunities, and general change has lessened the imperatives behind industry in the rice field. Nowadays large rice sales are made only by the wealthy. Firstly, the rich man is more likely to have extensive rice fields. But this does not necessarily follow; rice fields are more often inherited than purchased, and the man who has acquired wealth would not invest it in rice fields far beyond the subsistence needs of his household. Secondly, the wealthy peasant devotes more time to the rice fields. The poor man cannot afford to leave rubber tapping during the cultivation season, and will not attempt to grow more than his family needs, or to work more land

140

than his wife can manage with his occasional assistance. So, there are cases where a poor man owning a lot of rice land will rent it to others, simply because he cannot manage it all himself without leaving off tapping, and buying a bull. The wealthy man will not tap his own rubber, but will work his rice fields using a bull. This is an expression of the high valuation placed upon rice cultivation. In the past this was also expressed in a complex of rituals and beliefs of which now only disorganized superstitions remain, and a great 'interest'. It is a matter of pride to have extensive thriving rice fields, in a way that owning a lot of rubber land is not. To sell a lot of rice is also an occasion for pride, so long as it is done after generous provision has been made for the consumption needs of the household during the coming year.

It is not, however, only the wealthier minority who sell rice. Poor people sometimes seize the opportunity of the harvest to acquire money in a lump sum which they cannot accumulate from their regular income. This may be regarded as borrowing. Before the next harvest they will be forced to buy rice in the shops, paying a higher price than they received for their own crop. This difference in price is essentially an interest payment.

In Jelebu, the most important source of savings, indeed for the finance of all major expenditures, is the sale of the fruit crop. Rubber income is devoted to daily consumption needs. For most people rice is important for subsistence consumption. The income from fruit is large, and is not allocated beforehand to any specific purpose (speaking generally, the individual may well have decided what he wants to spend the money on). Ownership of this valuable asset is widespread, but there are devices which tend to extend the benefits even to those who do not own fruit holdings. Labour payments for picking the fruit and transporting it to the roadside are large, so that $15.00 a day would not be unusual, in place of the normal $3.00 or $4.00 rubber tapping. Also, a man who owns more than one holding, or whose holding is far from his home, has difficulty in controlling the harvest. Broadly he has four alternatives; camping in the holding for the duration of the harvest, losing his fruit, dividing his crop with someone who will supervise the harvest, or finally, accepting a lump sum payment from someone who will then treat the crop as his own.

Fruit income plays a major part in the planning and execution of all major ventures such as house building or feasts.

CAPITAL

The role of capital in each of the main forms of economic activity will now be considered. Developed land will be regarded as capital. In much peasant agriculture it is the relationship between labour and developed land which is important, while other forms of capital are typically of minor importance, consisting mainly of simple agricultural tools. On the other hand, more advanced economic activities, such as merchanting, or the processing of the primary products, are not generally in peasant hands, so that the capital problems are not for the peasants to solve. This statement in any case applies to the situation of the Malay peasant economy.

A common economic distinction that can be usefully employed is that between fixed and working capital. Fixed capital represents a once and for all investment, and working capital the other resources, apart from labour, which must be continuously applied if a return is to be received (this will include payment for the support of labour where this represents an outlay by the entrepreneur before a return is received). Developed land has very much the character of fixed capital; rubber smallholdings or fruit orchards cannot be used for anything else, and to a lesser extent the same is true of rice fields. It is true that the trees may be cut down and the land planted with something else, but this is best regarded as the destruction of the factor capital leaving the factor land, which, in the absence of attractive alternative crops, and given its abundance, is not of great value. Applying the same argument to rice fields, the land, usually fertile, will readily grow other crops, but this means abandoning the irrigation works which placed the land in the category capital.

Alternatively, developed land can be defined as a combination of land and capital, the latter component alone being treated here.

RUBBER SMALLHOLDINGS

The size of the holding is small, two to four acres being typical. Richer men may own more than one holding, however. This reflects the small scale on which the holdings were originally developed. Even the man who developed more land than the other villagers did so piecemeal. It is also a reflection of a tendency to concentration of ownership whereby some men gradually acquire the holdings of others, naturally giving a scattered geographical pattern of ownership.

An important feature of the ownership pattern is the age distribution of ownership. Owners of holdings are normally older men, or sons who have inherited from their fathers. This is largely a consequence of Government policy. Introduced during the second decade of this century, the new crop was adopted with enthusiasm by the peasantry. (It was selling then for as much as $5.00 per katty while nowadays $1.00 is considered an excellent price. From informants' accounts the quality sold then would only be accepted as scrap now, and if changes in the general price level are also borne in mind it becomes clear just how attractive a crop rubber was!) During this

142

initial period most villagers acquired a holding. If any man of the older group does not now own rubber, investigation usually shows either that for some special reason, such as employment outside the district, he was unable to take part in the original development, or that he once owned land and subsequently disposed of it. Then as a result of the Stevenson Restriction Scheme no new planting could be undertaken. In effect the acreage of smallholding rubber was fixed.

An important characteristic of this early development was the extent to which the peasants relied on their own labour and kept cash investment to a minimum. Thus, jungle could be cleared, seedlings raised, holes dug, fences made of bamboo, weeds cleared and so on, with no more than the ordinary equipment which every peasant owns.

This is the direct investment of labour in the creation of capital. It is an avenue towards acquiring property that is open to all in the society depending on industry alone (for, assuming that the Government would alientate it, there is an abundance of jungle land). This avenue has been closed since the beginning of the restriction scheme. It is only possible to acquire rubber land through the purchase of an already developed holding. The peasant without a cash surplus, and this he will not have if he does not already own rubber, but with a plentiful supply of (his own) labour, cannot hope to acquire this most desirable form of property, and must expect to be a tapper on someone else's land all his working life.

Therefore, at present there is no investment in rubber smallholdings. (Buying an existing holding, although an investment for the individual, is not an investment for the society as a whole.)

In general the villagers' trees are old, and approaching the end of their economic life. If income is to continue to be received the investment must be maintained. Reinvestment, or replanting, is taking place on a very small scale. The Government's Rubber Replanting Board will make a payment of $600.00 per acre, financed from a cess on rubber sales, for replanting which is adjudged satisfactory. There is also continuous propaganda explaining the necessity and desirability of this step. The grant is sufficient to finance replanting, even allowing for the purchase of manure and superior stock, and paying for the old trees to be cut down. There is therefore no capital problem here. Where the problem arises is in the finance of waiting. If the peasant cuts down his source of income he has no other means of support for five years until the new trees begin to yield. He therefore refuses to do so. What replanting there is in the village takes place on the land of those who are more interested in the accumulation of property (future income), than in present income, that is to say, salary earners who are able to save and accumulate property in the village. A few of the wealthier villagers are also able to cut down one or two of their holdings while living on the income from the rest, but, in general, they share the conservative attitude of their poorer neighbours, and are reluctant to accept a cut in their current income. Prevailing good prices are also a factor here. Some peasants argue that while it is good to replant, it should be done during a slump, and that the wise thing to do is to take full advantage of the current good prices and undertake replanting during a prolonged depression in world demand. Lest an impression of undue foresightedness be given, it should be noted that these same peasants should therefore have started replanting in the period of low prices which followed the end of the Korean War boom, but did not do so.

Apart from the holding there is very little other capital needed in the production of village rubber (sold to the Chinese dealer as unsmoked sheet). Depending on the density of the trees, latex cups and spoons cost approximately $15.00 per acre, a day or two's yield. If necessary coconut shells and cigarette tins can be used, and in any case, the villager of good reputation would have no difficulty in getting credit for these goods from a dealer who wishes to buy the rubber. A knife, latex pails, coagulating tins and acid complete a tapper's equipment, and should not cost more than $10.00 altogether. More expensive are the mangles, one ribbed and one smooth, necessary to make sheets. Here renting is typical, and the life of the asset is very long. A few of the wealthier villagers possess these machines, and they are used by the other villagers for a rent of $1.00 per month. One set of machines can easily be used by four or five men, and, if necessary, more.

Thus, investment in rubber has two major features: firstly the inexpensiveness of items of working capital, secondly, a great discontinuity in the creation of fixed capital. An initial burst of investment occurs and then nothing further—neither the planting of new land, so that stability might arise through new land coming into production to replace the old, nor the replacement of old trees.

FRUIT HOLDINGS

Fruit holdings will be called orchards here, but this term should not convey an impression of cultivated rows of trees. The orchards are concentrations of fruit trees in the jungle, planted, as the people say, 'by the squirrels'. Individual ownership, with the exclusive right to the produce, and to dispose of the land, is a modern development. Informants speak of the orchards as originally belonging to the aborigines. Land registration, and an urban market for the fruit, has led to the situation where orchards are private property, and the rights of the aborigines are confined to the deep jungle.

Despite the importance of the fruit to the economy there are almost no examples of people planting orchards. Most owners confine their

144

attentions to clearing beneath the trees when the fruit is ripe, and aiding the growth of fruit seedlings by clearing away neighbouring jungle growth. As there is no restriction scheme for fruit, and as any owner could certainly plant trees to increase the proportion of income yielding trees to jungle on his land, the explanation for this failure to invest must be sought elsewhere than in the case of rubber.

Two features of the crop are important in this connection. First, the two important local varieties of fruit are characterized by a long period of waiting before they yield a return—the *durian* fruit at least nine, and the *langsat* at least eleven years. Secondly, the return is uncertain. There are seasons, but they are unpredictable and irregular, both in time and between places. One orchard may bear fruit two or three times in quick succession, while another property of the same owner may merely have flowers which fail to come to fruit, or only a few fruit, 'for the squirrels'. It is not even possible to tell whether trees, once planted, will ever bear fruit until after a long period of waiting.

A long period of waiting, and an uncertain return, are two of the classic features of an unattractive investment, and they provide a plausible explanation of the failure of the peasantry to avail themselves of this economic opportunity. On the other hand, it cannot be argued that there are other more attractive opportunities making the opportunity cost too high. As with a rubber smallholding, an orchard could be created with the investment of little more than the peasant's labour. The contrast with the intense desire to own rubber is marked. But rubber offers a sustained rise in daily consumption, and perhaps a release from the unpleasant work of rubber tapping. Although the returns from orchards are large when they come, there is no certainty, and they cannot be made the foundation of a secure living standard. The year 1959 saw the first crop in the most extensively planted orchard in the district. Several thousand dollars return excited the interest of the other peasants, and this practical example, together with the continued frustration of the desire to plant rubber, might well produce emulation.

The production of fruit requires no working capital, other than boxes for the fruit, and these are normally provided by the purchaser, or perhaps a few rounds of shotgun cartridges to ward off the depredations of squirrels and monkeys.

RICELAND

A developed irrigation system represents a considerable investment of labour. But for the present population the problem is solely one of maintenance. In the old-established areas of Malay settlement the economic limit of rice cultivation has been reached. Fear of the

145

Japanese (not shortage of food), forced a slight expansion into marginal areas, but in the absence of such incentives, these plots, abandoned immediately after the occupation, will not be cultivated again. Where entirely new areas are opened for settlement the peasantry relies on the Government to provide the main features of the irrigation scheme, while the individual grower merely has to care for his own holding.

Topographically, the region discussed here is made up of a number of small valleys. The valley floor consists of rice fields, watered by the river, which is diverted by a small dam of wood, stones and mud into a ditch skirting the valley floor, from which it is allowed to run off into each holding, and thence make its way back to the river bed. Every year the dam must be remade. For this work the villagers rely on co-operative labour, each cultivating household being required to provide at least one member for the work. Communal labour makes the dam, and clears and repairs the ditch where it is not running alongside some individual's property. Two half-days of communal labour were sufficient to make the dam and repair the ditch in the village where I worked, unless the dam broke, in which case extra work would be required, again on a communal basis.

In the actual cultivation of the fields there is a choice of methods which decides the quantity of working capital involved. If a bull is used, then rake and roller are also required. These are made of wood by the cultivator himself. The man must attend to this part of the cultivation as women do not work with cattle. This makes the use of cattle typical of the wealthier peasant, both through the cost of the bull, but more particularly through the need to sacrifice daily rubber income. Because of the heat cattle can only be used for a few hours in the morning. This is also the time when the sap flows and rubber must be tapped. Thus, it is possible for a man to help his wife for a few hours in the afternoon using a hoe, but not using cattle. The majority of the peasants use hoe cultivation. The light Malay hoe (*rembas*) is used to clear the grass and break up the soil, and a heavier hoe (*changkol*) is used for making and repairing bunds (earth banks).

Harvesting also offers a choice of techniques. The traditional method is to cut off the heads of rice with a small knife held in the palm of the hand. This is said not to offend the rice spirit, but it is also very cheap, and can be used by one person. The other method uses a sickle, cutting the stalk long and threshing by beating against a simple canvas and wood construction. This method is slightly dearer, and so uses more capital. It is also recognized as more efficient, at least during the past three or four years when nearly everyone has adopted it in the village where I worked. Except for the very poor, the advantage of the first method is simply that it can be used by one person (while the other method preferably requires two

146

or more), so that even the man who normally uses the sickle will leave his wife to work alone with the knife when there is no urgency about the harvest.

Traditionally land was owned by women as members of matrilineal clans, and inherited by their daughters. The traditional code concerning land was embodied in the law with the establishment of British administration, and still applies, but only to land recognized as falling under clan control when the land titles were registered. This land was almost entirely riceland, and the land used as homestead and house-site. The subsequent development of rubber, and of individual holdings in fruit orchards, are not affected by the traditional code. Riceland and house-sites are still normally owned by women, but not through the force of legal sanction. Cases of sale have shown that the code is a dead letter if the villagers wish to ignore it. It is the character of the family system which maintains the female ownership of these categories of land, particularly the matrilocal marriage pattern. Since there is no demand for house-sites to rent, and little for riceland, these types of land will be of little use to a son if inherited by him, for he will be using his wife's land. On the other hand, a father wishes to be able to provide these types of land for his daughter on marriage, expecting the land to go to her daughter when her mother dies. Thus, although a father must be of a different kingroup from his daughter he provides her with land which will devolve as if it were the ancestral property of his wife's clan.

Many operations in rice cultivation can be mechanized. Economic practicability rather than technical considerations are the limiting factor. In this district two processes have been mechanized, one slightly, the other generally. An increasing number of farmers rely on tractor ploughing for the cultivation of their fields. The tractors, using disc ploughs, are owned by the Department of Agriculture, and can be hired for $7.50 an hour. Two or three hours should finish the normal holding, but even this short period will cost a week's income or so for the peasant. The attraction is getting the work done simply and quickly, and an economic case can be made out for it where a man has other work to do, and his wife has difficulty in managing on her own. But it seems an economically backward step as there is no other economic outlet for the wife's leisure. It is also argued by skilled cultivators that the plough cuts too deeply and buries the fertile top soil so that ploughing leads to diminished yields until the land can be restored. I know cases where this seems to be the case, but it may merely be the voice of tradition rationalizing a dislike of change.

But ploughing is still a rare innovation, and the high cost may well prevent its general adoption after the newness has worn off. Almost completely general is the use of a mobile power mill for polishing

147

rice. The equipment is owned and operated by a peasant co-operative started on Government persuasion after overcoming great village scepticism. The original equipment was purchased with a loan from the Rural Industries Development Association, but the profits of a few years' operation have been such as to allow the Society not only to repay the loan, but also to expand its operations, and acquire a considerable bank balance. From the charges for milling the actual costs of operation are covered, and the profits are due to the resale of the chaff as poultry food. The Society, indeed the venture as a whole, is interesting as a rare case of successful co-operative organization in a field where the general picture is one of monotonous failure. This may be attributed, in the first place, to the fact that the venture was economically sound, but this in itself will not guarantee success. Also important was the near monopolization of leadership by men who had been exposed to, and absorbed, the universalistic values of rational bureaucracy in the Government service, mainly as minor local officials or village headmen. I am unable to say why such men are not elected by the societies that fail, or if they are elected, why their influence does not have the same beneficial effect, but my own observation of the way in which the society overcame several organizational crises leaves me in no doubt as to the importance of this factor. A fairly strict refusal to tolerate nepotism, resistance to popular pressure to divide the profits as soon as the loan was paid off, refusal to tolerate inefficiency or dishonesty when the village attitude would be to shrug one's shoulders—actions of this type follow from the ethic instilled in Government servants, but are in conflict with the values current in the village.

This example also shows how the peasantry are very willing to accept any innovation making life appreciably easier, and also the strong position of women, for from the husband's point of view the only importance of the innovation is to force him to provide cash for machining the rice which previously his wife would have pounded in a foot or hand mill, and to lessen the feed available for village chickens.

OTHER FORMS OF ECONOMIC ACTIVITY

There is a host of other small-scale activities making a contribution to the peasant economy, although none can compare in importance with the three discussed above. Most of them share the characteristic of requiring very little capital.

Thatch making is a common pursuit of those who wish to supplement their tapping income, or who, for some reason or other, are unable to tap. There is some village demand for thatch, particularly for the work of a man noted as making a superior product, but it is usually disposed of through the village shop which collects for Chinese dealers.

Other men make a part-time speciality of house repairs and minor carpentry. Typically these men have very few tools, and can only undertake work which will not interfere with their normal work in the rubber holding or rice field. Both features indicate that these men operate without any capital.

Small-scale trading, especially in fruit, is also popular. Occasionally a man will acquire a small stock of some item such as books, caps, or cloth and start hawking it around the villages, but these ventures are always abandoned very quickly; either he makes an outright loss, or he consumes his returns as they are acquired and is unable to replace his stock. Fruit trading also demonstrates clearly a lack of capital. If the dealer is well established he will be provided with funds by the Chinese dealer who collects every day the fruit he has bought from the other villagers.

The small trader often has to make the people who sell him fruit wait for payment until he in turn has resold the fruit, and should he make a loss will often try to cut the price previously agreed on, although this course means the end of his trading! Fruit trading is a pleasant way of making a living, although not a very rewarding one for the small trader, and so competition is fierce. Traders use not only price competition but also their social connections with growers having fruit to sell to secure fruit.

Village shopkeeping by Malays has received a boost from the removal of Chinese competition, which has been one of the results of the Emergency Resettlement. Absence of capital is again a major problem, for it prevents the village shopkeeper maintaining as attractive a stock as the Chinese shop in town. Often he merely buys goods at the same retail price as his fellow villagers and resells them in the village at a higher price and in smaller quantities (e.g. cigarettes singly—but the town shops will also sell very small quantities, it is simply that the journey is not worth while for a purchase costing a few cents). Most of the peasantry make frequent bicycle trips to the town, for example to sell the results of a few days' rubber tapping, and tend to make their purchases on these trips, when they can get lower prices and a better selection. An important feature of village shopkeeping is the collection of village produce for sale to dealers. Fruit is one example, and thatch is also an important item in this respect. In buying fruit the shopkeeper is sure that he will dispose of the product the same day as he buys it, and so if he is using his own capital it will not be tied up for more than a few hours, or if he has to make the other villagers wait, he can promise them payment in the late afternoon. A large order for thatch takes much longer to fulfil, and on occasions the village shopkeeper may have to turn down very attractive commissions simply because he cannot afford to pay for the thatch due to his limited capital.

The number of licences to operate taxis is very limited, but an attractive investment for someone with capital is running a 'pirate taxi'. A man, perhaps retiring from wage employment with a nest-egg, may spend this on a second-hand car, or pay the initial deposit on one while he attempts to meet instalments out of his taxi earnings. Or a father may buy a car for his son as a means of earning a livelihood while in his wife's village. Earnings are consumed as if they were wages, with no provision for the depreciation of the car. A heavy repair bill will often find the owner unable to pay. Finally, when the car is too ramshackle for anyone to wish to pay to ride in it, or requires too expensive repairs, for which he cannot get credit, the venture will be abandoned; but there are always others willing to try.

ATTITUDES TOWARDS ACCUMULATION

Wealth is the most important dimension of the status system. All peasants desire wealth, and yet this desire is combined with attitudes which inhibit a strenuous striving for its accumulation. This might be termed an ethic of moderation. Peasants express their desires not in wishes for great riches but for comfort and security. Platitudes about wealth not bringing happiness are common in any discussion of the rich or riches. It is expected that the wealthy man will suffer in some other way, as if restoring the balance. I should be most surprised if these beliefs and attitudes ever led a peasant to refuse an opportunity for sudden riches, but they are still an element in the values underlying economic activity. Folk religion stresses luck, the predetermination of everything, a comfort for the poor man, and a check on too much pride from the successful. Official religion preaches that this world is only temporary, a testing; that worldly wealth is nothing as compared with the heavenly riches awaiting the pious, the attainment of which is hindered rather than helped by too much concern with this world.

Every economic system requires that its participants place some positive valuation on qualities such as industry, foresight and thrift, and the Malay peasant speaks of them as virtues. But since every economic system is also part of a wider social framework it also requires some excuse for those who fail, and the Malay peasant places more emphasis on this than on the economic virtues. To the outside observer he seems to be not really concerned with striving for economic success and accumulation of wealth, but to be aiming at short run maximization even when it is clear that serious long run difficulties will emerge from this course. This affects not only the individual's own efforts but his relations with his fellows. Economic striving beyond a certain limit produces hostility. The man who works hard in the rubber holding and rice field is praised. But he will meet hostility if his industry is allowed to interfere with his participation in ceremonial events, or with helping his neighbours on these occasions. If he starts, for example, to plant peppers rather than buying them, the neighbours will expect to be supplied free, offering a few cents when they come to ask for peppers, and expecting him to refuse payment. This he will resent, but he will do what is expected of him, give up tending the plant, and when it dies not plant any more. The shopkeeper finds everyone wanting him to treat their debts as ordinary debts between relatives and neighbours in the village, although the ordinary villager can always refuse to give a loan. He has difficulty in refusing credit, and will be expected to give credit to many more people than would ever ask for an outright loan of cash. The owner of a car is expected to drive his relatives free of charge. If a man saves and buys land, when he has more than his neighbours they will begin to comment 'he wants to own everything'. If he has acquired wealth and refuses to spend it lavishly on occasions such as the wedding of his children, and so perhaps halting, if not reversing, his economic advance, they say, 'What is the good of all that money, if you won't even let your children taste it?'

This is an economy where success can be achieved by the man who strives for it. Inheritance is a help, but inheritances are never so large, after division, as to make competition meaningless. The most striking quality about the economically successful peasant is a lack of concern for public judgment, a feeling that he will exact respect and recognition in spite of the popular view, an awareness that he is an object of criticism and jealousy, which he returns with a private contempt for his less industrious and successful neighbours.

CREDIT

The discussion so far should suffice to show that credit is not an essential part of the operation of the village economy. Given the existence of the fixed capital assets the peasants can continue to produce and sell their crops without any need for loans. Serious indebtedness is rare. The peasantry do not, with rare exceptions, resort to money lenders, and most indebtedness consists of debts of a few dollars with the village shopkeeper, or of the share-tapper with the owner of the holding. Where the village shopkeeper is a local man debts can lead to very serious quarrels. (Many shopkeepers are Malabari Muslims, who were not affected by resettlement). The debtor maintains that eventually he will pay, but that at the moment he is unable to do so. The creditor, who is operating on a very small profit in any case, sees his whole business existence threatened by small debts owed him by his customers. Eventually he will demand payment, and this outrages the debtor, leading to the complete breaking of social relations between them, and the debtor's outright refusal to pay. (Of course he always intended to pay, but now he has been insulted he no longer feels obligated!)

If a man has the means he should be prepared to give a loan to a fellow villager or relative in need, and not place too much importance on getting the money back. Accordingly, the peasants try and avoid giving loans, or should they do so, regard it as a charitable action. If the sum is large, or the lender is really intent on being repaid, he will demand a definite assurance of payment, probably after the harvest, or he will insist on security. After the harvest if the debtor does not repay voluntarily, the creditor may take a sack to his house and collect payment in rice, and if he is angry into the bargain, make sure that everyone knows his mission. Fruit orchards are a favourite security. The return from a rubber holding is certain and calculable, and the owner can raise money not by a loan, but by selling the tapping rights for a certain period. Chinese will pay highly for these rights, but tap the trees in such a way that they are worthless for a long while after the expiration of the agreement. This is called *pajak*; the same term is used when the owner sells the fruit on the trees for a lump sum, and for the method of raising a loan when temporary ownership of the fruit trees passes to the creditor. The creditor is entitled to whatever the orchard may produce until the loan is repaid. This may be more than the original value of the loan, or it may be nothing. The *pajak* relationship gives security to the lender rather than a return on his loan. If a piece of property has been in *pajak* for some time, and the loan still not repaid, either party may suggest an outright sale, but not necessarily so; years later a dispute may arise as to whether the original payment was for a sale or *pajak*.

The peasant may also occasionally borrow money from the dealer to whom he sells his rubber. These loans are small, the dealer knows the economic situation of the borrower, and will not risk more than the peasant can readily repay. As an additional security he may also take the licence book of the peasant, so that he will be unable to sell his rubber elsewhere and avoid repaying the loan. But no interest is charged, the loan is regarded as an expression of trust between old acquaintances, and it also serves as a substitute for price competition amongst the Chinese dealers to attempt to bind the peasants to a particular shop with quasi-friendship ties.

The village shopkeeper, if he is well established, may be able to get credit from the bigger Chinese wholesalers who send their goods to the district by van, visiting small roadside shops as well as the shops in the local town. This credit is very important in allowing the village shopkeeper to increase his stock, and its availability to one shop and not another might lead one to prosper while the other failed.

SOCIAL CAPITAL AND THE PLURAL SOCIETY

There are a number of assets used by the members of a society which are not individually owned. Public utilities, schools and hospitals may have this character, although they are, of course, also run as profit-making enterprises. The most important items of social capital in Malay peasant society are provided from outside the society. Public roads, schools, hospitals, and so on, are all provided by the Government. Although the peasant pays taxes, the provision of these items is not an economic problem for the peasant, and the spread of democratic political processes is only just beginning to involve the peasant in the political aspects of these problems. Within the village, however, there are a number of items of social capital which have to be provided from the village economy. The major items are irrigation works, which have been discussed above, village roads and buildings, and religious buildings.

Work on village roads and bridges has very much the same character as work on rice irrigation. But there is one major difference. Work on the rice fields is accepted as legitimate; there may well be minor disagreement on the exact timing of the work, but there will be no question that it should be carried out. With the paths there is always much disagreement. This reflects the current state of village organization. Social change has robbed the clan chiefs of their previously unrivalled authority. The Government has created village headmen without precisely defining their authority or their relations with the traditional chiefs. Other villagers claim the right to lead on the basis of education or religious office. The authority situation is fluid with many individuals endeavouring to assert their claims, and it is in the field of co-operative village work that these struggles are fought out. They paralyse the ability of the villagers to undertake collective action, and mean that continual maintenance cannot be achieved; work on village projects has to move by fits and starts, if at all. In an extreme situation even rice irrigation may not be carried out, the villagers unable to work together simply complain that they have no water, and say that the Government ought to do something.

Work on paths and bridges is not of crucial importance for people who usually travel on foot or by bicycle, and can make a bridge of a coconut tree over a stream. But even work on mosques and the smaller *surau* is plagued by this same inability to co-operate. A minor repair cannot be carried out, but is left until it becomes a major operation. But it should be admitted that this same tendency to leave things as long as possible is seen in the villagers' private affairs also. The special feature with religious works is that charity is sought on a wide basis, indeed, for a mosque appeals for contributions may be sent throughout Malaya.

Just as many of the problems relating to the provision of social capital are outside the villagers' concern, so are many of the capital problems relating to the production and sale of rice, fruit and rubber. An obvious essential is a transport system. Rice has to be milled, rubber smoked and treated. All these services are in the hands of other ethnic groups in Malaya, mainly of the Chinese. In many ways the position of the Malay peasant economy within Malaya invites comparison with that of a country exporting unprocessed primary products, not, in this case, to another country, but to another section of the national economy.

A co-operative smallholders' smokehouse was successfully operated during the post-Korean price slump, but when prices rose again the peasants preferred to revert to selling their rubber as soon as possible. The costs of building and operating a small smokehouse do not put it outside the reach of the richer peasants even if they only use it to process the production from their own land. But the share-tappers do not wish to pool their rubber, which differs in quality, and are always anxious to sell as soon as they can. The owner would therefore have to buy this rubber from them before it was smoked, running the risk of a loss if the price fluctuated, and needing capital to finance this purchase.

CONCLUSION

A number of conclusions may be drawn from the preceding discussion. The most obvious is the way in which the economy is based on the exploitation of a limited stock of existing assets, with no significant additions to the stock of productive capital, and in one important case, a serious failure to replace the asset as it declines.

With the exception of rubber replanting the economy impresses by its soundness, by its ability to give a standard of living to those depending on it which compares very favourably with other Asian peasant economies. This well-being is probably temporary unless rapid and far-reaching steps are taken to increase the stock of capital. Population increase continually reduces the individual share of available resources. A middle-aged informant could point to the riceland cultivated by his mother and show how it now supported six families, and within a few years would have to support more. Part of this burden has been temporarily relieved by the enormous increase in wage employment outside the village resulting from the Emergency, which has made jobs for thousands of village youths in the Security Forces. The ending of the Emergency has now closed this opportunity, and the contraction of the Security Forces is causing the return of these young men and their families to the village. A situation of relative labour shortage, where at any one time there were always a few rubber holdings without tappers, and a few owners of rice who would rather have rented out some of their land than cultivate it all, will change to the reverse, and involuntary agrarian unemployment and under-employment may become serious problems.

Also noticeable is the absence of peasant indebtedness and of the exploitation of the peasantry through credit relations. This is partly to be explained through the role of capital in the economic process. Where rice is the mainstay of the economy income is received only annually (or at most twice a year). The peasant thus has the problem of financing his domestic consumption until this income is received. This is usually done by getting into debt with the rice dealer who also runs a village provision shop. Goods bought on credit are over-priced, and the rice taken in settlement of the debt is undervalued. In time this relationship can be built into a permanent dependence of the peasant on the dealer, or lead to the dealer's ownership of the land through usury. The 'mixed farming' peasant receives income regularly from rubber tapping (at intervals of three or four days, at the most a week). He therefore does not have to get into debt to meet his consumption needs; or, put in other words, his need for capital is less. Nor, indeed, since the peasant does not receive his income in a lump sum, is it wise to give him credit. That this characteristic of rubber production is important for explaining the absence of indebtedness may be seen by a comparison with the rice dependent areas of northern Malaya where exploitation through the *kuncha* system is a constant feature of peasant life.

Also important is the inexpensiveness of working capital in rubber production. In an industry such as fishing where the most productive forms of activity require continuous, and heavy, investment in nets and boats, there is scope for the man with capital to acquire control of the independent producer through capital advances, especially if the fisherman's problems are complicated by a season during which he receives very little, if any, income. Control by capitalists in different degree has been the common fate of the Malay fishermen.

A further reason for the peasant to get into debt, even when he has successfully adjusted his consumption to income, arises from the need to meet extraordinary expenditures such as feasts. Here fruit is important to the economy, in that it brings in large amounts of un-allocated income. Where these extraordinary expenditures can be planned for in advance the peasant can wait until the fruit harvest provides him with the means, and should he be forced into debt the fruit harvest provides him with the means of repaying it.

There are two special features of the society which must be mentioned in connection with indebtedness. In the area where I

155

worked the land was 'Malay Reservation'. It might not be owned by
a member of any other ethnic group. The security that a peasant can
offer for a loan is his land, this can only be security to another
Malay, and Malays do not practise usury. Secondly the mildness of
competition in comparative expenditure on feasts is striking when
compared with the reported situation elsewhere in Malaya. A wedding
is still an expensive occasion, but it is a matter of hundreds of dollars
rather than thousands. This means that one of the main temptations
for a peasant to get into debt deeply is lacking.

The divisions of wealth in the society are still small. The difference
of a few acres only stands between the rich man and the poor. But
the differences are tending to harden, and a slight tendency to concentration may be observed. Due to the Government's policy on land
alienation the poor man cannot directly convert his labour into
property. Nor can he acquire large savings which will enable him to
buy a developed holding if one becomes available. The man who is
already wealthy can save his surplus, and invest it in further land
acquisition. This applies even more to the salary earner than to the
wealthy peasant; with the savings from his salary he can become an
absentee landlord until he retires from employment. (The savings of a
young man in the Security Forces are most unlikely to run to land
acquisition.) The trend is to make more rigid the property division,
and hence the status system, which is founded on wealth. This trend
is reinforced by the inability of the poorer peasant to take advantage
of the rubber replanting grant, which therefore amounts to a subsidy
of the improvement of the property of the rich.

While these trends are clearly discernible they have not yet advanced far. And it would be too much to predict confidently the
ultimate monopolization of all property in a few hands. Inheritance
will be a powerful leveller; and if no radical measures are taken to
open new land or to replant the old, the very future of the economy,
and the type of society it maintains, becomes problematic.

8

Capital, Saving and Credit among Indigenous Rice Farmers and Immigrant Vegetable Farmers in Hong Kong's New Territories

BY MARJORIE TOPLEY

INTRODUCTION

Field of enquiry

This essay discusses master farmers growing rice or vegetables as principal crops. Specialization in vegetable-growing is largely the concern of immigrants, while indigenous farmers, that is people whose ancestors settled in the area generations (sometimes centuries) ago, still specialize mainly in rice production. Rice was formerly the traditional crop of the New Territories, but has declined in importance in the last decade, giving way to market gardening. Increased vegetable production has been carried out mainly on former paddy land. The encouragement to change in farming patterns has been provided by the growth of the urban areas since the war, and has been almost entirely due to efforts of immigrants from the vegetable-specializing areas of Kwangtung province. The first large influx of these farmers was about 1937 when the Japanese invaded South China. Since the establishment of the present regime in China, their numbers have increased so considerably that on census day in 1961, indigenous people were in the majority in only one district.

A large proportion of all master farmers in the New Territories are either rice or vegetable specialists, and rear pigs as their main secondary agricultural activity. In 1961 some 24,000 master farmers were working in the area; about 8,000 grew principally rice, and a slightly larger number principally vegetables. Some 1,500 grew rice exclusively and 2,500 vegetables exclusively (based on *Hong Kong Report on the 1961 Census*, vol. III, table 423). Both groups are essentially peasant producers operating on a small scale with simple technology, low level of capital and little hired labour. (There are also farmers principally concerned with other forms of production which are more highly capitalized, notably pigs, poultry and eggs, and fruit.

157

They are relatively small in number, and, unlike rice farmers and most vegetable farmers, were originally city dwellers.)

Most immigrant and indigenous farmers are distinguishable not only by the difference in crop-specialization, but also by differences in certain aspects of social organization, economic opportunity and political status. A comparison of the arrangements and attitudes of the two groups in relation to capital, savings and credit helps point up the relevance of social factors for economic problems. Discussion is confined to the New Territories because it is the main agricultural region of Hong Kong, and it also has certain economic and legal peculiarities.

At present information on either social or economic organization in the area is extremely limited. Few studies have been carried out to date.[1] My observations here are not based on field-work but on seven years' residence in Hong Kong, two spent in the New Territories, together with some data obtained from documents and verbal communications largely from Government sources.[2] My object is largely exploratory: to see what kind of outline of the situation can be built up on the existing information, and the kind of information which might be needed for a more detailed picture to emerge.

Some facts about the New Territories

The British Crown Colony of Hong Kong adjoins Kwangtung province on the south-east coast of China. It consists on the one hand of the principal island giving its name to the Colony, and of Kowloon on the mainland, both of which were obtained by cession from China; and on the other, of the New Territories, an area north of Kowloon, bordering China, together with 200-odd islands. Hong Kong and Kowloon are principally urban areas with populations almost entirely immigrant in origin. The New Territories are held on lease

[1] A trial survey into the economic conditions of some families in the New Territories was conducted in 1950 by Dr D. Y. Lin. The results are unpublished and available locally only in mimeographed form. A Hakka village was studied during 1957–58 by Miss Jean Pratt, an anthropologist of Cambridge University; a study of the 'boat people', a socially distinct group engaged in fishing, has been carried out by Miss Barbara Ward (Mrs Stephen Morris), an anthropologist of London University; Mr Potter, an anthropologist of Berkley, California, is now making a general study of a Cantonese lineage village community; a geography graduate, Mr Ronald Ng of Hong Kong University, is conducting a study on Lantao Island in the New Territories, of several village and immigrant groups with a view to discovering ways of improving their economic conditions; and a national income survey of the whole colony is being conducted by an economist, Mr Roy Chang, of the University of the West Indies. The results of these various investigations are not yet available.

[2] I am particularly grateful to a number of past and present District Officers for discussion and opinions on farmers' economic and social problems, and to members of the Department of Agriculture and Forestry, and members of the Co-operative Development Department for additional opinions and information.

158

of which there is only another thirty-five years to run. Although principally rural with a population which was mainly indigenous until recent years, the New Territories have several sizeable market towns and a planned industrial town built since the last war on a site once occupied by villages.

The area is hilly and in many places transport and communications are poor. Arable land exploited amounts to only 13 per cent of the total area; an additional 82 per cent of the area consists of marginal land of sub-grade character, and the remaining 5 per cent comprises expanding urban areas which tend to encroach on arable rather than marginal land.

When the British took over, the indigenous people were living in village communities. Today there are said to be some thousand villages still occupied mainly by indigenous people, with immigrants living scattered between villages in fertile valley regions. The majority of villages are essentially 'private' communities consisting of family dwellings (see below) with no shops or industries. Many villagers from certain areas go abroad to work for periods from about three to twelve years. All persons born in the area are British subjects and can obtain British passports. Immigrants generally have no passports. Many came in illegally and cannot migrate further. Like villagers, however, they can work in the urban areas.

Administration is through districts. Below District Officers are Rural Committees and a Consultative Council. The former consist of Village Representatives, and the latter partly of such Representatives and partly of local people who are well-known New Territories residents, usually wealthy, and Justices of the Peace. Village Representatives are elected or appointed according to what is described in annual reports as 'clan custom'. Elections are informal affairs and not supervised by the Government. Village Representatives are rarely peasant farmers. They appear to be generally the wealthier members of their village and many live only part of the time in villages. This is so even in lineage villages (see below). As in traditional China, village leaders by no means always obtain their position in lineage villages by virtue of generational seniority, which would happen if strict custom was observed (cf. Freedman, 1958). Wealth alone, however, as in traditional China, is probably not enough to qualify a man as leader and Village Representative. He has to be, as in China, a man able to meet Government officials and discuss village problems clearly and with confidence: that is, he should be an educated individual (although educated according to the modern rather than the traditional system). Again, a knowledge of local custom is likely to be an important qualification, not however in order to organize and lead rituals in which the Representative may take only a minor part, but in order to interpret custom to

159

Government. Chinese custom is still adhered to in a number of local situations, particularly in regard to land, and there are many customary procedures on which Government has little systematic knowledge (see below, pp. 161–2). We need to know much more about the type of individuals who become Village Representatives and the nature of their wealth. Superficial investigation suggests that such men may play an important role in the village economy lending out money, organizing land deals and sometimes managing corporate lineage property (see below). Their economic functions may indeed provide a main sanction in their election, and their election in turn enables them to exercise such functions with more authority. Much reliance is placed on Village Representatives in interpreting custom in cases of disputes. The principal task of both Rural Committees and the Consultative Council is to arbitrate between District Officers and villagers in cases of disputes. Their main concern tends to be with problems affecting villagers—for example land-ownership and geomancy (*fung-shui*) disputes (see below, pp. 171–2)—rather than with problems of immigrants, who are not fully incorporated into the system.

There are a number of additional organizations, both governmental and philanthropic, which are concerned with economic problems of farmers. They tend in the main to be concerned with either indigenous or immigrant farmers respectively, partly because of their economic specialization. Some of the more important are the Agricultural and Forestry Department, the Department of Co-operative Development, including the Vegetable Marketing Organization (V.M.O.), on the Government side; and the Kadoorie Agricultural Aid Association, the Kadoorie Agricultural Aid Loan Fund, and the Joseph Trust Fund, on the philanthropic side. They have all been established since the last war.

The indigenous population consists of two speech-groups: Cantonese and Hakka. The latter were migrants to the area in historical times and originally lived outside villages like the present-day immigrants. Today the two groups are on peaceable terms and sometimes occupy the same villages. There are also many exclusively Hakka or Cantonese villages. Cantonese generally 'own' (see below) the best land and Hakka tend to live in the hilly regions. Generally speaking, Hakka women appear more prominent in agriculture and other outside pursuits than do Cantonese women, although the situation is complicated by migration of males from some Cantonese villages leading to a greater role of their womenfolk in agriculture. Many villages of both speech-groups are occupied by single surname patrilineal kin-groups: collections of families with a common surname and descended in the male line from a founding ancestor (or ancestors). Some large patrilineages cover several villages; other smaller units occupy sections of villages in which several surnames are found. Thus the potential for economic co-operation on a kinship basis at the village level varies. It is also affected by ownership or otherwise of corporate land-holdings by lineage groups and lineage segments.

No comprehensive survey of land tenure has been undertaken to date, and there is little published material on the operation of the system. A brief statement of the situation as it appears to be must be attempted, however, because of its relevance to questions of access to agricultural land and the ability of groups and individuals to accumulate it or vary its uses.

The general position, with a few important exceptions introduced by ordinance, is that Chinese custom and customary right are supposed to be enforced in regard to land matters in the New Territories. Because of this it is held that the Rule Against Perpetuities does not apply as it is held to apply in Hong Kong and Kowloon, and, again, that the English doctrine of Freedom of Alienation by Will does not apply as it does in the latter areas. A number of points relating to custom in regard to land remain obscure, particularly in relation to the constitution of certain traditional groups permitted to alienate land in perpetuity and their customary methods of management. There are even some doubts as to the actual dating of custom which is meant to apply in the area, although it is generally taken as being that of the Ch'ing dynasty which operated when the British took over. Few cases regarding land matters have come before the courts or are referred to in land reports. Most disputes have been settled by private arbitration between District Officers and representatives of the parties concerned (for example Rural Committees). The situation tends to be self-perpetuating: because so little knowledge has been accumulated on the workings of customary law the majority of lawyers prefer not to touch land cases and usually advise clients to settle disputes privately. Much of the data accumulated in the District Offices cannot provide a basis for generalization because custom is said to vary considerably from district to district and even between lineage groups.

A major departure from the traditional situation is that all land in the New Territories became the property of the Crown. Soon after British occupation a land court was set up to hear claims in the area and leases for agricultural land were granted, largely in accordance with what appeared to be customary rights held by individuals and groups at the time. These leases were for ninety-nine years less three days. Land held on these leases is known as 'private land'. Additional Crown land has been leased also since this date, particularly for development purposes.

Several groups were found to own land when the British arrived.

The main types were lineages ('clans') and lineage segments, temple associations, residential religious institutions ('nunneries'), and *oot* 'associations'. Lineages and segments owned land in the name of ancestors, and it was nearly always leased to members who cultivated it sometimes rent-free and sometimes with an annual rent according to their economic circumstances. Members could not sub-let such land. Sometimes lineage land was allocated to segments in rotation. While using such land a segment paid for the expenses of the ancestral rites. Some lineages also claimed rights over additional land which they did not themselves cultivate. Members of other lineages often cultivated such land, paying its so-called 'protectors' a 'tax' for its use. In return they also received protection from bandits and pirates. Income from lineage land was supposed to be used for the benefit of lineage members, especially the poor. Land was held by temple associations in the name of the deity worshipped, and again appears to have been rented out mainly to members, income being used for the benefits of the group and the upkeep of the temple and its rites. Associations used income for burial of members, for financing overseas migration of members, and for other purposes beneficial to the group.

These kinds of traditional groups were allowed to operate as trusts and continue to alienate land in perpetuity. No limit was placed on the size of membership of such trusts and individuals were permitted to make bequests of land to them. Today several lineages own much of the fertile valley land. Some have additional land, usually poor and hilly, allocated in compensation for 'tax' income on land they formerly had protected and which was allocated to the farmers who had cultivated it. A number of associations and temples and nunneries also own land. Membership of some is on an inter-village basis, and some temple associations are based on several adjacent lineage groups. About one-third of the arable land is said to be held by ancestral trusts at present, although the desire to bequeath land in this way is also said to be less strong than formerly. However, departing from custom, no group, traditional or otherwise, which did not own land in 1910 can set up a new land trust if it consists of more than twenty members. If this ruling is strictly followed, it would appear virtually to prevent any lineage group not previously owning land from starting an ancestral trust.

A further departure from custom is that managers of land held by traditional groups, including lineages, may now (at least in theory) dispose of it as if they were sole owners. In fact, objections by members to its sale or conversion to other uses (for example, renting it to vegetable farmers) are heard by the Land Officer and the validity of such objections is supposed to be determined in accordance with 'custom'. Two further factors which might inhibit more economic

162

use of 'private' land by leaseholders, both groups and individuals, are, firstly, that Government may resume land itself for development purposes by paying for it in terms of the agricultural value of the land plus, usually, an inducement fee, and, secondly, that land leased for arable purposes may not be converted by leaseholders themselves without payment of a conversion fee. This fee is worked out in terms of the increased value of the land on conversion, and might be considerable. Conflicts and disputes between rural dwellers—both groups and individuals—and Government on the one hand, and between individuals and managers of group-held land on the other, regarding land, customary right, and rights in terms of agricultural leases, appear to be a growing problem in some areas, particularly those close to urban centres where land-values are rising. Some of the implications of these factors will be examined later in respect to capital accumulation.

In addition to land-owning groups, about 40 per cent of rice farmers work their 'own' land, another 12 per cent use ancestral land without rent, and 6 per cent cultivate a combination of own and ancestral land. Others pay rent to landlords according to various kinds of leases (*Census Report*, vol. II, table 408). Holdings are generally small, a fairly common size for a family of five being about one acre. This of course has a further effect on a family's ability to convert land to other, non-arable, uses.

Land was traditionally calculated by rice farmers in terms of the measure of grain (*táu*) required to plant (*chùng*) a field. The *táu-chùng* measure is now commonly used in official calculations in the New Territories and is standardized at six *táu-chùng* to an acre. Crown rent is collected in money and has progressively declined in value in relation to the value of agricultural land. Other rents were originally paid in grain when rice was the principal crop of the area and because the value of grain was more stable than the value of money. Today rents for vegetable land are still reckoned in paddy, but are convertible into money at the market rate of best quality rice. (Rice grown in the New Territories is of high quality.) Many rice farmers still pay rent in grain grown on their fields. A common rent for rice land is about one or two piculs of rice per *táu-chùng* annually (1 picul=133 lb.). Fertile, well-irrigated land when rented out to vegetable farmers might cost as much as seven piculs per *táu-chùng*, this rent being equal to the yield obtainable if rice is grown on it. Much rice land yields only about four piculs per *táu-chùng*.

The smallness of rice farmers' holdings results partly from the system of land inheritance whereby, following Chinese custom, sons inherit land equally (daughters and wives having no share). Few indigenous farmers have holdings large enough to support their families by growing rice, and most would be able to handle larger holdings with the amount of labour available from household members. This is not because they have large households as a rule but because rice does not need much labour. The size of households returned at the 1961 census does not suggest that the large joint family is a typical form of social organization for indigenous farmers, and this may relate to smallness of land-holdings. The greatest number of households of farmers growing principally rice were of five members, the second greatest was of four, and third was of six members (*Census Report*, vol. III, table 404).

In addition to the land they cultivate, villagers often have prescriptive rights over uncultivated Crown land for grazing cattle, cutting grass and burying their dead. Disputes sometimes arise between them and Government when it is planned to use such land for development purposes, or with immigrants who wish to rent it for vegetable growing. There are certain religious sanctions which villagers additionally apply in such cases (see below, p. 171).

Immigrants rent land from individuals, lineages and other traditional groups occasionally, and from the Crown direct. A few may squat illegally. Absentee landlordism is not a problem: most landlords are villagers who continue to live in the area. Very few immigrants own the land they cultivate. The Census Report (table 408) shows 66 per cent of vegetable farmers renting land. Of the 22 per cent shown owning land, 5 per cent using ancestral land without rent, and 2 per cent using a combination of their own and ancestral land, the majority are likely to be indigenous farmers now growing vegetables. Settlement of immigrants has generally been on a regional basis: those from a single area of the homeland have tended to settle in a particular district. They generally live on the plot of land they cultivate. Regionalism can sometimes provide a basis for economic co-operation.

Vegetables, unlike rice, can be grown profitably on quite small areas of land. An average size holding for an unattached male is about two *táu-chùng*, and for a family of four or five about four *táu-chùng*. With two *táu-chùng* an unattached man would be fairly fully employed (vegetables need more labour than rice) and could earn enough to support himself. The same applies to a family of four or five with four *táu-chùng*. The size of immigrant households tends to be smaller than that of indigenous people. This is probably partly related to difficulties in entering the Colony. The Census Report (vol. III, table 404) shows that the greatest number of households of vegetable farmers were of two members, the second greatest of three, and third greatest of one member only. The optimum size of vegetable farms with present methods of cultivation tends to be determined primarily by the number of persons in a household available to work the land. Little hired agricultural labour is available in the New

164

Territories partly due to competition from town occupations, and partly (in the case of vegetable farming) to a reluctance of workers to handle night-soil—still an important fertilizer—unless they are working for themselves. For reasons of status most farmers prefer to work for themselves even when the income they can gain thereby is lower than that obtainable by hiring out their services, provided the former is sufficient to cover the cost of daily necessaries.

CAPITAL, SAVING AND CREDIT

Capital: Rice Farmers

The main equipment of the rice farmer is land, a few tools, a plough, and preferably a buffalo for ploughing. Poor farmers may own only their tools, renting land and hiring a plough which they work by hand. In many areas a bicycle is also an important piece of equipment. Fields often lie quite a distance from villages and bicycles are used to reach the area of cultivation and to carry equipment. Probably most farmers who need a bicycle own one. Many villagers have access to the ancestral hall of their kin-group for storing grain, and share with the rest of the village in the use of a communal winnowing machine, threshing floor, a water well, and a night-soil well. Many rice farmers rear a few pigs for both breeding and sale for meat. Pig rearing is more highly capitalized than rice production. Sties are usually owned by individual households, and some of the feed is obtained from the husk of their own rice crops. Most indigenous farmers also own their own houses.

Much of the indigenous farmer's equipment, including land, is inherited patrilineally, brothers taking equal shares. Sometimes lots are drawn to decide which items and which parcels of land each will take. Sometimes quarrels arise over division of property. I was told of a case where some family land has been left idle for five years because a group of brothers could not agree among themselves on its allocation. In view of the general shortage of arable land, however, such cases are probably rare.

Equipment is often purchased on credit or partially on credit. However, purchase of additional land is often difficult. The Kadoorie Agricultural Aid Association provides certain capital equipment free to both individuals and to villages jointly, if they can make out a deserving case. It has supplied such items as buffaloes to poorer farmers, buffaloes, pigs, pig sties and poultry to widows (who are one of its special concerns); also village paths, irrigation canals, and improved wells, sometimes using village labour. Much more information is needed on capital needs and preferences of indigenous farmers in both rice farming and secondary occupations. A few of the capital aid schemes to date appear to have been less successful than was

165

hoped: some widows, for example, sold their pigs and cows shortly after receiving them. More and more villagers are joining pig-raising co-operatives which are supervised by the Co-operative Development Department. They join partly because of the functions of these societies as bulk purchasers of pig-feed, and also because they act as vehicles for loans from outside impersonal sources (see below, p. 182). They are not producers' co-operatives. Out of forty-five societies operating at present, thirty-two appear to be based on villages. The New Territories Administration also has a local public works self-help scheme whereby it supplies materials to enable villages to undertake minor construction works with their own labour or labour paid for by themselves.

Specialist advice is provided by the Agricultural and Forestry Department on improved techniques in farming, welfare and breeding of animals, and control of crop and animal diseases. The operation and care of buffalo in Hakka society are specifically women's work, and a woman's eligibility for marriage is said to depend partly on her skill in these tasks, and may affect the bride-price offered. Conversely, a man's chance of acquiring a wife might be affected by whether he owns a buffalo, which in turn may be connected with the level of his income, and in some cases with a change in emphasis to other occupations, where buffaloes are less important. There is little conscious budgeting for replacement of durable assets, and few farmers keep systematic accounts of income and expenditure. The Agricultural and Forestry Department is planning a campaign to teach farmers simple methods of accounting. (Some co-operatives at present use adolescent schoolboys as their accountants because of the general scarcity of persons in the rural area who know how to keep accounts). It has also been considering the possibility of encouraging a system of outside contracts whereby farmers can hire from private firms certain capital equipment such as ploughs or insecticide sprayers, together with labour to work them, for periods when they are most needed.

For the landless farmer rent occupies a high proportion of gross product—as much as 50 per cent in some areas. Most farmers for this reason alone wish to acquire their own land. They could in fact in some areas increase their income by growing vegetables; rent would be a lower proportion of costs, and less land is needed to grow them profitably. Some of the reasons why they do not generally change to vegetable specialization will be taken up presently. Labour does not usually present a problem in the expansion of rice production. One man can look after as much as ten *tàu-chùng*. Extra labour used at harvest and planting-out time is usually supplied either free, with villagers helping each other in turn, or in return for food or for favours rendered by the farmer during the year. The main problems are having the means to purchase land, and of land being available for purchase.

Traditionally, individuals wishing to sell land were supposed to offer it first to members of their lineage. Deeds of transfer were traditionally worded as if they were mortgages and no period for redemption was fixed. The transferor or his descendants had a chance to redeem the property at the original price even after several generations. This kind of transference is no longer permitted, but in the more remote parts of the New Territories there is still a marked reluctance to make outright sales of land to strangers. I have seen no indication in any area that farmers are selling land because of the uncertain political future of Hong Kong in view of the short period left on the lease of the Territories. In remoter areas farmers may be compelled to sell land if their incomes fall below the margin of subsistence (most farmers operate within very narrow margins), or in some places to finance a male kinsman's trip abroad in search of work. Many men go to England from areas with poor land and small holdings (especially from Hakka villages) to work in Chinese restaurants and remit money back to their households. It is probably more usual, however, to mortgage a portion of the land or obtain a loan to finance the trip than to sell land outright for the purpose. In many areas Crown land not already under cultivation is of poor quality and there may be little incentive to purchase it. It might also be used by the village as a whole for grazing cattle and grass-cutting. The kinship nature of Chinese villages might also make it difficult or less attractive for a farmer to move to a district where more land might be available for sale or low rent. By moving he would lose advantages in the use of labour and credit facilities which kinship offers.

A man with large holdings and farming rice exclusively probably enjoys most prestige in the remoter rural areas such as the islands. He can provide work on the land for a large joint family of several married sons with their wives and children. He does not need his sons to go away to seek cash income and his control over them and their income is therefore greater (see below, p. 176). The highest status in the New Territories generally is probably enjoyed by the farmer who becomes a landlord and does not work further for his living. In areas with land suitable for vegetable growing many farmers rent their land and appear to try to live on income from rent, perhaps supplementing this income with the cash earnings of a son in the town. Tea-houses in one market town near a vegetable area can be seen crowded with such small landlords sitting about chatting for hours of the day (a favourite occupation of landlords in traditional China). The value of landlord status thus sometimes acts as a disincentive to further capital accumulation.

167

In areas where land values have risen because of the suitability of the land for vegetable production a rice farmer would find it difficult to acquire additional land by purchase or rent. Rent from such land might be equivalent to the whole gross product obtained by growing rice. Disputes sometimes occur between managers and members of lineages with joint property over the renting of land to vegetable-farming immigrants. Although the benefit to the whole lineage from such rents might be greater than if the land were used by lineage members themselves in rice growing, it appears that members usually see only the immediate effect which the alternative use of the land would have on them: less would be available for their personal use in rice growing. This attitude is also found when managers desire to convert lineage land to other uses when the land lies near an urban area. Moreover, it is sometimes felt that the managers would be able more easily to swindle members out of their share of benefits from the land if it were used mainly or entirely to obtain income from outsiders. In some areas there is a tendency for the usually illiterate members to distrust managers, who are usually educated men with business experience. Sometimes there appears to be cause for such distrust.

In areas with rising land values due to development and the spread of the urban sector farmers are often aware of the benefits of converting their land to other uses if they are able to do so. Attitudes towards traditional uses of land are changing under the influence of urban ways of life. In one district near a market town some smallholders belonging to the same kin-group have formed syndicates, pooling their land for conversion and paying the conversion fee jointly. In other areas where co-operation among kinsmen is not so strong and where few members of the group have modern business experience, particularly in those areas with smallholdings of a size not suitable for conversion, some farmers have sold their land to speculators. This is sometimes left idle by the speculators, who wait for a good price for further sale for development. They are usually townsmen with no intimate connections with the farmers of the area, and their practice of leaving land idle is often bitterly resented by the local inhabitants. In areas planned by Government for development farmers may be further inhibited from converting the land themselves by the fact that in addition to the payment of a conversion fee they also have to relinquish three-fifths of their land for use by Government in road construction and so on. They might therefore prefer to sell their land to others. Managers of joint-owned land may be prevented from converting the land to urban uses because such conversion may be regarded by the authorities as inconsistent with the terms of the trust on which they hold it. A recent case in point concerned a temple association. Its temple had burned

168

down and the managers wished to erect on the site a block of tenement flats rather than another temple (an indication of changes in attitudes). Such a conversion was thought by the authorities to be against the whole purpose of the trust: without the temple it had no *raison d'etre*. (A committee to investigate Chinese law and custom in Hong Kong—see Bibliography—recommended in 1948 that in order to facilitate alienation of land dedicated to ancestor worship which might be required for development the Land Officer should be given express power to sanction any transaction which he considered in the interest of beneficiaries as a whole even though such transaction might not be justified by customary law. So far this recommendation has not been acted upon.)

Near to the urban areas, particularly near to the industrial town in the New Territories, farmers are becoming increasingly eager to sell their land because of the considerable rise in land values in the past few years. Disputes sometimes arise between fathers and sons over land sale. Traditionally a man only held family land on trust for his descendants and was not supposed to dispose of it without the consent of his sons.

A system of brokerage has arisen whereby an outsider wishing to acquire land for industrial and commercial purposes (these developers are often recent immigrants from Shanghai) gets in touch with somebody known to and respected by farmers who own a group of smallholdings, who then negotiates its sale to the developer, usually taking a commission from the farmers. The majority of such brokers are lineage elders and members of Rural Committees. Such sales do not always turn out to be in the farmers' interest; often the proceeds of the sale are dissipated rather than reinvested (see below, p. 174).

Little appears to be known of investment by farmers generally, although my impression is that landed property such as flats and shops is usually preferred, with the investor perhaps placing his money in the enterprise jointly with other kinsmen. Hong Kong has few public companies and the Chinese generally in Hong Kong prefer to invest in private companies or small enterprises run by individuals known to them personally. In one case coming to my notice a wealthy village elder started a factory near his village, recruiting labour almost exclusively from among village women.

Many farmers invest in their children's education, including that of daughters. Girls were traditionally reckoned and referred to as 'goods on which one loses one's investment' because they moved away on marriage. But many families in emigrant areas give girls some education and the age of marriage appears to be rising there. Such girls handle remittances from male members of the household abroad and read letters concerning the use to which money is to be put. Farming families with members abroad do not like outsiders to know their income from this source and prefer not to let even outside kinsmen handle their papers. To do so might increase the risk of theft and pressure for financial assistance.

Money is also put into pig-breeding; also some spare cash will usually be put into jewellery, particularly gold items which are easily sold when money is needed unexpectedly. Gold jewellery is always sold with a paper guaranteeing the gold content, and stating the price of the workmanship separately. This is produced on resale. It is usual to buy jewellery with the minimum amount of workmanship. Farmers usually spend little on other durable consumption goods. Cars and refrigerators, which are signs of wealth for urban dwellers, are useless in villages far from the main roads and electricity supply, and are not—as in some societies—acquired for prestige alone when they cannot be used. Most villagers own transistor radios which are important not only for the amusement they provide but also for obtaining weather forecasts. Returned emigrants will often construct a new house in their village. Most farmers probably prefer to put money into goods which either help to keep the family together (a house, more land and farming equipment) or which are easily realizable if disaster strikes and cash is needed quickly.

The farmer with extra cash has a number of calls on it alternative to capital accumulation. He may prefer or have pressure put on him to loan it out or make gifts to relatives and friends. In return however he can usually call on them for similar services or for use of labour in busy seasons. Gambling during the slack season by farmers, and more continuously by landlords, probably leads to considerable circulation of small amounts of spare cash. However, in some cases money used in gambling appears to concentrate in the hands of gambling-house proprietors, who may have leadership positions in the village, and who take it out of the area for investment in towns. Gambling is an important social activity and associated with all festivals. A farmer who never gambled would probably not gain much approval in his community. Weddings and funerals require considerable cash outlay. It does not appear usual for farmers to budget for these occasions and to do so may be regarded as inauspicious; but many farmers join traditional associations, paying in monthly to receive a lump sum when such events occur (see below, p. 178).

In some areas indigenous farmers could increase their income by switching to vegetable growing. There are several reasons why few do so at present. One is that rice needs less labour, and they are in a better position than immigrants to send sons to work abroad where greater income can be earned than in Hong Kong's urban areas by unskilled workers. Emigration is largely confined to particular areas, however, and depends largely on contacts established over the years with jobs overseas. Again, many rice farmers feel they lack the skill

170

of the immigrants in vegetable growing and cannot compete with them commercially. Further, vegetable crops are more readily stolen than rice crops; immigrants live on their plots of land while villagers often live out of sight of their fields. In one area members of a large lineage have taken up vegetable farming and it has been possible to start a marketing co-operative based on lineage organization (each segment providing one committee member). There, it is said, the crops are relatively secure: 'kinsmen would not steal from each other'. Another reason is that some farmers hold that rice growing is more honourable than vegetable cultivation. But religious and social activities do not appear to be as closely connected with rice growing in the New Territories as in some Eastern countries (Japan, for example, where such a connection can provide a disincentive to change of crop), and it is difficult to assess the importance of this attitude. However, it is one which has been remarked upon by several observers in the area (see also Pratt, 1960, p. 150).

Although farmers want to increase their income and recognize the value of capital accumulation, there is one item in their religious ideology which can have a deleterious effect on capital formation and also on the most efficient use of some of their fixed assets. This is the belief in *fung-shui* (C): literally, 'wind and water'. *Fung-shui* is the effect which arrangements of land, buildings, trees, graves and other developments on land are believed to have on the destiny and fortune of individuals and groups. *Fung-shui* can be improved by planting trees and constructing ponds. But farmers might also abandon fields, houses and buildings used in farming if an alteration in their *fung-shui* takes place through construction of buildings in the locality. Villagers have successfully prevented the building of a new post-office badly needed to handle remittances, and have delayed the construction of new paths, irrigation schemes and petrol stations. At the time of writing (1962) one group is demanding the demolition of quarters built to house staff of a large foreign bank's rural branch (established mainly to handle loans to farmers). Sometimes farmers gain financially from such objections: compensation is paid to overcome the objections, and the project which is of direct or indirect use to them is completed (although the farmers may abandon some of their fixed assets). In other cases projects are abandoned or another site is chosen. Each district has its own fixed scale of compensation for *fung-shui* disturbed by removal of graves. In one area the District Officer is empowered to spend up to H.K. $500 (H.K. $16=£1 sterling) to compensate for removal of the more expensive kind of grave. It is not of course irrational of farmers to desire compensation for changes which they believe will have a bad effect on their livelihood. It may be, however, that the relatively low prices paid for land resumed by Government for development purposes, and the difficulties encountered by farmers who wish to convert land themselves, sometimes encourage them to use a religious sanction which they know from experience can be effective with foreigners and Chinese alike. The question of *fung-shui* beliefs, and the way they function as an economic and political weapon in Hong Kong generally, appear to justify fuller investigation.

Capital: Immigrant Vegetable Farmers

According to an estimate by the Co-operative Development Department, in 1959 an immigrant farming family of six needed about $2,130 to start cultivating four *táu-chùng* with vegetables. Equipment essential for the first crop are land, seeds, fertilizers (a common saying in the New Territories is that the soil holds the vegetables up while the fertilizers grow them), a few tools, and bamboo sticks for certain types of vegetables. A hut to live in is also essential. The farmer would probably not start until he was able to build a hut because of difficulties of finding accommodation elsewhere nearby. His land would almost certainly be rented. Few vegetable farmers can afford to buy land. The best vegetable areas are near urban areas. Indigenous farmers who wish to sell land will usually seek out those who want it for development and can offer higher prices. Although there are fairly plentiful supplies of short-term credit now available in the Territories (see below, pp. 177–82), long-term credit facilities, such as would be necessary for purchase of land by most vegetable farmers, are not so plentiful. Moreover, high rents do not provide as strong an incentive to purchase land as they do for the rice farmer, since they represent a smaller proportion of the value of the output. It may be that many immigrant farmers think in terms of returning eventually to China, which might further reduce the incentive to purchase land.

The immigrant would probably need a long-term loan to build his house unless he had brought savings with him, or articles he could sell—jewellery, for example. Some immigrants might work as hired labourers until they had saved enough to set up on their own; others might obtain a loan from a kinsman living in Hong Kong. Many immigrants have some kinsman or relative by marriage in Hong Kong. Those coming from areas near the border sometimes have marriage connections with villages in the New Territories.

It might be possible for the new farmer straight away to buy seeds, chemical fertilizers and insecticides on credit from shops in the local market town; he could almost certainly do so after harvesting his first crop successfully (about two months after planting). In the early days of migration some farmers brought seeds from their home farms and produced further seeds from the vegetables they grew. This meant that they tended to specialize in those particular vegetables

172

they had grown in their homeland. Today better strains of seeds are available in shops and most farmers grow a variety of vegetables.

The question of initial finances of immigrants is one on which little information is available at present. Certainly once the immigrants are established, a number of short-term credit facilities are open to them. Little equipment is needed by vegetable farmers for marketing their produce. Transport and baskets are supplied by the Vegetable Marketing Organization (set up in 1946) which has a monopoly of the transport and wholesale marketing of vegetables (see also below, *passim*). The VMO charges individual farmers a 10 per cent commission on sales for its services. It has now handed over the bulk of operations to twenty-six marketing co-operatives which between them handle about 75 per cent of vegetables grown in Hong Kong. (The monopoly does not extend to Hong Kong island.) The VMO also takes 10 per cent commission from these societies, but returns 3 per cent for their handling expenses and provision of other facilities. The majority of vegetable farmers, certainly the majority of immigrants, belong to these co-operatives. For his small membership fee, the farmer obtains credit facilities and cheap fertilizer (night-soil) purchased in bulk by co-operatives from the VMO which has a night-soil maturation and distribution scheme. The Kadoorie Agricultural Aid Association also supplies individual farmers cultivating from three to seven *táu-chùng* with free insecticide sprayers and additional interest-free loans to replace them when worn out. Those with more than seven *táu-chùng* can obtain interest-free loans for the purchase of sprayers, and those farming less than three *táu-chùng* may have the use of sprayers supplied by this association to co-operative societies. Water-pumps may also be available to co-operative members through joint purchase by societies.

Vegetable farmers obtain advice on the use of fertilizers, machinery and insecticides and are said to be more open to new ideas about the handling of equipment and new farming methods than are indigenous rice farmers. Nevertheless, they appear to be somewhat reluctant to expand their scale of operations even when conditions make this feasible. A farming family can live on four *táu-chùng*, but it might increase its net income in some instances by the cultivation of more land using either more capital equipment and less labour per unit of land, or more hired labour. This might also release some members of the household for work in more lucrative pursuits elsewhere. In some areas hired labour is more readily available than in others; unfortunately they generally are remote places with poor communications and poor soil. There are some vegetable farms of up to twenty *tau-chùng* run with hired labour; they are usually managed by former city dwellers rather than by traditional farmers. It is said that traditional vegetable farmers who go into larger-scale cultivation with

173

hired labour are generally poor managers who do not pay their labourers sufficiently and are unwilling to hire supervisory staff, so that large-scale ventures often fail. Today many immigrants are educating their children for non-farming occupations. This will probably mean that in the future they will have to reorganize their methods of farming if they themselves are to remain in vegetable cultivation.

One of the difficulties of increased capitalization in vegetable farming is that most farmers operate within narrow margins and, like indigenous farmers, wish to keep their assets in liquid form. They tend to operate with a minimum of both producer and consumer durables, and rarely, for example, build more than a cheap wooden hut for themselves. Like rice farmers, they have other calls on their resources, of which their obligations to family and other kinsmen in China are the most significant. These obligations are usually greater than in the case of indigenous farmers. They send money and food home fairly regularly, with extra amounts at the Chinese New Year, and, unlike the rice farmers who help their kin, they receive no services or goods in return for these gifts. They also lend money to other farmers coming from the same area in the homeland in return for labour for planting and harvesting of crops, and join a number of loan associations providing social as well as financial benefits.

Saving

It is my impression that farmers do not generally budget for capital expenditures out of current income, putting away small sums of money, say, monthly or yearly, for the purpose. Most farmers operate within narrow margins, and this method of providing for capital expenditure would be very protracted for most of them. When indigenous or immigrant farmers think in terms of acquiring capital goods or of putting money into some external investment, they tend to think in terms of having a lump sum of money available for the purpose there and then: perhaps through gambling, an unexpectedly large remittance from a kinsman abroad, sale of land, or the receipt of a long-term loan.

Many farmers find themselves in difficulties through selling their land and then using the proceeds in gambling, entertaining friends and relatives to expensive dinners, or gifts to relatives. A man who does not use for such purposes some part of a suddenly-acquired large sum of money would not meet with approval in his community. However, a man who lets all his money go in this way would also probably be despised, particularly if he had a family to support. His kinsmen would then have to help him out in various ways such as by finding him a job or lending him money. But it might be difficult for an indigenous farmer, in particular, to keep a suddenly-acquired large sum of money to himself. Pressure might be brought to bear on him by relatives and friends to make loans or gifts. In this respect the immigrant farmer might be slightly more fortunate, although he would probably send part of a sudden windfall to relatives in China, for which he could expect little in return.

Many farmers have small sums in excess of living expenses when they harvest their crops or sell their pigs. Both indigenous and immigrant farmers sell their crops for cash. Indigenous farmers also generally have an additional cash income from part of the wages of a household member working in one of the towns. Many also receive remittances from abroad. The main regular expenses of farmers are food (no farmers are completely self-sufficient) including cooking oil, pork, fish, soy bean, and rice. Rice farmers do not eat the rice they produce but buy or exchange it for lower quality rice. Small sums of money may be put into jewellery (occasionally gold bars), or may be lent out to friends and relatives, or put into traditional associations, many of which provide both short-term credit and periodic goods or services. Money is invested in this way for weddings, funerals, education expenses, New Year festival food, and clothes. Some associations specialize in items of this kind. Farmers sometimes lend out cash which is not exactly 'spare': that is, they are at the same time both lenders and borrowers.

The Co-operative Development Department has been trying to persuade co-operative societies to build up revolving loan funds and to start associated savings schemes. The system for vegetable co-operatives is for the VMO to deduct an additional percentage—about 5 per cent—from total proceeds from members' sales of vegetables. This is returned to the society, partly for its revolving fund, the remainder to be put into individual savings accounts when there is an associated savings scheme. Most societies now have revolving funds in operation, but few have savings schemes. The more successful savings schemes are run by small-scale societies in which administration works more efficiently. In some societies members may withdraw savings at will, and in others for specific purposes only. In one, for example, they may be withdrawn for education expenses, for marriage of a family member, and for medical or funeral expenses. It appears that in general savings schemes of this kind are not popular, possibly because farmers prefer the social benefits of membership of traditional associations which 'save' for such purposes, and also the use of spare cash for making loans to kinsmen and friends.

Banking facilities have increased greatly in the rural areas in recent years. It is difficult to obtain much information on their use by farmers, as distinct from their use by co-operative societies. Some banks handle remittances from emigrants, and sometimes part of a remittance is kept in a bank until the emigrant returns. Banks also provide loans for those wishing to emigrate, often with land given as security.

In Chinese traditional peasant society control over household income and decisions regarding its use were in the hands of the male head who was the most senior in generation. Today in the New Territories this system probably still continues in the main among immigrant vegetable growers. The vegetable-growing household operates as a single production unit, and cash income goes directly to the head of the family. His children who work on the family plot are given pocket-money and his wife housekeeping money by the household head who will also decide how the rest of the income is to be allocated among various uses. For the indigenous household, however, opportunities in the urban areas and abroad for earning cash incomes appear to have brought changes in command over income and in decision-making. It might be difficult for a family head to know how much is earned by a son working away, particularly if he is working abroad, and difficult for the head of household to dictate to outside earners how their income should be spent. Certainly most sons help to support their households, but it is unlikely that the household head has complete command over their incomes. For the first few months of working abroad, especially in restaurants in England, it is said that little can be sent back to the village. This is particularly so when, as is sometimes the case, the employer initially lends money for the employee's fare, which must usually be repaid within the first few months of employment. One farmer told the Agricultural and Forestry Department that he received annually about $1,500 from two sons working in England. (He was supporting a household consisting of eight persons.) This is much less than can be gained by one man cultivating vegetables on two *táu-chùng* of land. I have been told that many emigrants in London spend a great deal of their earnings there. Some spend a large proportion of their wages in gambling. Others, however, appear to save part of their earnings, and groups of restaurant workers coming from the same area of the Territories start a restaurant of their own.

It is often the father of a young family which has set up as a separate household who emigrates. In some areas it is more common for a man to go soon after the birth of his first son, leaving his wife and child in his parents' home. In many cases wives appear to have greater say in the handling of the remittances at the village end than do the fathers-in-law with whom they are living. I am told that the majority of remittances go towards the household's daily expenses, and that it is the man's wife who usually decides on their allocation among various needs. When a larger sum is sent, it may be accompanied by a letter giving instructions how it is to be used. It seems unlikely that many men would leave to their women-folk vital negotiations over capital investments they might wish to make with their overseas earnings, for example the purchase of land or the building of a new house. It is more likely that they would give instructions for large sums to be left in the bank until their return. Some men who emigrate for longer periods return about every three years for short visits during which they are able to handle any savings they have sent back for investment purposes. The question of the handling and use of remittances in the Territories is one, however, on which little information is available.

Credit

There are a number of sources of credit open to both indigenous and immigrant farmers. Loans may be obtained from relatives and friends, more particularly in the case of indigenous farmers. They may not be entirely serviced, but the debtor may be required to provide labour or credit in return when needed by the creditor. Credit, in the form of either money or goods, may be obtained by both kinds of farmer from agencies connected with trade and marketing. Shops giving goods on credit may require a guarantor or *taam-pó-yān*. He will be a person known to both creditor and debtor, and it is usual for the debtor to give him a gift for his services. The *taam-pó* system enables a small creditor to have a circle of debtors much wider than if operations were restricted only to those known to him personally. Money is usually lent in small amounts for relatively short periods, from, say, a few weeks to six months. This again allows the circle of debtors to be fairly wide. The practice does mean, however, that loans from such sources can in general be used only for meeting short-term production costs or unexpected commitments calling for relatively small amounts of cash. Other short-term credit sources are traditional associations and impersonal organizations. The latter usually require that the loan be used only for production purposes, although checks to see whether the farmer complies with this condition are not usually made. Longer-term loans can be obtained from 'money-lenders', religious organizations with landed property and sometimes lineages owning property. 'Money-lenders' are not a special class, but individuals, perhaps themselves farmers, who are prepared to lend to strangers without *taam-pó yān*. (Sometimes they are Village Representatives.) Usually, however, they require the loan to be secured in other ways. They charge about 10 per cent interest per month.

There are some traditional associations which are purely credit associations, and some provide additional benefits. Some save for a specific purpose—a festival or annual dinner, for example—and lend the money to members in the interim period. Members are usually known to one another personally, although outsiders may be permitted to join if guaranteed by a member who is known to the group. Indigenous associations usually operate within a village or group of adjacent villages, while immigrant bodies are usually based in membership on regional origins. Because of the regional nature of immigrant settlement they tend also to be restricted to a particular locality.

Rules for both kinds of association varied regionally in China. Those operating in the New Territories are similar to some of the forms described for traditional China (see for example Fei Hsiao-Tung, 1943, pp. 267–74, and Arthur Smith, 1899, pp. 152–60). Such types of association have also been noted for other peasant groups (Firth, pp. 31–2, above). In credit associations members make fixed monthly payments, and each member on one occasion gets the use of the total collected. The association thus exists for as many months as there are members, but it might be renewed at the end of the period and so operate on a semi-permanent basis. Often it consists of 'life' members (those individuals known to one another personally) and 'occasional' members (outsiders guaranteed by a member).

Loan associations at present may handle from about \$300–\$1,000 a month. When a member defaults on his monthly contributions, the amount is customarily borne by the head of the association (if he is receiving a commission for his services as leader), by the other members, or by his guarantor if the defaulter is an occasional member. Festival associations may accumulate as much as \$15,000–\$20,000. (Their outlays include expenditures on a Chinese opera, dinner, wine and pork distribution as well as on ritual paraphernalia and services of priests.) A few festivals are held at intervals of two years or longer. The sums available for lending may then be considerable, and occasionally loans are made for relatively long periods. In the semi-religious associations an important sanction for the repayment is said to be fear of punishment from the god for whom the festival is held. Another popular type of association is the 'pork society'. Each member contributes \$2–\$3 a month and the money is used to buy pigs for slaughter at the Chinese New Year. (Pigs are cheaper when bought in bulk.) The meat is usually distributed in equal weight among members, the best cuts apparently going to those reckoned to have the highest social standing in the group. In lineage-based associations the allocation of the various cuts may be according to kinship status. Loans from funds of pork societies may be available to members for from two to ten months. Amounts lent are said to vary from about \$50–\$200 per member, with interest working out at about 5 per cent a month.

Buddhist nunneries and halls of residence for laywomen and those for members of other Chinese religions are a popular source of longer-term loans. They often have considerable funds for lending, derived from income from landed property and arable land, from the accumulated life-savings of inmates, many of whom are retired domestic servants, and from regular contributions of outside members for their ritual services. Some also run funeral benefit schemes, and lend part of their accumulated funds. These organizations are prepared to lend to strangers, and arrangements are often fairly sophisticated. A credit document is often drawn up and endorsed in the District Office. Property is usually required as security. This may in fact make it difficult for immigrants to get loans from this source. Interest rates are said to be about 3 per cent to 5 per cent a month.

Immigrants may be able to get long-term loans from ancestral associations, interest payments being settled at the Chinese New Year. Lineage members have first claim on funds, however, and may not be required to pay interest. Temple associations and land-owning *ooî* also lend money, mainly to members but occasionally to strangers.

Both rice and vegetable farmers obtain credit from feed and fertilizer dealers. Material may be obtained on credit to the value of $100–$2,000 for one to six months, 15–20 per cent being added to the market prices of the materials when payment is made. Repayment usually takes place after the farmer's produce has been marketed. Food-stuffs, of the dried variety, for the household, are also obtainable on credit, prices being a little higher than those to cash customers. Payment is usually made monthly.

For those vegetable farmers who do not belong to co-operatives, loans may be available from middlemen who collect their crops, take them to the wholesale market in Kowloon and arrange their sale. (Prices arrived at in middlemen transactions in the market are subject to approval of a market salesman.) A commission of 2–3 per cent is charged for this service, but loans are usually made free of interest as an inducement to farmers to use the services of such middlemen. Middlemen may be personal friends of the farmers, marketing their own crops at the same time; or in certain districts they may be vegetable farmers who have performed this kind of service regularly since the establishment of the vmo. Such middlemen lend out from about $50–$500 for from three to twelve months.

Before the establishment of the wholesale market in Kowloon, vegetable farmers marketed through wholesale middlemen, termed *laan*. (The term *laan* also referred to their place of operation.) There was no central wholesale market, and each *laan* had his own centre and his own circle of retail clients. The farmer, it is said, did not then have easy access to knowledge of current retail prices in the town where most of the vegetables were sold, and was often cheated heavily on prices. The vmo was established to eliminate the *laan* system in Kowloon and the New Territories, although it still operates on Hong Kong island with Government-provided wholesale markets as the centre of operations. Under the old system, *laan* often made loans to farmers. Today the VMO has taken over their credit functions (see below). A brief outline of the old system may be of interest.

Laan operated with their own godowns (warehouses), lorries—some had fleets of lorries—and baskets for transporting vegetables. Sometimes regular retailing clients had shares in a *laan* enterprise. Some *laan* had agents or brokers operating in collecting stations in market towns. *Laan* and brokers were usually townsmen. They charged about 10 per cent for transporting vegetables and an extra 1 per cent per picul for handling charges. Sometimes brokers charged an extra commission. Brokers were more numerous in the post-war period when there was a shortage of *laan* transport, and some of them operated privately, selling their services to a *laan*. It is common to accuse middlemen in peasant societies of sharp practice; in the case of Hong Kong *laan* such accusations appear often to have been justified. But the farmers needed their services. They lacked transport facilities; baskets were expensive unless bought in bulk; many farmers could not spare the time to bring their crop to market; they lacked contacts with retailers in town; and they needed the credit provided by *laan*. Sometimes farmers were paid in advance for their standing crops: this of course involved risk on the part of the *laan*, but the prices paid were usually very low. Sometimes a group of farmers sent a representative to accompany their vegetables on the *laan* lorry; but he could do little to get better prices for the farmers. A common practice in selling to retailers was known as 'silent dealing': bargaining between the *laan* and the retailer was conducted by use of an abacus (a beaded frame for arithmetical calculations), and the representative of the farmers could not see the agreed price as the abacus was hidden from his view. If the price offered by the *laan* to the farmers was refused, they still had to pay the transport costs. Since vegetables are highly perishable, few farmers could risk taking their crop away from the *laan* centre and trying to sell it elsewhere. The majority of *laan* also are said to have been members of *laan* associations which fixed the prices to be paid to farmers. Farmers might be able to hawk their vegetables themselves; but they could not easily compete with regular retailers established in particular areas, who could cause trouble for the hawkers.

A few groups of farmers set up marketing associations among themselves to break the *laan* system. Farmers got together and bought a lorry and baskets to bring in their crops themselves. A representative would retail them in town or sell them to retailers with whom they established connections. I have no information as to how they managed to establish such connections. When they themselves retailed, they presumably had to operate in less advantageous parts of the town than the *laan.*

The VMO has been able to destroy the *laan* system. After the war there was a general shortage of transport, and because of this the *laan* were weakened in their operations. The majority had also lost their godowns, were short of money for making loans to farmers and for providing some of the other services traditionally offered to farmers or their representatives. These services had included the provision of free meals and the supply of dried foods on credit. The loans and services of the pre-war period had probably inhibited farmers from protesting more forceably against the *laan* system. Prices received in the new wholesale market were also considerably higher than those obtained through *laan.* The VMO was able to extend its monopoly over sales because of its control of the transport of vegetables (comparatively few vegetables were sold in the New Territories themselves). It had the lorries, and was, additionally, given exclusive right by Ordinance to transport vegetables or issue permits to private lorries for transportation. The police are supposed to stop all lorries carrying vegetables to market without permit.

The VMO received from the Government an initial loan of $50,000 to finance operations, and the commission charged on sales was to cover the rest of its expenses. Today profits from sale of night-soil from its maturation scheme are an additional source of revenue. Co-operatives were later started under its leadership at a number of collecting stations set up for transporting vegetables. The more successful have been those in which membership is based on regional origins. Some with 'mixed' membership have been less successful.

The original purpose of the formation of marketing co-operatives was to organize farmers to withstand pressure from *laan* who wished to crush the wholesale market and to build up groupings which could ultimately take over the operation of the market. One of their most important functions today, in addition to that of marketing, is handling loans for members. They act as members' guarantors and, in principle at least, they scrutinize members' production records before recommending them for loans. When loans are not serviced by the debtor, the co-operative has to meet obligations on his behalf. Usually loan obligations are in fact honoured by the member. The paid-up share capital of the co-operative acts as security for loans to members. Co-operatives usually charge a commission for handling members' loans.

Loans are made from the VMO Loan Fund, which provides credit, usually for periods of less than a year, at interest rates of 0.25 per cent a month (which is lower than in traditional societies). Outsiders can obtain loans at 0.5 per cent interest, but in fact most are taken up by co-operative society members. The Co-operative Development Department (which now incorporates the VMO) also handles loans from the Joseph Trust Fund, which are used mainly for purchase of seeds, fertilizers and bamboo poles. The considerable use to which both funds have been put so far suggests that traditional sources of credit are far from adequate. In 1961, 1,600 members of co-operative societies received loans totalling $770,000. The VMO Fund was recently increased to almost double its original size to meet growing demands as the number of societies and members increased. Co-operatives are being persuaded to operate their own loan schemes to relieve strain on the two funds.

Provision of credit is the main function of pig-raising co-operatives, and funds are also obtainable by members from the Joseph Fund. The Kadoorie Agricultural Loan Fund is handled by the Agricultural and Forestry Department. It charges no interest and its policy is to operate directly through individuals rather than groups. Debts may be cancelled if the recipient can prove hardship.

Indigenous rice farmers market their produce through millers operating in market towns. They either charge about $1.50 a picul for milling, returning bran to the farmer for pig feed; or keep the bran (most millers own pig-feed shops) and make no milling charge; or, when rice is wanted for consumption, mill free, returning one katty of lower grade rice for one of home-grown produce. Millers also provide credit. Farmers have few complaints against this system and have shown no desire to establish or join rice-marketing co-operatives. Prices of rice do not fluctuate to the same extent as vegetable prices; farmers can easily find out what the current price is; they can store their crop against better prices; and transport is not a problem since they sell within the New Territories. Millers are usually country people who are known personally to the farmers.

SUMMARY AND CONCLUSIONS

With existing economic patterns, probably neither indigenous rice-farming households nor immigrant vegetable-farming households generally can play a very significant role in capital formation in the New Territories. Most farmers of both groups operate within extremely narrow margins. Although vegetable farmers are the more successful of the two in agriculture and able to exist by farming alone, few have much income in excess of the requirements of daily necessaries. The indigenous farmer's total income from non-agricultural sources and from rice and pig-rearing also is generally not large. Both groups of farmers, and particularly vegetable farmers, rely greatly on short-term credit to cover production costs; the latter probably have slightly better supplies of credit from co-operative and impersonal sources, and the former from traditional sources. The vagaries of the weather and of imports of vegetables and pigs from China, both of which are largely unpredictable, tend to inhibit farmers from investment in items not easily convertible into cash and from saving over long periods for the acquisition of capital assets. There are also a number of factors, not directly 'economic', which affect particularly the uses to which any 'spare' money is put, the type of assets acquired, and use of existing assets. At present it is possible to make only a few general observations regarding some of these factors. Field research would probably show up considerable variations in circumstances in different localities—depending for example on such differences as kinship and village organization, land tenure practices, proximity to towns, patterns of regional settlement of immigrants and their relationships with indigenous people, and patterns of emigration among the latter.

There are a number of uses for available cash which may have priority over saving for eventual investment. This may be particularly so for farmers living in well-integrated village communities. The farmer may have to meet constant demands for gifts and loans from kinsmen and neighbours. He may simultaneously be both a borrower and lender in regard to a number of individuals. There is a tendency to lend out cash in small sums for short periods so as to maintain a wide circle of debtors on which the farmer can call for similar loans and for other forms of aid which may be received in lieu of full servicing of debts. Such small amounts are usually used for meeting production costs or for ceremonial expenses. There appears to be an acute scarcity of funds for long-term loans in the region. Loans from traditional associations and institutions also tend to be short-term.

Villagers who wish to acquire greater status in their communities probably spend as lavishly as possible on ceremonials, and part of any sudden windfall on 'throwing' dinners. The desire to spend well on such ceremonials as weddings and funerals encourages the formation of special clubs, and there are also clubs for religious festivals.

It is possible that for immigrant farmers some of the uses of 'spare' cash described above are of lesser significance, partly because of differences in their patterns of residence, and partly perhaps because they are less traditionalist. However, the majority are under pressure to send cash and commodities to relatives in China, for which they may expect little material return. It is difficult to assess the drain of resources from immigrant households in this way. My impression is that at present it might be considerable.

Calls on money of the type outlined above add to the difficulties which peasant farmers have in building up wealth. Yet wealth is probably an important qualification for those aspiring to political leadership in most areas in the New Territories, certainly for membership of Rural Committees and the Consultative Council. (Most members of Rural Committees are elected from among Village Representatives, and all by them.) Members will also need considerable spare time in order to attend to their tasks of office. Most Rural Committee members and a good proportion of all Village Representatives appear to be individuals whose main income comes from investments in local towns, the industrial town or the main urban areas of Hong Kong and Kowloon. They usually have some investments in projects which they do not manage themselves: shops, land investment companies and schools, for example. It may be significant for their ability to build up wealth that few of them spend much time in residence in their villages of origin and of which they are representatives. They may thus have been able to avoid some of the pressures on their finances which permanent village residents have to meet. I have been told by a Hong Kong University research worker on one of the islands (see footnote 1, page 158) that in his area such men, once their wealth is established, become the money-lenders and gambling-shop proprietors of their locality, and that income obtained from their gambling businesses (gambling-shops are in fact illegal) tends to be drained away to the towns. The fact that a section of a village may be in the debt of wealthy individuals aspiring to local leadership may form a sanction for their election. We need to know much more of the methods of wealth accumulation of such people and their economic role generally in the countryside. But it is not my impression that they are usually big landlords or that absentee landlordism with its usual concomitant of the drain of wealth from the rural area is a serious problem in the New Territories, although it may be so in one or two areas (D. Y. Lin, 1951). Rather, there tends to be a number of small landlords who live and use their income mainly in the area.

Managers of lineage and other corporately owned land are usually men with business experience and education. Such men may be in a position to help their community to increase in prosperity by converting such land to more profitable uses. However, there are problems in doing so connected with the terms of trust on which such land is held. Objections to new uses may come from Government, or from other members of the trust who may see only the immediate effect of such conversion on them—a reduction in the amount of land available to them for rice cultivation.

Near the expanding urban and industrial areas villagers can often sell their land on favourable terms. A common problem of smallness of holdings (partly due to rules of inheritance) and therefore unsuitability for development is often overcome by the emergence of land brokers, sometimes village leaders themselves, who arrange for a group of farmers to sell a block of holdings to a developer. Farmers

184

usually lack advice, however, on how best to invest their profits from land sales, and such money is often quickly used up in financing dinners, gifts, gambling and small loans to friends and relatives. The desire to sell land sometimes causes conflicts within the household, especially between sons and fathers. In some areas land can alternatively be rented out for greater income to vegetable farmers or pig- and poultry-raisers (although members of corporate land-holding groups may sometimes prevent managers from doing this with joint owned land). The high regard for landlord status in the rural areas often encourages farmers to try to live off such income rather than to invest all or part of it and work in other occupations to increase income further. A study of rising land values in the New Territories and their effects on social organization would clearly be of value at the present time. My general impression is that changes in land values may be having a considerable effect on the traditional social organization of a number of parts of the New Territories.

In emigrant areas, particularly those remote from urban developments, villagers may sometimes receive remittances large enough to yield cash in excess of immediate needs. Returned emigrants may return with savings, or have them accumulating in a bank for their return. Often there is a lack of knowledge of investment opportunities in such communities, and there is a tendency for the money to be used in first financing a new house, and then in meeting the various types of social commitments already described. It may be difficult for households with members working abroad to control the amounts of money which are sent back; but it is my general impression that more might be sent back if there were better knowledge of investment outlets. In one case coming to my notice the District Office offered materials to a village for building local improvements. Villagers are supposed to supply the labour in building local projects with materials provided in this way. Since there was a shortage of labour in the village itself, it was necessary to hire paid workers. At first the village said they were unable to afford this. After several months, however, they indicated their willingness to pay for the labour: the money had been obtained by writing to relatives abroad.

The development of capital projects (including public works projects) in the area may have to meet the problem of *fung-shui* objections from villagers, particularly perhaps when villagers cannot see great and immediate benefit to themselves from such projects. Land policy may also aggravate demand for *fung-shui* compensation when public works are carried out on land previously used by villagers. *Fung-shui* beliefs can also lead to the abandoning of assets by villagers themselves.

Probably the greatest contribution to capital development in the area generally must come from outsiders with greater resources—

Capital, Saving and Credit in Peasant Societies

from both Government and private investors. Nevertheless, something might be done to increase the prosperity of rural inhabitants by working through local leaders to bring about the more economic use of land. It might also be possible to start village investment companies through which rural people might use part of their income in investments in town areas. It must be remembered, however, that any plan to help villagers to use their land more profitably may adversely affect the livelihood of immigrant farmers who at present rent land from them.[1]

---

[1] *Note.* In this essay, romanizations follow the Cantonese dialect pronunciation and are according to the system used in B. F. Meyer and T. F. Wempe, *The Student's Cantonese-English Dictionary*, New York, 1947.

9

Institutions for Capital Formation and Distribution Among Fijians

BY C. S. BELSHAW

This essay[1] concerns itself with capital formation and use among the Fijian people of the Sigatoka[2] River Valley and adjacent coastal areas, in the administrative province of Nadroga and Navosa. Within Fiji there are a number of variations of traditional culture, but in the area of which I write the culture is relatively homogeneous. There are of course differences in the emphases of production as between coastal and riverine people; between those who cultivate the fertile alluvial flats and those whose garden plots are carved out of hillside forests; and between those who today are in close contact with roads and the settled population of East Indian immigrants, and those whose villages are seldom visited by any outsider. There are also a number of differences in culture which serve as symbols of differentiation as between local groups. Among these are minor differences of dialect and vocabulary, some details of marriage ceremonies, ceremonial group-names, guardian agricultural spirits, and ritually significant food-stuffs (erroneously described in the literature as totems).

In Nadroga there is a high chief bearing the title Tui Nadroga. Although his ceremonial precedence is recognized by the numerous other chiefs in the area who call themselves 'Tui', his political writ runs only in a small segment of the total province, and it so happens that almost all of the villages I studied regard themselves as in political opposition to him. Indeed, there are records of armed conflict in historical times. The social organization thus differs from the

[1] Based upon field-work carried out in 1958–59, on leave of absence from the University of British Columbia, with the assistance of the Tri-Institutional Pacific Program, the United States Social Research Council and the Canada Council.
[2] Fijian orthography adopts the following conventions: 'g' reads 'ng'; 'q' reads 'ngg'; 'b' reads 'mb'; and 'd' reads 'nd'.

'ideal-type' described for other parts of Fiji, such as Bau. The hierarchies of ceremonial and political status have been fluid and highly adaptive; the largest stable political units (*vanua*) are small in population (100 to 1,000) and, until Government registration, have been insecure in structure and status.

A formal summary description of Fijian social structure cannot do justice to its capacity to change and adapt, yet a summary is all that can be attempted here. The patrilineal descent pattern is well known, and is now uniform throughout most of Fiji. At the base there is a small patrilineage (*i tokatoka*, or *bito*) of four or five families, living in a defined section of a village. The common ancestor is known and of recent generation; in Navosa the *bito* had a small symbolic and ritual hut in which elderly males communed with the ancestors. A *bito* should be regarded as a segment of a larger patrilineage, the *mataqali*, which is also descended from a named ancestor, although the genealogical links between constituent *bito* may be impossible to demonstrate. Classificatory kin terms apply within the *mataqali*, which is co-residential, exogamous, contains a chiefly leader, and is recognized by statute as the basic land-holding unit.

A group of *mataqali*, again linked by kinship and a myth of common descent, is the *yavusa*. One *mataqali* is considered to be senior, and its head holds chiefly responsibility. Other *mataqali* are allocated various ceremonial responsibilities and statuses. Constituent *mataqali* do not necessarily live contiguously; they may spread over several villages, and one village may contain partial representation from more than one *yavusa*. The *yavusa* is a substantially independent political unit.

One *yavusa*, or, more usually, a number of *yavusa* in federation, may constitute a *vanua*, symbolized through the recognition of its leading chief as paramount, and through reference to him by the ceremonial name of the *vanua*. Such a unit held territory by force of arms, and entered into alliances with other such units for specific war-like purposes.

All the above social units made use of patrilineal principles in counting membership. But of just as great an importance in the web of Fijian relationships are the affinal principles variously interpreted in different parts of the country. Essentially, marriage links are predominantly with families outside the groom's village. Since marriage is virilocal, village women are nearly all from other communities. A great deal of the ceremonial directly or by implication emphasizes affinal relationships, and a large proportion of non-ceremonial exchange and contact flows along the same paths. Social units and villages are thus inter-linked by a vastly complex criss-cross of interests (and rivalries), which today have become so widespread

188

through advanced communications that the Fijians are rapidly constituting a unitary society as a whole.

While it is over-simplified to say that within this social schema the individual household is the productive unit, and the unit administering domestic expenditure, the statement is approximate enough for most of the purposes of this essay. A household consists centrally of a man of the appropriate *mataqali*, together with his wife and children, but is frequently extended both agnatically and affinally to include such relatives as parents, siblings, cousins, and their families, and occasionally immigrant friends. Possession of a house, and membership in its household, is well known, clearly defined and, in the case of male household heads, established by ceremonial and principles of inheritance, centred upon the ritual status of the *yavu*, or stone foundation. Nevertheless, movement between households, and even between villages for temporary (though often long-term) visiting and residence is a common attribute of Fijian life.

In theory, and in most common practice, agricultural production is based upon the use of a portion of the land of the user's *mataqali*. Frequently, users acquire permission to till soil held by other *mataqali*. In both instances, it would be a severe insult for the *mataqali* to assert its powers and remove a family from land it has been administering. To all intents and purposes, then, the use and inheritance of land once brought into production is a matter of individual judgment, bearing in mind the neighbouring interests of others. Official policy, however, especially in matters affecting alienation and leasing, recognizes the *mataqali* as the sole authority for decisions, although all members, and all chiefs superior to the *mataqali*, obtain a share in the financial return from any alienation procedure.

The primary pursuit in the area of which I write is agriculture, which may be described summarily as highly diversified, and largely cash-oriented. No family, even in the remote mountain fastnesses, lives entirely from the proceeds of subsistence agriculture. Each village or cluster of villages has at least one small distribution centre or store for commercial products, supplemented in the lower valley and on the coast by Indian outlets. I would estimate that dependence on cash is seldom less than 5 per cent of total family intake, that 50 per cent would be quite common towards the coast, and that 90 per cent would describe the position of professionals, such as schoolteachers.[1]

The diversification of agriculture is immediately apparent to any observer who can distinguish the Fijian enterprises, located as many of them are in and out of areas occupied by Indian farms. The crop

[1] Such estimates are of course impressionistic, and await further treatment of data for confirmation or amendment.

189

list includes bananas (for export and town markets), tobacco (for commercial companies and town markets), *yaqona* (a cultivated shrub[1] used in the kava ceremony), taro, yams, sweet potato, melons, tomatoes, beans, potatoes, rice, pumpkin, citrus fruits, cabbage, lettuce, cress (all for roadside and town markets). In the lower valley, near the railhead of the Colonial Sugar Refining Company's tramway, Fijians produce sugar, and along the coast there is some processing of copra, although this is not one of Fiji's major coconut areas. Villagers maintain substantial herds of livestock, principally horses, which are traded for Indian cattle, which are then used to build up herds both for domestic consumption and, increasingly, for butcher supply. It is not usual to find Fijian-owned herds of goats, though this is common among their Indian neighbours. There are two major ancillary enterprises in the area; a large Fijian-operated manganese mine at Vunamoli, owned in partnership with an American firm; and the organization of dancing and entertainment for the benefit of tourists at the Korolevu Hotel on the coast. In addition, some of the coastal people have interested themselves in forestry, specializing in the supply of logs to numerous small sawmills. In short, the Sigatoka River Valley and its environs constitute one of the most productive parts of Fiji, and it has been estimated that Indian and Fijian farmers between them have supplied from this area the bulk of the locally produced foodstuffs marketed in the towns of Viti Levu.

II

In such a society, where production is predominantly based upon the household, and where other forms of joint organization are in process of experimental formation for commercial purposes, capital associated with the household is most important quantitatively, and perhaps from the viewpoint of incentives. Nevertheless, capital held by units wider than the household is becoming of increasing importance. Its formation is a spur to economic growth, even though many of the wider organizations (to be analysed elsewhere) are in themselves failures, since there is a feed-back of experience to individual households, many of which are learning to form capital in new ways.

I would argue that almost all the stock of household assets is predominantly productive in character, since the major day-to-day interest of the household members is in production, and since there are very few frivolous or superfluous assets which do not in some major way contribute to the productive process. Indeed, it is perhaps most revealing to consider the household as a kind of microcosm of the firm. All members except the very young, the very old, and those who are incapacitated or ill, are fully engaged in the production of

[1] *Piper methysticum*, the Polynesian *kava*.

190

goods and services for themselves, for the market, for social exchange and for the community well-being.

From this viewpoint, the house itself is a major asset, and by far the heaviest expenditure a family has to meet. A traditional Fijian house of stone foundation, heavy beams, reed wall, and thick grass-thatch roof, demands elaborate organization of materials and work, requires substantial periodic repairs, and replacement about every fifteen or twenty years. The money value of the construction costs of such a house, including ceremonial rewards to the labour, would, in my estimation, run from £300 for a small three-fathom dwelling of minimal-quality construction, to £1,500 or more for a six-or seven-fathom house of best quality. Costs, which are never paid in cash, are indicative only of the size of the investment, and vary considerably according to materials used, quality of workmanship, and the ceremonial and status implications of the building.

The house is more than a sleeping and eating place for the family, and the symbol of household continuity. It is workshop, office, meeting room, storage room, and hostel combined. Although many small tasks are performed in it during the day, the workshop function is most apparent at night, when men and women have left the fields and gather together for the tasks which remain. Here women gossip as they join to plait mats for sale or ceremonial exchange, and people of all ages help to dry and roll the tobacco. Here the records of financial transactions and property are kept and dealt with, and business negotiations or productive techniques discussed around the *yaqona* bowl. It is the place where capital is assembled through social exchanges and collections. In its rafters are kept stores of tobacco, mats, and other commodities. It is the eating place of the workers, including not merely household members, but others who have been associated with the productive tasks of the day, and who are provided with meals as part of their reward. Here, too, they may sleep between tasks.

Supplementing the village house are other buildings. A small thatch kitchen, sometimes little more than a lean-to, sometimes a substantial storage room, is, in law and practice, associated with each dwelling house. A few of the more energetic farmers maintain an establishment in the fields, as well as in the village. This usually consists of a smaller dwelling, with its kitchen, and sometimes a storage shed for the drying of tobacco, the shelter of implements, and the preservation of tubers.

The maintenance of such buildings is a perennial problem, particularly since the main factor, socially co-ordinated labour, is becoming expensive and scarce. Some individuals and communities have shifted their emphasis to small frame and weatherboard houses with corrugated iron roofs. In many cases, these can be built for £400 to £500, though some more ambitious examples, incorporating several rooms and cement block walls, are considerably more costly. Some of the notable co-operative enterprises have invested their returns in building programmes. But the function of such houses inevitably changes. Because of their smaller size, they cannot act as hostels, or the centre of the larger ceremonial events. Their design and construction limits their use for storage or group work. Their purely domestic function becomes emphasized at the cost of their productive function. It is possible (for this has been discussed in some communities) that a further development will be the retention or expansion of some traditional-style houses to act as ceremonial and working focal points in villages where the domestic houses are of frame.

Houses are relatively bare inside, since most activity is carried out by persons sitting or lying on the floor. Domestic capital consists largely of a small number of utilitarian items, such as pots and pans, china and glassware, traditional-style cooking pots, and a food safe or cupboard. In addition, there are a considerable number of prestige items, which are often of high cash value. Even in the most isolated interior villages, approached only by narrow bridle paths over steep hills, houses contain a few items of heavy furniture—a round table, with a dining chair or two, one or two canvas lounge chairs, at least one large bedstead. These are considered uncomfortable, somewhat a waste of valuable space, and their use would in many cases involve serious breach of Fijian etiquette; they are there to be seen, not for use. On the walls, and particularly around the centre house post or its equivalent, hang family portraits and pictures of royalty, famous boxers, or other favourites. And on beds and floor are quantities of valuable mats, providing soft resting places, and a store of value which can be drawn upon for gifts on ceremonial occasions.

A number of substantial and relatively costly items are to be found in every village, but not distributed through every house. These include sewing machines (perhaps 50 per cent of female clothing is made locally), radios (essential for modern communication, including, for example, the announcement of banana shipment dates), and musical instruments such as guitars and ukuleles. Almost every house has one or more pressure lamps, with supplementary wick-type kerosene lamps. In addition there are a number of articles of traditional manufacture. Every village has at least one household, and sometimes as many as three, which possess the four-or-five-foot-long wooden slit-gong, or *lali*, used to summon friends to a *yaqona* drinking session, or a Church service, or to announce the comings and goings of persons of rank. The village of Nakoro, Navosa, is a centre for the manufacture of large pottery cooking vessels, about three feet in height and beautifully glazed. Although the rough terrain demands that they be

192

transported on the backs of women, for safety's sake, rather than on horses, they are to be found in the kitchens of every house in Navosa, and in a few houses in the Lower Valley and on the coast. Similarly, the small water pots made in the vicinity of Sigatoka are to be found throughout the area, distributed through the mechanisms of ceremonial exchange. Every house has its wooden or pottery *yaqona* bowl but only three or four in each village own the highly prized wooden bowls from the Lau group which alone figure in the highest ceremonial. To own a slit-gong and a major kava bowl, and to make these available for the use of others, is an investment in prestige.

Approximately 50 per cent of households which are involved in agriculture on the alluvial flats or along the coast own ploughs, harrows, and scarifiers, which can be drawn behind horses or bullocks. Various types of harness equipment are common, for the horse is in daily use, and there is the occasional saddle, mainly for official visitors. Hunting spears, heavy for pigs, light for river and reef fishing, are common, as are small hand nets for river fishing and prawn collecting. Canoes have totally disappeared from the scene, as have the heavy seine nets once used in this part of the coast. Canoes have been replaced (but on a small scale such that there is now only one for every two or so villages) by flat bottom punts of uniform design, occasionally powered by small outboard engines. In many villages there is a dearth of equipment such as carpenters' tools and axes; so much so that it seems to be a major task to find hammers and hatchets when house construction is under way. Perhaps investment in small articles of this kind is unrewarding, since loss through careless borrowing must be hazardous. A major item of investment consists in fences, which now surround each cultivated area.

Such personal productive equipment is supplemented by a few central pools held by corporative organizations for their own purposes. Thus Naduri and Narata villages each have a tractor, with appropriate ploughing and cultivating equipment, which is made available to others for rent. Vunamoli owns, through its manganese venture, a substantial share in mining equipment, including a truck and a road to the highway, and air compression machines. There is a marked interest in the careful acquisition of more equipment of this kind, but the history of past failures has made the people cautious. There is a noticeable fear that too much equipment reduces the weight of the labour component, and makes the interests of labour too dependent upon the new types of authority necessary to administer large capital aggregations. Vunamoli is a test case which demonstrates in its history a remarkable willingness to invest, but a determination to keep investment within bounds to preserve independence.

Finally, there is a substantial investment of social capital through public and private interest. Passable roads have been hacked out of

G

the hills and forests, originally by exploring manganese companies, and latterly by Fijians themselves. They are far from adequate, but point to a determined interest. Each of the old administrative sub-divisions known as 'Old Tikina' (in effect, a group of five or six villages, sometimes constituting a *vanua*), maintains an elementary school building and provides part of the school operating costs. With the exception of minor Catholic enclaves, each village is predominantly Methodist. The village church is sometimes no more than a private house cleaned up for Sunday; sometimes it is reserved for church use, but in the style of an ordinary home. In about one out of two or three villages, there is a frame church, by now usually weather-beaten and lacking paint, occasionally equipped with pews.

III

The level of capital indicated in the preceding section indicates a considerable alteration from that which may be presumed for pre-Colonial Melanesian times. I shall demonstrate elsewhere that the Fijian is highly interested in advancing his material well-being through commercially orientated action. Since capital growth is an essential aspect of economic growth in general, it may be asked why the stock of capital has reached this point, but gone, so far, no further. A first stage in arriving at an answer will be to consider the techniques and processes available to the Fijian in his task of capital formation. Since Fijian society is still in process of learning to cope with this problem, the methods used are on the one hand diverse and highly experimental, and on the other hand incomplete and inadequate. In what follows, I shall take the processes represented in each set of institutions used by the Fijians, and examine them from the point of view of their relationship to capital formation, saving, credit use, and negative saving (or dissipation of resources).

The household
Even today the level of production is so low that for most families saving and capital investment, at their present rate of output, is impractical and uncustomary as a regular charge upon income. Efforts have been made from time to time to encourage cash saving, particularly through credit unions, but the Fijian peasant is not in a position to make systematic and regular allocations to capital.

Nevertheless, replacement of capital assets, and minor additions to them, do take place. This is done primarily by selecting specific goals and working to achieve them through initiative in mobilizing and combining labour and physical resources. Traditional methods are still paramount, involving manipulations of the social structure. One example will suffice. A man of Bemana decided to become an independent farmer (that is, a person living primarily outside the village and paying a cash rate exempting him from village public service labour, but otherwise fully a member of Fijian society). He chose a large area of unused *mataqali* land for the site of farm and house. In considering which relatives he should ask to assist him, he hit upon his mother's sister's husband, who was closely related to a high chief of a neighbouring *vanua*. With the help of lineal relatives in his own village, he made appropriate ceremonial presentations, and secured the promise of help in house construction. At an appointed time, selected by reference to the calendar of social obligations (marriages, house building, etc.), the chief led his people to the site of the farm, bringing with them certain bush materials which could not be obtained locally. The residents of Bemana rallied round to help feed the visitors. In a short space of time, the house was erected. It then became apparent that the would-be farmer was in for a difficult time since he lacked planting seed. The helpers sent messages back to their homes, and a second contingent arrived with materials to plant tapioca, yams and bananas, and with a horse and plough. With the proceeds of this crop, the farmer was able to purchase his own plough, and eventually livestock, and to gain a position of considerable influence in his community. The original investment did not require any substantial outlay of cash, but was directed towards founding the basis for a cash income. Numerous similar instances could be cited, all involving a manipulation of lineal and affinal kinship connections.

Small farmers, whose land, ambitions, or energies are limited, meet their occasional capital needs by specific planning as the requirement arises. A noticeable feature of that part of the Valley served by a major feeder road is the involvement of Fijians, alongside Indians, in taking produce to market, either on their own individual account, or acting as middlemen for the stay-at-home farmers. Competition is intense, and profits not great, but the possibility of securing a cash return is there once a week for anyone who wishes to take the chance. Instructive is the experience of a young man who had watched others engage in this enterprise for a number of years. Shortly following the birth of his first child, he made his first foray into the commercial world of Lautoka township, obtaining from his sale of produce a net return of the order of nine pounds. This he used as capital the following week to enable him to sell, not only his own produce, but that which he had bought, at roughly half the market price, from neighbours. On the third market day, he retained approximately the nine pounds of capital for a similar enterprise, but used his additional profit to purchase the object of his activity, a safe for the storage of food and utensils. At the time at which I left the area, it was debatable whether he would continue his enterprise until his basic furnishing had been built up, and then return to more modest ways, or whether he would join the increasing number of villagers seeking such activity as a permanent means of improving income.

Inheritance is, at the moment, a limited method of gaining access to capital. The increasing village population decreases the amount of land *per capita* which is being passed on from one generation to another, and wherever roads penetrate the land appears to be fully used; only construction of new roads will increase the availability of commercially viable land. Although an interest in production for cash goes back at least one generation, it would be difficult to assert that each generation will be in a better position than the last, through obtaining an inherited capital advantage. Certainly, the number of implements is increasing, and their inheritance will enable young men to start with them in their hands. But houses, fences, the quality of the soil, require constant attention and alertness, and the application of resources to maintain them. One major exception to this consists of the growing herds of stock. It has been stated[1] that Fijians are not aware of the potentiality of natural increase as a means of raising the value of their assets. Nothing could be further from the truth. I came across several dramatic examples of the major growth of herds, up to 300 head of cattle amassed in four or five years, and constituting a rich source of income. Entry into this field of activity is only just beginning to be serious and well organized, but its implications for the growth of wealth are considerable.

Ceremonial
There is in Fiji a stock of articles which are used only in connection with ceremonial. These are the *tabua*, or whale's teeth, attached to a short piece of rope or plaited pandanus. The Fijian Administration takes note of the flow of circulation of *tabua*, and endeavours to check their possible export from the Colony, and to balance their occasional concentration in certain districts by injecting additional quantities at cheap rates into areas of short supply. However, undue concentration can occur only on most unusual occasions, such as during the nationally mourned funeral of Ratu Sir Lala Sukuna, for the essence of the *tabua*'s use is its rapid circulation. There is always some use for such an article: in a wedding, a funeral, a presentation to a visitor, in a ceremony of request, in the recognition of affinal relatives, in securing labour, and on many other possible occasions. *Tabua* seldom remain in the same hands for more than a week or so, and very frequently they change hands within hours.

Rapid redistribution is of course the central feature of Melanesian ceremonial exchange, and Fijian systems are no exception. With the exception of *tabua*, all the articles which enter into exchanges have

[1] Fiji Legislative Council Report, 1960.

a consumption function. This applies to the pandanus mats (used for sleeping and for floor coverings), the decorated bark cloth (used as bed coverings and wall ornamentation), cotton cloth, salt bars, drums of kerosene, agricultural produce, and *yaqona* roots. *And all the principal articles are durable.*

This last point is exceedingly important for accurate interpretation. The general feeling among European observers, supported by some casual Fijian statements, and incorporated into such commentaries upon the Fijian way of life as the Spate Report (1959) and the Report of the Burns Commission (Fiji Legislative Council, 1960), is that large scale ceremonies characteristic of weddings and funerals are wasteful, and consume valuable resources which could be diverted into alternative directions. In other words, ceremonies represent dis-saving.

This is not the place to enter full documentation, but I wish to record a major caveat. The consumer's goods which enter such exchanges are all consumed eventually, and in many cases they enter into use almost immediately. Even if they are not used immediately, since they are durable, they are available for further redistribution and later use. To this extent they represent an investment now for future use.

The argument still remains that participation in ceremonial constitutes a drain upon limited income which could better be used in production investment. This may well be true, but a judgment about the significance of scale must enter the analysis. Although a marriage might well involve the circulation of goods worth a thousand pounds or so, this would be distributed by three or four hundred persons to a roughly equivalent number. Except for the principals, personal involvement is of the order of outlay of one to five pounds in value. Rural incomes range from £50 to £1,000 per annum, with a mean of the order of £150. Involvement in *one* ceremonial a year, of this order, would hardly constitute an untoward drain on income, but involvement as a principal, or involvement in large numbers of ceremonials, would constitute a drain. Data based upon a census enquiry plus observation of the organization of ceremony indicate that individuals distribute their interest in ceremonials in such a way as to limit the possible effects on income. They manipulate two variables to keep their position in check: the scale of their contribution as minor participants, and the calendar of events to distribute their involvement as principals over time.

By and large, therefore, I would regard ceremonial as being neutral in its effect upon capital formation, being of primary interest as a distributing mechanism.

Credit Unions

Credit Unions have been established in Fiji only since 1954, but a network of unions, all affiliated and supervised through the independent Fiji Credit Union League, now covers almost all the villages of Nadroga and Navosa. Some of these are organized on a union per village basis; sometimes one union covers a group of villages. My observations cover some nine unions, but detailed information covers only four.

As can be expected from the low mean income, the amounts deposited are on the whole small, and some seem designed to give the movement little more than moral support.

SIZE OF CREDIT UNION DEPOSITS (1958)

Credit Union	Sawene		Nalebaleba		Rukuruku		Qalimare		Total
	No.	Amt.	No.	Amt.	No.	Amt.	No.	Amt.	Amt.
					(to nearest pound)				
Less than £1	—	—	4	2	4	2	4	3	8
£1 and less than £5	26	81	62	186	108	307	48	134	709
£5 and less than £10	31	214	13	89	10	67	20	139	509
£10 and less than £15	2	23	—	—	3	33	4	46	103
£15 and less than £20	1	15	1	17	—	—	1	15	47
Over £20	—	—	—	—	2	87	1	21	109
	60	333	80	294	127	496	78	358	

The number of outstanding loans is consistently smaller than the number of deposits, with the amount of the loan being on average rather higher than the amount of the deposit.

SIZE OF CREDIT UNION LOANS OUTSTANDING (1958)

Credit Union	Sawene		Nalebaleba		Rukuruku		Qalimare		Total
	No.	Amt.	No.	Amt.	No.	Amt.	No.	Amt.	Amt.
					(to nearest pound)				
Less than £1	—	—	2	1	8	4	1	1	7
£1 and less than £5	15	50	34	110	32	84	17	55	298
£5 and less than £10	22	138	10	75	19	116	22	154	482
£10 and less than £15	2	24	4	48	8	87	3	36	195
£15 and less than £20	1	16	—	—	1	15	2	30	63
£20 and over	—	—	1	20	1	39	—	—	59
	40	228	51	254	67	345	45	276	
Balance deposits over loans		105		40		151		72	

A substantial number of loans are smaller than the deposits held in the name of the borrower; in other words the borrower is doing little more than take back a portion of his deposit. In three out of the four unions detailed, the next largest category of borrowers asks for very little more than the deposit. Only in Rukuruku is there a significant number of borrowers who require substantially more than their deposits. In each case, those who borrow more than they deposit are relatively small depositors, which, of course, is fundamental to the rationale of credit unions.

SIZE OF OUTSTANDING LOANS RELATIVE TO DEPOSITS

Credit Union	Sawene		Nalebaleba		Rukuruku		Qalimare	
	No.	Amt.	No.	Amt.	No.	Amt.	No.	Amt.
Loan smaller than borrower's deposit	19	79	21	62	27	56	18	100
Loan same as deposit	—	—	1	4	—	—	—	—
Loan less than 50% higher than deposit	13	103	14	99	9	50	8	51
Loan 50–100% higher than deposit	7	49	7	40	14	109	9	77
Loan 100–200% higher than deposit	4	32	3	28	14	94	12	111
Loan more than 200% higher than deposit	3	29	3	30	5	50	1	3

Although each union has its own characteristics of borrowing and lending, the history of most shows a common pattern. This consists of a burst of interest and activity following formation, with a decline in business transactions in subsequent years. For some unions, which have committed the bulk of their funds, this is explained by slow repayments and lack of money available for further lending. Rukuruku, which has a high involvement in expansionist growth, has an unusually high number of recent deposits, but even so suffers from the slowness of repayment. The commercial vigour and prosperity of this community has enabled deposits to continue and to provide funds for future borrowing.

RUKURUKU CREDIT UNION

Date of	1. Contraction of outstanding loan		2. Last deposit	
	No.	Amount owing	No.	Amount deposited
1955 April–June	1	15	1	2
July–Sept.	17	51	1	10
Oct.–Dec.	17	62	1	1
1956 Jan.–March	4	21	2	2
April–June	7	76	3	4
July–Sept.	13	75	3	31
Oct.–Dec.	2	9	3	8
1957 Jan.–March	—	—	13	40
April–June	—	—	7	27
July–Sept.	1	10	7	4
Oct.–Dec.	4	15	5	11
1958 Jan.–March	1	12	23	60
April–June	—	—	25	75
July–Sept.	1	10	34	145

(Information obtained, last quarter 1958)

Capital, Saving and Credit in Peasant Societies

In almost all cases, borrowing is for consumption purposes; to meet school fees, purchase clothing or furniture, permit a contribution to ceremonial. Seldom is it to finance production equipment and so far as I know no effort has been made to encourage lendings in that direction.

The custom of *kerekere*, or ceremonial borrowing on demand, which was once described as the economic scourge of Fiji, has to all intents and purposes disappeared in this area. It is quite possible that the credit unions now perform the same function, in a less personally onerous way, since in essence they provide an institution whereby one villager lends to another on demand, but with a relatively impersonal administration intervening. It might be argued that the credit unions constitute a rationalization and control of *kerekere*, and that their popularity is due to a similarity of function between the two institutions.

Although the unions are in their infancy, and although they do not as yet contribute directly to the growth of productive capital, their future seems well established, and they provide a basic institution for the foundation of new credit methods. Each union has its own officers, and in particular a secretary-treasurer with equipment to take care of money, and trained in quite complex methods of accounting. The credit unions have indeed been more responsible than any other organ for the recent rapid growth in accounting knowledge. The union organization provides for minimal supervision from the centre which could perhaps be strengthened, and its officials have a complete transcript of the borrowing record of villagers. If at any time it becomes possible to distribute funds for rural credit, the credit unions have already provided an adequate and working mechanism for distribution and control.

Store Credit

A small number of villagers maintain accounts with the major trading stores in Sigatoka township, and a few who have needed building supplies or ploughing equipment have gone as far afield as Nadi and Lautoka townships. The latter are, however, usually guaranteed by some form of crop lien, which will be discussed later. Stores are reluctant to give credit unless they see an operating enterprise, or know the applicant has a salary: in some cases the person who has the account sells some of his produce to the store.

All Fijians who operate village stores have monthly accounts with either European firms or Indian retailers. From these sources they obtain all their stock; but they do so at retail prices, with minor discounts for bulk. In most cases, to save the high lorry freight charges, they transport the goods by bus to the roadhead, and thence by pack horse to the village. This means in effect that they cannot buy

200

in bulk quantities and hence they lose discounts. The final price cannot be too high above Sigatoka levels, so that the store-keepers are in a poor position with regard to both margins and size of turnover. Capital investment to increase stock and therefore turnover is well-nigh impossible, so that most stores are static enterprises of small scale.

Village stores usually extend local credit, both to Fijian and to neighbouring Indian customers. Much has been made in the past of the damage that can be done by unwise credit, particularly to relatives, which is not repaid. Certainly, there is one recent example in the area of a co-operative production and store-keeping venture which bankrupted through wild administration of credit facilities. The venture was precipitately sold up by orders of the Registrar of Co-operative Societies, its stock changing hands for a fraction of value. The store is now privately run by the same person who was responsible for its operation as a co-operative; although credit is still extended, it is severely limited, and the storeman has little hesitation in taking defaulters to court.

At another store, the owner permitted credit when his stocks were high, and when he knew that wages were about to be paid for contract labour, or that crops were to be harvested. The amounts in individual cases were small (a few shillings to three pounds). A typical entry in the record book reads:

I Nagede   3/3 B/F, tea 4/– fish 4/– baking powder 1/6
yaqona 2/– blue 1/– chewing gum 1/– powdered
milk 3/6 yaqona 2/– matches 4d soap 2/6
matches 2d dripping 2/3 sugar 2/–   £1/9/6.

This storekeeper charges a small premium on cigarettes and similar articles obtained on credit. On one occasion when I examined his books he had recent entries relating to twenty-nine villagers; but all had cleared their accounts following payments made to them by the Public Works Department for clearing the road.

While no doubt the personal credit system is open to abuse, it is difficult for me to believe on this kind of evidence that undue credit restricts enterprise in Nadroga and Navosa. Far more serious is the small turnover and the high prices paid for stock. Only access to wholesale outlets in Suva and Lautoka, and co-operative transport, will solve the problems of such enterprises, and give the operators a margin for capital investment and expansion.

Producers' Credit

The formal institutions of the sophisticated market economy operate with criteria developed in relation to the highly developed world of commerce, which would require considerable amendment to fit them to the realities of village life. Thus, paradoxically, capital and credit is not available where it is most needed to create new productive potential.

Banks treat the small borrower as a private applicant, and require collateral for loans which village applicants do not have, particularly since the land is jointly owned. (The Burns Commission has recommended that *mataqali* be permitted to incorporate, and use the land, with certain restrictions, as collateral.) Agencies of government, which have limited funds, are just as cautious in their lending policies. There is no rural loan bank designed to meet the need of peasants, Indian and Fijian alike. The Fijian administrative province of Nadroga and Navosa holds £12,000 in small deposits for village funds, special projects, schools and individuals, mainly as a convenience since there are no banks open daily in Sigatoka. No interest is paid on the deposits. Out of this sum £3,900 has been advanced, mostly in small amounts of five pounds or so to individuals. In 1958, one loan of £700 was to the Economic Development Officer's office, one of £664 to a cane growers' co-operative for a tractor, and other smaller amounts helped with the purchase of potato seeds and fencing wire. But for the most part this large sum is unused and unproductive, and money which could earn interest for its owners is not doing so.

Under such circumstances, many worthwhile enterprises have a great deal of difficulty in getting started. The Vunamoli Association is an instructive example, although I have space for only a few details. A Fijian of enterprise learned to prospect for manganese, and discovered large deposits near his village, which was isolated in the hills about halfway between Nadi township and the Sigatoka Valley road. A group of villages associated to exploit the deposits, and approached Province, Fijian Affairs Board, Industrial Development Board, and other sources of funds, for financial assistance. They were consistently turned down, but the Mining Board made available to them a few hand tools and some technical advice. The Fijians attacked the hills, and obtained quantities of ore of very high grade. Some of this they packed on horses to the road (taking about a day for a load). The District Commissioner, belatedly impressed by their determination, lent them a bulldozer, with which they carved out one of the most mountainous roads in Fiji. Still they could not obtain about £1,000 of capital required for further tools and equipment (compressors and a truck), in addition to the amount that could be raised through the sale of existing ore. They were persuaded to enter into partnership with a United States ore marketing concern, which provided the £1,000 in return for a 50 per cent share of the proceeds. For lack of £1,000 the Fijians gave up a return which over the years was worth many times more; and because of the credit structure of the colony's institutions, they had no alternative. (Indicative of their orientation is the result that their share of income has been used

202

entirely to build houses, found a school, open up timber resources, obtain coffee seedlings, and plant up a co-operative farm.)

Other productive enterprise, on a smaller scale and with less dramatic intensity, shows up the same problems, and similar techniques of meeting them. Very few of the most successful farmers, for example, have received a penny of government or institutional assistance. (There are however numerous examples of officially sponsored schemes which have received aid, most of which have now been abandoned.) The initial founding capital has come, with remarkable regularity, from the special marketing of a crop, planted and set aside for the purpose. The return has usually been quite small (£50 to £100), but sufficient to permit an investment in stock, in planting and fencing materials, or in equipment, permitting a growth in the scale of enterprise.

In many cases, primarily because of land limitations or domestic obligations, an initial investment of this kind has not been possible. There are very few alternative ways out.

One way is to enter into a partnership with someone else who has money. I know of only one clear instance of this, and aberrantly it was of a partnership between an Indian without money, and a Fijian who had obtained several hundred pounds from a remarkable farming initiative undertaken when he left school, without any agricultural training. The two began a taxi business which quickly bankrupted. The Fijian, when I met him several years later, had still not recovered his sense of enterprise and was working casually as a truck driver.

Another way is to borrow from the only source available, the Indian moneylender. Much has been hinted of usury in this regard. My enquiries did not show this. The rate of interest was never more than 12 per cent and often lower, and since this rate applies to most hire purchase agreements in the stores, since the risks are admittedly great and since the loans were primarily short-term, I do not think that a moral judgment against the lender is in order. Further, he serves a useful purpose at this point, since without him many efficient and productive enterprises would never have seen the light of day.

Producers' Levies

A large potential source of funds consists of levies made upon the sale of existing crops. A cess of £10 a ton is levied on all Fijian-produced copra marketed in Suva (i.e., about 15 per cent of the return). It is held in individual accounts which draw interest and which are administered by the Fijian Development Fund Board. Despite the developmental notion in the title, funds are not used in fact to any great extent as productive capital. In Nadroga and Navosa, for the year ending July 1, 1957, £6,626 accrued to the cess amount. The withdrawals amounted to £5,438, and the total balance stood at £25,658. Here again is a substantial sum available to initiate production. Most withdrawals, which have to be sanctioned by the Board, were for expenditures such as the financing of secondary school fees or building houses.

In addition, a voluntary cess is paid by some cane growers into a Provincial fund, the cess being collected by the Colonial Sugar Refining Company. Little control can be exercised over withdrawals from this fund, which again is used primarily for non-productive expenditures.

The idea of the cess appeals considerably to a number of Fijian officials, who have on many occasions urged its extension to cover other crops such as bananas and *yaqona*. For a cess to work, however, there must be a reasonable profit margin from which deductions can be made, there must be strict control of marketing, and there must be reasonable assurance that a compulsory cess will not divert production to alternative crops. These conditions do not apply to any crops in Fiji other than sugar and copra, and it is to be noted that the Burns Commission strongly recommended against the extension of the system.

In 1958 the Economic Development Officer Nadroga and Navosa, an official of the Fijian province, introduced voluntary crop liens as a method of financing farm improvements. Although the method was limited to the sugar crop, and although the intention was directed primarily towards house building rather than towards investment in productive capital, it met with considerable success. The stores and banks, being conservative in their approach, are likely to limit the loans to certain crops such as sugar which have assured markets and which can be inspected easily; but there is no reason why the method should not be extended to tobacco, root crops and cattle in a supervised rural loans scheme.

Social Capital
Social services, and social capital such as administrative and medical buildings and roads, are financed primarily through taxation. Few rural Fijians pay income tax, although they are liable, but males contribute to provincial rates which support the Fijian administration.

School buildings are financed through the activities of Fijian controlled school boards, their contributions matched from Government sources, and the school boards must find a proportion of teachers' salaries. There is no fixed levy or rate to provide these funds, and the boards are faced with the herculean task of raising the money voluntarily. Similarly, churches must finance their operations and building costs; and occasionally a community uses a similar method to raise funds to construct a road or initiate some other enterprise for the common good. Sometimes individuals use the same methods to raise school fees, to welcome a returning son, or even to send a young man off to jail!

Methods used to raise voluntary funds are a blend of the traditional and the modern. The *holi* or *soli* is a small feast accompanied by a *yaqona* drinking party, during which a cash collection is taken up. The *gunu peni* is a *yaqona* drinking party in which individuals (men and women) 'buy' bowls of *yaqona* of differing sizes at differing prices, and send them with their compliments to some victim who is expected to drain the bowl at a draught. The competition rapidly becomes hilarious and song often lasts well into the night. The *taralala* is somewhat more ambitious. Villagers construct bamboo and coconut leaf shelters and prepare food and *yaqona* for sale. They provide or hire a band, often with amplifying equipment. Guests, invited and uninvited, arrive by foot, horse, and chartered bus, and participate in gaiety and ballroom dancing on the grass 'floor'. Such parties are always performed by one host group for an assigned group of guests, who are expected to make the appropriate financial contribution. Thus the men may honour the women, the young the old, one church another, the schoolteacher his school board, one village its neighbour. The sums collected are not great (£15 to £20, after expenses have been met).

If larger sums are needed, more ambitious methods must be used, and the social units involved become more complex. The 'bazaar' which eventuates, perhaps to finance a church building, may involve five or six hundred visitors, who must be catered for with food, dancing, entertainment and accommodation. The visitors must pay for transport, and must bring ceremonial gifts. Prominent visitors, organizers, officials and Church leaders must be honoured ceremonially. The costs of collection are thus enormous by comparison with the amounts received; my estimate would be that it costs at least one to two pounds in goods, services and effort to collect every pound net handed over to the cause.

Voluntary collections of this type are thus extremely expensive, and since in addition they are uneven in their incidence and uncertain, they are an inefficient way of providing for public services. A number of provinces have indeed abandoned these methods of raising school funds, introducing compulsory school rates. For other purposes, however, they will no doubt continue to have a useful role.

IV

Fijian traditional institutions provided complex channels for the distribution of goods, and in their modified and possibly expanded ceremonial forms still do so. They also provided an outlet for social competition, through the mobilization of productive resources for reasons of social and political prestige. This function is not now apparent to the same degree, although elements of it are retained in ceremonies attending the rituals of passage.

Today, Fijians are becoming increasingly aware of the need for capital in order to enable them to transform their techniques and scale of production to penetrate the modern world of economic growth. They are acutely aware of the fact that adequate production to meet their ambitions is based upon the combination of capital, land and appropriate skills, and in their discussions their remarks are always directed to these points. Of these three factors, capital is in shortest supply, and has received least attention from Government.

Some Fijians have shown ingenuity in endeavouring to make up the deficiency, but there is little margin for saving on the scale needed for anything but modest consumption needs, and the increasing pressures of the costs of social services. To provide increased capital out of their own resources, Fijians must engage in innovative acts of production, over and above their normal village routines. One of the most fascinating conclusions to be drawn from observation in the Sigatoka area is that this is precisely the direction that individual Fijian initiative is taking. Despite the failure of a number of officially sponsored enterprises, experience gained by watching them in operation has enabled individual Fijians to experiment on their own.

Unfortunately, precisely because this initiative is private and because it receives little Government support, it is not described to any great degree in official records, which refer primarily to the officially sponsored schemes which, in this area, though not in some others, have been unsuccessful. There is thus little awareness of the potentialities of rural Fijian development, and still less are there signs that steps might be taken to create institutions capable of bringing productive capital into the countryside. The problem is not one for the Fijian alone, but is equally crucial for his Indian neighbour who, on the outlying rural farms, is frequently just as poor, just as restricted in his view, and even less secure, than the Fijian.

10

Rural Local Savings Associations
(Maori Komiti) in
New Zealand's Far North[1]

BY JOAN METGE

Fully incorporated into the social and economic life of New Zealand, with the same rights and duties as other citizens, the Maori[2] remain a distinctive minority. With their dusky skins and Polynesian features, they look different from the Pakeha (New Zealanders of European stock).[3] Though they form less than 7 per cent of the total population, in certain limited areas—all rural—they equal or outnumber Pakehas. And, while they share a large area of common culture and experience with the rest of the population, they continue to cherish their *Maoritanga*, which has the double meaning of 'pride in being Maori' and 'Maori ways'. Many of these Maori ways have their origin in traditional Maori culture, but others are based on ideas borrowed from the Pakeha and adapted to serve Maori needs and aims.

Good examples of this Maori adaptation of Pakeha ideas are the

[1] The research for this essay was carried out during visits to Kotare, a Maori community in the Far North of New Zealand, in 1955 (five months), 1958 (six months), 1959 (three weeks) and 1960 (one month), with the assistance of a Carnegie Social Science Research Grant (1955) and Fellowship (1958–60). I am indebted to the Maoris of Kotare for their unfailing courtesy and co-operation, particularly to the Hakea and Karaka *komiti marae* and to the officers of the Kotare Komiti Marae, who gave me full access to their minutes and account books. The essay is published with the full knowledge and approval of the members of the Kotare Komiti Marae, granted at their annual general meeting on April 25, 1960, in the hope that their experience may be interesting and helpful to others.

[2] The Maori population, as reckoned by the Census, comprises all persons whose ancestry is half or more than half Maori and the offspring of all unions between Maoris and other Polynesians. In this article, I use the plural 'the Maori' when speaking of the Maori as a whole, the English form 'Maoris' in all other cases.

[3] The Maori term Pakeha is widely used in New Zealand in preference to the ambiguous 'European'.

local savings clubs which occur in most Maori communities, urban as well as rural. Maoris call them 'committees' or *komiti* (the Maori transliteration of 'committee'), but they are distinctively Maori both in aims and organization.[1] For this reason, I shall use the Maori version of the term. *Komiti* are formed to build up funds to be used for two specific purposes: to finance *tangihanga*[2] (funeral wakes) and/or to maintain a *marae* (place of assembly). Membership may be limited to kinsfolk but not in number. *Komiti* are not legally registered or incorporated, and their existence is not widely known outside the Maori group. In this essay, I propose to make a detailed study of *komiti* in action in a Maori community called Kotare[3] between March 1, 1955, and April 30, 1960.

THE BACKGROUND

Kotare is a rural district on the west coast of Northland, eleven miles by road from a small country township. At the time of my study, settlement was concentrated mainly on a small, central lowland encircled by steep, scrub-covered hills and (on one side) the sea. It was divided into five main neighbourhoods: Karaka and Puriri (the farming areas), Hakea (a cluster of houses round a 'family' *marae*), Onepu (the sea-side) and Te Kainga (the village), adjoining the school and the stores. In June 1955, there were 537 Maoris living in Kotare, outnumbering the Pakehas by three to one. Pakehas owned and occupied eight farms on the periphery of the district and numerous sea-front sections, but most of the land was held by Maoris on Maori title.

Much of the Maori land in Kotare was under-utilized. There were twenty-two Maori dairy farms, but only nine were run by full-time farmers. A third of the lowland consisted of small blocks let on short-term leases or occupied by owners who used an acre or two for gardens and domestic animals and left the rest lying idle. There were many reasons for this situation. The most important were multiple ownership and fragmentation. Under the special laws governing Maori land, the children of a deceased Maori succeed to equal shares in his land holdings. As a result, most holdings are held jointly by many owners, and most Maoris have shares in many holdings. In the past, joint owners often sub-divided holdings, producing blocks too small for economic farming. Since normal lending agencies would not lend money on land with many owners, most of Kotare remained

[1] The term *komiti* is also applied to groups that are committees in the usual sense, but always with some qualifying word, e.g. *Komiti a Iwi*—Tribal Committees.
[2] Hereafter I shall use the widely-used abbreviation *tangi* for this institution.
[3] All names are pseudonyms.

208

undeveloped until the State launched a Land Development Scheme there in the 1930s. Most of the farmers had spent their early manhood in other occupations, with no opportunity to acquire farming knowledge. Finally, Kotare Maoris preferred team-work to the lonely working life of the dairy-farmer.

With one exception, Maori farmers in Kotare were all 'nominated occupiers', leasing a large part of their farms from co-owners. The average size of their farms was fifty acres, the largest herd forty-five cows. The full-time farmers made between £400 and £650 a year from the sale of cream, pigs and *kumara* (sweet potatoes). Out of this they paid running costs and instalments on development and housing loans.

Besides the farmers, only sixteen workers (including three women) found full-time employment in Kotare. The majority (eighty-nine men and twenty-three women) commuted daily to work in the township or surrounding countryside. Most of the men earned between £9 10s 0d and £11 10s 0d a week in wages, but six carpenters working in partnership made between £800 and £1,000 a year by contract work.

In addition to their cash income, most Kotare families derived an important non-cash income from their gardens (which supplied them with *kumara*, potatoes, corn, marrows and cabbages for most of the year), from the scrub (firewood), and from the sea (fish and shellfish).

Although new houses had been and were being built for Maoris in Kotare, sub-standard and overcrowded houses were still prevalent. Three-quarters of those occupied by Maoris dated from before 1945, about a quarter being 'land development houses' built by the Department of Maori Affairs, and the rest mainly small cottages and shacks in a poor state of repair. Most of the post-war houses had been built with Department of Maori Affairs housing loans and were much more spacious. The meeting-house and dining-hall on the main *marae* were in a state of extreme dilapidation. The two 'family' *marae* had only halls; neither was finished and one lacked cooking facilities.

The level of capital in the community was in general low. Apart from shares in Maori land (which yielded no unearned income and were difficult to sell), most of it was invested in houses and vehicles. Few of these were in first-class repair. Tradesmen working on their own account maintained a considerable working capital, but the rest held only minor amounts in the Post Office Savings Bank. They bought most capital goods on hire purchase, and used the Department of Maori Affairs as a savings agency to accumulate the cash needed to bridge the gap between the Department's loan maximum (£2,000) and the cost of a new house. They usually signed orders on their wages or cream cheques, so that the money was paid straight to the Department: they found it easier to save if they did not handle the money themselves.

The general standard of living of the Maoris in Kotare, as reflected in housing, dress, savings and capital equipment, appeared to be rather lower than that of Pakehas living in the same county. Apart from the few full-time farmers, workers earned the same as Pakehas in the same occupations. The cost of commuting was not enough to account for the difference, and it was offset by the income derived from land and sea. About one-tenth of the workers were periodically out of work, but they were nearly all single men without dependents. What then were the reasons? Larger families reduced the *per capita* income. (Out of seventy-two men with dependent children, twenty-seven had four or more.) Housewives were handicapped by lack of facilities and training in household management. Budgeting was not merely an unfamiliar but an alien concept. The Kotare Maoris prided themselves on 'never counting the cost'; they 'always put other things before money'. Generosity and sharing were emphasized as peculiarly Maori virtues, thrift suspected as 'selfish' and 'stingy'. Neglect of conservation and repairs characteristically shortened the life of most goods, and contributed considerably to the general shabbiness of dress, furnishing and vehicles, and to the dilapidation of public and private buildings.

The Maori community actively preserved the ideals of co-operation and group-action ('doing things together'). These were realized effectively only for short terms, mostly in association with *hui* (gatherings on the *marae*) but also, less frequently, with local Pakehas in projects of benefit to the district as a whole. For the rest of the time, the Maori community was highly fragmented. There was a pronounced divergence of interests between the 'young people' (under twenty-five), the 'elders' (over about fifty-five) and those 'in-between'. Religious affiliation divided the community into three church groups. The most fundamental distinction of all was that between the *tangata whenua* (the people of the land) and the *tangata haere mai* (the 'immigrants').[1] Finally, even the *tangata whenua* were divided into a number of distinct descent-groups.

The *tangata whenua* 'really belonged' to Kotare: they could trace lineal association with its land area back through at least three generations of forebears whose title had been recognized by the Maori Land Court, and they still held interests in local holdings inherited from them. According to Maori custom, proprietary interests in local Maori land were necessary to validate claims to 'belong' and alone conferred rights on the local *marae*. The *tangata haere mai* on the other hand had no ancestral ties with Kotare or its

[1] The first vowel of *tangata* (man, human being) is lengthened in the plural. Most Maori words have the same form in the singular and the plural.

land, though half of them were born in the district and many were kin to *tangata whenua*. Some owned land in the district but none on Maori title. The *tangata whenua* were in the majority, accounting for 70 per cent of the Maori population. Of the 'immigrants', 13 per cent were married to or fostered by *tangata whenua*, but 17 per cent were independent settlers.

Customary rights on the *marae* can be briefly summarized as: the right to speak publicly on the *marae* as host (*tangata marae*), the right to participate in its management, and the right to invite others to gather there. There were three *marae* in Kotare, the central or community *marae*, commonly called the Puriri *marae* after the sub-district in which it lay, and two 'family' *marae* in Karaka and Hakea respectively. Only members of the owning 'families' had rights in the latter, but all *tangata whenua* automatically had rights in the Puriri *marae*. In practice, however, the *tangata whenua* did not insist on the exclusive exercise of their rights in the central *marae*. In the first place, they had, some years before, allowed its management to pass from a *komiti marae* composed of *tangata whenua*, to the local branch of the Maori Women's Welfare League, which included 'immigrants'. The *tangata whenua* also permitted 'immigrants' to speak on the *marae* at gatherings other than those they themselves sponsored. But it was recognized on both sides that the extension of the privileges of the *marae* to 'immigrants' was based on courtesy and 'Maori *aroha*' (love). An 'immigrant' who presumed upon this favour was liable to public rebuke. At least one 'immigrant' married to a *tangata whenua* was regularly numbered among the chief *kai-korero* (public speakers) in the community: but he was an expert on traditional lore and had lived in Kotare so long that his origin was often forgotten. The independent settlers were generally too young to aspire to the position of *kai-korero*. A number of 'immigrants', mostly those married to *tangata whenua*, occupied executive office in clubs of various sorts and three had been elected to the Tribal Committee (a community council with limited powers set up under the Maori Social and Economic Advancement Act 1945).

The *tangata whenua* 'families' were essentially bilateral descent-groups, consisting of descendants of both sexes, traced through both male and female links, from a progenitor who had owned Maori land in Kotare and had died not more than fifty years before. Spouses and foster children were reckoned as part of the 'family' for practical purposes, contributing money and labour to 'family' activities: they were *quasi* members as distinct from the 'real' members. Because of bilateral affiliation, many *tangata whenua* belonged to more than one 'family'. Usually they gave one their primary allegiance, but carried out certain duties in the others. This was possible because the situations in which 'families' took corporate action were occasional in both senses of the word. Their main function was the sponsorship and organization of *hui* connected with four kinds of social crises: *tangi* (funeral wakes), 'unveilings' of memorial grave-stones, weddings and twenty-first birthday parties. In 1955, most of the Kotare 'families' organized these gatherings on an *ad hoc* basis, but five had set up permanent *komiti*.

1955: THE 'FAMILY' KOMITI

These *komiti* varied considerably in size and scope. The Onepu, Kennedy and Taua *komiti* had sixteen, seven and fifteen members respectively. The latter two were really formed by two branches of a 'family' in the process of segmentation, under the leadership of two *kuia* (elderly women) standing in the relationship of mother's sister to sister's daughter. With thirty-one and twenty-six members respectively the Hakea and Karaka *komiti* were much larger. Both were associated with 'family' *marae*, the former with that of the Samuels 'family', the latter with that of the Rewitis. These were the two largest and most closely knit 'families' in Kotare.

Each *komiti* consisted of a number of adult subscribers who elected a chairman, secretary and treasurer every one or two years. These officers kept minute and account books and acted as an executive committee in emergencies. In most cases, only the older, married members of the 'family' (including *quasi* members) sub-scribed to its *komiti*. However, the younger, unmarried adults always turned up to work at any activity the *komiti* sponsored. Emigrant members of the 'family' helped with the work when they came home to 'family' *hui* and made occasional contributions to 'family' funds, but only nine were financial members of any of the five *komiti* in 1955. Only the Hakea and Onepu *komiti* had any subscribers from outside the 'family', each having accepted a couple of 'immigrant' kinsmen.

Subscriptions were paid formally at meetings. Supposed to be held every month, these were often held over if there was no other business. The standard rate was 1s each per month, but sometimes it was raised temporarily to build up a depleted fund or levies were imposed for special purposes. The money itself was deposited in a Post Office Savings Account, often in the treasurer's name. Dis-cussion and individual speeches at meetings conformed to Maori rules of oratory and etiquette and were mostly in Maori, as were the minutes.

These 'family' *komiti* were commonly called *komiti wahine* or women's committees, but they all included nearly as many men as women. The executive officers, however, were usually women, in several cases wives of 'real' members of the 'family'. The only male

212

officer in the five *komiti* was the secretary in the Hakea *komiti*. The men explained half-seriously that 'the women do the work, that is why it is called a women's committee. The men do the talking and the planning. But if we do something wrong they jump down our throats'. The women, other than the officers, rarely raised their voices in discussions; having briefed them well beforehand, they preferred to let their men speak for them. The chief burden of preparing for *hui* fell on the women, because they were home on weekdays. Also, the men conceded, they were more punctual and reliable.

These *komiti wahine* went back, as far as my informants could remember, to the early years of this century at least. One informant alleged that they were set up in the 1890s as a result of a suggestion made by Sir Peter Buck (Te Rangi Hiroa) during an election tour. Originally they may well have been composed only of women, but because the idea of private meetings was foreign to Maori custom men had always attended and taken part in the proceedings.

The primary purpose of these *komiti* was to organize the 'family' to cope with the staging of *tangi* for its members. Members' subscriptions were used to build up a *tangi* fund which could be called upon with the minimum of delay. When a death occurred, the officers ordered the stores required in the name of the *komiti*, and generally directed operations on the *marae*, with the assistance of the closest male kinsmen of the deceased. (The closest kinswomen were preoccupied with receiving the visitors as chief mourners.) Though other kinsmen and friends helped with the work during the *tangi*, the 'family' supplied the most and the hardest workers. In most cases it was tacitly agreed that certain members of the *komiti* did certain jobs: killing the beasts, making the *hangi* (earth oven), getting wood and shellfish, making puddings and so on, with a *kaumatua* (male elder, head of a 'family') to act as *kai-whakahaere-o-te-hui* or general director. The immediate family of the deceased (*te whanau pani*) ordered and paid for the coffin and prided itself on giving as much in kind as possible, especially meat, one of the most expensive items. It was against Maori custom for a man to save up beforehand for his own coffin, but often they used part of his estate for this purpose. Other members of the 'family' contributed what they could, or what they felt their relationship with the deceased warranted, in the form of goods (meat, vegetables, milk, hay, firewood, preserves and pickles) and labour. There were no rigid rules about who should give what. The people believed in leaving such decisions to the individual's conscience and *aroha* (love).

After the last big meal of the *tangi*, which followed the burial (usually on the third day), the *komiti* auctioned the perishable foodstuffs in the dining hall, a certain amount having first been set aside for the *whanau pani*. Then the members held a meeting to reckon up

the accounts, settling the cash expenses against receipts from mourners' *awhina* (donations, sometimes called '*marae* money') and the sale
of goods. Food and other goods donated by the 'family', other kin
and friends did not figure in the account. Sometimes, if the funds
were in a healthy state, the *komiti* paid a token sum to the farmers
who supplied the meat, but if they were close to the deceased they
took a pride in refusing it. Any deficit was paid out of funds. If a
komiti did not have enough in the bank to cover the deficit, as sometimes happened, 'the bereaved family with the help of a few live
wires put up the difference'.

Here is the account for a *tangi* sponsored by the Karaka *komiti*
(the Rewiti 'family') in 1956, as recorded in the *komiti's* books:

Expenses	£	s.	d.	Receipts	£	s.	d.
Groceries	6	4	8	Hakea k.m.	1	0	0
(sugar, tea, salt, biscuits,				Puriri k.m.	2	0	0
tinned meat)				Onepu	1	0	0
Cakes and bread	6	6	3	Kennedy family		5	0
				Deceased's wife	3	0	0
1 mutton from local				Kotare friends		9	6
Pakeha farmer	3	0	0	Other friends		10	0
				Komiti from neighbouring			
4 bales hay at 6s	1	4	0	settlement	1	0	0
				Total *awhina*	9	4	6
				Subscriptions for month	2	12	0
				Credit balance in bank	8	7	9
	16	14	11		20	4	3
				Carried forward	3	9	4

In addition to the goods mentioned in this account, a cow was provided from the deceased's farm, together with vegetables and preserves. The Puriri *komiti marae* was in recess at the time of this *tangi*,
but one of the Puriri *kaumatua* gave a donation in its name.

The 'family' *komiti* also organized other 'family' *hui*, but with one
significant difference: instead of drawing on *komiti* funds, the officers
took up a special collection from members to meet expenses.
Occasionally a *komiti* voted a special donation of £2 to £5 out of
funds for such gatherings, but never more. 'The *komiti* orders from
the store in its name, but the members pay for it.' At weddings the
expenses were shared more or less equally between the bride's 'side'
and the groom's. The account book of the Karaka *komiti* supplied the
following lists of expenses in connection with the wedding of Mere
Rewiti to Manu Peters. As it happened, the parents on both sides
were subscribing members of the Karaka *komiti*.

Bride's side	£	s.	d.	Groom's side	£	s.	d.
Stores	12	15	9	Wedding cake	7	10	0
Dress material	5	9	0	Fowls	1	10	0
Sewing dress	2	15	0	Marquee (hire)	2	10	0
Drink	5	0	0	Ring	3	0	0
Half minister's				Beef and pork	8	0	0
travelling expenses	2	0	0	Half minister's			
				expenses	2	0	0
	27	19	9		24	10	0

Vegetables were supplied by the bride's parents. The minister's travelling expenses were later refunded by the church committee. Guests attending the wedding contributed a total of £5 15s 0d in 'marae money', which was divided by the two sides. The expenses incurred by the bride's side were paid by her father and four brothers. It will be noted that expenses which Pakehas would consider the responsibility of the bride's parents or the groom were shared by close kin on both sides.

In addition to organizing *hui*, two of the five *komiti* also managed 'family' *marae*. These *komiti marae* cared for buildings and grounds and hired out the *marae* to outside bodies. Income from the marae was paid into the 'family' savings account, but an attempt was made to keep it separate from the *tangi* fund in the books. Occasionally, if funds were low, the *komiti marae* would sponsor a dance on the *marae* themselves. The halls on both *marae* had been built with the help of subsidies in the days when the Government made grants of small sums. Neither was finished when the policy was changed (subsequent subsidies being granted only when half the required amount had been collected), and the *komiti* were still making additions as they could afford them.

THE MANAGEMENT OF THE PURIRI MARAE

Some four years previously there had been a *komiti wahine* attached to the Puriri *marae*, composed of members of 'families' associated with the land area of Puriri, but for some reason this *komiti* had (in the words of one informant) 'gone to sleep'. Its members had allowed the local branch of the Maori Women's Welfare League to take over management of the *marae*. This was an almost revolutionary break with tradition. The MWWL ran the *marae* for some five or six years, providing it with a new stove and a large store of crockery bearing the League's crest. However, the community began to murmur against its control over the *marae*, partly because it was an all-women's group in a way that the old *komiti marae* had not been,

215

partly because its meetings were held during the day when the rest of the community could not attend, so that its deliberations appeared to be cloaked in secrecy, and partly because it instituted a system of charges for the use of the *marae*: 5s for the evening, 30s for a full twenty-four hours. These charges were designed to cover the cost of electricity and to provide an income to be spent on the *marae*, apart from reimbursing the League for the money already spent out of its own funds. But many people accused the League of 'charging a dead body for the *marae*'. Instead of calling a public meeting to defend and explain its action, the League went into recess early in 1957. The Puriri *marae* was left unsupervised.

THE KOTARE KOMITI MARAE

For some time, several *kaumatua* told me, they had been concerned that the attendance at and the organizing of *tangi* in Kotare had been falling off—'dying', as one expressed it. 'We were criticized for our poor *tangi* when we went to deaths on other *marae*.' 'Things were going more in the Pakeha style: people went and paid tribute at the funeral and then came away. Until suddenly we realized we were drifting away from the Maori custom, which means gathering and talking from the time of the death up to the funeral.' The collapse of the MWWL did not improve matters. Pomare Anaru, *kaumatua* of one of the Puriri 'families', was about to revive the dormant *komiti marae* when Hakope Watene (*kaumatua* of another Puriri 'family') proposed the establishment of a *marae* committee on a community basis. He made this proposal towards the end of 1957 at a *tangi*. Pomare Anaru conceded that this was a better scheme and withdrew his own proposal. A levy of 1s a head was collected from those present to help with the *tangi* expenses, and a date fixed for a general community meeting.

This meeting was held on December 10th and was exceptionally well attended for Kotare. Hakopa Watene's idea was enthusiastically supported and the Kotare Komiti Marae formed on the spot. It was agreed that the new *komiti* should include everybody, 'immigrants' as well as *tangata whenua*, on an equal footing. Pomare Anaru told me: 'The (Puriri) *marae* belongs to everyone now. You aren't considered an outsider if you pay your fee.' Officers were elected at this first meeting: *Heamana* (chairman), *Hekeretari* (secretary) and *Peeke* (treasurer), and two *Tarahiti* (trustees) for the Post Office Savings Account which the latter were authorized to open in the *komiti's* name. (*Peeke* is apparently the Maori form of the word 'bag'.) All five were women. (The chairman and treasurer were re-elected at the annual general meetings held on Anzac Day—April 25th—in 1959 and 1960, but a new secretary was elected each time.)

216

Subscriptions were fixed at 1s a month—12s a year—for each adult, and it was decided that *tangi* were to be financed by special taxes calculated on the basis of net expenses. Finally a caretaker (*kaitiaki*) was appointed to watch over and clean the *marae* at a nominal charge. The use of Maori words in connection with the new *komiti*, even when speaking English, was significant, emphasizing its orientation to wholly Maori ends. The term *aitua* (misfortune or calamity) now came into favour to describe *tangi*, especially in the expression *aitua* taxes.

Before it had been in existence a week, the new *komiti* had the names of 191 adults on its books, people who had signified their interest or whose names had been suggested by kinsfolk. But by April 1958, when the *komiti* had weathered three *tangi*, it had become apparent that at least forty of these were not going to pay either subscriptions or *aitua* taxes. The Kotare Komiti Marae decided fairly early that it would assist at *tangi* even when the deceased and his immediate family were not subscribers, provided that they had some kinsman who was. This, while according well with Maori custom, removed the incentive to pay subscriptions. In the case of several kin-groups who maintained their own 'family' *komiti*, it was decided that only a few representatives would pay subscriptions: the rest baulked at paying twice over. By the second annual general meeting (April 25, 1960), only fifty-two subscriptions had been paid, with disheartening effects on *komiti* funds. Moreover, none of the members had paid his subscription more than once, the idea that it was only an entrance fee having gained wide currency in spite of the treasurer's denials.

For the first three *tangi*, the *aitua* taxes were reckoned on the basis of nominal membership (between 180 and 190), but it was soon evident that the full deficit would not be recovered by this means, and subsequently the taxes were determined by the number of those who had paid their taxes more or less up-to-date, an average of 150. In April 1960, this included twenty-three who had been living outside Kotare from the beginning and another thirteen who had left within the last two years. These emigrant members were all either *tangata whenua* or their spouses, and all but six lived within a radius of twenty miles. Over two-and-a-half years, the *komiti* had lost seven subscribers by death and ten as a result of emigration. It gained only five by immigration and marriage.

The collection of subscriptions and taxes from so large a group was obviously too much for three officers. At the third meeting, shortly before the first *tangi*, it was decided to divide members into four territorial groups, and four *kaumatua*, all men, were selected as *tohunga e whai* (collectors) for these groups. (1) Tere Wepiha was appointed as collector for Te Kainga, where many of the 'immi-

217

Capital, Saving and Credit in Peasant Societies

grants' lived; (2) Hakopa Watene for Puriri: (3) Rua Rewiti for Karaka; and (4) Nopera Samuels for Hakea. Tere Wepiha was an 'immigrant' married to a *tangata whenua*; he had emerged in recent years as one of the chief speakers at Kotare *hui* and one of Kotare's strongest personalities. The other three were *kaumatua* in *tangata whenua* 'families', Hakopa Watene and Rua Rewiti being two of the foremost *kai-korero* in the community. Nopera Samuels was a practical man rather than a 'talker'; he shared the leadership of the Samuels 'family' with his first cousin Manu Matthews.

This scheme was never put into practice as planned. Some of the *komiti* already in existence preferred to maintain their identity, and various individuals attached themselves to another collector than that for their area. Eventually there emerged seven distinct sub-groups.

Four were *komiti* in their own right: (1) the Karaka Group, which was identical with the Karaka *komiti marae* (33 members on April 25, 1960); (2) the Taua 'family', most of whose members lived in Puriri (9 members); (3) the Kennedy 'family', located mainly in Te Kainga (5 members); (4) Whanau Kotahi, a new *komiti* formed after the Kotare Komiti Marae, under the leadership of Pomare Anaru. Pomare told me that he had formed this *komiti* in the first place to simplify the payment of *aitua* taxes. Hakopa Watene had asked him to collect the taxes from his Puriri kinsfolk, and he had found that it took months to get them all in. Now the treasurer of Whanau Kotahi took members' taxes out of funds and paid them to the treasurer of the 'big *komiti*' in a lump sum as soon as they fell due. Whanau Kotahi had begun as a 'family' affair with 21 members, but other kinsmen kept asking to join until by April 1960 there were 43. It might be noted that neither Rua Rewiti of the Karaka group nor Pomare Anaru held office in their respective *komiti*. Puti Kennedy and Aroha Taua acted as chairmen in their groups, but left the practical work in the hands of their daughters.

The other three sub-groups had no internal unity but were simply miscellaneous aggregations of individuals who paid their taxes through a particular collector: (5) the Puriri Group, consisting mainly of Hakopa Watene's 'family' (14 members); (6) the Te Kainga Group, mainly Tere Wepiha's 'family' (8 members); (7) Nopera Samuels' Group, which included people from 'all over Kotare' (29 members). Finally, there were some half dozen members who paid their taxes straight to one of the officers.

So far we have accounted for three of the old 'family' *komiti* (the Karaka *komiti marae* and the Kennedy and Taua 'families'). The Hakea (Samuels) *komiti marae* preferred to retain complete independence as a group. Nopera Samuels and Manu Matthews and their wives subscribed to the 'big *komiti*', but none of the other

218

members followed their example. Every time the Kotare Komiti Marae managed a *tangi*, the Hakea *komiti* made a donation, at first £1 but later £2. Since 1955, the Hakea *komiti* had lost some members by emigration but replaced them by young married couples; it had also accepted two more 'immigrants' who apparently felt that it had more to offer than the KKM. The fifth of the old *komiti*, Onepu, 'more or less went to sleep when the big committee was formed'. About half its members joined the KKM, and when they lost three members one after another early in 1959 they let the big committee organize the *tangi*. But though they hardly ever held a meeting they continued to collect and bank subscriptions, and they made substantial donations to the 'big *komiti*' to help pay for *tangi* for Onepu members.

Another independent *komiti* came into being after the founding of the Kotare Komiti Marae and at least partly in reaction from it. Some nine adults who joined the 'big *komiti*' in the early days withdrew after three months because they disapproved of its providing liquor for the workers at *tangi*. They formed a church *komiti*, the Kotare Assembly Komiti, and thereafter contributed to *tangi* run by the big *komiti* by means of a group donation.

The relationship established between the Kotare Komiti Marae and the four 'family' *komiti* contained within it is worth exploring in more detail. All four maintained a separate existence within the wider framework and in some respects independent of it. They had their own elected officers, records and savings accounts, and they held separate meetings. In each case they agreed that only certain members—the older ones who were better established financially and more enthusiastic about the whole thing—should subscribe to the big *komiti* as well as to the 'family' one. *Aitua* taxes and in some cases special levies were paid in a lump sum out of *komiti* funds, the treasurers collecting them later from members. The 'family' *komiti* also sponsored certain activities independently of the Kotare Komiti Marae. They organized weddings, unveilings and twenty-first birthday parties for their members, sometimes donating £2 or £3 towards their expenses out of *komiti* funds. Whanau Kotahi ran a series of card evenings one winter to build up its funds, while the Karaka *komiti* continued to work for the improvement of its *marae* facilities. Loyalties still came into conflict on occasion. At a meeting of the Kotare Komiti Marae, Tere Wepiha once suggested that the Karaka *komiti* give its hall to replace the tumble-down meeting-house on the Puriri *marae*, thus sharing it with the whole community; but Rua Rewiti retorted that 'It's all very well for you, it isn't your *marae*', and so far forgot himself as to remind Tere that *he* had no rights on any of the Kotare *marae*. Yet Rua Rewiti was one of the keenest supporters of the Kotare Komiti Marae. Members of the big *komiti* expressed resentment when they learned that the Karaka

219

komiti had applied to the Tai Tokerau Trust Board for a loan to develop their *marae*, fearing that a second application from Kotare might affect their own chances. And the members of the Karaka *komiti* were disgruntled when Rangi Peters (who had married a Rewiti), drawing £10 from the Maori Land Court for land he had sold, turned it over to the big *komiti* for *its marae* fund instead of giving it to Karaka.

The organization of the Kotare Komiti Marae remained cumbersome even after the establishment of these seven sub-groups, and in May 1958 the members set up an executive committee of ten members, consisting of the chairman, secretary and treasurer *ex officio* and seven elected members. The seven elected at the time were Hakopa Watene, Tere Wepiha, Nopera Samuels and one member from Whanau Kotahi, the Karaka Group and the Taua and Kennedy 'families'. According to one informant, they were chosen 'more or less as representatives of the various districts and for their gumption'. All seven were still on the executive in April 1960, as no re-election had been held.

The Kotare Komiti Marae was established primarily to handle *tangi*, as the 'family' clubs had been. But it soon realized that it had taken over the duties of the Maori Women's Welfare League at the *marae*, and as time went on various other minor functions were added.

Let us look first at the way in which it handled deaths after two years' experience (i.e. in 1960). As soon as anyone died in Kotare or a Kotare emigrant died elsewhere, the *whanau pani* (bereaved family) or close relatives notified the chairman or the secretary. As Hakopa Watene put it: 'Members of the *komiti* automatically start moving into position and take action without calling a meeting.' The chairman immediately telephoned an order to one of the two local stores, a standard list which she varied according to the status of the deceased (which affected attendance) and whether the *tangi* would extend into the weekend or not. (A typical order was as follows: 36 two-pound loaves of bread, 35 lb. sugar, 12 lb. butter, 5 lb. salt, 3 lb. tea, one dozen small bottles of tomato sauce, 3 large tins jam, 2 tins assorted biscuits, 1 large tin of powdered milk.) The chairman then went to the *marae* with the caretaker to make sure it was clean and ready. Nopera Samuels, a farmer who had been appointed 'butcherman' by tacit consent, called on the other farmers to find who had the cheapest and most suitable animal. Those who were free helped him kill it at the most convenient cowshed. He also arranged for a couple of men to cut firewood and for a truck to deliver it to the *marae*. By the time that the *tupapaku* (corpse) arrived at the *marae*, everything was in train.

The Kotare Komiti Marae officers stayed at the *marae* throughout the *tangi*, together with the chairman's husband, a farmer, and a faithful band of some ten *kai-awhina* (helpers) who formed the nucleus of the work-force at every *tangi*. They were strengthened by those relatives and friends of the deceased who felt it their duty to assist. The regulars were either farmers who could take time off work as they chose, or men who lived close to the *marae* and valued their role enough to lose an occasional day's work for it. Each had his own particular job: four or five of the men always made the *hangi* and tended the cooking fires, a couple of the women specialized in making puddings, and so on. Waiters and waitresses, dish-washers and general helpers were drawn from the ranks of the casuals. Usually only the closest relatives and the chief *komiti* workers were there on a weekday, but there were always plenty of workers in the evenings and at weekends.

All the *tangi* sponsored by the Kotare Komiti Marae were held at the Puriri *marae*, except in three cases when it had been let for a long weekend to a conference group including visitors from outside Kotare. The *kaumatua* formally asked those who might otherwise have taken the body to one of the 'family' *marae* to go to Puriri. In one such case, involving a member of the Rewiti 'family', the husband of the deceased consented, but later, when the corpse was being moved from Puriri to the Karaka cemetery, their daughter dramatically stopped the cortege to plead with the elders to allow her mother to lie for an hour at least on her own *marae*. They could hardly refuse.

In most cases a corpse lay in state on the *marae* for two nights, during which time mourners came from Kotare and from outside, even from Auckland and beyond, to 'pay their respects' and to talk in a series of formal speeches into the early hours of each morning. The Kotare Komiti Marae provided all comers with meals during the *tangi* until the final feast after the funeral. The big *komiti* itself provided only the plainest of fare: beef or pork and occasionally mutton, potatoes and *kumara* cooked in a *hangi*, sauce, bread, butter, jam, biscuits, sometimes plum pudding, and an endless supply of tea. Additional luxuries (jellies, cakes, preserved fruit) were provided on the initiative of the bereaved family. Visiting parties of mourners brought *awhina* which they presented privately to the *kaumatua* or the *komiti* officers. (In other areas, *awhina* are presented publicly.)

After the last meal, the surplus food was auctioned in the dining hall, followed by a meeting to make up the accounts. All those who had bought or paid for anything for the *tangi* presented the bill and the *komiti* decided whether it would accept responsibility for its payment. It had never actually refused to pay a claim, but the officers had several times to warn members against ordering stores without their knowledge. The deficit between receipts and expenses was divided by the number of members and the amount of the *aitua* tax declared.

Capital, Saving and Credit in Peasant Societies

In the two-and-a-half years that the KKM had been operating in April 1960, it had organized fifteen *tangi*, including eight for non-members. *Tangi* expenses varied from £11 to £53, *awhina* amounted to as much as £40, and the taxes levied were between 1s 3d and 3s 6d per head. The size of the accounts depended partly on the size of the *tangi*, partly on the time of the year, potatoes and *kumara* having to be bought if relatives had exhausted their own store, and partly on the extent to which relatives claimed for expenses. At one *tangi* in 1958, the deceased's brother, a farmer in Kotare, refused to claim a refund for anything he had supplied, with the result that *awhina* and sales covered expenses entirely and no tax was levied. The KKM paid for such store-bought luxuries as cake and jellies if the bills were presented, though it did not order them. Often the family concerned preferred to pay for such trimmings itself, as a mark of respect for the deceased. Relieved of most of the expense of providing for visitors at the *tangi*, many families had allowed themselves the luxury of hiring a hearse. I did not hear of a hearse being used in Kotare in 1955, but one figured in at least five *tangi* in 1958 and 1959. The KKM made no charge for electricity for *tangi*: power bills were paid out of *marae* funds. The minister's travelling expenses were paid by the bereaved family or sometimes by the appropriate church committee as its donation to the *tangi*. (A specimen account is reproduced below.)

In general, both the receipts and expenses were less than was typical in many Maori areas. The meals and accommodation (in the meeting-house) were plain and adequate rather than lavish. The Maoris of the Far North had never been wealthy either as individuals or as groups; unlike those in other parts of the North Island, they

ACCOUNT OF A TANGI MANAGED BY THE KOTARE KOMITI MARAE, 1959

Expenses	£	s.	d.	Receipts	£	s.	d.
Groceries	12	2	5	*Awhina:*			
Beef (2)	34	0	0	Hakea k.m.	1	0	0
Potatoes	4	12	10	*Whanau pani*	2	10	0
Transport	2	10	0	Kotare friends.	5	10	0
Hay (4 bales)	1	0	0	Refund on beef	20	0	0
				Auckland bus party	5	0	0
				Six outside *komiti*	6	0	0
				Refunds and sales	4	16	4
	£54	5	3		£44	16	4
Deficit	9	8	11	Tax per head		1	6

Note: Two farmers accepted only £7 each for the cows they supplied, returning £10 of the price as a donation. Both were personal friends of the deceased's family, though not kinsmen.

received virtually nothing in the way of unearned income from their land. Kotare lacked a tradition of lavishness at *tangi* to uphold. Although the general standard of living had risen markedly since the war, the greater proportion of the increase was directed to other ends than increasing the amount spent on *tangi*—to improved housing, cars and trucks, and higher education.

The second major function of the Kotare Komiti Marae was the management of the *marae*. One of its first problems was to decide on charges. This was the rock on which the MWWL had foundered. At the beginning of 1958, members of the *komiti* agreed on a charge of 4s a night for money-making gatherings, just enough to cover the cost of electricity; no charge was to be made for deaths, weddings, unveilings, birthdays or Tribal Committee meetings. It was hoped that the sponsors of such gatherings would make a donation instead. (In fact few did.) The importance attached to this question of charges was indicated by the fact that members (especially those who had missed earlier meetings) kept raising it periodically, to be referred to the original motion by the chairman. Another early motion decreed that crockery breakages were to be replaced by the groups responsible. Though they had been heavy, they had not been replaced by April 1960, largely because the *komiti* members wanted the chairman to see if she could get more bearing the MWWL crest.

The Kotare Komiti Marae decided at an early stage to keep a special fund for *marae* purposes. Subscriptions were to form the basis of this fund. But, as already indicated, the payment of subscriptions had lapsed. Over a period of two-and-a-half years the *komiti* received from local clubs a total of £6 7s 0d for the hire of the *marae*; but this covered only electricity costs. In 1958, the *komiti* ran a series of twelve card evenings with the aim of building up the *marae* fund. By the time the supper and prizes had been paid for, the profits amounted to only £7 16s 11d. (Some members felt it would have been better if they had asked players to 'bring a plate' (of food) for supper and had encouraged them to donate prizes, as was the practice in other Kotare clubs.) After more than a year of discussion, it was decided (at a meeting held on October 24, 1959) to impose a special levy of £1 a head to bolster up the *marae* fund. £21 15s 0d had been paid in by April 25, 1960. Towards the end of 1959, Pomare Anaru and Rangi Peters, who were first cousins, transferred £10 each from the sale of 'family' land from the Maori Land Court to the Kotare Komiti Marae's *marae* fund. The KKM also applied for financial assistance from the Tai Tokerau (Northland) Maori Trust Board, but had not yet received a favourable reply. The cost of sending two delegates to attend a Trust Board meeting in 1958 was defrayed by a special levy of a shilling a head.

The *marae* itself was in an extremely dilapidated condition when the KKM took it over. The *komiti* had since organized three working-bees which had repaired fences, cleaned out gorse and rushes, put in underground drains, and built two double toilets, at a total cost of £48 19s 1d. Neither the fencing nor the clearing had been quite completed. In February 1960, the regional Health Inspector condemned the buildings on the *marae* and instructed the *komiti* not to use them for overnight gatherings. This was a serious blow. The *marae* fund contained just on £60 at the end of the financial year, on April 25, 1960. The officers elected at the annual general meeting had a formidable task in front of them.

Organizing *tangi* and managing the *marae* absorbed most of the energies and resources of the Kotare Komiti Marae. There was strenuous opposition to the assumption of other responsibilities. Members were reluctant even for the *komiti* to give *awhina* to 'outside deaths', that is, to *tangi* held on *marae* in other communities for folk related to Kotare residents. This was a duty which had always been accepted by the old 'family' *komiti*. After more than a year of argument, those who stressed the importance of the old customs carried the day. A motion was passed imposing a special levy of 1s a month to form an *awhina* 'fund', and an *awhina* already given in the name of the *komiti* was refunded to the elders concerned. But the levies were not paid, and when another member claimed a refund early in 1960 it was refused on the grounds that there were not funds in hand for the purpose.

In May 1958, only six months after its inception, the Kotare Komiti Marae broke its rule against making payments unrelated to *tangi* or *marae* by giving £10 each to three local footballers picked to go to Australia with the Maori All Blacks that winter. Many members felt that the *komiti* had been rather stampeded into this gift. To begin with, two elders announced at one of the card evenings that the *komiti* was giving £10 out of the expected profits from cards to a certain footballer, without putting it to a general meeting or to the officers. An old lady present immediately pointed out that two other footballers from Kotare had also been selected and should receive a similar grant. At that stage the KKM did not have the extra £20. A private individual put up the money, the Tribal Committee paid him a little later and the KKM imposed a special levy of 3s a head. But it had difficulty collecting the levy and only £6 7s 6d was paid over to the Tribal Committee. This experience confirmed the leading members in their determination that the *komiti* should not commit itself to other activities, however worthwhile.

However, when a household in Kotare was burnt out early in 1959, it was reluctantly agreed that the *komiti* would hold money contributed to a distress fund. The treasurer opened a credit account at a local store with some of it and paid the rest into the *komiti*'s own savings account, out of which she paid various accounts for the family as they were presented. But she kept a separate record of these transactions and did not enter them into the *komiti*'s own accounts.

Finally, the *komiti* imposed a levy of £1 a head to assist the 'Beach case' in which the Maoris of Te Rarawa and Te Aupouri tribes were claiming ownership of the Ninety Mile Beach through the law-courts. About a dozen had paid this levy, mostly members of the family of one of the prime movers in the case.

Even at the end of April 1960, the Kotare Komiti Marae had not achieved its plan to bring the whole Maori community into a single unified organization. Out of approximately 250 adults, only 147 could be reckoned as members, all but one either married or widowed or over twenty-five.

The most important group still standing outside the 'big *komiti*' was the Hakea *komiti marae*. According to one of the Samuels *kaumatua*: 'The root trouble why the Hakea folk won't join the big committee is that they want their dead to lie in state at Hakea and not Puriri. They are a hard-hearted folk, they don't take to anything different. The *komiti wahine* was handed down from our forefathers and we don't like to leave it. Besides, in the big committee there are a lot of different ways of doing things, so whispers go round and then there are arguments. In our *komiti* we never have arguments. What the *komiti* says goes.' He went on to say that 'we wouldn't worry if the big committee folded up tomorrow, we could carry on just the same. We have kept going all these years. Though sometimes we don't have a meeting for months, we keep on paying our shilling a month.' Since the establishment of the Kotare Komiti Marae, the Hakea *komiti* had suffered a serious setback when a hurricane destroyed its hall in March 1959. Not only was it not insured, but the *komiti* was still paying for materials used in lining and painting the interior, a task they had only just completed. In spite of pleas from the KKM to pool their resources for the benefit of the Puriri *marae*, the Hakea *komiti* was planning to rebuild.

The Kotare Assembly *komiti* also held aloof, as did five women who had been active in the Maori Women's Welfare League. Nursing resentment over the way that 'the people closed down the League by their jealousy and forgot all it had done for them', they claimed that 'the new *komiti* has nothing to show for the time it has had at the *marae*. The crockery is nearly gone and now the buildings have been condemned. We don't feel like paying £1 a head (the *marae* levy) after seeing all we paid into the League go for nothing.'

Although its originators had planned to draw in all the 'immigrants', those who joined the Kotare Komiti Marae were mostly married to *tangata whenua*, and the majority of the independent settlers remained outside. Either they maintained close contact with home communities in the vicinity, belonging to home *komiti,* or they cherished complete independence. (Many had in fact settled in Kotare for just that reason.) One 'immigrant' said that he would not join the big *komiti* because its members had to pay *aitua* taxes whether they attended the *tangi* or not. In the case of 'immigrants' like him, that meant paying for *tangi* for people they hardly knew and sometimes had never heard of before their bodies were brought home for burial. He preferred the system current in his own home community: a flat rate for all members of the community who ate at the *marae* during a *tangi.* He attended gatherings in his own community (which was only fifteen miles distant) at least as often as he attended those in Kotare and could rely on the support of his people there in any crisis affecting his own family. He had no real need for the social or financial security that the KKM offered.

The Kotare Komiti Marae had been faced with many problems; some were still not fully overcome. In the first place, members were slow about paying subscriptions and taxes, so that there was a considerable time-lag between the payment of bills and the banking of the money intended to cover them. Inevitably, at times, it was necessary to draw temporarily on the funds earmarked for special purposes, such as the *marae,* to meet *tangi* expenses. Many of the less sophisticated members could not see why it was still necessary for them to pay an *aitua* tax after the accounts for that particular *tangi* had been paid. It had taken and was taking considerable patience on the part of the officers and collectors to explain the financial complexities and to convince them that the *komiti* was not 'making a profit out of them'. In some cases, the collectors paid outstanding taxes out of their own pockets rather than let the big *komiti* down. Its success thus depended a good deal on the enthusiasm and self-sacrifice of the leaders. Secondly, most members had only a cursory acquaintance with committee procedure and were either bewildered by it or inclined to be over-critical. They took up a lot of time seeking satisfaction on minor points or bringing up the same issue over and over again. Those associated with 'family' *komiti* were often suspicious of methods that differed from their own. Lack of knowledge and the amount of criticism directed at officers limited the number of candidates able and willing to stand for office. Those who had been elected had done a fine job under difficult conditions, establishing the *komiti* on a firm basis; but they themselves admitted that they would have found the task less onerous if they had been more certain of the correct and simplest ways of doing things.

Thirdly, it had taken a long time for the people to get used to the idea of the *komiti* ordering and directing everything at *tangi,* which had so long been run by the 'family'. In the early days, officers had been bothered by duplicated orders and extravagant unauthorized

226

purchases. At one *tangi*, members of the 'family' had tried to 'run things their way', impeding the *komiti* officers. At another, the deceased's brother-in-law, home from the city for the *tangi*, started to cut up the meat that was left over to take home to the *whanau pani* and was startled when the chairman told him that it belonged to the *komiti*, which had paid for it, and that the *komiti* would decide how much to send to the *whanau pani* as a gift. On another occasion, a relative tried to walk off with a bag of potatoes, evidently hoping that the *komiti* officers would 'let it go from Maori *aroha*'. But by patience and tact the officers had accustomed members to the new regime without a major incident. Fourthly, many of the members were diffident about speaking their mind at meetings, which were always held on the Puriri *marae*. 'A lot of people disagree with a motion but they don't say so because they feel that they can't stand up against the *kaumatua*. They go off home and discuss it and get hold of someone who is a good speaker to put it as an amendment and get the whole thing reversed.' Fifthly, as one *kaumatua* observed, 'Kotare Maoris are conservative and jealous of anything new. They hold off, waiting and watching to see how it succeeds before giving it any support'—an attitude that is by no means rare, especially in rural communities. Another, however, was hopeful for the future: 'It is very difficult to get these people to co-operate, but once they see you are genuine, they'll stick.'

In spite of its weaknesses and difficulties, the Kotare Komiti Marae had managed to survive two-and-a-half years, and in that time it had kept on moving forward, making mistakes and then recovering and learning from them. If it was still a long way from realizing its founders' ideal of a completely unified community, it had secured corporate action on a wider basis than Kotare had known for many years. It had achieved at least its original intention of improving attendances at *tangi*, for recent ones in Kotare had been crowded out. Up to a thousand visited the *marae* during *tangi*, with people coming from as far as Hokianga as well as emigrants living in Auckland and beyond. Also important for the future was the fact that it provided a system of organization in working order to cope with the very big problem posed by the condemnation of the Puriri *marae* buildings.

THE KOTARE KOMITI AND SOCIAL AND ECONOMIC CHANGE

Both the 'family' *komiti* and the Kotare Komiti Marae had adapted a form of organization which was non-Maori in origin to particular Maori aims and Maori ways of doing things. All were unrestricted in size. When a *komiti*'s members became too numerous to participate in all its decisions, they set up an executive sub-committee. The

Kotare Komiti Marae was divided into a number of sub-groups formed largely on the basis of kinship, some with officers of their own, who were in no way controlled by those of the wider group. *Komiti* meetings were only lightly constrained by procedural rules, the latter being interpreted for the group by the few members who had any experience therein. They were invariably lengthy and open to the public. Members followed the Maori pattern of talking until virtual unanimity was reached rather than resorting immediately to the ballot. The talking was done mainly by those recognized in the community at large as *kaumatua* and *kai-korero*. The executive posts were filled and the practical work directed by those in the 'middle generations', while the young and unmarried were often absent from meetings but cheerfully turned up to work at any gatherings the *komiti* sponsored. This division of labour was characteristic of the Maori community at large. It took some time for opposition to the ideas of the *kai-korero* to crystallize, because so many were diffident about speaking in public in Maori, and often waited until they could arrange for someone to speak for them.

The Kotare Komiti Marae was started for a specific purpose in response to a specific situation: to place the running of *tangi* on a sound economic basis by spreading costs over the whole community and thereby to restore Kotare's reputation in the Maori world of the Far North. An important underlying motive was the desire to achieve a return to the traditional Maori ideal of unified community action. To this end, its members were prepared to subordinate their kin-group loyalties to a large extent and to accept as full and equal members those who were 'outsiders' according to Maori custom. The Kotare Komiti Marae had developed out of the 'family' *komiti*, but it had already outgrown them. In its short history, it had proved itself more flexible and progressive than the older *komiti*, which by all reports had changed little over the last generation or two. Yet the people themselves saw the 'big *komiti*' not only as in tune with Maori cultural aspirations but as actively promoting them. Rua Rewiti summed it up when he observed: 'The Kotare Komiti Marae is a new idea in Kotare but it is also an old Maori custom.' One of the most significant characteristics of the Kotare Komiti Marae was its spontaneity. It was conceived and carried through by the people themselves for ends they held to be important, without outside guidance or interference. Therein lay both its strength and its achievement.

Neither its originators nor its members intended or expected that the Kotare Komiti Marae should affect their relationship with the Pakeha world. Yet in fact it marked a significant advance in the social and economic development of the Maori community in Kotare. In the first place, it indicated dissatisfaction with the *status quo* and a willingness to discard or modify traditional patterns in the pursuit of a worthwhile goal. The fact that it was also directed towards an ideal implicit in the traditional culture does not diminish the significance of this acceptance of change. Secondly, it increased the familiarity of the average Maori in Kotare with the mechanics of modern, democratic committee government—with the conduct of meetings, the use of written records to settle arguments over past events and decisions, and the drawing-up and interpretation of financial statements. Thirdly, by achieving its original and most specific aim, it had built up the people's confidence in themselves, attacking the defeatist attitudes that had prevailed so long concerning their ability to handle money and to 'get things done'. And fourthly, it provided members with an insurance against the heavy cost and anxieties associated with *tangi*, which could be a serious drain on economic resources even when shared by kin.

It would be easy to claim that forms of organization such as the Kotare *komiti*, by emphasizing the exclusiveness of the Maori groups and aims differing from those of the rest of the population, actively hinder the full integration of the Maori into New Zealand society. But, as I have tried to show, the Kotare *komiti* helped in many ways to combat some of the real obstacles to integration: cultural conservatism, unfamiliarity with Pakeha forms of organization, feelings of inferiority and insecurity, lack of economic resources. Indeed, I would suggest that such forms of organization play a vital role in the process of integration, providing as they do a bridge between the old and the new.[1]

---

[1] Today (at the beginning of 1963) the Kotare Komiti Marae is still functioning efficiently, with 152 members paying *aitua* taxes. Many members have been lost through emigration, but members of the Hakea *komiti*, abandoning their intention to rebuild the Hakea *marae*, have joined the big *komiti* as a group, and so have those of Onepu. The renovation of the Puriri *marae* has been entrusted to a new Marae Trustees' Committee. Under its direction a former school building has been moved to the *marae* and converted for use as a dining-hall, a sanitary block built and a 3,000 gallon concrete water-tank installed. When improvements to the meeting-house are completed, the project will cost £2,200, half of which will be paid by Government subsidy. With the Puriri *marae* temporarily out of commission, *hui* are being held at the Karaka marae.

11

Capital, Credit and Saving in Javanese Marketing[1]

BY ALICE DEWEY

This essay attempts to place certain economic aspects of the internal peasant marketing systems of Java into a wider social context. Thus it will be suggested that the causes of the shortage of capital—one of the characteristics of an under-developed country—are not narrowly economic, but stem partly from prevailing social patterns, which affect the form in which savings are held and the goals towards which they are used. It will also be shown that larger-scale trade is usually financed and handled by Chinese who are more capable than the Javanese: the larger capital resources as well as certain advantages in trading organization and methods enjoyed by the Chinese are largely the result of their social organization; Javanese social organization, in contrast, inhibits similar developments among Javanese traders. These problems, and other inter-related problems, will be considered in the light of both the economic and the social forces operating on the peasant economy.

Java, an island of almost fifty thousand square miles, has a population of something over sixty million. The composition of this population is complex. It includes a small European sector which, in

[1] The material for this essay was gathered during the year July 1953 to July 1954 in a medium sized town (here given the pseudonym Modjokuto) about eighty kilometres south of Surabaya in East Java. Though the work was done within only one market, this market was in daily contact with the surrounding town and city markets and information from traders who visited these markets indicates clearly that the patterns found in Modjokuto were typical of a wider area. Statements from traders who had previously worked in other parts of Central Java, and my own observations in widely scattered areas, indicate that the basic organization of the market was similar over much of Java, at that time. In 1959, however, the Indonesian government passed laws expelling Chinese traders from rural areas. These laws are now being put into effect. It is clear that the removal of the Chinese must have important repercussions on many aspects of market trade, and that many of the patterns described here will have been substantially affected.

230

1953–54, dominated that part of the economy which was organized on a capital-intensive basis on a Western pattern. (The expulsion in 1957 of a large portion of the Dutch residents has undoubtedly altered this segment of the economy.) It also includes a larger number of foreign Orientals, mostly Chinese, Arabs and Indians, the Chinese being by far the largest group. Each of these groups maintains its own cultural community, preserving its own language and customs, and marrying endogamously. These groups also form a separate economic category, specializing in intermediate trading and medium and small-scale manufacture. The bulk of the population consists of Javanese. Most of them are small farmers. A significant proportion of them, however, make their living partly or wholly as artisans or small traders, and an increasing number work as unskilled and skilled wage-labourers. Since Indonesia gained its independence, many more are engaged in clerical and administrative work in the civil service and also in the professions. Their number is still relatively small.

THE MARKET SYSTEM

With the exception of the very wealthy who can afford to patronize the large urban stores with their supplies of imported goods, almost everyone depends on the peasant market system for the supply of goods, that is, some or all foodstuffs and many other things. The Europeans and foreign Orientals, who are prohibited by law from owning farm land, as well as the town and city-dwelling Javanese buy all or most of their food in the *pasar* (the indigenous peasant markets). The farmer buys not only those things which he cannot raise himself, such as salt, refined sugar and imported spices, but often also other foods which he cannot or has not raised himself. Most farmers put the bulk of their land into those few crops which it is judged will bring the most profit when sold. At harvest time the farmer sells most or all of his output to meet expenses calling for payment in money. If the need for cash is urgent, he may even sell crops he normally reserves for his own consumption and buy a cheaper substitute instead. If his financial position improves, he may later buy the very foods he has sold previously.

Handicrafts are done on a commercial basis by specialists rather than by individual families for home consumption. For this reason not only the urban population but also the rural Javanese buy cloth, tools, kitchen utensils, furniture, building materials, etc. in the markets. Even the tailoring of cloth into clothing and the preparation of certain foods (for example, soy bean cake, one of the commonest items in the diet) are largely done commercially. Some of these commodities are imported and some made in factories in Java; but most are produced by local cottage-industries. All of them, however, are handled by the *pasar* system, at least in the last stages of their distribution.

Thus a great variety and a large quantity of goods and services are purchased daily in the markets by the people of Java. Most of the food and the goods produced by artisans come from within the peasant segment of the economy; they are produced in small amounts and come from many scattered sources. Imported goods and those of the few large factories in Java come in large quantities from a small number of sources. Those from medium-sized and small factories fall somewhere between these two patterns. And so the *pasar* system has to cope with goods which have vastly different marketing characteristics and modes of production.

Imported and factory-made goods which are dispersed in large amounts from a few sources are handled mostly by Chinese, until they have been broken down into small retail lots. Because the values and the distances involved are considerable, large-scale capital-intensive techniques can be used to advantage and economies of scale are possible. The Chinese with their larger supplies of capital and their widely spread commercial contacts are in a better position to handle this phase of distribution, and they dominate the intermediate trade between the few large supply centres and the many local markets. For the same reason they are important in the inter-market wholesaling of the major cash crops produced by Javanese peasant farmers.

Where trading is necessarily small in scale, however, Javanese traders working as independent businessmen handle most of the goods. Retailing of most things must be done on a very small scale since the consumers are distributed widely in thousands of towns and villages, and each buys in very small quantities. Most foods and goods produced by cottage-industry are in fact traded in small amounts within a restricted area; and both the concentration of supplies and their distribution are in the hands of Javanese traders. They are able to compete successfully with the Chinese in this type of trade, because the patterns of production and consumption restrict trade to a small scale in which economies of scale are insignificant or non-existent. Large-scale organization would require centralized control or supervision of employees or agents in each of the many villages and towns in the marketing region; and this would be both difficult and expensive in a country with poor communications and transport facilities. In many aspects of trading the small-scale Javanese trader can compensate for his very limited capital by using his own (unpaid) labour and local knowledge in labour-intensive methods. He is also prepared to work for low returns, because there are few alternative uses to which his labour and knowledge can be put.

There are thus two fairly distinct spheres and types of operation in

232

the marketing system: large-scale trade using (relatively) capital-intensive techniques which is dominated by the Chinese; and small-scale trade, centring in the *pasar*, which consists almost entirely of the operations of independent Javanese traders working with a minimum of capital and depending on labour-intensive techniques, local knowledge and individual initiative. Certain goods do not fall clearly into either category of trade. Some of the most interesting of these are the large cash crops which commonly pass from Javanese into Chinese hands, and back again. During the heaviest periods of this trading the Javanese traders adapt their practices so as to take advantage of certain distinct economies of scale and of central direction, without raising capital requirements beyond their limited means.

PROLIFERATION OF TRADERS

The most usual pattern of trade in the *pasar*, however, is characterized by extremely labour-intensive methods. There is a great proliferation of individual traders using only their own limited capital, neither employing others nor being employed by others. The proliferation of traders partly reflects the serious unemployment and under-employment in Java. There are no restrictions on entry into *pasar* trade, and many fall back on trading who do not have enough land to support themselves and cannot find paid employment. Much of the proliferation constitutes, in effect, the substitution of plentiful resources in the form (in the industrial sense) of unskilled and self-motivated labour for scarce resources such as skilled labour, equipment, communication and transportation facilities, and experienced managerial personnel. Some of these resources are virtually unavailable because of import restrictions and the like, while others would require heavy investment of scarce capital.

To utilize labour-intensive techniques, heavy complex tasks must be broken into smaller simpler tasks. The work must be organized so that it can be done by one-man units. Each task must be simple enough to be readily learned. The total complex task has to be subdivided into a number of separate simplified tasks; and then a large number of people have to engage in each sub-division, so that the achievement of the total task can be hastened. When a task is as complex and requires as much energy (in the technical sense of the word) as that of the market system of Java, it is obvious that many individuals are needed.

The lack of communication facilities and the low literacy rate mean that the circulation of market information alone is complicated. Most information is, in fact, transmitted from trader to trader as an incidental part of their contact. This limits the area over which any trader can operate successfully, for it is impossible to maintain daily face-to-face contact with people in more than one market, or at most two markets. Poor communications also mean that certain tasks, such as the searching-out of goods in rural areas and testing inter-market wholesale prices, cannot be done simultaneously by one person; this is so even though neither task is technically too complex nor the immediate energy requirements too heavy for a single person. Difficulties of communication increase the total number of people needed. They also reduce the chances of achieving efficient centralization. Independent traders operating within a restricted area can gather their own information individually, and need no over-all supervision or direction to co-ordinate their separate information and activities; and so they have a competitive advantage over centralized organizations.

There are also the problems caused by lack of standardized and universally-accepted grades for most commodities. Farm products are not graded, and goods from cottage-industry establishments vary widely in size and quality. Because of the consequent need for careful inspection of all goods, bulk buying is inadvisable especially when it is done at a distance and no check of quality is made on the spot. Under these conditions more mechanized methods, which depend on bulk handling of standard goods, are at a disadvantage, and centralization of buying impractical. In *pasar* trade, on the other hand, buyer and seller meet face to face and handle small quantities, and it is not difficult to inspect each purchase thoroughly. There is, therefore, little need of, or demand for, standardization. The Javanese *pasar* system, by being labour-intensive, overcomes certain difficulties associated with technologically under-developed economies with poor communication facilities, difficulties which pose serious problems for capital-intensive and large-scale enterprises.

There is a further factor which draws more people into trade than are in a sense necessary to supply the labour-effort for the physical performance of the marketing tasks: this is the need for capital. For though *pasar* trade is very labour-intensive, money is still needed to buy goods and to meet other costs such as market entrance fees, occasional weighing-fees, and so on. Individual savings are small, credit is used in only a few types of trade (see below), and each trader works independently with his own capital resources. Thus, the individual trader can handle only a small amount of goods. To increase the total amount of capital available for trading purposes, the number of traders must be increased.

To summarize; the proliferation of traders is a result of the technological under-development of the economy, the unemployment and under-employment which makes self-employed labour cheap, the ease of entry into *pasar* trading, and the need to attract many small individually-owned amounts of capital to finance those operations (in trading) in the performance of which self-employed labour cannot be substituted for capital and other factors of production.

CASH, WAGE-LABOUR AND USE OF TIME

The inter-relation of certain other factors, some primarily economic, some primarily social, must be taken into account to understand the operation of the Javanese market system. Among these are cash, wage-labour and time.

The banking system in Java is never used by most peasants, who are largely illiterate. For this reason currency is the only generally-accepted means of payment, and for all practical purposes liquid capital means cash. Many of the most common consumer goods, from soy bean cake, the main protein in the diet, to kerosene for lamps, can only be obtained by the expenditure of cash. (Barter of goods is virtually non-existent in Java.) Heavy cash outlays are also required at essential social ceremonies celebrating life crises such as marriage and circumcision. Opportunities for acquiring cash, however, were sharply curtailed with the decline in the number and size of the plantations (mostly sugar plantations in the area in which I worked); money income from wage-labour on the plantations and from land rented to them was one of the major sources of cash for many people before the war. At the same time the desire for expensive western-style goods not produced within the peasant economy has risen in recent years. While sources of cash incomes have declined, the uses for it have increased. Credit is hard to get, and there is no other form of negotiable paper. Cash, or rather activities or assets capable of producing a money income, have thus become relatively more valuable than activities or assets not capable of producing a money income. And as the *pasar* is (or was in 1953–54 when this study was made) the main source in which money comes into the hands of many rural and urban Javanese, the *pasar* system takes on a special importance.

This special importance is shared with wage-labour. A man with work to be done and the cash to pay wages is in a position to allocate it on a patronage basis. In the post-war situation most wage-labour is engaged by wealthy farmers. (There are in Java few of the really wealthy absentee landlords of the sort reported for other parts of the Orient. The wealthy farmers referred to here are wealthy only in relation to other people in their villages, with whom they share most aspects of daily life.) They are almost invariably influential men in their villages, and various of the poorer villagers are tied to them in a special relationship through links of kinship and neighbourhood. These villagers have obligations to support their patron politically, to assist him with labour and gifts of cooked food when he gives a feast, and to do odd jobs and run errands. They must also be available when he needs a large labour force. At harvest time crops must be gathered quickly to keep them from spoiling and to get them to market when the price is highest; thus success in large-scale farming depends mainly on the ability of the farmer to assemble a sufficient labour force. (See Robert R. Jay, 1963, for a complete analysis of this problem.) For this reason the patron must keep the loyalty of his 'clients'. He must help them by lending or giving them money, food and other supplies when they are in need, by advising them in their dealings with the outside world, and also by giving them priority in access to land and in allotting wage-labour so that they have opportunities to earn cash. If the patron does not do these things he loses the political support of his clients and their assistance during harvest, the one time when labour is scarce.

A 'closed shop' is created in which there is preferential allocation of opportunities for wage-earning, labour is commanded by a few, and the relationship between employer and employee is defined more by social and long-term than by narrowly commercial and short-term considerations. As a result, wages seem to be somewhat higher than they would be otherwise, and the mobility of wage-paid labour is restricted. Townspeople who have severed their ties with village life are cut off from one of the main sources of paid employment.

Trading, as already noted, is the other major means of acquiring cash. People are willing to put what, to an outsider, may appear to be a disproportionate amount of time and labour into a commercial transaction which promises them only a few rupiah.[1] This does not mean, as has sometimes been asserted, that the peasants do not appreciate the value of time. The Javanese know that time is vital not only in the agricultural process but also in marketing, where a few hours' delay may mean a considerable adverse change in price. They are prepared to expend their own time freely if doing so enables them to be at the market to catch the most favourable opportunities for buying and/or selling according to their speciality. If they miss the critical periods, their profits which are small enough as it is will be even smaller, no matter how much time and labour they have invested in the process. Realizing that there are few alternative ways in which to employ their time and labour productively, they use these personal resources liberally especially when they yield earnings in cash rather than in kind.

The Javanese social structure influences the economic structure in several ways. Perhaps the most important effect is the restricted

[1]The official rate of exchange in 1953–54 was Rp. 11·40 to one us dollar. (The black market rate was about Rp. 25·00 to a dollar.) At that time Rp. 5 would keep a family of two or three for a day.

possibilities of assembling capital caused by the small size of the group within which informal social and economic sanctions are capable of enforcing contractual obligations. These informal sanctions are of paramount importance in Java where the legal machinery for enforcing commercial contracts is not yet sufficiently developed to provide reasonably cheap protection for the average person.

Javanese social structure has no clans, castes, age-grades or other groupings of the kind which bind large numbers of people together. The kinship system is bilateral and the kindred has no clearly defined limits and no existence as a group. Kin ties link individuals to one another, but not groups to groups. In the rural villages, where the population is fairly stable, neighbourhood groups based on a combination of kinship, neighbourship and economic interdependence are of considerable importance. Within these groups informal social and economic sanctions are quite effective. The people depend on each other for help both in daily life and in times of crises. The poorer people exchange labour for labour, or for payment in kind. They give labour to the wealthier villagers in return for cash wages and access to land. The wealthy patrons have land and capital and need labour; the poorer clients have labour and need land and cash. Thus the interdependence of land and labour provides an economic basis for strong informal sanctions in the agrarian sector of the peasant economy. The community can withdraw its support from anyone who fails to meet those obligations which are traditionally recognized, thereby causing him serious economic and social difficulties. Within the neighbourhood group credit of various sorts can be, and is, extended with reasonably low risks of default. These sanctions, effective within any one rural neighbourhood, are, however, powerless outside it, and credit transactions between villagers of different neighbourhoods are much less common.

The economic interdependence characteristic of rural areas has no counterpart in urban areas. In urban areas the neighbourhood group is of little importance socially or economically. The people with whom an individual associates in his work often do not live in his neighbourhood. Kinsmen tend to be more widely scattered and economic co-operation between them is less common than among rural kinsmen who tend to cluster in local areas and who may have common land interests. Most full-time traders are urban-dwellers, and so to a large extent are independent of social and economic commitments in their relationships with one another. Some villagers do engage in trade, usually on a part-time basis; but trade, by its very nature, takes them out of their villages, and most of their business is transacted with people who do not belong to their neighbourhood and with whom they have no other ties.

Thus, among traders in general, competition and trading intercourse are virtually free; and since capital, the major scarce resource, is fairly equally distributed, the bases for a patron-client relationship (on the rural pattern) are lacking in marketing. In trade, each person supplies both his own capital and his own labour, so he can neither exert pressure on other traders nor be controlled by them. Thus informal sanctions are very weak.[1]

TRADING RELATIONSHIPS

In most of the trading activities carried on by the Javanese, small-scale labour-intensive methods are more advantageous than capital-intensive ones. So most traders dealing in the same commodity prefer to operate independently and in competition with each other. The absence of sanctions is not a serious handicap. But it becomes a problem in the trade between people specializing in different phases of the marketing process.

In a market system which is labour-intensive and must contend with poor transport and communications, goods must be passed from hand to hand through a long chain of intermediaries. In the marketing of agricultural produce, for example, the first stage of the assembling process is done by men and women carriers who travel through the rural areas, mostly on foot, from farm to farm until they have found enough goods for sale to make a reasonable load. The carriers bring the goods to market and sell them to middlemen who operate almost entirely within the market place itself. The middleman may then sell to a housewife, to another middleman, or to an inter-market carrier who takes the goods to another market for resale there. Usually there are no social ties between the people involved in the different parts of the chain of intermediaries, and the commercial contacts are too intermittent and short-term to provide the basis for a stable business relationship.

Each market serves an area with a radius of approximately five miles, and in a land where the population density rises above 1,000 per square mile, thousands of people are involved in the trade focused on each market. Each small producer sells to such carriers as happen to be in his area, and the carriers have a choice of several markets in which to sell their goods. Within each market there are numerous traders who may buy the goods, and they in turn have a wide variety of customers to whom they sell. Except when one middleman sells to another, those involved in successive transactions

[1] In certain conditions, however, some traders pool their resources of capital and labour for limited periods and purposes, forming trading groups within which sanctions do operate. These trading groups, though never large, are nevertheless capital-intensive in comparison with the operations of individual traders. These groups will be discussed later.

in the chain of distribution are strangers to each other, or at best casual business acquaintainces, and they cannot use informal sanctions to enforce payment when credit sales are made. Since legal sanctions are ineffective, the risk of default is high, and as a result very few people are willing to give credit.

The absence of sanctions and of stable commercial relationships preclude long-term planning in small-scale trade. No one orders a given quantity and quality of goods at an agreed price to be delivered at a certain date, for such a contract could not be enforced any more than could the repayment of a debt from a credit sale. In any case, such an order would not be practicable because communications are not sufficiently developed to give traders the information on which to base such long-term plans. In small-scale marketing short-term planning gives more flexibility, and the traders prefer it because it allows daily adjustments to local conditions, and reduces the amount of capital invested and the length of time it is tied up in goods. As long as the Javanese restrict themselves to small-scale trade the looseness of the social and commercial structure is not a serious drawback, except in so far as it restricts credit, for this limits the flow of the already scarce capital. But it puts them at a competitive disadvantage in large-scale inter-market trade. The latter is dominated by the Chinese for reasons closely associated with their type of social organization.

The social organization of the Chinese is very different from that of the Javanese. They maintain connections with a wider circle of kin and, as elsewhere in south-east Asia, they also have various types of associational groupings and secret societies. The most important of these in Modjokuto, and in Java generally, are the groupings based on what is called *bangsa* affiliation.[1]

CHINESE AND JAVANESE TRADERS

The *totok*—Chinese immigrants who have kept their own culture in relatively pure form, mostly more recent arrivals—still trace their descent from a specific area in China. They form *bangsa* groups with other people from that area speaking the same dialect. They usually marry within the *bangsa* group. The relations between the members are formalized in various associations: burial societies, sports groups, commercial associations and the like. Most trade relations follow *bangsa* lines, a practice which is reflected in and strengthened by the tendency for the members of the same *bangsa* to engage in the same

[1] See Edward J. Ryan's forthcoming report on the Chinese in the 'Modjokuto Study' series. Most of my information of the Chinese comes from Mr Ryan, and I am greatly indebted to him for his help in formulating the ideas presented here on the inter-relationship of social and commercial organization.

type of business. For example, the majority of the Hokkien of Modjokuto are wholesalers of secondary crops or cloth-sellers; the Hok-chian deal in secondary crops but not in cloth; the Hinghwa run bicycle shops almost exclusively; and the Chinese dentists in Modjokuto are Hupei. Usually a few people of each *bangsa* follow different trades from the majority, and, except for specialized occupations such as dentistry, no one field is dominated completely by any one *bangsa*. Nevertheless, a Hokkien wholesaler in secondary crops maintains trade relations almost exclusively with other Hokkien in Modjokuto and in the larger cities rather than with Hok-chian in the same trade.

The *peranakan*—Chinese who have lost their ties with China and absorbed Javanese ways—are not as tightly organized as the *totok* groups, nor are they as specialized in trade. However, they also group themselves into units according to local area or associational affiliation, and prefer endogamous marriages. Their trade, in general, follows the lines established by marital and associational ties.

Within the various Chinese groupings, and to some degree within the Chinese community as a whole, especially in a community as small as that of Modjokuto (1,800 people), ties of kinship, common nationality and co-membership in various types of associations reinforce commercial relationships and are reinforced by them. The result is a series of closely-knit inter-connected Chinese communities extending all over Java and often beyond. Social ties are used as a basis for extending commercial relations beyond the nuclear family and the local group. Thus Chinese social structure tends to encourage larger commercial units, while Javanese social structure gives no basis for extending co-operation beyond a small circle.

This leads to an interesting conclusion concerning the relationship between social structure and economic development. Many Westerners hold that Javanese economic expansion is held back by their large extended families, since profits from a family business must be shared among a large number of people, many of whom have not helped to earn them. This, they claim, inhibits individual initiative, prevents the formation of capital, and causes employees to be chosen because of social obligations rather than for their commercial skill. This theory falls to the ground, in the first place, because extended family groups are not characteristic of Javanese society. In the second place, the same criticisms can be levelled against the *bangsa* groupings among the *totok* and the various groupings among the *peranakan* Chinese which, like the extended family, are based on kinship, linguistic similarity and other social ties. Yet the Chinese have turned these groupings, based on non-commercial criteria, to advantage in business. Through them capital is gathered, credit safely extended and favoured treatment given to selected individuals. This gives an im-

Capital, Credit and Saving in Javanese Marketing

portant advantage where competition is severe and profit margins narrow; capital flows more freely within the group and contractual obligations are honoured even at great cost. Thus under certain conditions social ties are not antagonistic to business efficiency.

It is not known what these conditions are, but one factor which may be important is the minority position of the Chinese in Java. In relation to the Javanese they are a small community. (In Modjokuto itself they number about 1,800 out of a total of approximately 18,000, and there are few of them in the thickly-settled rural areas surrounding the town.) The number of people who will call on a given merchant for favoured treatment is limited by the size of the Chinese community, and further by the split between *peranakan* and *totok* and the division of the latter into *bangsa*. This prevents demands from becoming so burdensome that they nullify the economic advantages derived from the groupings. For this reason social ties, when restricted to distinct groupings as they are among the Chinese, are commercially useful. However, it is by no means certain that they would operate in the same manner for the Javanese, among whom the lack of focused groupings (beyond the local rural ones) would expose a merchant to demands from an almost unlimited number of other Javanese.

By operating within their own community the Chinese establish wider geographical contacts without unduly increasing the number of people involved. The relatively small numbers involved and the tight organization of the community give greater power to informal sanctions. The Chinese live mostly within their own community. The larger Javanese community is somewhat hostile and discriminates against them. Thus the internal organization, in the form of *bangsa* groupings, associations etc., and external pressures combine to give a high degree of solidarity. Furthermore, the fact that the vast majority are merchants in intermediate trade and that this trade is largely in Chinese hands increases their interdependence.[1]

Each Chinese deals with and depends on other Chinese in business. If a man is found to be dishonest or irresponsible, the community can bring strong informal sanctions, social and economic, to bear on him. No one will lend him money or deal with him and he and his family will face social isolation which can mean difficulty in finding spouses for his children, mourners at his funeral, and so on. The result is strong adherence to accepted business ethics. A merchant who has promised delivery of certain goods on a particular date will make every effort to fulfil his commitments even if it means a financial loss, for it is essential that he maintain his reputation. The buyer is freed from uncertainty and from the need for constant supervision of his

[1] The reasons for the concentration in intermediate trade have been discussed elsewhere. See Dewey, 1962.

241

associates; and he can proceed with the resale of the goods knowing they will be available as planned. A man who asks for credit normally gets it, and a man who gives it knows he will be repaid. This reduces costs and risks. In effect, the members of the Chinese trading communities underwrite each individual transaction, as occurs by more formal arrangements in an organized Western stock exchange or commodity market. This gives the Chinese a marked advantage over the Javanese in the (relatively) large-scale trade, where long-term large-scale planning is important and economies of scale are material.

JAVANESE TRADER GROUPS

In the main Modjokuto market the Javanese enter large-scale trade in certain restricted types of goods, mainly corn and onions, commercially the most important crops in the area. In the marketing of these commodities they change their mode of operations to cope with the difficulties and opportunities peculiar to this trade.[1] This trade requires widespread trade contacts, and also appreciable amounts of capital to finance buying and to achieve the economies of scale of bulk handling and mechanization. The Chinese with their superior capital resources and organization largely account for the large-scale inter-market wholesale trade. But the Javanese usually handle much of the collection and concentration of the important local crops, selling them to the Chinese who then resell them in other markets where other Javanese traders handle the local retailing.[2] At times the Javanese enter even the inter-market trading in competition with the Chinese.

Even when they handle only the farm-to-market trade in goods of this kind, where the quantities involved in a single transaction are smaller than in trade between markets, the Javanese in the Modjokuto *pasar* must adapt their practices to meet the demands of the more mechanized and relatively more capital-intensive methods of the Chinese to whom they sell. They mediate between the small-scale trade, where quality is unpredictable, quantities small and uneven, and the flow irregular, and the large-scale trade which demands a regular supply of specific quantities and qualities. To achieve the adjustment, the Javanese must handle larger amounts of goods and have greater control over the flow than in their retail trade. They do this by forming small groups, and pooling their capital and labour

---

[1] The most elaborate development of large-scale marketing techniques among Javanese seems to be a post-war phenomenon and may not appear in other areas in quite the form I observed in the main Modjokuto market.

[2] Similarly Javanese traders handle most of the retailing of goods brought into the Modjokuto area from elsewhere, among which hardware and dry goods are more prominent than agricultural produce.

242

resources. With more labour and capital available in the unit of organization, the participants can send one of their number into the country to negotiate large purchases direct from individual farmers; this helps to assure a supply of uniform quality goods at a favourable price, since the farmers prefer to sell their whole crop in one transaction. Even when they buy in the *pasar*, the fact that they can buy in quantity usually secures them a lower price. While the buying member of the group is thus engaged, other members guard goods already in the *pasar*, watch market conditions and arrange sales to wholesalers. If they are not satisfied with the price offered by the wholesalers, they may use some of their capital to send another member to the big centres to investigate the possibilities of sales there. If he arranges a deal, the group hires a truck to transport the goods, and sends one or more of its members as representative to oversee the shipment and receive payment. Group collaboration allows co-ordination of buying, pricing, weighing, grading, transporting and selling (as well as bulk handling with a certain amount of mechanization) and a wider knowledge of market conditions. All this speeds the marketing process and helps to assure a regular flow of goods by giving the *pasar*-based traders greater control over the farm-to-market stage, and in some cases over the inter-market phase as well.

At the same time, the Javanese continue to enjoy the advantages of using self-employed, individually motivated unskilled and cheap labour in those phases of the operation where heavier capital investment would not increase productivity proportionately. They do, however, forfeit flexibility, for capital is invested for longer periods, and once a contract has been made it cannot be altered. Since it may be a week or more from the time a contract is made until the consignment is delivered to the Chinese trader, the risks from price fluctuations increase. The formation of groups in itself helps to compensate for this, as the risks are spread over a larger number of people. A group is formed to handle only a single consignment, and when it is completed the profits or losses are divided and the group dissolved. A trader usually belongs to more than one group at a time, and invests only a portion of his capital in each. Actually there is much overlap in the membership of the groups; but each group is a distinct unit and each consignment is handled separately, so that a loss on one does not affect any other. (This is a rudimentary example of the same system on which Lloyds underwriters work.) Risks are also reduced at times by a particular type of credit transaction (*harga hidup*) discussed below.

These trader groups are interesting because they represent almost the only case of collaboration (as distinct from master-and-servant relationships) between people who are not members of the same nuclear family. The groups are unstructured, transient, and not based nor modelled on kin groupings, rural neighbourhood groupings, nor the rural patron-client relationship. The members are often kinsmen and/or neighbours; but the basis for the group is purely one of economic convenience and each person profits in proportion to the capital and work he contributes, and not in proportion to the closeness of his kin or neighbour ties.

At the corn harvest in 1954, my first experience of the formation of these groups, each consisted of only two or three independent traders. When the heavier trade connected with the onion harvest reached its height some weeks later the normal number in a group rose to between six and eight, but it never seemed to go beyond this. The core of a group usually were two or three close friends or relatives. Others were brought in as the need for capital dictated. Since these groups are very small and short-lived and the people know each other well, there is no need to set up a formal organization to make decisions and communicate information. An experienced trader with a forceful personality may have more influence than the others in the group; but there is no leader and no one has authority over the others.

As already observed, there are as a rule few sanctions, formal or informal, which traders can impose on one another to enforce compliance with the rules of business ethics. As a result they usually avoid relationships in which trust is necessary. However, when they belong to a group they have to depend on one another. I never heard of a case where one member of a group violated the trust of his fellows. The people who operate in groups are drawn from a restricted number of established traders who are well known in the local *pasar*, and each man is careful to collaborate only with those he knows and trusts. At the same time, since working in a group has distinct advantages, traders are anxious to maintain their reputations so as to be eligible for group membership. Dishonesty is hard to conceal for any length of time; once discovered, it is gossiped about and the offender excluded from future group ventures. Thus within the limits of group collaboration, traders can enforce a limited type of economic sanction on their fellows. They have little power over those outside their own market; but within one market the threat of exclusion from group operations combines with personal loyalties to reduce the risks of dishonesty sufficiently for the traders to engage in this type of operation.

The groups also have a strong incentive to preserve their reputation for honesty in their dealings with others, because in certain conditions they are forced to ask for credit from the farmer suppliers. Only established traders with good reputations are likely to be granted credit. At one period in 1954 when I was observing the market, prices had been very uncertain and many traders, having lost heavily, lacked capital with which to continue trading. The inter-market wholesalers also were in difficulties and could not advance them the necessary cash. In these circumstances the farmers began to extend credit to the market traders in what may be described as a type of commission selling. The credit extended was only very short-term, it is true (payment was usually made within a week or ten days); but it is interesting that such credit was given at all, for it is the reverse of the practice in many peasant economies where it is the traders who extend credit to the farmers in the form of advance payments on their crops. (In Java the Chinese do this at times, though it seems to have been more common before the war.)

EXTENSION OF CREDIT

When selling on credit first became common during the 1954 harvest season (in April), most of it was on the system called *harga hidup,* or literally 'live price', which ties the price the farmers receive to the price the traders get when they resell the goods. The traders contact a farmer and offer him a tentative price per kilogram, based either on their estimate of current resale values or on a bid they have received from a wholesaler. If the eventual buyer forces down the traders' selling price, the price eventually paid to the farmer falls accordingly. In this way the traders shift the risks of falling prices to the farmers. The traders, however, bear the costs of handling and thus the risks on this investment. For the first part of the 1954 harvest season the farmers were willing to extend credit on a *harga hidup* basis; but by the beginning of May conditions had deteriorated. Prices had fallen further, and the Chinese stopped buying for a time so that inter-market trade almost ceased. Traders were reluctant to continue operations and the farmers did not want to extend credit for fear that the prices realized would be too low. On the other hand, if selling were delayed too long, the onions would be spoiled and lose value disastrously. When the situation became desperate, the farmers began to extend credit again; but at this point the *pindjam* system became more common than *harga hidup.* In the *pindjam* system the price per kilogram is established at the time the contract is made. (The total price is not determined until the trader has taken possession of the goods in the market place and weighed them.) By using this system the farmers shift most of the price risks back on to the traders.

Once the Chinese intermediaries had stopped handling the transfer of onions to the cities where the demand was heaviest, the Javanese traders began to send agents to make direct contact with the urban wholesale buyers. They were obliged to take over the inter-market operations themselves if they were to dispose of the onions at a reasonable price. They had not only to accept the risks associated with this trade, but they also were no longer able to shift some of the risks on to the farmers as in the *harga hidup* system. However, the farmers' risks were also increased in spite of the change to the *pindjam* system, because the risk of default increased as the general market conditions deteriorated. The danger that the crop would spoil produced a crisis which involved farmer and trader alike in heavier risks.

Had the farmers insisted on selling for cash they would have been able to do so only if they accepted a very low price. By extending credit they improved their prospects of bigger profits. This increase, when realized, may be considered to be hidden interest on the credit; but in none of these transactions was interest overtly charged by any of the parties. In fact, overt interest is rare in market trade. This is at least partly due to the strong Koranic prohibition. Even people not avowed Moslems have come to view the charging of overt interest as immoral.

Selling on credit is not unfamiliar in Java (apart from the type of credit sales already discussed). When it is done systematically, the price is increased in lieu of (overt) interest charges; but it is practised in this form only by Chinese, Arabs and the more Westernized Javanese. The Javanese do a certain amount of small-scale, and usually very short-term, credit selling; but it is in the nature of a small service done for one's customers or fellow traders and does not normally involve an increase in the price. It is possible that there is some hidden interest in some cases.

Small amounts of interest-free credit are extended by traders to their customers. On the simplest level, a customer who buys a cup of coffee and finds (or pretends to find) himself short of cash, will pay part of the price and promise to pay the rest later. Interest on such a small sum, perhaps as little as five or ten Indonesian cents, would be ridiculous, and it would certainly alienate the customer who would probably default on the whole debt and take his trade elsewhere into the bargain.

Credit is also given by one trader to another in certain cases. I knew of one woman selling hot coffee and snacks who occasionally bought a particular type of pastry from another snack-seller because she did not have the equipment to make it. Normally the pastries cost 25 cents apiece; she paid a reduced wholesale price of Rp 1.90 for ten and bought as many as thirty at a time. She got them early in the morning and did not have to pay for them until noon, when the major business of the day was over.[1]

Another type of credit extended by one trader to another is a form of consignment trading. The sums are much larger, the time involved

---

[1] Whether she would have paid a lower wholesale price if she had bought for cash it is impossible to say, since she always bought on credit.

much longer, and it is highly probable that there is hidden interest. This credit is extended by itinerant cloth-traders who travel from market to market selling to cloth-traders who confine their activities to one market place. The sedentary trader buys cloth on credit on the understanding that he will pay a portion of the debt to the itinerant trader on his next visit, according to the amount of the cloth sold in the interim. If none has been sold, payment can be deferred until a later visit. The total sum to be paid is agreed at the beginning, and does not depend on prices ruling when the payments are made, nor on the length of time taken to complete payment. An itinerant trader would probably find it unpopular to charge interest on a time basis, since the delay between payments is at least partly due to the timing of his visits.

When buying in this way the trader pays a higher price than if he went direct to a city store or to the factory, the other ways in which cloth merchants most commonly buy supplies. When buying direct, however, the trader has to pay rail or bus fares to and from the city, which reduces the advantage. Since itinerant traders always seem to sell on credit, it is impossible to tell whether part of the difference in price is really interest on the loan or whether it should all be considered compensation for the time and expense of transporting the cloth to the trader's market. However, when the sums involved are as large as they are in these transactions, and when the time involved is several weeks, it is reasonable to look on part of the price differential as hidden interest.

INTEREST AND INDEBTEDNESS

Overt interest is paid on certain types of loans, mostly cash loans. Moneylenders are traditionally the source of cash loans in the Orient. (In 1953–54 I saw very little evidence that they were important in providing trade capital for those operating in the *pasar*.) Most of the moneylenders in Java are Chinese, and there are also some Arabs. Before the war it was reported that they were very active. The Dutch tried to suppress them by establishing government banks and pawnshops, because it was felt that they charged exorbitant interest rates, and the Chinese were also accused of running opium dens in association with their pawnshops. The post-war inflation enabled many Javanese to pay their debts cheaply, while the general insecurity and anti-Chinese feeling during the war and the Revolution made it difficult for Chinese to collect overdue debts. This combination of circumstances apparently reduced the moneylending activities of both Chinese and Arabs, though this cannot be fully established because neither the pre-war nor the post-war statistics are adequate.

Much has been said about the high interest rates charged in peasant economies. In some cases there has been exaggeration and a mis-understanding of credit terms. Yet the fact remains that loans are expensive in most under-developed economies. This is due partly to the scarce supply of and the high demand for liquid capital in these economies. There are other reasons also. Handling costs are greater for ten small loans than for one large one; so that the lender requires a higher interest rate to yield the same net return. Since most loans in Java are small, this is an important consideration. Records must also be kept for each transaction, papers perhaps drawn, and an assessment made of the borrower's ability to repay, no matter how small the loan. In a largely illiterate society where records are few and bank references non-existent these operations are very costly, unless use is made of unskilled, self-employed labour and local knowledge. The small moneylender who uses these cheap resources is, therefore, a most important source of credit in the Orient.

Default on debts is another major problem. Most loans are made without security, for the people have few possessions. Court action to recover debts may be difficult and expensive, and the social organization, especially in the urban areas, has been so disturbed by the war, the Revolution and the subsequent unrest, that the normal social sanctions are not sufficiently effective. The moneylender can only compensate for bad debts by raising his general interest charges. The danger of default has two adverse effects. First, it makes people reluctant to lend money or give credit, and so interferes with the free flow of capital as has happened in market trade. Secondly, the high interest rates keep capital out of productive channels because people hesitate to borrow on these terms, and they borrow mainly to meet the costs of serious illness or similar emergencies and not for 'productive' purposes.

It may be unwise merely to improve the efficacy of the legal enforcement of debts. The lack of effective enforcement renders a service in checking the power of lenders. In some descriptions of Oriental moneylenders it has been suggested that they demand interest rates far in excess of those appropriate to the circumstances. But without effective legal sanctions, the agreed terms cannot be enforced. When the lender has to rely on informal sanctions to collect his debts, the consensus of opinion within the community will not support him against a debtor if his claims are considered to be exorbitant. Even if the originally-agreed rate of interest is high and the borrower technically remains in debt for a long time, the real burden of the debt on the borrower depends on the extent of his defaulting. Thus effective legal enforcement of a technically lower rate of interest might prove to be more onerous for the borrower. Moreover, the threat of effective legal action against a borrower could be used by a lender to wring other concessions from the

248

borrower, such as forcing him to sell his crops or give his labour to the lender or to support him politically. None of these is inherently bad; but they can be abused when backed by threats. On the other hand, difficulties in enforcing the terms of loans deter the making of loans and the circulation of capital. Ultimately, the high cost of small-scale borrowing reflects the low level of liquid capital and the high costs of handling small loans.

Cash loans can also be obtained by traders (and only by traders) from the Government-run Market Banks. No security is required other than their signatures (or thumbprints in the case of the illiterate) and those of two co-signers. In 1953 the Market Banks made loans in units of Rp. 40.00 each; the following spring the unit was increased to Rp. 50.00, presumably to keep up with the inflation which had been taking place throughout the year. These loans are to be paid back within fifty days, one-tenth of the principal plus interest of 1 per cent of the original loan being due every five days, that is every *Kliwon*, the main trading day of the five-day market week in this particular *pasar*. Thus at the end of fifty days the borrower has paid back the principal plus 10 per cent. (There seemed to be no moral censure of the Government for charging interest on these loans. Apparently people felt that just as the Government had a right to assess taxes and charge entrance fees at the market to support itself, so it had a right to charge interest to support the Market Banks which were seen as a public service.)

Calculated on a yearly basis, the interest charged is about 80 per cent, which is high in Western terms. However, even higher interest rates have been reported in pre-war Burma by Furnivall, and it would seem probable that such rates are appropriate where security is poor and default hard to control. On the other hand, the system operates in Java in such a way that the effective interest rate falls as time passes for those who have trouble paying. There is no additional interest charge if the borrower cannot repay a Market Bank loan in the specified time, so that no matter how long the loan remains outstanding the total interest due never rises above one-tenth of the original sum borrowed. A trader who is hard pressed can simply delay repayment without enlarging his debt. The only inconvenience he suffers is that he is ineligible for another loan from the Market Bank.

Traders do, in fact, manage to get more than one loan from the Market Bank at a time. I knew one woman who regularly took out three of the standard units of Rp. 40.00. She herself signed for one, with her two sons as co-signers. Then she and the elder son co-signed for the second, naming the younger as principal, while she and the younger son co-signed the third, naming her elder as principal. She then took charge of the total amount together with the responsibility for repayment. Technically this was a series of loans, with each son lending her his loan interest-free; but from their point of view she was the true borrower throughout and the re-lending was considered a mere formality. She depended on the co-operation of her two sons, who did not themselves wish to make use of the Market Bank and who trusted her to repay the loans. The woman told me that one could not borrow more than three units at a time in this way because one could not appear as co-signer for more than two loans at once. (I asked if less interest was paid if the loan was repaid before the full fifty days. I had some difficulty in making her understand the question, and when she did it was obvious that the possibility had never occurred to her. Thus, while the interest does not increase if payment is delayed, it is probable that it is not reduced if payment is made ahead of time.)

The borrowed money was, to my knowledge, always used to finance trading. Market Banks were set up expressly to stimulate commercial investment, and pressure may be exerted by market officials to prevent traders from using the money for other purposes (though I have no evidence of this). Since the rate of interest is high if the payments are kept up, the money must be used in such a way that there are rapid returns. This feature, and the small size of the loans, make them unsuitable for long-term investment in capital improvements. At present the loans are used to meet current trading outlays. Whether the use would change if the sums were larger and the basic interest rates lower, I cannot predict on the evidence available to me. It is possible that with the peasant market system as it is (or was in 1953–54), few traders would be in a position to use large long-term loans.

SAVING AND INVESTMENT

Credit from producers or other traders and loans from moneylenders, Market Banks and (informally) from private persons provide only some of the capital used in market trade; most of it comes from the earnings of the traders themselves. Each tries to save enough out of his profits each day to finance all or part of the next day's trading. Such savings are normally retained only a few days in the form of cash before being reinvested. Traders also try to accumulate savings above and beyond what they need for normal operations.

Since most traders are illiterate and not familiar with banking procedure, they do not use banks; and since the simplest transaction can take up to an hour in a Javanese bank, the banks themselves could not handle large numbers of customers. Moreover, banks are found only in the cities, foreign ones only in the large cities, and each banking company usually has one branch only in each city. The time and the money expended in getting to and from a bank and arranging one's business is too great for banking to be feasible for the average trader. Therefore, traders usually hold their savings in the form of goods. A wide range of articles is bought for this purpose. The purchaser considers not only the size of the return he can expect (which varies with the nature of the goods), but also the sum of money available, the amount of effort needed to make the particular investment profitable, the goods being offered for sale at the moment, and the ultimate use to which the savings are to be put.

In Java, as in many agrarian societies, land is considered one of the best investments. It is secure in that it cannot be lost, stolen or destroyed, and it can be made to give a continuous return by working or renting it. Owning land in itself also confers prestige. In many ways it is considered the most desirable form of investment; but for this very reason it is not important as a way of holding capital temporarily. Once land is bought, the tendency is to retain it until all other possible sources of capital have been exhausted should the need for liquid capital arise.

Building a house is also a safe way to invest savings. A house cannot be lost or stolen and, barring fire, is not easily destroyed. One can live in it or rent it. Moreover, because of the manner in which Javanese houses are constructed, parts such as bricks and bamboo matting can be removed and sold piecemeal, so that a house is a source for small amounts of ready cash; disinvestment can proceed as required. Since the sale of a house, or pieces of it, is not felt to be nearly as serious as the sale of land, capital invested in houses is more liquid than that put into land.

Livestock is another popular form of investment. The larger animals (humped Indian cattle and water buffaloes) are not a favoured investment unless they can be used for working land or for haulage, because the milk is not commonly drunk. They are also expensive and require more stable room than most villagers or townspeople can provide. Town traders therefore seldom own such animals. They prefer sheep or goats which are cheaper to buy, need less stable room, and can find enough grazing on the patches of grass even in the towns. Wool is not used locally or exported, so that they are valuable only for their meat and hides; therefore it is best to buy young animals or females for breeding. Many Javanese keep a few chickens because they require little care, cost little to feed and house, and the sale of eggs provides pocket money for daily expenses. They are also a convenient form for small savings; they can readily be sold whenever cash is urgently needed, chicken being the most common meat in the diet.

Except for good draught animals, livestock is bought as a form of savings, and there is no loss of prestige when they are sold. As there is always a strong demand for meat, savings kept in this form are quite

251

liquid. However, if injury or disease kills the animal, the investment is lost, for only properly butchered meat is eaten. There is also the risk of theft, though this, to my knowledge, is serious only in the case of poultry.

Cloth and jewellery also are popular forms of savings. The amounts involved run from ten or twenty rupiah to several hundred for the more expensive jewellery. These goods are easily stored, require no upkeep, and do not deteriorate appreciably. Cloth bought for investment is worn only rarely on special occasions. *Batik* cloth and sarongs, the types favoured for investment, are sold in standard lengths and are worn simply as a wrapped skirt; their resale value is not reduced in the same way as when a garment has been tailored for a particular person. *Batik* and sarong designs are traditional and do not go out of fashion. Jewellery is also usually traditional in design, and its value lies in the amount of gold it contains rather than in the craftsmanship. Its resale value is affected only by the fluctuations in the price of gold on the international market. The prices of both cloth and jewellery are as stable as any in the economy. There are, therefore, relatively safe investments, and also readily saleable (or pawnable). Neither, however, yields any money income on the investment. This is balanced by the pleasure of wearing them, and in Java, where the everyday clothing of the average peasant is quite plain, this satisfaction is appreciable. There is no sentiment against the sale of cloth or jewellery. When a family sells land it admits that it is in serious difficulties; when it sells jewellery, it means it has decided to use some of its savings in another form. Often savings are from the beginning stored in the form of these goods for a specific purpose such as to finance a wedding or circumcision or other celebration.

The decision to sell or pawn an object lies in the first instance with the owner of that object. For small items such as a length of cloth or an inexpensive piece of jewellery, this usually means one person, for these things are normally bought by a single individual. For more expensive items the situation is more complicated. In a sense the whole family has an interest in them. A bicycle used mainly by the men of the family or a piece of jewellery worn only by the women is a family investment. In most cases it has been bought with the savings resulting from the earnings and efforts of both husband and wife, and therefore is not owned exclusively by either, according to Javanese customary law. When the question of selling a major piece of property is raised, it is discussed by both husband and wife, and possibly also their adult children, especially if they are living in the household. If a member of a family sold an item of this kind without consulting the others, there would almost certainly be strong protests. Such incidents, if too flagrant or if repeated, can lead to the break-up of the household through divorce or alienation of the children.

252

Pawning is widespread in the Orient. Pawnshops were largely run by Chinese in Java up to the turn of the century. The Dutch Government took control of the pawnshops about 1900 on the grounds that the Chinese were charging exorbitant rates of interest and were not guaranteeing the safety of the pledges (Furnivall, 1948, pp. 337–40). The present Government has continued to run pawnshops. The pawning of an expensive piece of jewellery or a bicycle may bring several hundred rupiah; but most of the transactions are smaller, running perhaps to five or ten rupiah.

An article may be left in a Government pawnshop for 200 days; after that it is sold. The proceeds from the sale, less the cost of the loan, can be claimed by the borrower. For amounts between ten cents (Indonesian) and fifty cents there is a charge of one cent every fifteen days for the full 200 days. For amounts between fifty cents and Rp. 25.00 there is a charge of two cents for every rupiah or fraction of a rupiah for the first 135 days, after which the charge is the same as that for smaller amounts. When an article is pawned for Rp. 25.00 and left the full 200 days, the total interest charged is about Rp. 4.50 or a little more than 20 per cent.

Whether the valuables are sold or pawned, the use to which the money is put depends mainly on the amount. Small sums are seldom used for daily expenses but normally are reserved for minor emergencies: buying medicine, paying school fees, buying school books, etc. It is rare, in my experience, for small sums from such sources to be invested in commercial transactions. Similarly when more expensive items such as livestock or major pieces of jewellery are sold or pawned, the money is usually used for some long-planned purpose, such as building a house or holding a wedding. Only rarely is the money diverted into trade, and only under extreme pressure is it used to cover daily living expenses. If a serious illness or some other major emergency occurs, the money saved for other purposes will, of course, be used to meet these expenses.

Valuables are, in general, not looked on as a source of capital to be invested in day-to-day business. Undoubtedly there are cases where a 'nest-egg' is used as commercial capital; but, in general, savings put into valuables are held separate from those funds to meet daily expenses and from capital for commercial purposes.

There is one other way in which savings are handled. This is a form of pooling liquid capital. They can be put into an *arisan* or rotating credit association. Most of the money so invested, at least among the poorer traders, is eventually used for trading purposes. The *arisan* is formed by a group of people, each of whom contributes at intervals a set sum of money, usually small, to a 'kitty' or pool. Each participant has a number, often assigned by lot; and when his number falls due he gets the total amount contributed for that round by the

Capital, Saving and Credit in Peasant Societies

members. Pooled savings plans are common throughout the Orient, though many of them have a much more complex organization than the Javanese *arisan*. In the Javanese system no interest is paid and each person, in due course, gets back as much money as he contributes. The usual market *arisan* rotates endlessly with much the same membership, and the rotation period is short. There is therefore little advantage in drawing a low number; and inflation does not seriously reduce the purchasing power of the contributions.

Market *arisan* vary in size: the largest I recorded took 187 days to rotate, with a fee of Rp. 1.00 paid daily for each share; the smallest took thirty-five days with a fee of Rp. 2.00. The number of participants varies, since two or more traders may pay one share between them, dividing the 'kitty' when its turn comes. Some participate in three or four of these credit associations at once; others never join any. Those who join make every effort to keep up payments, presumably because of pressure from the other members.

CREDIT INSTRUMENTS

A final point sould be noted about the flow of capital, especially in the form of credit, in Java. Except for loans from Government banks and pawnshops, formal documents stating the amount and terms of the transaction are rarely drawn. This is related to the fact that most Javanese (in 1953–54) were illiterate and not accustomed to using documents in their daily life. Significantly, the only case I recorded of the transfer of a loan involved a pawnshop ticket. These tickets are printed forms on which a Government clerk enters particulars of the transaction, and they are evidently accepted as negotiable paper. Even in 1953–54 there was always someone available literate enough to read the ticket, so that disputes did not arise as to its value. If literacy becomes general, as it undoubtedly will, and the legal system upholds the validity of properly drawn credit instruments, more use would probably be made of them.

The most important credit arrangements for traders, the *harga hidup* and *pindjam* systems, and other similar informal agreements, are not even committed to paper, and hence it might be difficult to establish them as legally binding. Thus the greater part of the credit extended is not in a form that can be transferred or negotiated in any convenient way. Much credit is very short term and would not be particularly useful even if it were formally negotiable. However, if written contracts became more common, long-term loans might gain in popularity. At present the low level of literacy makes it difficult to introduce formal credit instruments, but the intensive Government programme of education (which seems to be operating very effectively) may change this situation rapidly. The fact that pawn tickets are

254

occasionally accepted as negotiable credit instruments indicates that there would be no resistance to the extension of the idea, once the majority of the people were equipped to handle the paper work involved. At the moment the absence of negotiable credit instruments reduces the flow of capital and hampers the expansion of the economy.

12

The Employment of Capital by Market Women in Haiti[1]

BY SIDNEY W. MINTZ

INTRODUCTION

The Republic of Haiti, which occupies the westernmost third of the island of Hispaniola, shares that island with Santo Domingo. Haiti's approximately 28,750 square kilometres (*ca.* 10,700 square miles) is occupied by a population estimated at 3,400,000 (1959). One recent work suggests that the rural population alone in 1960 numbered 3,500,000.[2] Much of the country's land is not arable now, and never was; more than two-thirds of the natural territory is mountainous, much of it unusable for agriculture. Deforestation and erosion have ruined large areas as well. Population density is believed to stand at about 130 per square kilometre for all land, at more than 450 per square kilometre for arable land.[3] This latter figure suggests that Haitian agriculture must be highly productive indeed, whatever its shortcomings. It would have to be so, since there is virtually no industry; nearly 88 per cent of the total population is rural; and almost three-quarters of the national income comes from agricultural enterprises. Net national income (1951–52) was estimated at US $200,000,000. The calculated *per caput* income *per annum* of US $60 came almost entirely from agriculture, and a poorly capitalized and 'unscientific' agriculture at that; in 1953–54, the corresponding figures were US $267,000,000 and US $80.[4]

The 1950 census indicates that more than 80 per cent of Haiti's

[1] Field work was carried out in Haiti during 1958–59. The writer is grateful to the Guggenheim Foundation and the Social Science Research Council for support of his research, to the Republic of Haiti, its official agencies, and its citizens for their courtesies and hospitality. Thanks go to Mr Vern Carroll for helpful criticisms.
[2] Moral, 1961, p. 320.
[3] *Ibid.*, p. 322.
[4] *Ibid.*, p. 320.

256

rural citizens own agricultural land. Holdings are prevailingly small: it is believed that about 40 per cent of peasant families are exploiting less than one *karo*[1] (1.29 hectares, or 3.33 acres US), and only 6 per cent employ more than five *karo*.

In spite of Haiti's small size and generally subtropical climate, there is considerable ecological variation. The amount of rainfall and the seasons of rain vary greatly; altitude, soil type and topography also are much differentiated. These variations naturally affect the character of agriculture, and the extent to which land is put to this use, to other uses, or left unoccupied. Different crops have widely varying seasons, and the harvest times for the same item grown in different locales may be months apart.

Haitian peasants produce foods for subsistence and for sale within the local marketing system, and certain commodities which are mainly for export. The most important export is coffee, which represents about 12 per cent of national income and, since the 1950s, about 60–70 per cent of total export values. Other exports include cocoa, bananas, sugar, sisal, rubber, items yielding essential oils (e.g. vetiver, citron peels), and goatskins, but none of these is very important at present. For their own consumption and for sale in local marketplaces, the peasantry produces maize, millet and rice; root crops such as yams, sweet potatoes and manioc; fruits and green vegetables of many sorts; fowl and livestock; and also some craft materials and craft goods.

Though there are several plantations in sisal and sugar and a few modern coffee farms, almost all agricultural production in Haiti is carried on by small-scale operators who own their own land, and who produce simultaneously for consumption, for local sale, and for export. These agriculturists are heavily dependent on the outside for many commodities they regard as essential (such as soap, cloth, iron tools and minor medicinals), and for many services as well, however poorly provided (such as education and medical care). In the anthropological view, such people constitute a peasantry. They mainly own their own land; they are agricultural producers; they are market-orientated, and always sell some part of what they produce; they are dependent on political systems and an economic system not subject to their control and outside their local sphere; and they are conservative in their living standards, traditional in their methods and beliefs.[2] The very large proportion of Haitians to whom these

[1] Créole words are transcribed in the Laubach orthography, on which see Hall, 1953. All Créole words are italicized, and will be distinguishable from French words by their orthography. The *accent aigu* over 'e' is as in French, as is the *accent grave*. Over 'o', the *accent grave* forms the equivalent of the French open 'o'. The 'ou' is as in French, the 'ch' as in English 'sh', and the 'j' as in French 'z'. The *accent circonflexe* indicates nasalization.

[2] Cf. Wolf, 1955, pp. 458–60; Redfield, 1956, pp. 5–22; Firth, 1951b, pp. 87 ff.

characteristics apply make Haiti the Caribbean area's best example of a peasant country. Haiti's people are the descendants of African slaves who revolted successfully against their French masters in the richest plantation colony in modern history, thereupon to create a peasant economy *in situ*; thus one could speak of them as a 'reconstituted peasantry'.[1]

Descriptions of rural Haitian family and social organization usually begin by referring to the '*lakou*' (French *la cour*) as the central physical expression of rural social grouping. The *lakou* was a compound consisting of several residences and outbuildings, usually set off from the outside by a picket or living fence.[2] The main house would be occupied by the senior male, his legally, ecclesiastically, and publicly sanctioned and acknowledged wife, and their unmarried children. The remaining houses within the *lakou* would be occupied by sons of the senior male, each with his wife and children; by junior siblings of the senior male, or senior female siblings, sometimes with parts of their families. At one time, women living in socially acknowledged but neither legally nor sacramentally validated unions with the senior male might live with their children in houses within the *lakou*. Much more commonly, these *plasé* wives lived at some distance from the *lakou*, often many miles away, caring for the senior male's children and tending a plot of his land. Today, the *lakou* has changed its character considerably. The unit of agricultural exploitation, '*le ménage agricole*', in Moral's words,[3] today averages five persons. The grouping of two, three or more nuclear families within a single compound, in separate houses but under the control of a senior male, has nearly disappeared. In earlier decades of this century, migration to Cuba, Santo Domingo and elsewhere contributed to the weakening of the *lakou* structure. Opportunities for migration to the cities and to less densely occupied regions have also reduced the control of the senior male within the family group. It appears likely that the United States occupation (1915–34) may have had some of the same effect, particularly through the reorganization of the army, and the opportunities for rural young men which this betokened. Legal changes connected with land inheritance also have probably contributed to a waning of the power of the *lakou* head, and to a decline of the extended *lakou* grouping.

At the same time, unions involving one man and several women in which the male has a legally and religiously sanctioned marriage to one wife, and *plasaj* relationships with one or more additional women, are still common. Moral cites statistics showing that for every 100 Haitians living in *plasaj* relationships, who are between the

[1] Cf. Mintz., 1961a, pp. 31–4.
[2] Mintz, 1960a, 1962.
[3] Cf. Moral, 1959, p. 50.

258

ages of twenty and fifty years, there are fifty-eight women to forty-two men.[1] *Plasaj* is still important in peasant life;[2] it is a sign of elevated status for particular leaders in the peasant group;[3] and it is, moreover, an effective means of increasing labour resources, when the woman is charged with the care of fields far from the main *lakou* of her *plasé* spouse and his 'accepted' wife and children.

The typical Haitian peasant pattern of agriculture shares much with other Caribbean peasant economies. The small plots of land are rarely devoted wholly to single crops. Instead, numerous different crops are intermixed, planted successively, harvested in sequence, given over to different marketing media, and otherwise variously diversified. Since one peasant may hold two or three or more pieces of land, often differing ecologically, he can employ them strategically for different crops and seasons. The variations in soil type, rainfall, topography, floral cover, altitude, etc. permit and even encourage diversification. The peasant distributes the risks of agriculture by growing different crops in different fields, by growing different items in the same fields, and by producing for several different kinds of market. He also distributes risk by combining livestock raising and/or wage labour with agriculture; and his wife may further augment income and reduce the risks of a single economic pursuit by engaging in trade. Women do some agricultural labour (*plasé* in particular often do a great deal), and men do certain special kinds of marketing. But the prevailing division of labour in these connections is along sexual lines: men farm, women market. This pattern of labour division, and the accompanying beliefs, form a background to marketing activity.

Small-scale agriculture, diversified production, and small and irregular yields combine well with the marketing activities of thousands of women, who buy up varied stocks in small quantities, and carry them to sell to other marketers or to consumers. Just as production is on a very small and diversified scale, so trade is highly diversified as well, and modest in terms of the investment of single dealers. The pattern of consumption of the Haitian people rests on buying only enough for one meal at one time, rather than preserving stocks of food (or of economizing) by buying in quantity. Thus there are underlying uniformities in economic activity from production through exchange to consumption: smallness of scale, distribution of risk by diversification, a low value put on time and a high value put on capital.

Trade and exchange, by which imported consumers' goods and

[1] Cf. Moral, 1959, p. 51.
[2] Cf. Comhaire-Sylvain, 1958. See also Bastien, 1951, 1961; and Moral, 1961, pp. 169–78.
[3] Cf. Romain, 1955, pp. 51–2.

regionally differentiated local products reach consumers, rural products reach the boards of townsmen, and certain staples are prepared and bulked for export houses, occur largely within or in connection with the internal market system. This system embraces nearly 300 rural and urban marketplaces, distributed widely throughout the Republic. The marketplaces are supervised by Government officials, and buyers and sellers are heavily taxed by the State, in a variety of ways and for many different activities.[1] Most trade is in the hands of women. Moral estimates that somewhat more than 50,000 women and perhaps 15,000 men are engaged primarily in trading activities; employing Colin Clark's classification, he suggests that some 6½ per cent of Haiti's women fourteen years of age and over are specialists in trade.[2] But in practice the figure probably ought to be much larger, since Haitian women move in and out of trade frequently and freely. Nearly all rural women have some trading experience and were traders at one time or another in their lives. The conventional categories applicable in more highly organized economic systems probably do not serve well for an economy such as Haiti's, and the total number of women engaged in trade probably well exceeds Moral's figure.[3]

PRINCIPLES OF TRADING

Certain features in common typify Haitian intermediary activity, attributable to the general character of the economy: its agrarian base; the plentifulness of labour; the uncertainties of the market situation, resulting from its being predominantly an agricultural market with fluctuating stocks and prices; dispersed, low and irregular demand; inadequate transport; equally inadequate means for processing, preserving and storing agricultural produce; and the economic advantage to many people of carrying on several kinds of gainful activity, simultaneously or in alternation.

But intermediary activity varies according to the particular services women perform and sell, the amounts of capital they invest in their work, and the kinds of opportunities their work leads to. The availability of capital, the means of obtaining it, and the uses to which it may be put, are central themes in Haitian marketing activity. Capital (*'mâmâlajâ'*, literally, 'mother money') is hard to come by.[4] One can collect business histories of women who started their

[1] Descriptions of the market places themselves will be found in Métraux *et al.*, 1951; Mintz, 1960b, 1960c, 1960d; Ricot, 1961; Underwood, 1960.
[2] Moral, 1959, p. 84.
[3] Cf. Bauer and Yamey, 1951.
[4] Hill, 1962, pp. 6–8, discusses very usefully the distinction between capital and 'spending money', in this case in West Africa.

marketing as young girls with less than US five cents and who possess today a working capital in excess of US $500. These stories are surprisingly common in an economy cited for its low productivity and its limited ability to generate new capital.

To the extent that intermediary activity does follow some common pattern, it is possible to note a few principles of action used by market women. These are rarely stated explicitly. But when each in turn was described to marketers, they would agree with the point being made, often giving examples to confirm and amplify its meaning. Therefore, though only two of the following four principles were enunciated as such, they are probably reliable guides to intermediary activity in Haiti.

The first such precept is 'build a personal niche within the arena of exchange'. This teaching has to do, of course, with the general character of the exchange economy in Haiti. Labour is Haiti's most plentiful resource and capital its scarcest. The presence of large numbers of unemployed and underemployed persons means that people with labour to sell must fill every possible corner in the economy in order to live. In many instances labour is substituted for capital in many ways that are striking to visitors from more developed economies. This is perhaps truer in the distributive sector of the economy than elsewhere; at least, it is most dramatically revealed there. The sudden acquisition of small amounts of capital which are available only for short periods of time, as sometimes occurs, can evoke an enormous investment of labour on the part of the temporary holder, anxious to show a profit before the capital must be returned to its owner. Again, holders of perishable stocks will travel great distances in order to sell what they have before it turns bad and its price falls. Yet there are circumstances where no investment of labour, however great, can protect an intermediary against financial loss. The competition is too stern; the means of protecting one's investment are too limited. The great risks faced by the individual marketer in her daily operations may partly explain why it is so important to make formal friendships to underlie economic dealings.[1]

Within the field of economic activity, and in spite of the highly individualistic character of trading operations, there is a strong personal cast to exchange. The intermediary seeks to secure and protect her sources of supply and her supply of buyers in the face of stern competition. She does so via personal relationships, built up over time by small economic concessions and the gift of minor services to individuals known to her through series of transactions. These relationships are not created overnight. Intermediaries establish regular sequences or cycles of operations, bringing them to the same place at the same time, in order to cement and maintain

[1] On this point, cf. Hill, 1962, p. 11.

their connections. One refers to a favoured client, whether buyer or seller, as '*pratik*' (French *pratique*: a good customer). The desire to create *pratik*, and the way in which it is done, together with the *pratik* relationships themselves, give patterning and regularity to marketing activity. *Pratik* are created by the granting of concessions taking three main forms: the provision of credit (sometimes with interest); lower prices for the same quantity of goods when selling (or higher prices when buying); greater quantities of goods for the same price when selling (or lesser quantities when buying). In addition there are many services granted by *pratik* to each other, usually consisting of small gifts of labour or time, sometimes of economic opportunities which the giver cannot exploit because she is involved in another activity at the moment. The extension of credit is the most-used means for strengthening and maintaining *pratik*, but credit is not extended until a relationship already has some form and predictability. Before this, small concessions in price or quantity are used to attract potential *pratik*, to provide a basis for discussion and more negotiation, and to create an atmosphere of mutual trust. *Pratik* relationships are dyadic and may be viewed as chains of two-way relationship; they are established to stabilize and secure sources of supply and loci of demand. Those who make *pratik* state that they trade immediate advantage and some part of their gain in return for long-range security, and some protection against the vagaries of the market. Some marketers go farther and say that it is not possible to enlarge one's business without *pratik*—that they are essential to the growth of the orbit of trade.[1]

To some extent, *pratik* relationships resemble those a woman is likely to have with other women in her own family circle. Such women may seek out local supplies of certain products; assist in transporting and packing stock; acquire supply for resale while sister, mother or other female relative is away in the capital or in another region; retail minor stocks of imports as a service; and otherwise co-operate economically. But in these cases the economic service is given on the basis of a kin relationship.[2]

Such ties differ from *pratik* because their background is one of kinship. *Pratik* ties are formed outside the context of blood relationship; mutual economic advantage is the basis for forming such ties where none existed before. And the deterrent to terminating such relationships, once they are established, is the loss of economic advantage, though coloured by the overtones of friendship and mutual trust. The ascribed nature of kinship ties, on the other hand, provides a less variable basis for intra-familial relationships of the

---

[1] These relationships are discussed more fully in Mintz, 1959, 1961b.

[2] Such kinship linkages, through which economic services are rendered, are described in an urban market place setting by Legerman, 1962.

The Employment of Capital by Market Women in Haiti

pratik kind. The unreasonable breaking of *pratik* obligations can damage a woman's economic stakes in certain circles, but might conceivably improve them in others—at least, up to a point. In contrast, the economic relationships one has with one's kinfolk cannot be broken without imperilling one's entire position in the local group. In other words, though *pratik* ties and family ties with an economic referent share some characteristics, they are formed in different ways, have a somewhat different nature, and cannot be regarded in the same way.

Yet it is dangerous to treat *pratik* ties lightly. A marketer who fails to fulfil *pratik* obligations gets talked about by other market women. She will have difficulty in forming new *pratik*, and in getting numerous small perquisites, normally supplied free by her fellow marketers. The excellence of one's *pratik* ties are not all or always publicized freely. The very fact that these ties are largely formed on the basis of concessions made with reference to the current market prices for goods and services signifies that some secrecy is likely to surround the relationships and the concessions they facilitate. Many of the negotiations between *pratik*, then, have a semi-secret character. Though personal relationships of these sort are common to many societies, they deserve particular attention here because they can be a general feature of the distributive system, and their importance expresses the awareness market women have of the nature of their own society and economy.

The second general precept which the Haitian market woman follows is 'keep capital working'. In practice this is translated into never allowing capital to rest in stock-in-trade, and thereby risk its being squandered in overhead expenses. One example may serve. In a North Haitian area which produces fine onions during the months from March to May, one intermediary buys large stocks from many small holdings, up to a total load of 450 pounds, and wholesales this produce in Port-au-Prince, the capital, nearly 200 miles away by the best route. It may take her up to a week to clear her stock, and she risks serious losses if the onions begin to spoil. Being perishable, onions are a speculative item. The profit margin on them is not particularly high, given the nature of the merchandise, and sometimes this intermediary loses on her transactions. During the rest of the year, she sells hard goods such as soap, kerosene and flour, both wholesale and retail, in a large regional market. These products keep well, and she never loses on them. But if she is asked whether she would prefer to market such products as onions the year round, were this possible, her answer is a vigorous, almost aggressive 'yes'—because 'the money moves then' (*atò lajâ maché*). It may be granted that not all intermediaries prefer to deal in speculative goods; but all seem to believe in rapid turnover as a marketing

263

principle. For capital to rest in stock for long periods and without some specific goal is a source of acute discomfort to these women. Their feelings are the same whenever they lend money at little or no interest (and they sometimes do), and have any difficulty getting it back. They speak of 'spoiling money' (*gaté lajâ*) when capital is absorbed in overhead; almost the same in meaning is the expression 'eating money' (*mâjé lajâ*). When money lent at no interest is not promptly returned, they speak of their money 'staying outside too much' (*lajâ rété tròp dèò*). Though the term for money (*lajâ*) rather than for capital is used in these expressions, the distinction between money and capital is precise, and is made in terms of the use to which resources are put. The assumption underlying this precept seems to be that if capital is not expanding, it must be contracting. The assumption is a salutary one in an economy such as Haiti's, and probably stimulates marketers to ever greater efforts.

A third precept, hardly separable from the second, is 'never sell retail if you can sell wholesale'. The distinction between wholesale (*â gro*) and retail (*â détay*) can be applied to a particular woman, however small her stock, according to whether she sells large portions of her entire stock, or only small quantities and single units, to her different customers. There is also recognized the formal (and in Haiti, legally important) distinction between wholesaler and retailer, as in the case of cloth-selling. At times the preference for wholesaling over retailing may seem economically irrational to the observer. One would search for ever to find a Haitian *révâdèz* (French *revendeuse*) who would opt for selling cigarettes at two for three cents (yielding a gross profit of US one dollar per carton, or 50 per cent) if she were able to sell a carton for two dollars at one time (yielding an immediate gross profit of US ten cents, or 5 per cent). Of course the economic rationality is very plain in most instances, since the would-be wholesaler will turn retailer once more if the wholesaling opportunities disappear. Underlying the strong and perhaps sometimes unrewarding predilection for wholesaling there seems to be a belief that sales in bulk, the replacement of goods with money and money with goods in rapid order, cannot bring failure and may bring success. In the preference for wholesaling, many considerations enter into the intermediary's calculations, particularly that of access to supply. But the theme of keeping the money moving is combined with that of selling wholesale (or in bulk) when possible, to produce some interesting manipulations. Bulk buying can be cheaper than retail buying, of course: transport costs, and often taxes as well, are proportionately less when one deals in bulk. The money itself comes to hand more rapidly, in a series of hopefully quick turnovers. It is 'working' when in stock, and each time it is transformed into money again, the market situation may have created a slightly different setting for reinvestment. Transaction is built upon transaction in swift succession. The Haitian intermediary seemingly dreams of an infinite series of brilliant business operations, each yielding a profit, each larger than the preceding. Not only does one point constantly in the direction of turning small sales into large ones, but one tries to use all the cash possible in business activity, as much as the intermediary's standards of consumption and the market situation will allow. These principles aim at straining the intermediary's accumulative powers tô the utmost, not for the sake of future consumption, but for the sake of a constantly increasing stake in the economic system.

The final precept is: 'try to buy dear and sell dear, rather than buy cheap and sell cheap'. What this may mean is simply that the intermediary profits more in a situation of scarcity. Market women express their preference by saying that capital accumulates more rapidly when prices are high. In practice, the principle is expressed simply in the fine capacity of the intermediary to sense unfulfilled demand and then to try to fill it. Even women who have worked out solid businesses in certain basic staples such as corn and millet are usually on the lookout for special items which may be in temporary undersupply in city markets. Intermediary activity at the buying end is also characterized by a desire to intensify activity at the very start of harvest seasons, when prices are normally high. Loans are often made to producers on the basis of planted fields, to which the lender-intermediary will have first access when the crop is ripe. And though many intermediaries with large resources may stockpile certain goods in Port-au-Prince depots for a week or even more, awaiting a price rise, they will do so only if they have additional capital available so that they can keep buying in the countryside in the interim. It is during temporary gluts in the city that some country-based intermediaries will be buying up the very stock that is in oversupply— at relatively low prices. This is true, of course, only with more or less non-perishable goods, particularly grains. And the woman who has too little capital both to stockpile and to keep buying will sell off at a lower margin in order to have her capital in hand for more buying. Though these statements may seem to contradict the adage of 'buy dear, sell dear', in fact they reinforce it. All of these principles appear to be directed to the idea of ever-heightened economic activity. Needless to say, such precepts do not always work out. All marketers lose some time, and some lose frequently enough to be pushed out of trading. Yet the precepts apparently make sense for an economy like Haiti's.

TRADING WITH SMALL AMOUNTS OF CAPITAL

The readiness of Haitian women to engage in trade at very low rates of profit, and at very low absolute earnings as well, springs from the lack of economic alternatives. Since earnings are prevailingly low and capital scarce and dear, it is to be expected that large amounts of labour will be invested to save or to accumulate small amounts of capital. Lacking alternative employment, large numbers of women are always prepared to invest labour in trading for very small absolute rewards. This readiness to sell services is combined with considerable commercial acumen on the part of those engaged in trade, and leads to important savings to the economy. Endless examples could be given, but one in particular should suffice.

In the Saint Raphaël market of northern Haiti, trucks pull in on market day, once a week, loaded with coarse salt from a nearby coastal city. When the market is brisk, the salt sells at US five cents for two heaped tinsful (standard US No. 10 cans). On such days, the truck owner, who wholesales the salt, will not sell in quantities of less than two tins at a time. But the ordinary consumer does not buy salt in such large quantities. Hence intermediaries are able to enter between wholesalers and consumers. At the foot of each truck squat small groups of salt retailers. These women buy from the truckers in quantities of two tins and more. The investment they make in their enterprises varies from US five cents to about US twenty cents (twenty-five *centimes* to 1.00 *gourde* in Haitian currency). Such women may also carry to market small quantities of vegetables for resale; these may have been produced on their own or their husbands' land, and will have a value of a few cents. If the total assessed value of their stock is in excess of US twenty cents, they will probably be taxed about US two cents by the State. They retail salt at three cents a tin, which yields a profit of one-half cent on each tin; or in smaller quantities, such that their profit per tin may rise to one cent. When one undertakes to calculate the value such women must put on their time, the results are rather depressing; but it must be remembered that, given so small a capital, there are no other activities known to these marketers which will yield a greater profit. And market day—the big market—comes but once weekly in Saint Raphaël. On eight tins of salt, resold by the tin, the retailer makes a profit of US four cents. It is worth noting, at the same time, that there is a group of sellers before each truck; they are competing for buyers, and may seek to establish regular selling relationships by giving slightly larger quantities to particular buyers.

Though this description is discouraging in the extreme, one remembers that the opportunities to obtain a cash reward are even rarer on those days when there is no market. Such a woman may make baskets; or work for a local peasant, planting or harvesting; or tend her own land, if she has any; or take her surplus of unsold salt and carry it to sell in rural neighbourhoods far removed from the market; or beg. But come market day, she must be prepared to buy and to sell; her capital (such as it is) must not be tied up, and her time is enormously valuable to her that day. Willing as she is to sell her time as cheaply as she does, the market situation may still be too tight to permit her to participate as an intermediary. On those occasions when the sale of salt is weak, trucker-wholesalers will begin selling by the single tin, at fifteen or even ten centimes (US three or two cents) the tin. On those days, very few women remain in the picture as intermediaries. Usually salt retailers who stay in are those who already have some other stock, to which salt becomes a sideline. These women sell salt at five centimes (US one cent) for approximately one-third of a tin, yielding a profit of one cent per tin, and somewhat more, proportionately, for smaller quantities—but sales are usually very slow. Such women carry their unsold stock back to their home villages to resell, hopefully, at a higher margin of profit.

One question that must be answered in this little drama has to do with those women squeezed out of their niche by the decision of the truckers to sell in one-tin quantities. The truckers, fearful of losing too many sales in a weak market, engross most of the local retail trade when they reduce the scale of the sales they are willing to make, as well as their margin of profit. Since they control access to supply by virtue of their greater buying capacity and the distance they can come economically, carrying a bulk product with low unit value, they are in a position to do this when they feel that the market situation requires it.

Two different levels of intermediary are affected when the truckers reduce the quantities they are willing to sell to individual buyers and the price at which they sell. The better-off intermediaries may continue to carry salt as a sideline, as indicated. But the women having the smallest amounts of capital (US five to twenty cents) apparently cannot afford to do this. When they are cut out of the chain of intermediation by those who stand above them in the sequence, they must find some other niche in the structure of middleman activity since their potential profit margins would be reduced almost to zero if they attempted to compete by selling salt alone. And since this may occur with relative frequency, and they know it, they must have alternatives. Some of them move swiftly into other areas of small-scale trade in hard goods—for instance, soap, matches, locally rendered castor oil, etc.— in hopes of still making a profit, however small. Others quite regularly resort to begging when their salt retailing is denied them. In this instance, one comes squarely to the point where it is cheaper not to work than to work. It is worth remarking at the same time that some consumer-buyers, when purchasing salt by the large tin at the cheapest price, undertake to retail part of their purchase in their home villages, thus entering the trading framework casually and temporarily. When the market is strong, the price of salt rises, the wholesalers restore the two-tin minimum sale, the part-time beggars become intermediaries once more, and the consumer-buyers, purchasing smaller quantities, surrender their casual middleman role. It would be difficult not to appreciate the economic efficiency of these practices, however rudimentary the total system of exchange may seem.

There are other illustrations of the same sort of minimum-capital trading. Métraux writes:

'... there are in the region [the Marbial Valley] a large number of young girls or women who take up their stand along roads or paths, in a hut or at the foot of a tree, to sell thread, matches, candies (*tablèt* and *dous*), fruit, vegetables, cereals, spices and tobacco. Mangoes, caimitoes or avocadoes are arranged in little heaps, for each of which there is a fixed price. Coffee, and beans in pod, are also sold by heaps. The women who sell cola, 'clairin', candies and biscuits are constantly on the move. They go to any place in the valley where for any reason a group of people are gathered together—for a service, a marriage, a political meeting, etc. 'Wakes' by the dead—for relatives and friends, an occasion for festivity and entertainment—are a godsend to these traders. As soon as they learn that someone in some *kay* has died, they proceed thither at any hour of the day or night, carrying their heavy trays on their heads. They also go from market to market, in the sole hope of making a few pence of profit. Their wandering existence is a specially hard one, and the slightest accident—a theft, a fall, or an illness—may permanently destroy their small trading concern.'[1]

Marketing of this kind, and the marketers who carry it on, underlie those levels of trade involving larger sums of capital, larger stocks, and different sorts of trading operations. Small-scale traders are always seeking some means to rise on the economic ladder, to increase their stake and thereby further to increase their manoeuvrability. Some women manage to do so. But it is very difficult to move from the bottom level without considerable help, or great good fortune. The women who deal in such tiny quantities rarely can accumulate enough wealth to improve their position, since their earnings are often just enough to enable them to keep operating. The ways in which capital is accumulated are hence of great interest.

HOW CAPITAL IS ACCUMULATED BY TRADING

It is the willingness of market women to render service at low cost which makes Haitian marketing efficient, in spite of the low level of

[1] Métraux *et al.*, 1951, p. 127.

268

transport and communication services, the absence of national standards of measure,[1] the lack of refrigeration and storage, and so on.

Because the competition for places within the sphere of marketing activity is intense, Haitian women must use their wits, strength and endurance to find and hold stakes in the intermediation process. The competition reveals itself in the great resourcefulness of these women, their readiness to render any reasonable economic service in the search for financial advancement. The two most important services rendered by intermediaries appear to be transport and the bulking and bulk-breaking of produce. But in addition, market women undertake such tasks as processing (e.g., salting pork, cooking food), packaging (tying up bundles of brooms or baskets, sewing 'heads' on burlap sacks), commission buying and selling, running errands, conveying marketing intelligence, money-lending, and so on. It is the large number of people struggling for places in the system and the accompanying very low supply cost of labour which the observer first sees. But equally important is the inventiveness and resourcefulness of those offering to sell service. Both in buying and selling, women are prepared to travel great distances with heavy loads and under incredibly difficult conditions in order to make a living. A price difference of a fraction of a cent is enough to keep produce moving into or out of particular market areas.[2] Women are always ready to render some slight additional service for the promise of future economic opportunities or immediate gain, however small. The various services they can supply are often combined creatively, so that the woman who salts pork for a large-scale wholesaler will buy salt pork at the same time, to retail when her job is done, and ask for small concessions in quantity or price because of her good work. Transport will be combined with bulking or bulk-breaking, wholesaling with retailing, and so on.

At the lowest level of capital holdings, the provision of these services does little more than permit the intermediary to stay alive. The salt retailers of the Saint Raphaël market, whose capital amounts to perhaps US twenty to forty cents, combine their business in Saint Raphaël with arbitrage, day labour, the cultivation of marginal land, and begging, in order to live. The likelihood of their increasing their available capital significantly is slight. They exercise no control over the price of the commodity they sell, nor can they influence the whole-

---

[1] The significance of the absence of national standards of measure as a limitation upon trade can be somewhat exaggerated, as in Moral, 1959, pp. 79–81, and 1961, pp. 246–7. Bauer, 1954, p. 386, suggests that it is not a limitation in West Africa. For some idea of how the measures system works in one Haitian market place, cf. Mintz, 1961c.

[2] Métraux *et al.*, 1951, p. 3, provides a good illustration.

saler who sells to them. As noted earlier, when their margin of
potential profit sinks too low, they may withdraw from the business
altogether until a later time.

Yet other women, with the same amount of capital but differently
situated, are sometimes able to increase the scale of their businesses.
A young girl, the daughter of landed peasants, may initiate her
career in commerce with no more stock than several hands of ripe
bananas coming from her parents' land. No cash outlay is calculated
in the acquisition and resale of this stock. She will try to sell it to
other retailers at the mouths of paths leading to the market road,
thus avoiding the payment of taxes or market fees. By repeating this
manoeuvre, she may be able to acquire enough capital to begin
buying hard goods such as soap or matches to sell in local markets;
or to buy fowls in her rural district to resell to poultry merchants
from the town. Idle capital can go into small livestock or into the
planting of fast-maturing legumes, such as the ever-popular red,
black and congo beans. The distinction here is not one of scale of
capital; rather, it has to do with the family associations of the
marketer. If she can draw on the family's resources in kind, her
capital, however limited, is endowed with a manoeuvrability which
that of the indigent or 'detached' marketer rarely possesses. In one
case recorded, a young woman was permitted to save all of her earnings from a *karo* of inherited coffee land, making no cash expenditures
from the time of harvest until the crop was sold, and then began
work as a marketer with an operating capital of 125.00 gourdes
(US $25).

But just as important as the kind of backing a woman may get
from her family is her own ability to make the most of marketing
opportunities. There is not room for everyone in Haitian marketing,
and bad luck, inadequate resources or poor marketing ability force
many marketers out of trade. Métraux, *et al.*, write: 'The secret of a
"revendeuse's" success is to know the precise place where she can
find cheaply a product for which she will obtain a higher price at
Port-au-Prince or elsewhere.'[1] This would indeed be a valuable
secret; but in fact a *révàdèz* can never be sure she will make a profit by
arbitrage and the supplying of transportation in this way. She will
often find herself caught in a glut; other marketers will offer her
stiff competition in buying stock; and price differentials are likely to
adjust themselves fairly swiftly, in view of the great numbers of intermediaries on the constant lookout for buyers and sellers. There is no
single secret to the success of a *révàdèz*. She must be ready to work
long and hard for small profits; to trade some part of her profit
margin in return for securing her routes of supply and her buyers; to
change from product to product as the seasons change, and even to

[1] Métraux *et al.*, 1951, p. 123.

270

change her routes as need dictates; and to be prepared to deal equally well with all of the eventualities these changes entail. If she is short of cash, she must be prepared to pay dearly for it, to restrict her own standards of consumption, and to sell at as low a margin as her competitors, in order to pay off debts and to conserve operating capital.

Capital is accumulated through trade because marketers are willing to do these things, and to learn the accompanying skills. Originality, daring and endurance enter in as importantly as capital and family backing. After interviews with twenty women who dealt in onion wholesaling, it was noted that each had an operating capital in excess of US $100. Women were asked whether they could carry on such wholesaling with less capital than that, and it was agreed by all that it could not be done—with one exception. This woman had successfully wholesaled onions and had made a high profit on an operating capital far below that of her competitors. To succeed, she had to make an exhausting trip by donkey, saving her fare and the freightage fees for her stock; she had hidden the stock at the house of a *pratik*, successfully avoiding the payment of taxes and depot fees—and running a serious risk thereby; and she had sold out at a very low rate of profit in order to attract buyers under circumstances that were not entirely legal. This tale involves an element of dishonesty, insofar as marketing fees are concerned; but the other important elements are the resourcefulness, energy and daring of the woman. What she succeeded in doing was to use her money in a way which would have been barred to her, had she gone about things in the same way as her competitors.

In the following section, the use of trading capital in slack season is discussed. It will be seen there again that the problem constantly confronting the marketer is how to keep her capital available for manipulation and investment, and yet not see it dissipated in the course of daily life. This is as true in the season of heavy trading activity as otherwise. When a woman commands a substantial amount of capital, her problems are of a different order. When she has only a little, it is keeping her capital intact, and occasionally being able to make it grow, that occupies her every effort.

THE USE OF TRADE CAPITAL IN THE 'DEAD SEASON'

Viewed as a whole, trading activity in Haiti's rural market places reaches its peak about December, declines very sharply in the first months of the year, climbs to a spring climax around Easter, and then remains relatively stable (sometimes with a slight rise and fall in the late summer) until the November-December peak once more. This description is subject, of course, to variation and refinement,

271

depending upon the region, the rainfall, the particular crops being considered, and so forth.

The coffee harvests are said by everyone to set the levels for trading activity; when coffee has a good price and the crop is good, the countryside feels a temporary prosperity reflected in its trading. When the price is bad, taxes high or the crop poor or scanty, there is increasing depression in rural areas, felt even where coffee is not produced.

The variations in trade, particularly during the year, pose investment and saving problems for traders. When market conditions are poor, a central question for them is how to keep their capital available for future trading without consuming it, squandering it in nontrading activities, or investing it in ways that make it difficult to transform it again into trading capital, swiftly and easily. Women dislike holding capital in the form of cash, and avoid doing so if possible.[1] The onset of summer usually means a slackening of trade for most marketers, however, when they must withdraw capital from trade and use it in ingenious ways until trade picks up once more.

During the slack season ('*mòt sézô*') the resourceful marketer restricts her own consumption to an absolute minimum, never spending cash if she can avoid it. At the same time she seeks to transfer some measure of capital back into agriculture or livestock, though aware of the risks these measures entail. Such transfers aim at relatively quick-yielding investment, particularly in the form of small livestock, such as pigs and goats, or in the form of rapidly maturing crops, such as two and one-half month maize, and sixty-day legumes.

It is hardly accidental that piggy banks are made to look as they do. The pig (and other small livestock) is one of man's principal ways to save and keep money (capital) growing when other kinds of investment are not feasible. In Haiti, the late summer and early autumn bring rich harvests of mangoes, oranges, avocados and shaddocks, and the fruits and their waste are perfect food for swine. Livestock raising in general is an important kind of rural investment and its conjuncture with large fruit harvests is particularly important in this instance. Such animals as are fattened during the summer reach the market in

[1] Hill points out that, in West Africa, the similar desire to avoid squandering liquid capital can easily lead to unwise investment—that is, to a kind of saving which might be considered hoarding in one sense, at least: 'Many business people (defined in the broadest sense) are so anxious lest they squander their capital that they instantly invest any sum they have on hand, however small, in tangible assets such as cement or corrugated iron sheets, this being one of the explanations of that distressing and common feature of the West African urban scene, the "never-to-be-completed" house.' Hill, 1962, p. 7. The psychological significance of this somewhat skewed form of conspicuous consumption may be greater than it seems at first.

272

the early autumn. Meat prices are of course affected by the increase in supply; but it is said that there is no depressing effect on prices since autumn brings so sharp an increase in business activity. The actual percentage gain on the money invested in small livestock over a summer period apparently varies greatly; but earnings of 100 per cent are not uncommon in the recounted business experiences of rural women.

The investment of capital earned by marketing in the cultivation of such items as red and black peas and maize in the spring, while very risky, can often provide a profit by the late summer. Rural women holding land may plant small plots of these items, harvest them before the summer's end, and market them themselves, or sell them to other *révâdèz*. Drought, insect pests and local gluts, however, constitute serious dangers in these operations. On the other hand there are few ways to employ capital in the dead season that permit its being rapidly freed for other activities in the fall. If the crops do well, they provide not only a rapid transformation of product into cash, but also a food supply for the marketer and her family. Research has not revealed a marketer who simply holds her cash resources in hand and uninvested during the dead season, in spite of the riskiness of dead-season investment.

Another alternative that has come to light is small-scale commission activity. A market woman whose travel becomes disproportionately unrewarding during the late spring and summer may make quantities of bonbons and candy which she turns over to children to sell on a commission of US two cents on twenty. These children scour the neighbourhoods and haunt tiny rural markets with such stock. Since they have no operating capital themselves, they are 'getting into business' by working on commission. The number of individual business records which begin with such experiences is large.

A final alternative may be cited, though the details are not wholly clear. A woman may invest part of her free capital in the purchase of a few minor crops, particularly dried legumes, which are harvested during the summer but have a low cash value at that time. These items are stored relatively easily in the dry season; the major potential loss is by weight since they are bought and resold by volume and continue dehydrating during the hot summer months. But with any luck at all, the woman who can manage to store a quantity may be able to turn a profit in early autumn.

Market women who intend to start trading again in the autumn may be willing to engage part of their capital to rent land and hire labour to put in a quick-growing crop. Such women are by no means above doing agricultural labour themselves, and it should not be thought that the division of labour prevents women from cultivating. What

they will not do in these circumstances is use their operating capital
to buy land. Many marketers do own land, worked for them by
family members or outside labour, and such land often is bought
with profits from trade. But in those instances, the marketer has
decided to invest some of her capital in land; this is a decision
affecting the nature of investment, not a manoeuvre to keep capital
ready at hand.[1]

The investment of capital in money-lending activities of various
sorts is another use for it in the slack season. It usually means that
money must be lent for a long period—perhaps several months' use—
which leaves Haitian market women feeling anxious, and may require
legal guarantees which are troublesome and expensive. Money is
advanced against a crop, however, on terms which almost always give
the lender a solid economic advantage. This is usually done close to
the end of the summer, when capital is especially scarce, and interest
rates are supposed to be even higher than usual.

Since most of these manipulations designed to keep capital liquid,
intact or growing during the slack season are based on countryside
operations, it will be plain why rural and family associations can be
of importance in facilitating investment and insuring dependable
transactions. City-based market women have greater difficulty
generally in making satisfactory arrangements in the countryside for
investing capital over the summer season.

TRADING ACTIVITIES INVOLVING MORE CAPITAL

As capital is brought together, traders find that there are a number of
different ways to increase their resources. These vary in line with
numerous considerations, the most important being the amount of
operating capital a woman holds. Though information on this is by
no means complete, a few examples suggesting different levels of
capital holding and business operations may be useful.

Dealers in certain kinds of miscellaneous stock called '*kêkay*' can
maintain business with capital ranging from as little as 10.00 *gourdes*
(US two dollars) up to perhaps 100.00 *gourdes* (US $20). The stock of
these retailers will include such items as soap, matches, kerosene,
cooking oil, cigarettes, star anise, cinnamon, Jamaican pimento,
sulphur, shallots, garlic, blueing, asefoetida, bicarbonate of soda,
wheat flour, students' notebooks, needles and thread, nails, resin,

[1] It would be valuable to know just what determines these decisions, since they
signify—as does the 'house-building' Hill refers to—some turning away from
trade. The purchase of land by market women out of their trading profits is
probably one of the phenomena most requiring analysis in the whole of Haitian
peasant economy. Unlike the house-building, however, this may be investment of
a long-range sort rather than a temporary economic adjustment; capital invested
in the purchase of land does not easily become free again for trading.

tailors' wax, buttons, cloves, dried thyme, candles, catechisms, or some assortment of these items. Most of such stock is relatively non-perishable. Turnover is slow, and profit margins are apparently not high. Taxes are paid by sellers of such goods, each market day. A woman wants to have a wide variety of such little items to satisfy all comers, but she also must avoid tying up a large portion of her capital in those things having the slowest rate of turnover. Those women who choose not to sell these kinds of items argue that the seller eats up her capital while she waits for sales. The *kêkay* sellers themselves always aim at enlarging their operations in various ways, if they can ever accumulate enough free capital. They begin thinking about the possibilities as their savings mount—for saved money that is not working is lost money. This view differs from the way the Haitian peasant views his land—unused land is not wasted land, nor is it thought of as dissolving capital, so far as could be determined. But unused money is viewed as consuming itself—that is, money that is not earning is not working, and if things turn worse, one may not only not be making a profit, but may be reduced to consuming capital.

A *kêkay* seller who has accumulated some additional capital can serve as an illustration of the sorts of alternatives which appear when savings mount. She may choose to enlarge the scope of her activities in a number of different ways, three of which will be described here. One is simply to enlarge her retail stock so as to be able to sell at better prices and in greater variety. Another is to relegate her *kêkay* selling to the summer season of inactivity and begin dealing in more speculative produce in other seasons. Or she may seek to break into wholesaling, particularly of *kêkay* (since that is the stock she is already familiar with). To assess the forces which define her making one choice instead of another, however, is difficult.

The enlargement of a *kêkay* stock for continued retailing on a bigger scale is the least desirable alternative; during the dead season *kêkay* does not sell rapidly or well. Still, trading risks are slightest with *kêkay* and enlargement of operations does not entail changing one's mode of business activity. Older women who cannot travel freely, and women who must stay near their homes for one or another reason, are therefore likely to make this choice. And there may be times when no other choice is possible.

To shift to wholesaling is more difficult, In view of the large number of separate items necessary to make up a wide *kêkay* stock, it takes quite considerable capital to permit buying in quantities that represent a satisfactory profit upon resale to retailers. To buy in large quantities is often contingent upon founding credit relationships with an important wholesaler (*met magazê*) in the capital of a large town on the one hand, and the establishment of commercial ties with retailers, based on personal relationships, on the other. Often *kêkay* wholesalers in the country get into credit arrangements both with those who supply them and with those whom they supply—getting credit from the sellers and giving it to the buyers. For women who are prepared to attempt wholesaling, the usual procedure is to begin stocking only one or two items which sell regularly, such as kerosene, soap, matches, local rum and wheat flour. They will try to interest other women who retail these products in small local markets in buying their stocks from them, and they will offer small concessions in price to win such customers to them. At the same time, they may extend credit—though the extension of credit on the one hand, and the offer of concessions in price on the other, seem to be mutually exclusive in practice. When starting to wholesale, these women will usually maintain their own *kêkay* retailing at the local market.

The proper moment to launch modest wholesaling operations is generally in the autumn, when coffee and other cash items are reaching the licensed intermediaries who deal in them, and money is beginning to flow more freely in the countryside. Then the peasant has newly acquired funds in relatively large quantities; standard household necessaries sell on a larger scale; buyers are a little less exacting; and commercial transactions are accelerated. Since the autumn season is preceded by a period of relative commercial and agricultural stagnation, women who plan to make such a jump are those who will have been wise and fortunate enough to save and re-employ their capital at the start of the summer slack season.

There remains the third general alternative open to a woman who has accumulated her capital through *kêkay* selling and now wishes to make a 'jump upward'. It will be remembered that she could theoretically: enlarge her retail stock; go into wholesaling the same items on a small scale; or go into another line of commerce. It is this third possibility which must now be considered.

Haiti has one major city, Port-au-Prince, the capital. Its character is reminiscent of many other Latin American metropolises, particularly of fifty years ago. It is a city by virtue of its large concentration of population (now in excess of 200,000, it is believed); its central role in administration and government services; and its port facilities for import and export. There is some petty industry in the capital, but in its generally non-industrial character it resembles other Latin American cities more than it does cities of equal size in Europe or North America. Coastal cities in Latin America generally are really ports of entry and departure for products, as well as centres of control; their history, as well as their functions, differs from that of the industrial city of the machine-based western world.

For Haiti, Port-au-Prince is the nexus of all economic activity, in spite of its non-industrial character. Through it moves not only most of the rural wealth in the form of export staples, and finished goods from other lands on their way to the peasantry, but also a very substantial share of the total agricultural production of the nation destined to be consumed within Haiti itself. The reasons for this are not hard to find.

First of all, the best roads of Haiti originate in the capital. The roads between different points in the countryside, other than on the principal routes to Port-au-Prince, are uniformly inferior in quality. Secondly, the greatest concentration of buying power is in the city, as well as the major supplies of finished goods, both imported and local. Thirdly, the capital is the major centre of credit and of money to be lent. Geographically, Port-au-Prince stands at about mid-latitude to the rest of Haiti, and the three main travel routes unite it with the north, the central plateau, and the southern peninsula. Because of these facts and in conjunction with them, there is a constant stream of transport, of produce, and of resellers, in and out of the city. The great city markets are surrounded by depots whose owners rent space to resellers, and by warehouses and magazines where finished goods are wholesaled and credit to resellers is granted. As regional markets unite and represent regions, so the commercial complex of Port-au-Prince unites and represents the Republic.

All of this description is by way of background to the third alternative open to the modest seller of *kêkay*, to change her form of business operations. The magnet which seems to attract almost all resellers intent upon expansion is Port-au-Prince. There are, it is true, resellers whose commercial operations are relatively large and successful and who base themselves in such provincial towns as Les Cayes in the south, and Cap Haitien in the north, without ever going to the capital. But inevitably such business women are tied to the Port-au-Prince trade circuits.

A woman who has decided to turn from the retailing of *kêkay* to some other, wider activity usually thinks in terms of the Port-au-Prince trade. Whatever alternative activity she selects, it must be so arranged as to yield her a reasonable return on her investment. She will learn that the profit margin on some items is so low that transport, taxes and other costs will consume her gains unless she has sufficient capital to deal in substantial bulk. The purchase of onions for resale will illustrate this sort of situation, even though the profit margin on onions is often high.

A woman who carries onions in the spring harvest season from the Saint Raphaël region of the north to Port-au-Prince should have on hand a 'free' capital of at least US $50 (250.00 *gourdes*); even with that amount of capital, the risks are serious. Onions sell for approximately $8 a bag (40.00 *gourdes*) in Saint Raphaël when the harvest

277

gets under way. They may sell for as much as $10 a bag to retailers in the capital. Transport will cost fifty cents a bag; the fare for the marketer herself runs about $4. Storage at a city depot costs US four cents per bag. Taxes are US ten cents per bag per day, unless the marketer can sell off before the collector comes by. The total cost of the operation described here, not including food expenses for the marketer (she will normally sleep free in the depot), comes to 236.00 *gourdes*. If she is able to sell her stock at US $10 per bag, she will make a profit of 14.00 *gourdes*. This would be considered a coup; it assumes a profit of over 5 per cent on the total investment; it further assumes that taxes will be paid but for one day; and it omits the cost of food during the trip. Normally, women reselling onions in the capital cannot complete their sales in a single day, so that their food and tax costs are likely to be higher than calculated here. Women often stay in the capital a week or eight days before selling off all their onions. And they are not above pleading with the tax collectors to remit the collection of the tax because they are so hard pressed. If one were to hold constant all of the factors discussed in this single example and assume that the trip took seven days in all, the daily earning, less food, would be at the rate of US forty cents, or 2.00 *gourdes*; this would be considered very respectable indeed. Interviews make clear that any Saint Raphaël marketer with a capital of 250.00 *gourdes* would happily halt her marketing activity for the opportunity to work regularly in her home village for a 2.00 *gourde*-a-day salary. Were onions to be selling at US $9 a bag in the capital rather than at $10, the woman who had invested her 250.00 *gourdes* in the case described above would lose money on her operations. No woman can predict at what price she will be able to sell a product such as onions upon reaching Port-au-Prince. She will know the current price of the previous few days, and she tries to purchase in anticipation of the price holding or even rising; otherwise she will not buy so speculative an item. Still it is plain that a woman who can invest twice 250.00 *gourdes* in such an operation stands a better chance of making the trip pay than her less well-fixed neighbour. As stated earlier, only one woman interviewed in Saint Raphaël claimed to operate in the onion trade with less than US $100 capital, and described a trip which demonstrated her intrepidity as well as her good fortune.

For women with capital in the neighbourhood of US $20 (100.00 *gourdes*), another category of goods is more fitting, namely, that of eggs and fowl. Since the trip to Port-au-Prince from a point such as Saint Raphaël in the north is expensive, however, even a fowl and egg dealer would need substantial stock to make the trip worthwhile. The turnover in these items is rapid, and the profit percentage is usually high, often between 50 and 100 per cent. A chicken selling for US thirty cents in Saint Raphaël will bring sixty cents or more in the capital. At that rate, eleven birds will pay for a round trip, and thirteen will pay for their own transport as well as the reseller's. Eggs purchased at three for two cents may be resold at three for five cents, normally. There are certain difficulties with dealing in these products. With eggs, the major dangers are spoilage and breakage. When buying eggs, a reseller seeks to separate out the bad ones by examining against the light; but usually peasants will sell all or none. The reseller seeks to sell in the same way when she reaches Port-au-Prince, but is not always successful. The risk of breakage is great, particularly since the roads of Haiti are so bad and transport so rough and unreliable. Fowl are less difficult to sell off, and less risky, but on occasion, particularly in the autumn, there are gluts. Since women dealing in these products usually have high overhead expenses and limited capital, a bad day may wipe them out. Often, as will be discussed in a moment, fowl and eggs turn up as important adjunct stocks in the operations of women bulking quantities of less risky products—a sort of speculative sideline which may repay the costs of a trip, but will not be counted upon heavily to make money.[1]

Another view of the alternatives available is exposed when it is remembered that a woman carrying stock into the city may also carry stock outward. In terms of overhead costs, this can be a strategic choice for investment. Travel costs for the seller herself are the same whether she carries stock or not. One gets the impression that a woman feels very satisfied if her net profit is equal to the costs of her transportation, almost without regard to the total amount of capital invested—at least up to a certain point. If the sales of goods carried from the capital to the country are promising, it makes good economic sense for the reseller to maintain operations in two directions rather than one. A related consideration once more has to do with her total operating capital. If she carries onions or other perishables, up to the limit of her capital, to the city, she cannot buy her stock to carry home until she has completely sold off, unless she

[1] In Haiti, poultry and eggs are one kind of trade item, distinguishable from others such as grains, hard goods, or vegetables by their own characteristics as commodities and by the commercial arrangements which exist to handle them. Legerman, 1962, has suggested that the relatively non-speculative nature of poultry and eggs may help to determine the particular circumstances under which they are sold, and Hill (personal correspondence, 1962) has organized some of her West African field materials by commodity item, in part making the same point. It seems certain that the specific character of the commodities themselves will affect the conditions under which they are bought and sold, particularly in agricultural market situations of the Haitian and West African sort. In technologically very advanced situations, where trucking, processing, preservation and storage techniques are well developed and mass production and sales the rule, the specific differences between, say, eggs and rice and potatoes cannot so significantly influence the conditions of their handling and sale.

has relatively expensive credit arrangements. At the same time, she dare not invest her operating capital in products which will have a slow sale after her return home, or else she will have no capital to buy stock for her next trip to the city. Some very clever tactics are employed to make the most of a return trip home, but there are risks as always. Some women will buy seed beans or peas, or grain, at Port-au-Prince at the very moment that a harvest of the same item is about to be made in their home region, and sell it off quickly at their home market. But this manoeuvre may fail. In one case in Saint Raphaël, a woman who returned home with some dried congo peas fell sick upon her arrival and was unable to sell at the local market for two weeks. By the time she recuperated, congo peas were plentiful locally and she was compelled to sell out at a loss.

A parallel manoeuvre, requiring more capital, is for women returning to the Saint Raphaël region from trips made with onion stocks to Port-au-Prince, to stop at the great highway market at Pont de l'Estère in the Artibonite Valley to buy up rice. When rice is selling well in the Saint Raphaël market, the reseller can regain her capital, with a profit, in time to buy new onion stocks for another trip to Port-au-Prince. Timing is very important. The Saint Raphaël market is held Thursday; the market at Pont de l'Estère bridge is held Tuesday; while Friday and Saturday are the best days for wholesaling onions in the capital. An onion reseller intent on handling rice on her return trip will try to reach Port-au-Prince Friday morning, sell off by Monday, get to Pont de l'Estère on Monday night or Tuesday, and reach Saint Raphaël by Wednesday night so as to sell rice in the market on Thursday, the main market day there. She could not conceivably make a return to the capital the next day, however; sheer fatigue would prevent it. Scheduling hence becomes an essential part of business operations of this sort.

One can readily imagine the forethought and daring which must accompany such commercial ventures. The concerted planning which must go into making a step upward in the scale of operations is particularly important. The considerations which dog all planners and which can be ignored at one's economic peril are many. No matter what exquisite care a reseller takes with her operations, there is absolutely no way for her to know in advance how well or how poorly she will do on any one trip.

The rural women who do best in their regular commercial operations are also the biggest holders of capital. The concentrated intelligence which goes into building an original capital of five or ten cents into one of several hundred dollars must be remarkable; those who pass the test are the élite of the marketing system. With their accumulated experience, these women show fine judgment in their businesses; what is more, they are in a position to stand losses which would knock out resellers of scantier means. It seems characteristic of the most successful rural marketers to distribute their capital in several different areas of endeavour. But in the case of the successful large-scale rural resellers, commercial versatility seems to be a prime feature of continued success. One from the Fond-des-Nègres region of the south carries on activities which illustrate this.

This woman goes regularly to Port-au-Prince the year round, at two-week intervals. Her major stock on such trips changes with the seasons—now millet, now corn and cornmeal, now beans, or ginger, peanuts, root crops, coconuts. Her sources of supply include several rural sections at some remove from her home near Fond-des-Nègres, such that she increases her margin of profit slightly by going outside the defined peripheries of that market area to buy. She maintains ongoing relationships with the peasants and petty resellers who supply her by paying a bit more for their relatively imperishable stocks. She does not, however, advance or request credit in any of her commercial relationships. (Some Haitian *révàdèz* refuse to extend or ask for credit; others use it freely.)

In addition to the 'staple' stock this woman carries to the capital, she buys up 'fringe' stock: eggs, fowl, pumpkins and tomatoes. She also carries empty gallon jugs with her to Port-au-Prince, where she has them filled with full-proof rum to be carried back for resale in the Fond-des-Nègres region. She also buys some wholesale stocks of hard goods in the capital—lard, soap and the like—but she does this as a service to her women relatives who are retailers in the Fond-des-Nègres neighbourhoods. In return, they act as buying agents of staple goods for her between her trips. If she sees items in Port-au-Prince which she thinks to be in short supply around Fond-des-Nègres but relatively cheap in the city, she will occasionally take a flyer. Her operating capital normally exceeds US $200 (1,000.00 *gourdes*), but—and this appears to be very important—she does not invest it all at one time. When prices for her staple items are discouragingly low in the capital, she has sufficient reserves to permit her to store her stock in a depot there in hopes of a price rise, and still buy what she wishes to carry back to Fond-des-Nègres. Friends at her storage depot in the city will sell off for her if prices rise in her absence to a figure she stipulates. And she will have word from other returning market women whether it seems advisable to acquire large stocks for her next trip to the city—a decision always involving some risk, of course. It may appear in this instance that all of her capital is not working at any one time, thus violating one of the precepts of Haitian market operations. In practice, she is hedging her investment and guarding against any unexpected catastrophe. She has withdrawn funds from her capital at various times to invest in pigs and other livestock, and in land, worked by her sons and by hired

281

labour.[1] Even more interesting, perhaps, she has made sacrifices to educate one of her sons, who can speak, read and write French. This last 'investment' may never bring an appropriate financial reward; it is a noteworthy if slightly pathetic demonstration of the upward striving some of these women feel and manifest.

THE SOCIAL BACKGROUND TO THE EMPLOYMENT OF CAPITAL

Haitian rural economy is fully caught up in a cash system of exchange, and in an international system of trade, and this was true even before the Haitian Revolution. Under slavery, the slaves not only worked in the sugar fields and on the coffee plantations, but they also produced, more or less independently, items which they could sell for cash, and they purchased with their earnings those commodities they desired.[2] In contemporary Haiti, the peasant's dependence on the outside world for many commodities is heavy, and he produces for that outside world in order to get the cash he feels he must have. Peasants employ each other more and more for agricultural labour, which continues to supplant the traditional work-exchange groups and societies.[3] They rent, and buy and sell, land. They produce for local markets and for export. They consume substantial quantities of imports of all sorts, and of items produced in the cities.

At the same time, as in every society, economic activity is shaped in one way rather than another by the institutional arrangements: religious ties, traditional forms of work and reciprocity; the social organization of family and local group, and so on. Background social institutions affect trade and the employment of capital as they do the rest of economic life. This can be seen in the socialization of children to adult roles.

Girl children learn how to trade from their mothers, aunts, older sisters and other female relatives and ritual kinfolk. They customarily accompany some older woman, first to the local market places and the market-like gatherings for cockfights, wakes, etc. Later they will be taken to the large regional market places, the town market places, and even the great market places of the capital. They are taught to buy and sell, to calculate value and to recognize currency, to measure and to judge quantity and quality, to assess various products, as matter-of-factly as boys are taught to plant, cultivate and harvest. It is usual for a little girl to receive a small gift of cash from

[1] Legerman, who has since worked with this same revendeuse, tells me that the woman commits a very considerable part of her earnings to religious (*vodoun*) ceremonies. I failed to get this information in my own less intensive work with her.

[2] Moreau de Saint-Méry, 1797, I, pp. 440–4, provides a description of the Cap Français (today's Cap Haitien) market of Clugny in which the slaves marketed.

[3] Cf. Métraux *et al.*, 1951, pp. 74, 85.

a relative or godparent to enable her to undertake business on her own, under the supervision of an older woman. The first marketing activities a young girl undertakes with the hope of profit are likely to be small-scale bulk-breaking (for instance, the retailing of small quantities of sugar or soap) or commission selling. These are low-profit, 'safe' operations. While doing these things, the child learns about bulking, processing, wholesaling and other ways to make a profit in marketing. Above all, she has a chance in the market place to see how trade is done, and those older than her have a chance to see if she is quick and zestful in trade.

The young girl who begins marketing with her family behind her enjoys a considerable advantage, as indicated earlier. She may be given small quantities of stock to sell by her parents; her earnings need not be eaten up if she has a family to depend upon, and the family has some land; if she loses her investment, the family will probably back her once more (particularly since the cost will be in kind); and she may be able to borrow some capital at little or no interest as her stake and skill grow. As a very little girl, she will have provided considerable unpaid labour to her mother or to some other woman relative, meanwhile learning about marketing work. And with time, she strikes out on her own, sometimes becoming a much more successful marketer than the woman who trained her.[1]

The socialization of girls into the marketing skills is paralleled by the way boys are trained to agriculture. This division is not absolutely rigid; there are no religious sanctions behind it, and most women know something of farming, as men do of trade. Women inherit land, just as men do, and men engage in trade on occasion. But men and women equally emphatically express their preferences along the lines of the division of labour. The division is to some extent accompanied by some division of family resources. Market women may sometimes take part of their surplus earnings to purchase land, but usually they will keep their marketing capital quite separate. Men, in turn, may stake their wives to initial marketing operations, but they will not willingly subsidize such operations again if the woman is an unsuccessful marketer. Though both husbands and wives uniformly maintain that budgeting is never a source of discord, each partner has only limited ability to draw on the other's 'line of work' (i.e. agriculture as contraposed to trade) to subsidize his own. For the woman, however, the main way she can really invest extra capital, other than in more trade, is in land. The constant reinvestment of some part of trade earnings in economic activity on the land makes

[1] Legerman, 1962, p. 146, notes that the urban poultry sellers, unlike their rural counterparts, rarely train their daughters in the same occupation. Presumably, the urban sellers have higher aspirations for their children. This difference in socialization may have some wider sociological significance.

good sense, contributing to the growth of capital, as when livestock is purchased and fattened or fast-growing crops are put in. But this is less clearly the case when land is purchased but the labour to work it is not. Idle land is not regarded in the same way as idle cash. It may be that the Haitian economy in this case reveals a certain contradictoriness—strong commercialism in the sphere of distribution, and conservatism and land hunger in the sphere of agriculture. Where investment in operations on the land is tied directly to distributive activity—the manoeuvres designed to keep capital working in off seasons, for instance—the use of the land is frankly capitalistic. Where land is acquired as a means of saving, this saving may sometimes be tantamount to hoarding.

The capital of the marketer has only limited ability to galvanize family resources in the generation of yet more wealth but this is hardly the fault of the 'conservative peasant'. There are many technical limitations upon the way Haitian agriculture is carried on by the peasantry. These could be corrected in part by improving the quantity and quality of extension services, broadening the market for peasant products (particularly overseas), and improving the peasant's relative position in the economy. At present, the peasantry's response to stimuli, including those originating with the market women, is realistic, since the market for peasant products is in any case feeble, dispersed, often undependable—and eminently taxable.[1] If the wife's —marketer's—role in the economy seems to be more 'progressive' than her husband's, it has to do with the nature of her activities: the constantly changing market situation, the high value placed on quick-wittedness, resourcefulness and daring, and the liquid form her capital takes during her operations. The most successful marketer will excel in skills that probably do not make for the best cultivators.

These points, and others made earlier, merely confirm that the relationship between economic activity and the social system within which it occurs is intimate.[2] For traders, the economic associations one has with one's family or other close supporters are immensely important. Only when the level of capital holdings is sufficiently high to permit the marketer to become a full-scale city retailer, a cloth merchant, a storekeeper, or a dealer in capital itself (as in large-scale commission selling, wholesaling and money-lending), does the importance of such associations dwindle. Economic individualism appears at times to take precedence over family obligations. In several cases, market women reported that they were able to borrow

---

[1] The taxation of produce and marketers in the Haitian markets is so arbitrary and pervasive on the one hand and so inefficient on the other that it manages to be both punitive and a barrier to economic growth. For a list of some of the taxes, cf. Mintz, 1959.

[2] Cf. Mintz, 1959, 1960d.

capital for marketing operations from close relatives only by the payment of high rates of interest on short-term loans. In one case, a woman reported that her mother refused to lend her capital, without explanation, though she could have lent the money without difficulty. At the same time, almost all of the market women interviewed on this point—about thirty—borrowed their first stakes from close relatives without paying any interest. There appeared to be no general rule governing this,[1] which is the more surprising since capital is clearly very difficult to come by in rural Haiti.

CONCLUSIONS

The aim of this essay has been to describe the ways in which the Haitian market women employ capital in their operations. The accumulation and manipulation of capital in the Haitian economy is of interest because the availability of labour and the ways in which it is substituted for capital are so pronounced. Capital is stored up for investment at the cost of very great effort, resourcefulness and daring.

The technical level of marketing services in Haitian society seems low, but society pays a low price all the same for what the market system provides. This low price is guaranteed not by the high productivity of those participating but rather by their numbers. The price is raised by such considerations as shockingly poor roads, high import duties on vehicles and fuels, backward and poorly capitalized agriculture resulting in poor yields and relatively high production costs, and onerous taxation of the activities of distributive intermediaries. These problems, however, do not originate with the market woman. And though she communicates demand to potential producers, relates new producers to the market, stimulates improvement in agriculture and closer ties between the producer and his market, she cannot solve the problems that beset the economy.

A substantial part of the rural Haitian's consumption needs are satisfied by cash expenditure, even though the products purchased are often Haitian and produced by the peasantry itself. These products come from very large numbers of highly diversified small farms, in small and irregular quantities. Such circumstances, together with the lack of viable economic alternatives, explain the very large numbers of persons engaged in middlemen's activities. Intermediaries contribute the services of bulking, breaking bulk, transport, packaging, and processing, also assisting each other and their

---

[1] Cf. Hill, 1962, p. 12, writing on West African marketers: 'On the one hand credit is ubiquitous—on the other hand there are many times, places and circumstances when nothing save complete down payment on the spot is found acceptable.' Hill calls attention to the disregard planners sometimes show for local patterns of credit even when these may seriously affect development planning.

buyers and suppliers with cash advances, credit, concessions in price and quantity, and the like. To the extent that they can show a profit on their investment, they are 'paid' for their services; the competition involved lowers the cost of these services while severely limiting their earning power.

At the same time, these marketers show a firm grasp of certain economic principles as they apply to the Haitian economy; some of the ways in which they manipulate their capital demonstrate this. That economy seems to have considerable resiliency because of the readiness of intermediaries swiftly to change their modes of operation, and otherwise to show verve and originality in investing capital productively. Such daring and skill cannot communicate their consequences more effectively to the agricultural sector because of the overall limitations upon the economy, particularly in its lack of a secure or an expanding market. Yet it appears that substantial entrepreneurial talent, for the most part actually unexploited, is available in Haiti and may be available in other countries like it. The significance of this for economic development may not have been wholly realized in some underdeveloped countries.

13

Capital Saving, and Credit in a Guatemalan and a Mexican Indian Peasant Society

BY MANNING NASH

Capital, saving and credit are aspects of an economic system, which in turn is a sub-system of a total social system. This very general proposition expresses the anthropological orientation that economic behaviour and economic arrangements are part of, and mutually interdependent with the social and cultural constitution of a given aggregate of persons whose behaviour is well enough adjusted to each other so that they may be called a society, and whose common understandings and social relations are so ordered that they may be analysed as a social system. The orientation leaves open the questions of the kinds of articulations between economy and society; the precise ways in which they determine each other; and the range of functional compatibility between action in the economic sphere and the other foci of action which make up the social system.

One way of approaching the empirical questions and putting flesh and blood on the bare skeleton of analysis is to compare communities of broad similarity in cultural pattern and social organization, but dissimilar with respect to strategic aspects of their economic system. Capital, saving and credit as categories of inquiry are convenient avenues leading to the descriptive understanding of significant economic variations. In this essay I compare the Guatemalan Indian community of Cantel with the Mexican Indian community of Amatenango. My aim is to describe the differing notions, uses and levels of capital; the meaning, extent and institutions of credit, and the amount, form and channelling of savings. From the descriptions I shall suggest the social and cultural sources and constraints of the patterns of credit, capital and saving. Finally, I shall move to some analytical propositions on the relations of economy to society.

Capital, Saving and Credit in Peasant Societies

I. CANTEL

Cantel (Nash, 1958) is a *municipio* of Quiché speaking Indians in the western highlands of Guatemala. The municipio is a governmental and administrative unit, but in this region of Guatemala, it corresponds with a local, ethnically distinct society (Tax, 1937). The people of Cantel have a feeling of distinctiveness from neighbouring Indian communities and from Ladinos (as the Spanish-speaking carriers of national culture are called), and this sense of ethnic identity is supported in fact by the minute and endless ways in which the culture of Cantel differs from other local Indian societies and in the striking ways it differs from Ladino culture. The broad pattern of the area was set more than 400 years ago and is a fusion of Spanish colonial heritage, Maya peasant culture, local Guatemalan adaptations, and a thin overlay of the modern industrial world. But as it is lived by Canteleños it is a particular blend tied to a territory and to a people, with particular local meanings and symbols. The chief features of Cantel society are a simple plot agriculture of corn (maize), beans and squash (the milpa), rotated in the better lands with cash crop wheat. The land is held in fee simple and is owned by an individual, but is run by a household unit, most frequently corresponding to a nuclear family. Wealth differences are not marked, and no class lines on wealth or economic interest lines have crystallized. The technology of farming is simple; tools of steel and wood powered by human energy break the soil, plant the seed and harvest the crop. Only in threshing is the animal power of the horse added to human effort. Cantel is a money-using society, and all exchange is money exchange, or in terms of the money values of items. The local market, a once a week affair, is part of the regional system of rotating markets in a 'solar' system in which community level markets have specialized days of meeting around an everyday market centre. The Indians of Cantel both buy and sell in the various regional markets. The market, as an institution, is free (prices are set by the interplay of supply and demand), open (anyone may enter to buy or sell), and competitive (no buyers or sellers are large enough or well enough organized to affect significantly the price of a commodity). There also exists a labour market, both for internal services (chiefly agricultural labour at the peaks of the cycle) and external for the workers on the coffee plantations in the 4,000–2,000 ft. altitude range to the west.

The households are connected into a system by the operation of a civil-religious hierarchy (Nash, 1958). This is a system of offices, arranged in a hierarchy, in which all men (as representatives of households) must serve. The offices have the manifest functions of civil order, maintenance, dispute settlement, administration, cleaning

288

and civic projects on the civil side, and maintenance of the church, the corporations of the saints (*cofradias*), the planning and carrying out of religious festivals, and the upkeep of the cemetery and burying of the dead on the religious side. As latent functions of the hierarchy, the community is stratified as to prestige (since service in the offices confers it, and men move up the ladder of offices all through their adult life) and age graded. The hierarchy also serves to drain accumulated wealth in ritual expenditure, and to level wealth differences among families, since the offices are unpaid, costly to undertake, and an incumbent cannot work while he is in office.

In world view, religion and mythology, Cantel has many of the features associated with small, long-settled, non-literate communities. Its mental apprehension of reality is narrow (in the geographical and intellectual senses), local and unsystematic. Parts of nature are animate; devils, witches and powers are part of daily life.

The above pattern Cantel shares in larger or smaller measure with other Indian peasant communities of the region. It differs radically from them in having in its midst a large modern textile factory which employs about one-fourth of the labour force. The textile factory is Central America's largest and as an enterprise produces a substantial amount of the cotton goods used in Guatemala. Consequently Cantel has a much more differentiated occupational structure than most Indian communities. This occupational heterogeneity is a basic fact in understanding some of the roots of capital formation, saving and invention of credit mechanisms.

To understand the level of capital in Cantel and the incentives underlying that level first requires micro-analysis, which in this context is the stipulation of the motives, incentives, costs and benefits of playing the culturally defined roles. A second step in understanding is macro-analysis, a movement from the meaning and content of social roles to the level of the structural conditions and constraints in the role sets open to a social system.

The productive unit in Cantel is a household unit. The household units are basically engaged in farming. The end of farming is not the accumulation of money or assets, although that would be a welcome outcome, but rather the meeting of a traditionally defined level of living. The level of living defined as adequate for Cantelenses (a family of two adults and three children) runs about 320 dollars a year (*v.* Nash 1958 for this computation, pp. 21 ff.). For a family to have this cash equivalent annually they must have at their disposal just over two acres of fairly good, level land. Most Cantelenses do not own this much land; the average is about half this, and the mode near a fifth of the land needed to meet what custom and aspiration call adequate. In this situation, most farming families do not have the resources to make capital improvements, nor is their withholding power from consumption apparent. Another consequence is the short time perspective for use of money or the building of assets. Farmers in Cantel can stretch their economic horizons to a harvest cycle, but not beyond. Even in non-agricultural improvements, like repairing a house, or digging a well, no Cantelense makes a total plan. Rather he does one little thing now, say repair a wall. Next year he may fix a roof, and the year after he may replace the wooden doors, and the year after he may whitewash his patio walls. But he does not envision, or save or invest for a new state of affairs. This way of regarding capital and assets is clearly a function of the level of living and the small to negligible funds available to plan with and think about. And this way is the key to the mode of a capital handling. Cantelenses think in terms of *maintenance* of the given stock, not in terms of expansion, innovation or renovation according to any organized entrepreneurial plan.

The maintenance outlook means that people do in fact save, do plan, do have clear ideas of when they must curtail consumption in favour of keeping a level of capital, or capital goods at a given mark. But the conditions of a very simple technology, land scarcity, widespread poverty, result in the reproduction of the capital level, in the good years at least. Such limits on the ability to take risks, on the commitment to maintenance, give the technology of this community the appearance of traditionality. For about seventy years the farming tool kit has remained virtually unchanged, and during the previous period, only metal tools have been substituted for indigenous ones. The life experience which leads to maintenance of levels of capital implicates, therefore, continuity in forms as well.

It is not clear just how much of the level and form of simple agricultural technology and investment is conditioned by the presence of hands to work which require no formal wages, being members of the household. Except at peak periods, and for the larger landholders most families, given the land at their disposal, have more labour than is needed. That is to say, a large farm family will proportionately employ less man-days in the agricultural cycle than will a small one. Boys, for example, are kept busy by taking the family's single cow to pasture, or a young boy may be seen with a small and virtually ineffectual hoe trying to break ground beside his older male household relatives. True, part of this is training, both in the technical sense and the sense of building the discipline to bear the hard work in the fields, but it certainly contributes to absence of search for capital-intensive techniques.

The farmer's situation is somewhat different from that of the factory worker's. Factory workers and artisans, more than one quarter of the labour force of Cantel, see themselves as selling services. Their income is not available for investment in a productive tech-

nology to the same extent as is the farmer's. Consequently there is
some differentiation in the life style and consumption pattern of those
relatively less engaged in the peasant occupation of farming. Factory
workers tend to have a wider range of commodity consumption,
although when compared to Ladinos (Tax, 1955) Cantel Indian
factory workers still have an Indian pattern of consumption. In
Cantel, if the house has a radio, if the head of the house wears a
wristwatch, if a bicycle is parked in the patio, or if canned goods are
in the kitchen it is probably the household of a factory worker. There
are two classes of items in the above list. One is composed of items
that any Cantelense with more income would be likely to buy; the
other is made up of things that fit the factory worker's but not the
farmer's way of life. Radios would be bought if income were available
along with electricity by farmers. Wristwatches and Mexican enam-
elled ware would be bought if farm income rose, but bicycles are not
of use to farmers, and the same money would be used for a beast of
burden or a cow, or an apiary. One consumption item is exclusive
to factory workers and artisans: enrolment in correspondence
courses for instruction in mechanical arts and crafts. Apparently the
selling of skills enables them to envision economic mobility in terms
of investment in learning, while farmers view mobility in terms of
more land—if any is available when they have money on hand which
can buy it. Factory workers eat more of the higher priced items in the
Cantel diet than do farmers, and some of the festal foods have moved
into the category of routine items for them. Their clothing shows
greater approximation to Western models, and tends to be in a better
state of repair than does farmers'.

In viewing the household as a consumption and production unit,
the mechanisms of control of income are the same irrespective of
occupation of the family head. The male head of the family is the
nominal controller of all family funds. He is the receiver of all income
of those who live under his roof, and the spender of all funds. In fact
the wife spends most of the income. She spends it in the market place,
but her husband is usually at her side in the shopping. Money saved,
in cash form, is rare in Cantel. Saving takes two chief forms: one is
corn in the *troje*, a wooden structure where the maize harvest is
stored to be used during the year; the other is in the raising of pigs
and chickens to be sold when needed. Daily supplies of cash come
either from the selling of eggs, milk, honey or corn in small amounts.
Women frequently 'raid' the *troje* for small amounts of corn to buy
things that cannot be bought from their usual family stipends. The
keeping of chickens, turkeys or ducks is clearly profitable in terms of
the corn they eat and the return they bring, but the raising of a pig is
not, and may even be a losing proposition, but it is a form of saving
which requires neither banks, nor credit instruments, nor even hard

cash. Part of the reasons for keeping pigs is that they are readily saleable, there being a local animal market in a convenient situation between the lowlands and the rest of the highlands. Catelenses tend to sell their pigs to meet an unforeseen large expense (sickness, death, etc.) or when in their close calculation they think the pigs may shortly die. Chickens are also kept for pin money, but may die more easily than young pigs.

Savings on hand do not usually suffice to meet large expenditures, and so various forms of borrowing are employed. Almost all of the money borrowed in Cantel is for consumption purposes and does not contribute to the raising of the level of production or result in items that have a future income stream. Some borrowing takes place when a parcel of land is on the market, but it is more likely that the richer Cantelense will buy the land outright than borrow to purchase it.

Money loans are difficult to come by in Cantel. Kinsmen or neighbours are not recourses for more than 'pin money' loans. A substantial loan, anything from $5 upwards, requires dealing with the resident strangers—Ladinos, many of whom are moneylenders. Loans in Cantel must be secured with something beyond the word of the borrower. Items like a sewing machine, bicycle, watch, ring or silver earrings, or even clothing and umbrellas, may be pledged to a Ladino moneylender. Like a pawnshop the item is physically surrendered until the loan is repaid. Interest on this sort of loan runs at about 25 per cent per month. Another means of raising money is to pledge one's land. In this case the land is surrendered to the lender until the loan is repaid, with the lender keeping its produce until that time. The land does not get transferred in title until the borrower, if he does not repay, dies. The court of the first instance then transfers the land to the holder of the debt.

Raising money on a growing crop is also common. But only on the wheat yield is this done. A man goes to a miller in the nearby town and contracts to sell his wheat at a given price on the day it is harvested. He pays a premium for this advance, but the exact amount of the premium is contingent on his bargaining powers and the guesses buyer and seller make on the price at harvest time.

Credit over a signature, or on a spoken pledge, is virtually absent. Some Indians do get credit in the *tiendas* (stores with stocks of matches, cigarettes, candles, rope, coffee, herbs, flashlights, cloth, beads, etc. and liquor) but this never exceeds a few dollars, and must be repaid or the Indian will have to avoid going to that particular tienda. What characterizes the credit structure of Cantel then is the relative scarcity of funds, high rates of interest, consumption borrowing and physical equivalences for money lent, plus the provision of credit by those who are not socially or morally bound to their borrowers. In these conditions the need for credit follows personal

292

misfortune or tragedy, and borrowing or indebtedness is always unfortunate, and sometimes a calamity resulting in loss of livelihood and reduction in level of living.

Factory workers have one additional source of providing money for emergency consumption. They have organized a series of wage-pools. Each member contributes fifty cents a week, and through a lottery the money is awarded to the lucky number. A man cannot win more than a fixed number of times in a year, and the pools work virtually as a forced saving device with periodic redistribution. Factory workers occasionally may borrow against wages without interest, but not for more than a week or two's earnings.

It is probably sufficiently clear from the above why the level of capital is low for any given unit, why the stock of capital takes the form of assets used in the traditional technology and mode of living, why credit is used for emergency consumption purposes and not for financing production, and why the supply of credit tends to be in the hands of resident strangers and two or three of the richer Indians. What needs further explanation is why this configuration continues to exist, why particular households do not prosper and become more like firms, or why in this market and pecuniary economy business opportunity is not sought nor developed. The answers to these macro-structural questions fall into three categories: 1. the social and cultural structure acts to drain wealth for ritual and social ends; 2. the inabilities to find a social basis for reorganizing economic activity; 3. the problems of communal detachment and acculturation in economic success. I shall explicate the content of the categories in serial order.

The households of Cantel are organized into a social system through the operation of a civil-religious hierarchy. Since male heads of households must serve in these offices and must in addition spend their own funds while serving, and usually cannot carry out full economic activities during their tenure, the system of services drains accumulated wealth and may even require borrowing of money. The richer members of the society take their turns in office with less delay between posts than do the poorer and hence spend their substance more rapidly. They also run the danger of becoming addicted to alcohol since the offices require much ceremonial drinking, and they start younger and hence run the risks of early and continual reliance on liquor. In addition to the civil-religious hierarchy is a system of voluntary attachment to given cults of the saints. Some of the cults are on a basis of group payment, but the larger ones are at the expense of an individual. The richer people vie for public recognition and as measures of their piety or attachment to *costumbre*, for the opportunity to expend funds in the upkeep of a given saint for a year, with the attendant festivals. The civil-religious hierarchy and donations to religious expenditure are the capstones of the 'levelling mechanism', which ensures a democracy of poverty and which keeps individuals from amassing disproportionate wealth. The levelling mechanism is combined of these elements:

1. low level of wealth and technology
2. fracture of estate by bilateral inheritance
3. expenditure of time and resources in communal office
4. forced expenditure in ritual by the wealthy.

The reciprocal operation of these elements means that wealth does not adhere to family lines, and that such capital as is accumulated is deflected from strictly economic ends and pursuits to investments in social obligations and prestige.

The organizational difficulties in using capital for economic ends in a community like Cantel derive from its social and cultural structure, but are of a different order. These exists no basis for forming groups oriented to economic ends in traditional Cantel. Only among factory workers, whose conditions of aggregation are special, have voluntary organizations, like the wage-pool, the labour union, the bicycle club and a basketball team, been organized. Among farming Cantelenses any persisting formation of persons depends upon the kinship network, or the institutional pattern of the society, i.e. the hierarchy, the cults of the saints, the market place, etc. Relations between persons are formal, impersonal and fleeting outside of these contexts. If a man wants to organize personnel and resources for an economic activity, procedures are not known, and trust and confidence in the performance of roles cannot be assumed. One example is the case of one of the richest Cantelenses, who in addition to being a farmer was one of the town butchers. He brought cattle up from the coastal hotlands at weekly intervals, slaughtered them in Cantel and sold the meat in a store which was part of his house. (To indicate how competition was regulated in this extra-traditional butchering, the three butchers took turns at having their shops open, with hardly any overlap, except in fiesta times and for the Sunday market when the demand was more than they could meet even in combination. Competition was maintained, however, by meat stores in nearby Quezlatenango.) He also had a good supply of wheat and corn which he sold in markets outside of Cantel. All of this activity involved him in paying for many transportation services and he perceived that it might be to his advantage to buy a truck. Now even as rich as he was, a truck was an investment he did not want to make alone. He considered who else would put up part of the money for a truck and he thought of some likely persons. But, how would they work out who would use the truck, how often, when and who would be responsible for its upkeep, payment in case of accident, etc? He could not reasonably see a way of getting people to agree to a contract, or enforcing

294

it even if they did agree. His kinsmen were poor and so they, though possibly trustworthy, were not able to contribute.

Another thing that gave him pause was the dependence upon persons and skills beyond the local community. Repair and maintenance would depend upon Ladino mechanics. A driver would have to be a Ladino, or one of the few Ladinoized Indians who know how to drive. All in all, the truck fell from active consideration as an item of investment because the outlay was too much for a single household, and because even if the household strained or borrowed money, the piece of equipment would not be directly controllable by its owner. This example does not imply an 'amoral familism' (Banfield, 1957), which limits a people's capacity to organize for technological or economic change, but that the ordinary operation of a peasant society like Cantel places severe limits on the risks that capital holders can take, and that an organizational basis for the spreading of the risks has no soil in which to flourish.

The third category inhibiting capital formation, or investment in economic or productive forms, is the consequence of detachment from the community. Cantel is a society which depends upon economic homogeneity in wealth, and upon use of wealth towards communally defined ends rather than abstract best opportunities. Not all persons equally subscribe to communal ends, and there is 'leakage' of personnel into Ladino society. Anybody who begins to orient his activity to economic self-interest begins to detach himself and his family from the local community. The carpenter who expanded his operations, hired assistants, bought a motor and power saws, soon found himself confined by Cantel, unwilling to take his turn in the hierarchy, reluctant to contribute to the saint cult. He moved to either another Indian community or to a Ladino town. In 1953–54, I observed just this sequence of economic development and communal estrangement. People who run enterprises, on however small a scale, tend to get Ladinoized, and if they are very successful, tend to become Ladinos. The young boys who own or chauffeur motor cars (used as taxis between Cantel and neighbouring communities, but chiefly the city of Quezlatenango) all wear Ladino clothes, speak Spanish, have not taken Cantel wives, and talk of living somewhere else. The pattern of capital formation for economic ends when it conflicts with communal obligations (as it often does at this level of wealth) requires either the detachment from the community, or the abjuring of a calculus in terms of best use of capital. Cantelenses are aware of the possibilities of personal wealth leading them into Ladino society, and most of them would clearly choose a pattern of ritual and prestige expenditure in the local context than the known alternative of being at the bottom of rural Ladino society.

Cantel's major capital expenditures, however, are through the operation of the community itself, and for communal ends. The hierarchy has the power and authority to use seven work days a year from each able-bodied man in the community. And this labour is involved in building things like roads, a bridge across the local river, the laying of the church floor, or the repair of public properties. This effort tends to add to the communal stock of assets, and occasionally to raise outputs, or reduce the costs in time and money of transport. But such slow accretion does not alter the structure of Cantel's economy, nor inject dynamism into it. Like most community development ventures it moves toward balance, harmony and equality in the social sphere and provides no continuing basis for structural change in those arrangements of values and persons which might make for sustained development.

II. AMATENANGO DEL VALLE

In south-east Mexico is a community of Maya Indians, related to the Indians of mid-western Guatemala. The connections are lost in the centuries of history, but they clearly stem from the same cultural tradition and in very broad outline are similar kinds of social systems. Amatenango is a community of Tzeltal-speaking Indians, one of the Maya tongues, about 44 kilometres south of Las Casas in Chiapas, Mexico. Compared to Cantel, it is smaller in size, not nearly so 'cosmopolitan', and in many ways culturally eroded from the richness and complexity of its Maya heritage. At the same time, it is more embattledly Indian, and the gulf which separates it from the superordinate national culture of Mexico is much more marked by hostility and tension.

Amatenangueros do not allow Ladinos to live in their community, and with the single exception of the Ladino school teacher and his family, there are none. They do not permit the transfer of land to outsiders, and if an Amatenaguero wants to sell his land and cannot find a local buyer, he is obliged to sell it to the civil hierarchy who will hold it until a local buyer is available. Amatenango is also a municipio, it has the general features of a distinct dialect, a local civil and religious hierarchy, endogamy, economic specialization and, in short, it too is a locally organized society united by blood and custom.

Amatenango is a farming community and a pottery producing community (for a fuller description of the economy see Nash, forthcoming in *Man*; the social structure is described in June Nash, 'Social Relations in Amatenango: An Activity analysis', Phd. Thesis, University of Chicago). To produce its corn, beans, squash in the milpa; its wheat in the fields, and its garden crops in the house gardens, a very simple technology is employed. The ox-drawn plough, the machete, digging stick, sickle and a net bag make up the tool kit. A simple irrigation system of ditching serves the lower, level lands. The cleaning and care of the irrigation network is done through communal labour, and each farmer takes his turns with the water run. Though the agricultural complex includes the plough and beasts of burden it is not much more efficient than Cantel. The plough and animals serve to cut the working time of Amatenangueros and they have much more leisure than do the farmers of Cantel. Part of this is also due to the more favourable situation of Amatenango (it sits in a broad valley about 5,000 feet average elevation: Cantel is over 8,000 feet high). Amatenangueros use their increased leisure in loafing, drinking and hunting, and so there is a more rustic and 'wilder' feeling about Amatenango when compared to Cantel. People move slower, seem to be less busy, and spend more time in their patios and around their houses than do Cantelenses. Also it is a more 'open' society in that high walls do not surround the houses, and neighbours know each other, interact and have much more enduring bonds of social and economic interdependence than in Cantel.

Since the agricultural complex and hence the farmer's incentives and motivations are broadly similar to those of Cantel, I shall concentrate on the pottery making industry in exploring the meaning, formation and use of capital in this community. It need only be added that Amatenangueros tend to have land outside of the community because of Government grant land (*ejidos*) and that most of them know how to handle a wider variety of crops and soils (since many of their lands are in the lowlands growing a more tropical crop complex) than do Cantelenses.

Pottery making is a woman's job. All women born in, and raised in, Amatenango know how to, and do, make pots. Of the 280 households in the town centre of the community only two or three are not engaged in the making of pottery. Pottery making is a community skill, not an individual art. The communal nature of the specialization is highlighted by the fact that adjoining communities, sharing virtually the same natural resources, do not produce a single pot, and in a region nearly forty miles long and thirty across there is no other Indian pottery-making community. The techniques of pottery making are part of the culture of Amatenango, and learned in the same intimate, informal processes of enculturation as are its language, its etiquette, and its world view. Productive skill and knowledge are no more for export than are other aspects of culture. Though the potters are women, male help is required to get the pottery fired, to get it to market and to pack it. So men are an essential part of the production cycle.

Pottery making is a hand industry. No wheel, mould, oven or other mechanical aid is required. Technologically the work requires great skill—in the shaping hand of the potter, in the close adjustment of the ware in the open street firing, in the mixing of clay and temper, in the grinding of pigment, in the painting of designs, and in the final smoothing and polishing. But the technology is neither complex nor expensive. The raw materials in pottery making (clay, temper, pigment, wood for firing, scraping stones) come from municipal resources and are equally available to any member of the community. The most elaborate additions to the raw materials—a steel blade for scraping, a smooth board, a burlap bag, net bags) cost under three dollars, and every household has that much capital. The pottery industry is, of course, part-time work for any woman and takes place in the multi-purposed structure of the household. It is one of the fields of activity in which maintenance needs of the basic social unit are met. Production varies with the composition of the household in terms of sex, age and numbers of persons. Production is also inversely related to the land wealth of a household, for the rich need less of the cash income brought in from pottery sales. And production is geared to the annual round and the festal cycle of the community. Prices vary from time to time and from place to place, and the Amatenangueros are keenly sensitized to the differences, and pots tend to flow to points of sale until there is virtual equality in the prices at different sale points (counting, of course, the extra expense and time involved in carrying pots to the more remote points of sale).

That the pottery industry continues to exhibit the features of many reduplicative production units, with low capitalization, and virtual technological stagnation is easily explained. The organization of production in households, with women as the agents of production is the first limit on expansion of size in any given unit, or the agglomeration of units. The household organization limits the size and composition of the 'labour force' since only kinship or adoption mechanisms can recruit potters; furthermore women are homebound, do not travel much, do not speak Spanish, do not read, and hence are not alert to or even looking for ways to alter the technology of pottery production. And the male is the controller of all funds the household receives, and he thinks of land investment, or more likely (since land is but rarely up for sale) buying cattle or horses. The low capital level of the pottery industry is also a positive factor in Amatenango eyes. When, in 1957, under the aegis of the Instituto Nacional Indigenista of Mexico, I suggested the use of a kiln for firing pottery to some of the people of Amatenango, keen enough interest was expressed; but with two socially important caveats: (1) the initial capital outlay for the kiln would not be borne by the household, and (2) the cost of all ruined pottery would be borne by the Instituto. If someone else would put up the capital and take the initial risks, Amatenango women would experiment.

This attitude, of course, rests on reasoned, long experience of the people of the community. They have worked out a rather intricate adjustment to their ecological possibilities; the suggestions of outside experts for improving it have, in the past, shown massive ignorance of the conditions of life in the community, or have proved costly when tried. Certain kinds of 'improved corn' did not store as well, a wood-burning kiln tried some twenty-five years ago turned the pots to ashes, and the attempted installation of latrines has fouled the sweet shade of the patio.

The productive enterprise of Amatenago, even though it is an 'industry', shows the same kinds of restriction on investment opportunities and sets of motivation as does the farming complex in Amatenango, and indeed in Cantel. The analysis leads to the observation of stereotyping in productive technique, and a technology and economic organization not conducive to changes in the kind and levels of capital. Capital maintenance rather than an 'entrepreneurial' outlook is the dominant theme. This is all the more remarkable when the twin facts of the open, free, competitive market, and monetary exchange are recalled. Apparently, in some social contexts the market and money are disjoined from the credit instrument and the business outlook. From Western experience we take these to be a single economic bundle.

Compared to Cantel, there are some striking differences in the amount, form and use of savings in Amatenango. In the first place, the daily flow of small coins is nearly constant in Cantel, but not nearly so in Amatenango. Money comes in from the pottery sales, or the sales of chayotes to the colder villages, nearly constantly, but it does not circulate so much in Amatenango. Amatenangueros have a much more restricted sort of diet, provide much more of it themselves than do Cantelenses; are much more poorly clothed and buy less cloth, and they do their own liquor-making. Stores were absent from Amatenango, and now there is only the co-operative run by the Instituto, and two small home-store combinations started by ex-employees of the Instituto co-operative. Amatenangueros seem to have less cash than the Canteleños, and there is certainly less commercial transaction within the community. Amatenangueros tend to invest in cattle or horses. Most families have one such large beast, which is a reservoir against emergencies. Richer families have many horses, and they rent them out to poorer farmers who need them during the threshing periods for wheat. When a household needs money for consumption emergencies it will slaughter a bull and sell the meat by shares among an invited group. Payments may be deferred for as long as a month, but people can trade on the strength of these obligations, since this is a strictly enforceable contract. If a meat purchaser does not pay, the list of buyers which was compiled in

299

public at the time of the purchase is produced at the local court-house, and payment is extracted.

One of the features underlying the relative absence of the circulation of money in Amatenango is the fact that liquor serves equally well as a medium of exchange. Many transactions involve the exchange of commodities or services for home-brewed liquor, and many transactions must be sealed by the gift of alcohol. Liquor serves as payment for all public fines, to seal a wage contract, to make final a transfer of land, as marriage payment, at the exchange of ritual office, and as beverage at most social events. Liquor, of course, is the completely consumable good, and at most exchanges it must be consumed at the time of the exchange, thus precluding accumulation. It certainly prevents the officials who get the fines for breach of public order or violation of law from becoming rich, if not alcoholic, in office.

Because of the absence of resident strangers in Amatenango, and because of the smaller supply and velocity of money in the community, loans are very difficult to secure within the community itself. Some small loans are made between neighbours, or among kinsmen, but usually enough to meet an emergency consumption need. If there are no horses to sell, no cattle to slaughter, and no land to sell, an emergency is met by trying to borrow money from Ladinos in the nearby town of Teopisca. Ladinos lend money on wheat crops, against Indian labour, and against cattle to be delivered. But the ability to borrow money from Ladinos is limited and the operation is delicate. Occasionally the bond of ritual kinship (*compadrazgo*) is formed between an Indian and a Ladino with the sole hope on the Indian's part that it may facilitate economic aid, on the positive side, or at least obviate the expenditure of his funds in ritual on the negative side (with Indian compadres there are always festal expenses). So subject to caprice is the business of borrowing money from Ladinos, that one of the mythological figures of Amatenango is derived from this context. In Amatenango, there is (as in Cantel) a cluster of beliefs regarding the amassing of wealth which always make wealth something that is in the realm of supernature. Men get rich through the discovery of treasure, by windfall, or by making pacts with the evil devils who inhabit the surrounding hills. Amatenango has a particular tale about a spirit called *Klabil*, or with full title *Don Klabil*. Klabil inhabits the tallest peak near the community, living deeply within the mountain. He has treasure to dispense, if men have the nerve to climb in the cave opening in the side of the mountain, brave the devouring animals and talk to him. He will either give treasure by sending a mule train of gold-laden animals past the petitioner's door at midnight on some cloudy night, or point out where gold can be gotten. Sometimes the aspirant for wealth falls into the hole and is lost for ever, sometimes he makes a pact with Klabil which calls for eternal servitude after death in the mountain domain of Klabil.

There are other spirits, and other variations of this theme, but Klabil is the most prominent. Now Klabil is the Tzeltal equivalent for David. When inquiry was made as to why an Indian spirit should bear the name David, the tale of the Ladino David is given. David was a moneylender who lived in Teopisca and lent money to Indians of Amatenango, at moderate interest rates. David is now dead, and he is the spirit of the hill called Klabil. Now it is difficult, since the death of David, to borrow money in Teopisca. Indians of Amatenango are virtually without credit resources.

The closest regular moneylender is the wife of the Ladino secretary, who takes things on pawn. She lives across the highway from the centre of Amantenango, just on the border between Teopisca and Amatenango. Indians are in her debt on two counts: instalment payment for her medical services, and loans made against their goods. The moneylending of the Ladino secretary's wife is virtually confined to the richer Amatenagueros, or the more acculturated of them. The ordinary household has practically no credit source.

Like Cantel, Amatenango has a civil-religious hierarchy to run its public life in the sacred and secular spheres, and this hierarchy has the wealth-levelling functions common to the system throughout the region. But, in addition, Amatenango has a special levy against the rich. This is the post of *Alférez*. There are four *Alférez* posts to be filled annually. The post involves large expenditures in feasting a neighbouring group, kinsmen and the officials of the hierarchy. There are expenses involved in renting the special costume, in providing great amounts of liquor, and in making special pots for cooking, benches for sitting and other items for the service. Taking the post involves the co-operation of most of the bilateral kindred, and they all contribute time, corn, liquor and money. The *Alférez* is the son of one of the rich families, for the post is always held by a young man. However, it is clearly the head of the household who bears the cost. Amatenangueros are explicit about the qualifications for an *Alférez*—first money, second good moral standing in the community. One cannot refuse the hierarchy's nomination. Men sometimes attempt to plead poverty, but they are jailed until they accede to the nomination. Wealth—in the form of cattle, horses, land, health of one's children—is not easily concealed in a face-to-face community like Amatenango, nor is it a matter of private knowledge.

The efficacy of the institution of *Alférez* in keeping wealth from crystallizing along family lines is quite marked, and its latent function of keeping the community oriented inwardly and away from economic opportunity in the Ladino world is equally as marked. The neighbouring community of Aquacatenango no longer has the *Alférez* institution. It is much more acculturated, much more receptive to Ladinos, works in closer harmony with the Instituto, and in general is a less defensive and hostile community in relation to the outside world. I do not suggest the loss of the *Alférez* customs have made it that way, but rather that the acculturating forces have eroded the institution and hence have made further acculturation much easier.

The wealth-levelling mechanisms of Amatenango, its system of household production, its orientation away from the Ladino world, its fierce pride in independence and group identity are all sanctioned and controlled by a system of witchcraft belief and practice. The system works so that persons are encouraged to orient to the prevailing norms, on the one hand, and physically punished (by death) for conscious deviation on the other. For the year for which I have data, a man was killed every two months as a witch. And the slain are those who have deviated, or become salient in a direction violating either the economic homogeneity tendencies of the community, or its power structure which rests on age and previous service in the hierarchy. All in all Amatenango appears to be a community not likely to lift itself by its own bootstraps, but at the same time one which can maintain its social identity in the face of great pressures, both political and economic, on its life way.

III

Cantel and Amatenango are variants of a kind of peasantry found in the culture area called Mesoamerica. As a type, they raise some interesting questions of a theoretical and historical nature. They exhibit an economic structure in which money and the market are essential elements, while the firm or enterprise and credit and savings institutions are absent. They exhibit a social structure in which households are tied into a system of hierarchial arrangements depending upon previous communal service. The operation of the system acts as a drain on accumulated wealth and as a means of levelling the fortunes of the individual households. It also defines precisely the membership of the local community and serves to insulate it against the larger, superordinate national society.

Amatenango is the more constricted of this type. It is farther removed from Ladino society; it is more hostile to national culture; it is more insistent on internal homogeneity, and it is less amenable to economic and political pressures than Cantel. Its economic life is more subject to a dual frame than that of Cantel. There is much less internal economic activity, much less internal specialization, many fewer artisans, much less of a division of labour, and much less leakage of individuals into Ladino society and culture. Part of the differences between Amatenango and Cantel can be laid to differences in the traditions they began with; Amatenango is more reduced Maya culture than is Cantel and Chiapas was more of a periphery of Maya culture, while the mid-western highlands was more of a heartland. But more of the difference can be laid to the communication networks, and to the differential spread of Ladino society in the two regions. Cantel has lived since the 1880s in a network of roads which tied it to virtually all parts of the Republic, and its Indians travel widely throughout the highland region, and even into Mexico in their trade and pilgrimage trips. This kind of road net is just being built in south-eastern Chiapas. Amatenango Indians have been, and still are, spatially restricted and, in comparison to Cantel, are parochial. Furthermore the Ladinos have lived in some numbers throughout the highlands of Guatemala for a long time. Chiapas is still Indian country, with Ladinos restricted to their own towns, and since the 1920s living in scattered rancherias of Government grant land. The lesser development of the market, of credit, of specialization, of extended trade networks in Chiapas is a result of the twin fact of absence of Ladinos (for it is they who provide what the people of the region call 'moviemiento'-excitement, flow and connection to the larger world) and the absence of a network of surface communication (which keeps communities relatively isolated, as compared to Guatemala).

Some more abstract propositions about these types of communities, perhaps of applicability beyond the confines of Mesoamerica, may be hazarded. It appears that, on the basis of evidence from these societies, a household system of production, in a bilaterally structured society, does not have the incentives for capital accumulation, nor the resources for seeking deliberate technical and economic innovation. At this level of wealth, with this kind of technology, capital maintenance, technological traditionality and economic homogeneity, seem to be built-in aspects of the economic system. Resident strangers seem to be the chief means of providing the lubricant of credit to such societies. But the system of ritual expenditure or forced service in communal office makes the credit inevitably for consumption ends, not production uses.

These kinds of communities are subordinate to a national society, both politically and economically, and their whole social and economic system seems oriented to the struggle to keep hold on their ethnic identity, their culture in a precarious economic niche. As such they eject the economic deviant, the social deviant and the culturally marginal person. This keeps a successful economic innovation which might lead to a change in the social system from spreading by conduction to other members of the society. At the same time the economic opportunities that would entice members of these kinds of societies need to be extraordinary before they will hazard their small resources and their social positions. But extraordinary economic opportunity is most likely to be seized by the Ladinos, who are less constrained than are Indians. So a sort of feedback mechanism is set in play—expanding opportunities are taken by Ladinos, Indians stay on the economic and social peripheries, they become more and more defensive. Or if the economic expansion is very great and not entirely exploited by Ladinos, the Indian communities lose population, begin to break into factions to balance between progressive and conservative elements (defined as those who tend to act for self interest as the national culture defines it, and those who act for communal ends as the local society defines it) in a situation of waxing and waning of power between the factions strictly dependent upon the economic expansion or contraction of the national economy and society.

From the point of view of economic development as that is related to capital accumulation, credit and investment in new technology, and as these are dependent upon the social and economic organization of a society, Indian societies present special instances of societies with great obstacles to economic innovation and change. Part of the set of obstacles comes from the internal social and economic organization as sketched above, and part from their positions as the peripheral elements in a national society and culture. Unless special efforts are made by a national society to provide credit, machinery and economic opportunities for these kinds of societies, national economic development may for Indians mean nothing more than the widening of economic gaps and level of living between them and the national sectors. The Indian notions of capital, wealth, savings and the social mechanisms for the control and channelling of them make these communities specially liable to be instances of what Myrdal has called the 'backwash' effects of economic development (Myrdal, 1958).

14

Ethnic Difference and Peasant Economy in British Guiana

BY RAYMOND T. SMITH

INTRODUCTION

British Guiana is sometimes referred to as 'The Land of Six Peoples'. The population of a little over half a million is uniformly English-speaking (with the exception of some of the more isolated Amerindians), attends the same sort of schools, participates in a common economic and political system, and shares many fundamental values, but the population is differentiated into 'ethnic groups'.[1] These groups are designated as East Indian (279,460), African descent (190,380), Chinese (3,550), Portuguese (7,610), Other European (5,230), Amerindian (22,860) and Mixed (66,180), and are popularly supposed to possess distinguishable social and personality traits as well as phenotypical characteristics.[2] The attribution of such characteristics is often no more than the application of stereotypes which help to perpetuate the basic differentiations. Although attempts are made to eliminate such stereotypes this is difficult to achieve and as British Guiana has moved closer to political independence a struggle for power has developed among previously dominated groups. The conflicts are often between class or economic interest groups but tensions of a severe kind exist between the two major ethnic groups, Negroes and East Indians, and contribute to the political deadlock which has delayed the granting of independence. There are clear differences between members of the two groups in some elements of custom, in religion, in family structure, marriage ceremonies and so

---

[1] The general terms used in British Guiana include 'race', 'nation' and '*jat*', the latter being understood by all Guianese to mean the same as the first two. The term 'ethnic group' is used here because of its connotation of a cultural rather than a simple phenotypical distinction.

[2] These population figures are based upon the end-of-year estimates for 1960.

305

on but these have rarely formed the basis of conflict or even verbal hostility.[1] It is in patterns of economic activity that the basis of future conflict is supposed to lie, and even relative voting power is seen as a means to economic domination.

Speaking very generally one can say that the majority of Negroes believe that the majority of East Indians (henceforth referred to as Indians) are grasping, miserly, cunning, ambitious and ruthless and that they are well on their way to the ownership of the bulk of important economic assets as well as to the monopolization of prestigious positions in the civil service, the professions and commerce. It is believed that by these means, plus the exercise of political power based upon universal adult suffrage, the Indians will soon come to dominate the country and that Negroes will become second-class citizens. The Indians tend to look down upon Negroes as being improvident, and more interested in dancing and drinking than in hard work, but on the other hand they accuse them of trying to hold on to a privileged position by discriminating against Indians for appointment to the civil service, teaching and even in the distribution of casual employment on public works department projects. Indians feel that Negroes have enjoyed a privileged position in the past which they are trying to hang on to by all possible means; Negroes feel that Indians intend dominating the country numerically, economically and politically.

Both Indians and Negroes came to British Guiana as labourers on the plantations of the coastlands—the Negroes mainly as slaves and the Indians as indentured immigrants. Both groups moved off the plantations into village communities whenever opportunity offered but in neither case did the groups revert to a 'pure African' or a 'pure Indian' way of life. Neither did they establish a pure subsistence culture. Rather they adjusted to a similar social and economic environment, working part-time on sugar plantations and growing cash crops for whatever markets were available. Sometimes members of both ethnic groups settled in the same villages but in most cases they established separate communities because of the time lag between the emancipation of Negro slaves and the creation of Indian communities out of ex-indentured labourers. A comparison of the internal economic structure of each type of community throws light upon varying responses to a similar ecological and market environment, as well as throwing some light upon the factual bases of stereotyped beliefs about ethnic characteristics. This essay, then, will examine

---

[1] Although it is convenient to speak of differences between two 'groups', this ignores the fact that there is no group organization and many Indians are culturally indistinguishable from members of other ethnic groups at the same socio-economic level. However, minimal inter-marriage operates as a powerful force perpetuating the ethnic divisions.

the patterns of capital, savings and credit in the Guianese coastal communities with special reference to the differences between Negro and Indian communities. Because of the very close interdependence between rural and urban areas, between central and local Government and between national and village economy, these villages are more like those found in parts of Europe than like 'primitive' communities. Finally, the existence of extensive sea-defence, drainage and irrigation works as a basic pre-requisite for agricultural activity along the Guiana coastlands introduces another factor of general practical and theoretical interest.

SOME GENERAL FEATURES OF GUIANESE VILLAGE COMMUNITIES

There are only two real towns in British Guiana; Georgetown the capital, with a population of about 148,000, and New Amsterdam, with a population of about 11,500.The rest of the population of over half a million lives either on sugar plantations, in village communities of some kind or, exceptionally, in scattered homesteads.[1] In all the villages along the coastlands an initial capital investment has to be made in drainage and irrigation works and in sea defences if the farmlands are to be put under cultivation. The first settlements in what is now British Guiana were located well inland up the rivers and it was not until the middle of the eighteenth century that the fertile coastlands were reclaimed from the sea. A system of sea walls, dams, trenches and water conservancies was constructed for each plantation using slave labour and Dutch techniques. A plantation was usually a long strip of land about half a mile wide and up to five miles in depth with the narrow end fronting on the sea. The dwellings and mills were built together near to the sea to take advantage of sea breezes and to facilitate shipment of produce. The considerable investment in hydraulic works was made because of the profitability of tropical agriculture at that time which made such a use of slave labour worthwhile. Control of the agricultural cycle and of the maintenance of the drainage and irrigation system was vested in the plantation owner or manager and the internal political system was not dissimilar to that which Wittfogel (1957) has termed 'Oriental Despotism'. It is true that the slaves were more like factory workers than peasants subject to corvée labour and expropriation of their independent produce, but the important thing was the strong central

---

[1] Approximately 28,500 people live in scattered Amerindian villages and on cattle ranches in the remote interior. Most of the population is settled upon the narrow coastal strip which lies below the level of the sea at high tide. Except where indicated, the discussion in this paper is based upon the author's own field-work in three Negro communities and one Indian, carried out between 1951 and 1953 and in 1956.

control. With the passing of the Emancipation Act and the freeing of the slaves in 1838 many planters went out of business, especially since the West India monopoly of British markets was destroyed soon afterwards. Their lands were taken up either by neighbouring plantations which were expanding and rationalizing their productive processes, or by ex-slaves who bought them co-operatively with money they had saved during the four years of apprenticeship. The surviving plantations continued to exercise strong central control over a tied labour force (contracts of indenture replacing a slave relationship), but the ex-slaves tried to establish democratic communities within the framework of a plantation hydraulic system. The planters, who constituted the most powerful political element in the total society, were anxious to keep the ex-slaves dependent upon the plantations for cash income and they used their influence whenever possible against any attempt of the Negro villagers to make progress as independent producers. However, with the existing state of the export markets and the added complication that the villagers could not avoid internal dissension over the allocation of labour to estate maintenance, there was not much chance of the villagers becoming prosperous farmers. The internal market for produce was small since plantation labourers usually had their own gardens and the towns were very small at that time, and there was no organization for exploiting export markets. A local government system of sorts was gradually developed to help the villagers maintain a minimal standard of well-being and the central Government came to give more assistance to the improvement of drainage and irrigation as time went by, but there was no chance of substantial development of village agriculture until strong political bodies in favour of allocating resources for its growth were established (Young, 1958; Smith, R. T., 1956, 1962).

Prior to emancipation the planters had been most concerned over the possibility that the emancipated slaves would withdraw from the coastal area into the bush there to revert to a tribal life outside the economy of the colonial society. Such fears were without foundation for by this time the Negroes had become integrated into a social system quite different from anything they or their ancestors had known in Africa. Such elements of African culture as they retained had been woven into a pattern of life in which the Christian mission church formed a central element, propogating those values which helped to bind the whole society together. If the ex-slaves had ambitions they were to become less like tribal Africans and more like Englishmen. Their style of life had already altered toward a European pattern in several important respects; as among the English lower classes, good clothes were very important as a mark of respectability. Personal prestige was bound up with the conspicuous display of

308

clothes and of imported trinkets and domestic ware. These goods had to be purchased with cash, as did many of the staple food items such as imported codfish, salted meat, flour and rice. Attempts to grow cash crops for an external market were largely unsuccessful. The sugar market was monopolized by the large planters, and was in any case so reduced that only the most efficient large producers could survive. Markets for such crops as coffee, arrowroot and pimento were uncertain and difficult of access for the small farmer. The villagers continued to grow the crops that they had been accustomed to raise on their slave 'provision grounds' (mainly yam, cassava and plantains), and tried to sell their surpluses to landless labourers, townsmen and artisans as they had done when they were slaves. Most of them remained dependent upon the plantations for wages to supply at least a part of their cash requirements.

Although emancipation did not lead to the withdrawal of the ex-slaves from the society of the coastlands, it did result in their withdrawal from regular and predictable labour on the surviving plantations. The planters could no longer *command* labour (in 1840 and 1841 the Negroes actually went on strike for higher wages) and they sought to make good their deficiencies by the importation of indentured labourers from Europe, Madeira, China and India. The latter country became the main source of supply, and 238,960 Indians were imported between 1838 and 1917 for work on the plantations. The indentured labourers moved into the position on the plantations that had previously been occupied by the Negroes, doing the same work and living under similar conditions. Upon the expiry of their indentures many of the labourers settled in the colony. The Portuguese quickly became a specialized trading group and by the middle of the nineteenth century they dominated the retail trades. The Chinese did not become an occupationally specialized group, but they were among the first of the indentured immigrants to become acculturated and to begin moving into higher prestige occupations particularly in the city.

In the earliest days of immigration the Indians adopted the customs of the creolized Negroes, and many became Christians and settled off the plantations upon the expiry of their indentures.[1] As continued immigration built up the Indian population, proportionately fewer of them left the plantations, which tended to become Indian communities in the full sense of the word, in which the inhabitants formed a cultural sub-group of Guianese society. (For a fuller discussion of the social position of the Indians see Smith,

[1] The term 'creolized' has been used to indicate acculturation and integration into the Guianese social system. It is preferable to the alternative and inaccurate terms 'westernization' and 'anglicization', though 'creole' culture has been dominated by English influences.

R. T., and Jayawardena, 1959; Jayawardena, 1963.) Various attempts were made during the latter half of the nineteenth century to start Indian villages along the lines followed by the Negroes, but none of them were very successful (Nath, 1950, pp. 94–110; Young, 1958, pp. 152–61). The main initiative in this came from the planter-dominated Government which was anxious to escape some of its liability to provide return passages, and at the same time to build up the resident population of potential labourers. This double object was to be achieved by providing grants of land in lieu of return passages. Several settlements were established, but it was not until a market for a cash crop, rice, had been developed that they became at all successful. Even then the area of land available to each family was usually insufficient to provide a reasonable living without supplementary income from wage labour. Since the growth of a West Indian market for British Guiana's rice (which dates mainly from the period of World War I) the same farmer has been able to derive a living almost entirely from the land. Rice is grown mainly by small farmers, who take wage work whenever they have time to spare from their farms. Significant numbers of people, including plantation workers and many Negroes, grow a little rice as a side-line, and at the other end of the scale there are many farmers, almost always Indians, who have farms large enough to require their full-time attention.

The historical developments outlined above have given rise to a number of different types of community on Guiana's coastlands. The sugar plantation settlements are mainly East Indian and are much less like farm communities than small towns, containing what has been called elsewhere a 'rural proletariat'. The standard of living of sugar workers is, today, probably higher than that of other rural communities. The second type of community is the Negro village, which usually dates back to the middle of the nineteenth century. (For detailed description of three such villages see Smith, R. T., 1956.) Today these villages often contain a proportion of Indian residents or some of the lands may be leased to Indian farmers. In a few cases the population has become so ethnically mixed that the term 'Negro village' is no longer appropriate, except from a historical point of view. The traditional pattern of agricultural activity in the Negro villages has been the cultivation of limited quantities of ground provisions for domestic consumption and local sale, together with the raising of a few cattle and small-stock. The bulk of the cash income of these villages has been from wage labour on the plantations, public works department projects, gold, diamond and bauxite mining, or from remittances from the towns. In some Negro villages rice cultivation has been increasing in recent years, but rice is always something added on to the traditional pattern rather than being the basis of it.

310

The Indian village communities vary greatly in nature. Some were originally Government-sponsored land settlements that have now become villages with their own local authorities. Others are still land settlements administered directly by a central Government department, whilst some have grown up on large private estates which are usually owned by Indian families who lease the land in small plots for rice cultivation or for grazing. Other Indian communities have been established on the frontlands of sugar estates and their residents may have to travel many miles to their farmlands. But in every case rice cultivation is the basic activity, and other forms of agriculture such as cane-farming, vegetable growing and stock raising are subsidiary.

Although the provision of basic drainage, irrigation and sea defence is made at the community level, farming and the ownership of land is an individual or family matter. No cases are known where a sizeable group of people farm on a communal basis (though this was tried in some of the early Negro settlements), but it is not uncommon to find a small group of persons co-operatively owning a tractor or combine harvester. Rights in land are easily bought, sold and leased, and many transactions take place without a properly registered change of title being effected.[1] Village farmlands are usually divided into small blocks, often as small as a quarter of an acre, and each farmer owns or leases a number of these. It is only in the recently developed areas behind the old plantations that a farmer may have a large consolidated holding; normally his 'farm' consists of a number of scattered strips.

The possession of rights in land is of more than purely economic significance; if this were the only consideration more land would be placed on the market instead of being left idle as it is, particularly in the Negro villages. It is generally felt that possession of permanent rights in land provides some sort of independence and security, and whilst this may not be strictly true there are certain social advantages involved. Title deeds can be used to provide security for loans or they may be lodged as bail. Local government elections are still based upon a property franchise, and the election of members of the national legislature was based on a limited franchise until 1953. Negroes are especially reluctant to part with freehold rights in land, even though it is lying idle and they may have to pay rates on it, often sending the money back to the village from other parts of the country or even from overseas. It is quite common to find large areas of Negro village land under bush, but rare in Indian villages where all available land is generally under rice. A very dramatic aerial photograph illustrating this point can be found in a paper by Lowenthal (1960, p. 47).

---

[1] This point is discussed in detail in Smith, R. T., 1955 and 1957.

Capital, Saving and Credit in Peasant Societies

CAPITAL, SAVING AND CREDIT IN THE NEGRO COMMUNITIES

Except for those villages near to Georgetown on the East Coast Demerara, most of the Negro villages present a rather drab appearance to the casual observer. The houses do not vary greatly in size or appearance except for those occupied by storekeepers, schoolteachers and any Government servants who may be resident in the village. During the past ten years there has been some progress in self-help housing schemes in which villagers have been encouraged to build concrete block houses but these are still in a small minority. Few houses are painted and because of the livestock that wanders freely about there are few gardens around the houses. The uniformly dismal appearance reflects the underlying sense of equality of the villagers; an equality of poverty and low status. The ambitious try to escape altogether. There is an immediacy and a sociability in the pattern of living which is most striking. Most house yards are open and there is a constant bustle on the road which runs through the village. The admired individual 'lives well' with his neighbours and is never 'cheap 'or mean. In action terms these sentiments involve generosity, a willingness to spend what you have when you have it, and a facility for avoiding words and actions that would make others feel inferior. Such sentiments tend to discourage upward mobility through the accumulation of wealth. In recent years there has been great improvement in the facilities of bars and 'beer gardens' which usually have electric lighting plants and kerosene refrigerators. Despite all the efforts of the central Government welfare agencies there is no marked development of community goals except the ever-present necessity of maintaining drainage and irrigation systems, which must be organized at the village level until such time as wider bodies are set up. Rates are paid reluctantly and are usually heavily in arrears.

The level of capital resources of households is uniformly low. Some variations do exist but even these tend to be masked. A man with more land or more income from livestock than others does not emphasize the fact because this is not considered to be a legitimate basis for claims to superiority in the same way that the enjoyment of a monthly salary as a schoolteacher is, for example. This does not mean that actual differences in wealth are unimportant or that they do not bring added respect, but once an attempt is made to transform them into a basis for community prestige this involves greater expenditure upon prestige goods and a change in style of life. If this is not carried through fully and successfully it will merely bring ridicule. Some variation in level of consumption and of conspicuous display does exist but it is nearly always related to occupational rather than simple wealth differences. The man with better furniture or who

312

is better dressed is usually the ex-policeman, ex-teacher, ex-soldier or the man who has had some steady job or travelled overseas. The largest items of household capital are the house and the land owned by members of the household. The majority of houses are built of wood and cost between 600 and 1,000 dollars in the early 1950s.[1] This represents a man's biggest single capital outlay, and houses are usually built in stages over a number of years, using money earned outside the village to buy materials and pay for labour. There are few households that do not contain one or more persons with rights in the provision and grazing lands which form an integral part of the village and strangers can usually rent or borrow enough to meet their needs. Lending of land is quite common especially between kin (Smith, R. T., 1955). Since the expansion of markets for rice which occurred during and after the last war many Negro villages put part of their lands under rice or extended their backlands with the help of Government loans for drainage and irrigation. Where this happened the extra lands are leased by the central Government, being divided in roughly the same proportions as the freehold lands, but again there is considerable transfer of rights in these lands.

Most families possess a few chickens, maybe a pig, a few sheep or goats and possibly a few head of cattle if grazing is plentiful and cheap. In one small village of 111 households with a population of approximately 685 persons there were 106 cattle, 207 sheep, 141 goats, 310 pigs, 993 fowls, 160 ducks and 88 turkeys. Cattle are regarded as a form of saving and are kept less for their milk than for sale or slaughter. Draught oxen are kept for ploughing rice land though not every farmer has his own. Those farmers who plant rice usually own a simple plough with a locally-made frame and a store-bought share, and there will be a few simple ox-drawn harrows in the village which are used by everyone on a borrowing basis. Other tools and implements are few and simple. The machete is the universal all-purpose tool but most families own forks and axes as well. A special kind of shovel with a very small blade is used for removing mud from silted drainage and irrigation trenches and because of the depth of some of these it is equipped with a very long handle. Most men own one of these shovels and some of them are extremely skilled in its use and in great demand for work on the sugar plantations as 'shovel-men'. Transport within the village is by head load or by punt along the canals. Most shopkeepers own a donkey and cart and these are made available for transporting padi at harvest-time. Collections for the mills are made by truck from a central point in the village or padi is sent direct to Government mills by the railway that runs through the villages in the central part of the country. Marketing of other produce is very sporadic and produce is either

[1] One British Guiana dollar equals 4s 2d or approx. $0.55 (us).

313

sold to neighbours or to itinerant hucksters who carry it to the markets in the sugar estates. Small markets are held in the villages but these are not very important as there are few buyers as a rule. Fleets of taxis ply for hire along the coast to transport passengers to Georgetown or New Amsterdam and for those who cannot afford the fares (which are low) the Government railway is even cheaper, though considerably slower.

Negro family structure in British Guiana has been described elsewhere, and one of its interesting features is the high degree of individualism in the control of household resources (Smith, R. T., 1956). The woman of the house normally controls the domestic budget, but she receives income in the form of cash or food from a number of sources. In the simplest case of a young woman with children living with her husband or common-law husband, the bulk of the household income will come from the man's farm and from his cash wages from whatever work he can get. Since most available employment is casual and irregular, income will be sporadic. Older women, who provide for bigger household groups, generally receive income from a series of individuals; her husband, common-law husband or lover, her adult sons and daughters if they are working, and perhaps from the fathers of her daughters' illegitimate children. The adult members of such a large household will each have their own source of income and may each own farms or livestock in their own right, be they male or female. Out of this income they will contribute to the household budget, but they normally retain a portion of their income for their own use for entertainment. The important point is that the members of the household are not closely controlled by a male head and they do not form a co-operative unit of production. On the contrary, a man with a rice farm may even pay cash wages to the members of his own household for the help they give at harvest time. Women regard their earnings from rice work as an extra which they are entitled to spend on clothes.

Stocks of consumer durables are not high except in the homes of higher status families such as schoolteachers. The inevitable 'cabinet' with its display of glassware and trinkets, a few locally-made cane or wooden chairs, a table, perhaps a settle, and a picture of the Queen or a church calendar are the usual furnishings. Most families have at least one bed for the principal adults and a chamber pot, since it is considered unhealthy to leave the house at night. Radios were rare up to 1956 and bicycles only found in a small number of cases for cycling to work on nearby plantations. Sewing machines are normally owned only by tailors or seamstresses.

Stocks of food are not normally kept on hand, and it is not usual for houses to have any storage facilities. Daily visits to the village shop are the rule, with short-term credit being extended when cash is

314

in short supply. Those farmers who cultivate rice normally lodge a number of bags with a miller to be drawn upon as required for home consumption in the form of milled rice. In fact this procedure is required by the law which stipulates that all padi must be declared and sold only through the statutory Rice Marketing Board. If seed padi is retained it may be stored in the house or in a small store-room built outside. The provision farm acts as a sort of food store in that some of the root crops can be left in the ground until required. Provision farms normally bear something the year round, and when cash is scarce it is usually possible to sell a few ground provisions to a fellow villager or in a neighbouring market.

Cash which is surplus to immediate requirements is most usually spent on clothes and entertainment, including rum and luxury foods such as canned corned beef. There are opportunities for spending at the many dances and weddings which take place, particularly towards the end of the year when the rice harvest is in and work is available on the sugar plantations. The level of saving is generally low, especially if taken over a long period. Houses represent the biggest single form of capital investment, and over the past twenty years or so there has been a gradual improvement in the quality of rural housing. This is partly due to the high wages that were available from the United States Air Base and from the bauxite mines during the war, and partly due to more recent development programmes through which money has been made available for this purpose. Improvements in the drainage and irrigation systems of these villages have also been mainly financed from central Government development funds; local rates are usually inadequate even for proper maintenance. Other forms of investment have been in improved types of seed padi made available cheaply by the Department of Agriculture and in some slight improvement in cattle through the artificial insemination service.

In any village one finds a number of small shops, usually called 'cake shops', which carry small stocks of bottled drinks, bread and cakes, sweets and perhaps ice and cigarettes. Many of these are owned by Negroes; often by a retired policeman or a man who has made a little money in the goldfields. These shops represent the limit of Negro trading activities, and none of them is very profitable. The bigger stores, which are usually owned by Portuguese, Chinese or Indians, soak up the bulk of village money income; the cake shops collect very little.

The most usual form of individual saving is through the custom of 'throwing a box' or by deposits in the Post Office Savings Bank. 'Throwing a box' is a form of savings institution which is extremely widespread and involves all the 'hand holders' in a weekly or monthly contribution of a fixed amount of money, the total sum being

315

drawn by each participant in turn. Money accumulated by participation in a box, or through a savings account, is usually spent on consumer goods of one kind or another, including household furnishings and clothes, both of which are generally renewed or renovated for the big festive season of Christmas. Chronic indebtedness is as rare as affluence among Negro villagers.

One of the earliest institutions to develop in the Negro communities was the Friendly and Burial Society. These are mentioned by writers of the slavery period when they appear to have been organized as tribal societies expressly charged with providing a proper feast on the occasion of a death. They flourish today in practically every Negro village, usually levying a small fee on all the members on the occasion of a death, the lump sum being paid to the member's kin to meet the funeral expenses. Some of the bigger ones have taken on extra functions, sometimes paying a sickness benefit or even acting as saving and loan societies (Wells, 1953).

It is clear from the above descriptions that the Negro villages have always been a part of a wider economic system, their inhabitants participating as unskilled labourers in plantations and mines capitalized and managed by Europeans, Americans or Canadians. They have produced a certain amount of food for local consumption, but their main contribution to the economy has been as a reservoir of labour. Although Negroes have not generally been in positions of control in the large companies, nor have they been conspicuous in commerce, they have occupied many important positions in the civil service by virtue of which they have had responsibility for the management of national assets. The important point is that they have exercised this responsibility within the framework of a bureaucratic structure so that individual enterprise has been less important than conformity with the rules of office and the maintenance of standards of behaviour. The whole definition of prestige and success has been based upon higher income coupled with 'higher' cultural standards, the adoption of which involved a break from the solidarity of the lower-class village and a move into the urban middle-class. At the village level the possession of wealth which is not spent in a sociable way can only create suspicion of anti-social activity.

CAPITAL, SAVING AND CREDIT IN THE INDIAN VILLAGES

The Negro village tends to be regarded as the physical base, the birthplace, the place where one's 'navel string is buried', from which individuals venture forth to make a living knowing that they can always return to its security and the warmth of its human relationships in time of trouble. The Indian village by contrast is primarily the place where one has a rice farm. The absence of strong local

316

sentiments among Indians is related to the fact that they possess other bases of social identity such as religion, perhaps caste origin, and more importantly strong kinship ties. This is not to suggest that Indians do not have a sense of local community solidarity, but it is much weaker than in Negro villages precisely because there is more internal differentiation and more cross-cutting associational ties. Those Indians who left the sugar plantations did so in the main for the purpose of establishing rice farms, and this is the focus of activity of the rural Indian family even if it provides only a minor portion of the family's cash income requirements.

The Indian household, most usually consisting of a man, his wife and children, with perhaps a recently married son and his wife, functions as a co-operative economic unit under the control of the eldest male. He, with the help of his wife, plans the family budget and directs the farming activities. As compared with the Negro villages there is much more careful long-term planning of expenditure, saving and investment, and such planning is related to the needs and pro- ductivity of the household and family rather than being individual- ized. There is considerable variation in the levels of prosperity of Indian households even within one village. Some families may live almost entirely by wage labour, with both men and women working on the sugar plantations or on other farmers' lands. At the other end of the scale lie the wealthier families which not only operate more land but have a greater diversity of assets and economic interests. Such a family may plant up to about thirty acres of rice land using a good deal of paid labour as well as a tractor for ploughing; it may also operate a small rice mill, own a shop, run a taxi or own land which is rented to others. The majority of Indian farmers fall somewhere between these extremes. In the country as a whole there are a number of Indians who are large landowners. Some of them bought up whole plantations in the days when land was cheap and rented plots to other Indians. With the improvement in prices and markets some of these large landowners have embarked upon large-scale rice cultivation using machinery as well as paid labour. But the number of really big farmers operating more than 100 acres is not large and they lie outside the village communities being discussed here.

Various studies have indicated that the majority of rice farmers cultivate about six acres of padi; a little over half of this area is owned by the farmer or held on long lease and the rest is rented.[1] Rentals and rates for the provision of water control are now regulated by

[1] O'Loughlin, 1958; Smith, R. T., 1957. For the autumn crop of 1954 only 274 farm units out of 26,983 were over thirty-one acres. See O'Loughlin, *op. cit.*, p. 121. Since then there has been considerable increase in the acreage under rice but it seems probable that this has been an increase in the number of farm units rather than in the size of holdings.

legislation and are related to the quality of the soil and the level of the basic services provided. Simple comparisons of acreage under rice are not very helpful since both productivity and method of cultivation vary according to the type of land and the adequacy of drainage and irrigation provisions. Where water control is bad a farmer may plant a large acreage of land using broadcast sowing and superficial ploughing in the hope that he will get some yield. In other areas a man may plant a small acreage using very intensive methods and be certain of high yields. As in the case of Negro villages farmers' holdings are liable to be scattered, though with the increasing use of tractors there is a definite tendency to try to consolidate holdings. Government loans, easy hire purchase terms and the sale of duty free fuel have all encouraged tractor purchase and over the country as a whole there is now probably an excess of machines for full economic utilization. Many farmers are willing to buy tractors on these easy terms even if they cannot make them pay fully in economic terms; the convenience of having one's own tractor to use whenever one needs it is one consideration, and the prestige of ownership is another. The critical problem in British Guiana is reaping and threshing, most of which is done by hand. Heavy showers of rain at harvest time can result in the padi being beaten down into waterlogged fields and under these circumstances combine harvesters are of little use. If a man has a large acreage under rice he must be able to command the labour to reap it. Up to a certain level family labour and the 'day for day' system whereby groups of women work on each others' land in turn is adequate, but beyond that point there must either be a pool of labour available or one has to depend upon machinery. Most farmers in the Indian villages employ intensive cultivation techniques upon limited areas of land and then diversify their economic activities if they are able to accumulate more capital for investment. The growing of seedlings in beds and their transplantation by hand using female family labour is very common among Indians but rare among Negroes except in the remote areas where there is no possibility of finding any other kind of employment.

Although rice cultivation is the focus of interest for Indian farmers they do grow some other crops. Most farmers have a plot of provisions and a garden close to the house which supplies greens and herbs for the kitchen. Small stock and cattle are kept, the numbers of cattle generally depending upon the availability of pasture. Many Indians will keep a few cows in the vicinity of the house and feed them on cut grass, selling the milk to itinerant vendors, but it is only in areas with adequate pasturage that dairying becomes an important part of the domestic economy. Land, livestock, implements and machinery (the latter mainly in the form of small tractors) are the obvious first calls upon the capital which the farmer has available for

318

investment, but few farmers continue to maximize acquisition of land beyond a certain point. In the first place land is in short supply and in order to get extra acreage a man may have to go far away from his home village (O'Loughlin, 1958; Smith, R. T., 1957). Secondly, there are other attractive investment opportunities such as starting a shop, buying and operating a taxi, or investing in a small rice mill. But most important is the fact that as a man becomes more prosperous the demands upon him to engage in consumption expenditure increase disproportionately. This is partly connected with a long-term trend in Indian consumption patterns.

The family house is an important capital asset and provides opportunity for the demonstration of status differences. The poorest villagers live in mud-wattle houses that are more wretched than those found in even the poorest Negro villages. Some families live in very neat and well-kept and spacious thatched houses but most families with any pretensions to prestige try to build a wooden house with a corrugated iron roof, well painted and fit for the entertainment of guests at religious ceremonies and rites-de-passage. In the past Indians bought few items of furniture; a square of bright linoleum was considered sufficient in many houses. Today it is almost obligatory to have chairs and tables, cabinets for the display of china and glassware, and good quality beds. Sewing machines for family use are very common, and although radios and pressure lanterns still have status significance their use is becoming accepted as normal. Radios are used mainly for the reception of Indian music from Georgetown, Surinam, Trinidad or India and the prestige rating of the set is proportional to its capacity for continuous high volume output. In a sample survey carried out in 1956 it was found that 31 per cent of households in the sugar areas owned radios as opposed to 26 per cent in the rice areas and 60 per cent in the urban areas (British Guiana Dept. of Labour, 1957). This survey also confirms the impression that expenditure on clothes has been rising among Indians. A purely Indian form of dress disappeared long ago except for religious purposes, but on the other hand Indians adopted a simplified form of western dress unless they became thoroughly absorbed into the middle-class. Women wore simple cotton dresses set off by a colourful head-cloth or a more elaborate and costly *huerni* for special occasions, while the men wore trousers and a loose white shirt. The practice of wearing suits and ties is spreading rapidly and women are becoming more clothes conscious. The more adventurous ones even wear make-up and have 'permanent' waves. The figures given in the survey show very little difference in expenditure on clothing as between Negro and Indian families, but it was taken at a time of year when expenditure of all kinds is at a minimum. One interesting figure indicates quite clearly that Indian communities

319

spend more money on alcohol and tobacco than Negroes; Indian households spent an average of 1.81 dollars per week, Negro households only 1.24 dollars. This is so although rum is a normal sociable drink in the Negro communities against which there is no disapproving attitude, whereas in the Indian communities rum is consumed with something of a sense of guilt and bravado, especially by young men.

Marriage is one of the most important events in the life of an Indian and requires a considerable expenditure on the part of the parents of the bride, as well as involving a complex series of gift exchanges. This cannot be dealt with in any detail here, but it can be mentioned that in the rice areas it is considered desirable that a young man should have the prospect of a share of land from his father before he marries and the parents of the girl are generally anxious to ensure that she will be well provided for, various forms of dowry payments being regarded as a form of initial capital for the couple. (For detailed discussion of these questions see Smith, R. T., and Jayawardena, 1958, 1959; Jayawardena, 1962.) A newly married couple usually live in a private apartment in the house of the bridegroom's parents, and they gradually hive off to establish their own household, being given a piece of riceland by the man's father. He will also take the major responsibility for providing houses for his sons, though of course their labour and perhaps wages from plantation work have contributed greatly to the savings which made it possible. As an Indian man grows older he faces two important sets of responsibilities; to provide adequate dowries for his daughters and sufficiently elaborate wedding feasts to demonstrate his status aspirations, and to provide a start in life for his sons. The latter requires his buying the traditional gifts of gold jewellery and clothes for the sons' wives, providing land, ploughing animals, and at least a part of the cost of a house. But it is the daughters' weddings that impose the greatest strain and which bring no economic return. Sons are always nearby and can be called upon for help; daughters go to live in another village and virtually sever their ties with their natal village.

In order to meet these responsibilities adequately years of planning and preparation are necessary, involving quite deliberate saving and increased capital investment. It would be quite wrong to suggest that all Indians display such prudence, for many simply accept their low status and live from hand to mouth. But the majority of villagers certainly do make an effort and they are tied in to a complex network of reciprocity which is best exemplified by the fact that each family keeps a little book in which is recorded all the gifts received by, and donated by, the family at weddings.

As a man's children begin to mature he will try to obtain more riceland in order to meet the increased cost of maintenance and also because he now has more hands to help with the crucial tasks of transplanting and reaping. His daughters' marriages represent the big events of his life, and the sons will probably have to postpone theirs until the girls are married off. The number of guests at a man's daughter's wedding, the size of the dowry, and the social standing of her husband's parents all help to determine the status of a man within his own community. Most of the expenditure on a daughter's wedding is in the nature of display consumption and new ways of boosting expenditure on such things as clothes, electrically reproduced music (except in the case of strict Muslims), electric lights, and more expensive kinds of food and drink are continually being introduced. The expenses involved in a son's marriage are much smaller and the son is likely to stay on helping his father for at least a year or so, the youngest son often staying until the father dies. It is rare to find a large joint family working a farm together; each son normally breaks away to establish his own independent household, taking some of his father's accumulated capital with him. There is thus a process of accumulation of resources up to a certain point after which they are redistributed to girls in the form of dowry, to boys in the form of economic aid in starting a family of their own, and to the public in the form of a prestige display.

The process outlined above represents the long term trend. In the short run the rice farmer's economic fortunes have their ups and downs and various institutional means of dealing with them are found. The major rice crop of the year is reaped in the autumn; a second crop may be planted for reaping in the spring, but less trouble is taken with it and yields are not expected to be high. The farmer therefore gets his farm income in one or two lump sums and has to balance his expenditure over the year. Many farmers bank their cheques as they come from the Rice Marketing Board either in the Post Office Savings Bank or in the savings branch of one of the commercial banks. It is more usual for a farmer to have a number of debts to pay off as soon as he gets his money. His wife will probably have run up a bill at one of the village shops; he may have taken a cash advance from the miller who handled his padi; in a few cases he may have borrowed from a moneylender. This latter is not very common today, except in cases of emergency. When all the debts have been settled further inroads may be made into the 'rice money' for buying consumer goods. This is the time at which the womenfolk and the children expect new clothes, when new items of furniture may be bought or improvements to the house may be made. Smaller expenses may be incurred in performing outstanding religious obligations by inviting a priest to perform domestic rituals and friends to witness them. Such money as is left in the account (or less frequently these days, kept at home in the form of cash), will be

L   321 drawn upon as necessary for current expenditure during the following months. Some money will probably be earned by casual labour of one kind or another, and this is used before withdrawing from the reserves.

The credit institution of 'throwing a box' is as popular among Indians as Negroes, but more particularly among those who earn a monthly or weekly income. These days the rice farmer is able to get credit in the form of loans from the Co-operative Credit Banks, and these are most frequently used to meet any expenses that arise in connection with preparing the land and planting. With a loan a man can often plant more land than he would otherwise be able to by employing a tractor to do some of the ploughing. Loans from this source may also be used to finance house construction or improvement. An increasing number of rice farmers are taking out life insurance policies, and these have several uses apart from the obvious one of acting as a form of savings. Loans can be secured from the insurance companies for a wide range of purposes from house building to buying a tractor. The policy can also be used as security for bail. Most rice millers will give advances on padi that is lodged with them for milling and, as with credit extended by shopkeepers, no interest is charged. In case of emergency it is always possible to pawn the wife's gold jewellery (providing she is willing), livestock can be converted into cash or family members can be called upon for help. Emergencies in this sense most usually arise in case of sickness or involvement in litigation. Rates of interest charged by moneylenders are now controlled, but moneylenders still function. They are less numerous than formerly because of the higher level of incomes and the existence of other sources of credit. They do more business among sugar estate residents and among the poor landless villagers. Pawnbrokeries are mostly situated in Georgetown and run by Portuguese.

The picture so far is of a village population engaged in rice cultivation and supplementing income from this source by casual wage labour, enjoying a gradually rising standard of living with increasing consumption expectations but displaying no signs of marked change in productive resources. Because of the rising prices for rice in the privileged West Indian market rice farmers have enjoyed a substantial increase in income over the past twenty years and the higher prices have stimulated an increased production. In addition to higher prices paid for rice, there have been injections of capital into the national economy in the form of Colonial Development and Welfare grants, special development loans and private investment, particularly in the sugar and bauxite industries. Some of this money has found its way into the villages in the form of improved drainage and irrigation works, loans through the co-operative banks and through expanded social services provided by the central Government such as better roads, water supply, medical services, education and various forms of community development. For the ordinary Indian villager the principal form of capital accumulation has been in the form of improved housing. There has been practically no change in traditional methods of rice cultivation or processing. No important new crops have been introduced and lack of adequate pasturage has retarded improvements in stock raising. The introduction of tractors has been a technological improvement but in many cases has not really led to an increase in production. Tractors are frequently unusable because of heavy soils and reaping remains a hand operation for the most part. Expansion in the area of land under rice has been matched by an increased population and a retrenchment of sugar workers due to labour stabilization schemes.

It has already been mentioned that there is a greater degree of internal status differentiation in Indian villages than in those that are predominantly Negro, ignoring in both cases those who belong to different ethnic groups and those few people who may live in the village but move in a middle or lower-middle class milieu. Whereas in the Negro village the emphasis seems to be upon modest behaviour that will not make others feel inferior, Indian villages seem to be in a perpetual turmoil of attempts to demonstrate superiority. In these struggles for prestige and higher status three factors are important; observance of religious prescriptions, wealth and formal education. The really active element in these struggles is relatively small, but constitutes an important group from an economic point of view. Speaking very generally, one might say that its members are similar to the rest of the village population in educational background and culture, and differ principally in their greater economic prosperity and in the fact that they usually fill leadership roles in the many voluntary associations which one finds in the Indian villages. Shopkeepers are prominent in this group for the simple reason that setting up a shop is one of the most usual forms of investment of surplus capital and therefore the economically successful tend to become shopkeepers.[1]

The attempt to establish prestige by what is known as 'holy living' is generally connected with increasing material prosperity, and is most evident among Muslims and members of Hindu reform organizations, the most important of which is the *Arya Samaj*. The orthodox Hindu organization, *Sanatan Dharma Maha Sabha*, is dominated by the hereditary Brahmins and their wealthy patrons and offers less scope for the upwardly mobile. The *Arya Samaj* on the other hand is aggressively in favour of equality of opportunity for all who are

---

[1] Many younger shopkeepers are themselves the sons of shopkeepers, having been set up in business instead of being given extended formal education.

prepared to live an abstemious and pure life, and because it has no hereditary priesthood any member can assume leadership in the conduct of ritual or management of the society's affairs. The same applies to the Muslim organizations. In fact, those who do assume leadership are generally the men who are better off financially but not distinguishable from their fellows in formal educational background. It would be both fanciful and incorrect to imply that these men are budding capitalists imbued with a 'protestant ethic' and no allusion to Max Weber's thesis is intended. It is an empirical fact that men who are ambitious tend to be active in the economic, the religious and the political spheres, and that all these activities, including the adoption of an ascetic mode of life as prescribed by Hindu and Muslim scriptures, can be interpreted as forms of status striving.

When we refer to the 'wealthy' villagers the term is used in a relative sense only. No clear-cut line exists to distinguish the wealthy from the poor; there is rather a fairly numerous section of the village population striving to move into this category and a relatively small number who have accumulated enough resources to put them in a position of being considered well-off. Many of the men who are shopkeepers or large landowners today accumulated their resources in the days when the standard and style of living in the Indian communities approached that of a village in India whilst the level of income was *relatively* high. Others made money by acting as moneylenders, charging high rates of interest in the days before other credit facilities were widely available. A few became wealthy through priestly activities and invested in land. The important thing was that even small amounts of cash could be turned into land which has since appreciated in value.

For the man who has managed to save, the most usual forms of investment are in more rice-land and the machines necessary to work it, in a shop, a taxi, a rice-mill or in urban properties which can be rented. The education of a son for the medical or legal professions is regarded as much as a form of investment as a source of prestige. Most of those who can afford it try to send their children to high school these days, and this is one example of the increasing demands that are made upon a man's income as he becomes more 'prominent'. He will be expected to build a better house, to spend more on entertaining, upon his children's weddings and upon their education, so that it becomes difficult to continue the upward curve of saving and investment. The most usual pattern is for the children of this class of villager to leave the countryside to find work in the civil service, in teaching and in the professions. As among Negroes, few young men with a secondary education choose farming or commerce as a career, except as Government officers or clerks in large stores.

SOME REASONS FOR DIFFERENCES IN ECONOMIC RESPONSE

It was stated at the beginning of this essay that in British Guiana people often speak as though each ethnic group possessed distinctive characteristics and as though each was a separate entity specializing in some form of economic activity. This idea sometimes finds its way into popular accounts of the country when Indians are spoken of as sugar workers and rice farmers, Portuguese as shopkeepers, Negroes as urban labourers, and so on. In fact, of course, the situation is much more fluid than such abbreviated descriptions suggest, and the really interesting aspect of Guianese social structure is not its 'pluralism' but the way in which the different ethnic groups are integrated into one social system, the way in which group customs become modified in accordance with common societal norms and values, and the way in which ethnicity is tending to disappear as a basis of total status placement. This is essentially a process in time and the differences between the Negro and Indian villages in the sphere of economic activity should be considered in the light of this process.

The emergence of a specifically recognizable 'Guianese society' dates from the beginning of the nineteenth century. Prior to that time the individual plantation had been the main unit of social organization, but with the cessation of importations of new African slaves and the intensification of missionary activity and Colonial Office interest after about 1820 new forms of colony-wide organization began to appear. By 1840, when the emancipation of the slaves was complete, the form of the society was fairly clear. The Negroes, the Coloured and the White were integrated into a social system based upon the common acceptance of the superiority of European racial characteristics and European culture. The conversion of the whole Negro population to Christianity, and more specifically to membership of churches controlled from England and under the supervision of white missionaries, was of the utmost importance, especially as it tended to reinforce the idea of the highest moral values being somehow bound up with European culture, whilst the remnants of African belief and practice became both illegal and immoral. For the Negro in this situation the term 'progress' became synonymous with the adoption of 'English' cultural standards. The economic difficulties facing the first Negro villagers have been mentioned, and though many efforts were made by the Governments of the time, under Colonial Office guidance, to establish a prosperous 'peasantry', the economy of the country was such that peasant farming was difficult. Added to the natural difficulties was the fact that the Negroes began to define 'progress' and 'success' in terms of the adoption of a style of life requiring substantial expenditure on consumer goods. Upward mobility was difficult to achieve in a society where status was so closely tied to colour, but the expanding Government services and teaching provided some opportunities and those who managed to move into the higher status positions demonstrated their achievement by even more conspicuous consumption. Any attempt at status differentiation that was not based upon an adoption of a more 'European' style of life, and that was not based upon education, was not accepted as legitimate by those at the lowest level.

The Indian's absorption into this colour stratified social system was considerably delayed, and meanwhile the system itself was undergoing modification. During the nineteenth century a small number of Indians became upwardly mobile in the same way that a few Negroes were. Mostly children of men who occupied positions close to the Europeans on the plantations, house servants, foremen and so on, they usually became Christians, acquired formal schooling and adopted a European style of life. Members of this group came to constitute the first batch of 'successful' Indians, and a few became professional men in the usual fields of law and medicine. The bulk of the Indians remained sharply distinguished from the rest of the population in culture as well as being partially segregated upon the plantations. Christianity made little headway, but nothing like the same effort was put into missionizing the Indians as had been the case with the Negroes. Most important of all was the fact that the Indian continued to value certain elements of his own cultural background, and the growth of economic opportunity through the developing rice industry enabled him to manipulate slight differences in wealth to establish prestige differences *within* the Indian community. It was the fact that Indians did not fully accept the low status assigned to them by the rest of the community, but rather retained a separate set of criteria of status, that assisted the process of their internal rank distinction. But of course this could only be a temporary stage of development. After 1917 there were no new importations of indentured Indians, and since that time the process of absorption into Guianese society has continued and increased in effectiveness.

It is against this background that the different economic activities of the two groups must be viewed. The Negroes came to British Guiana as slaves with no hope of returning to their own country and with no idea of making money. They were introduced to a money economy through their leisure gardening activity, and then more completely after emancipation. But the overwhelming emphasis at this point was upon the integration of the society through the transmission of values of correct behaviour. Trading, which was virtually the only means of acquiring wealth apart from entry to the urban middle class, was soon dominated by the alien Portuguese, who felt none of the solidarity with their customers that could lead to the over-extension of credit and ultimate bankruptcy. The Indians came to British Guiana with the express intention of earning higher wages than they could get at home. They brought with them a complex culture which was inevitably altered by the demands of plantation life and labour, but was not deliberately destroyed as had been the case with the Negroes. In the Indian community much was made of the fact that a thrifty man could return to India with enough money to re-enter society at a higher level, and this was part of the appeal used by recruiters in India. Many families did return, taking their savings with them, and the idea of money savings as the key to 'progress' and a better life was reinforced.

THE CONTEMPORARY SCENE AND THE DIRECTION OF CHANGE

A number of developments have taken place over the past twenty years of so which serve as some indication of the probable lines of future change. Since the beginning of the Second World War there has been a small but steady increase in the size of what it is most convenient to call the 'middle class'. This has been based upon a growth in the size of Government services, private business and the professions consequent upon growth in the whole economy and the considerable injection of development capital both in the Governmental and private sectors. This has created greater opportunities for upward social mobility than have ever existed in the past and there has been an increase in the number and proportion of children receiving education at all levels, though this expansion has been modest. These changes have affected the Negroes by increasing the flow through the already established avenues of mobility but the Indians have been affected in a much more positive way. Until very recently Indians were grossly under-represented, in relation to their numbers, in the civil service, teaching, the professions, nursing, the police and so on, and they were predominantly rural. This has changed positively and substantially, and the relatively rapid absorption of Indians into the mainstream of Guianese life plus their political superiority through sheer weight of numbers has caused considerable disquiet among other Guianese. Along with this increased social mobility it is evident that Indians are increasingly accepting the values and culture of the rest of the society and its definitions of social success which include white collar employment in Governmental and private bureaucracies as well as entry into the professions.

There are still relatively few Guianese, including Indians, who get enough education to encourage them to believe that they qualify for white-collar or professional employment. The vast majority remain unskilled even if literate, and it is among these that there are still marked divergences of occupational preference. Most Indians prefer to become rice farmers while most Negroes prefer employment in the city, at the bauxite mines or in similar occupations. This generalization does not hold uniformly of course but is broadly true. The main emphasis of the Government's development programme has been upon an expansion of agriculture and since sugar has about reached its optimum size this means an expansion of rice cultivation. Attempts at diversification are being made but so far the great emphasis is upon the expansion of rice cultivation. Most economists who have examined the situation seem to be agreed that from a long-term development point of view the expansion of rice cultivation is bad and that heavy industrialization would be desirable.[1] They also agree for the most part that in view of the lack of capital, knowledge of resources and skill and in view of the sharply rising population, investment in drainage and irrigation to provide more land is probably the best that can be done immediately. The acquisition of new markets for rice in Cuba and some of the Eastern European communist countries has been of great help and has helped to strengthen Dr Jagan's position among rice farmers.[2] The important point is that the expansion of rice cultivation is likely to be merely an expansion in the number of Indian villages; the population growth will quickly lead to overcrowding and probably fragmentation on new as well as old lands; there is no indication that either the internal structure of the villages or the development of markets will lead to the development of a group of more efficient and larger-sized farms. The educated and ambitious of all races seek the same kind of rewards in the same activities and define status in the same way. Neither Indians nor any other local group has contributed very much to the growth of the economy in the role of entrepreneur and it is a complete myth to suggest that the Indians are acquiring control of any key sectors of the economy through a superior business sense. These key sectors are still firmly in the hands of expatriate business firms (except for rice which has been improved through Government initiative) and it seems likely that they will remain there for the present. Even in commerce and distribution the really big firms are mainly non-Indian being controlled by European interests or by Guianese of Portuguese descent.

On the basis of available evidence it does not seem likely that the existing villages will produce substantial entrepreneurial activity or generate important kinds of growth in agriculture without considerable outside interference by way of education, providing and organizing new markets, providing good drainage and irrigation and finding outlets for excess population. It may be fortunate that in the

[1] See Newman, 1960, and subsequent discussion in Vol. 10, No. 1 of the same journal; O'Loughlin, 1959; Kundu, 1962.
[2] Dr Jagan is Premier and Leader of the left-wing People's Progressive Party which obtains its main electoral support among East Indians.

short run Indians are willing to move on to new rice lands rather than into the towns in search of employment, though this will inevitably accentuate the friction between Indians and Negroes in so far as their interests are respectively bound up with different kinds of economic development. But the increases in the rate of economic growth will be fostered by that group within which ethnic differences will become of least significance—the educated bureaucrats of the Government agencies and the large business concerns—men who have new orientations and who will be able to marshal capital, savings and credit where these will have maximum effect upon the whole economy.

15

Capital, Saving and Credit among Mauritian Indians[1]

BY BURTON BENEDICT

Indians in Mauritius are dependent on money incomes which they obtain from the sporadic sale of their labour and of seasonal crops. They face the problem of assuring themselves a livelihood throughout the year. This is not merely a matter of allocating their economic resources, but of entering into and maintaining a wide network of social relations. Without some form of credit day to day expenses could not be met. Yet credit relations are special and delicate social relations which involve careful assessments of many factors. Despite the economic hardships of peasant life, some individuals manage to achieve relative prosperity, and this is as much an achievement in social relationships as in economic management. In this essay I examine the demands of a cash economy on Indo-Mauritians: how they use their labour, accumulate capital resources, and earn and dispose of their money incomes. In particular I examine part of the network of credit relationships which permeates the economic structure of the island.

The material was gathered during nearly two years of social anthropological research carried out in two villages, an estate camp and an Indian area of the town.[2] During this time a sociological census of the 9,156 people living in these areas was taken, including data on occupation, income, land-holding, livestock, capital goods, etc. Household budgets and data on daily routines were also collected. Information on credit relations was obtained from shopkeepers, middlemen, planters, wholesalers, businessmen, Government officials and householders.

[1] The research on which this paper is based was made possible by a grant from the Colonial Social Science Research Council to whom grateful acknowledgement is made.
[2] For a fuller account, see Benedict, 1961.

Capital, Saving and Credit Among Mauritian Indians

MAURITIUS AND ITS ECONOMY

Mauritius, a British Crown Colony with an area of about 720 square miles, lies in the Indian Ocean 500 miles east of Madagascar. The economy is based on a single cash crop, sugar. Ninety-nine per cent of the island's exports are sugar and its by-products. Ninety per cent of the arable land is planted in sugar cane; 70 per cent of the labour force is engaged in the production of sugar. The island does not feed itself, for there is no subsistence farming. The greater part of its basic foodstuffs and virtually all manufactured goods must be imported (v. Meade, 1960). For their labour Mauritians receive money; for their needs they must pay money.

The sugar industry's demand for labour was satisfied in the eighteenth and early nineteenth centuries by slaves imported from East Africa and Madagascar. After emancipation, the planters turned to India. Between 1834 and 1907 some 450,000 Indians were brought to Mauritius as indentured labourers.[1] Today, in a population of over 650,000, 67 per cent is of Indian origin, both Hindu and Muslim; 28 per cent is of mixed African and European descent, known as Creole; 3 per cent is Chinese; and 2 per cent is European, mostly of French extraction. With the population growing at the rate of over 3 per cent per annum, there will be over a million inhabitants in twenty years and nearly three million by the end of the century (v. Titmuss, 1960). Overpopulation is the most serious Mauritian problem. Despite an increasing gross national product, real national income per head is already declining (Meade, 1960, pp. 43–4). The Indo-Mauritian has remained the agricultural labourer of the island. He is a wage labourer, hired by the day in his village and paid cash at the end of the week.

The villages of Mauritius stretch along the main roads and vary in population from a few hundreds to over 7,000. The villagers' main economic ties are with the sugar estates where the majority are employed. Village leaders are often those with access to the managements of the estates—overseers, job contractors, middlemen. Other leaders are in Government which, after the sugar industry, is the largest employer in the island. Most villages are run by village councils with funds derived from Government. There are possibilities for patronage in the employment of village labourers and in the awarding of contracts for public works within the village, and leaders compete with one another for election to the council (v. Benedict, 1957).

The patrilineal joint family is still the ideal among most Indians, but in the cash and wage economy of Mauritius it faces different

[1] In 1922–23 some 1,200 more were imported, but most of these returned to India.

problems from those in a subsistence economy. Wage earning leads to independence of sons, who often resent making contributions to the common budget, particularly after marriage and the birth of children. Balanced against this are the advantages of sharing a common houseplot and a common kitchen, of pooling labour in domestic chores, and of obviating the need for cash expenditures to buy certain goods and services used domestically or in production. These advantages are greater when the family owns agricultural land on which family labour can be used to produce a cash crop.

The villager is placed in a network of money relations. There is constant pressure on him to acquire cash, for most goods and many services are only obtainable with it. He purchases most of his food from one of the village shops or from hawkers. He buys cloth from hawkers on bicycles or from shops in town and pays the local tailor to make it into suits. For services he must pay the barber, the doctor, the bus or taxi driver, or the tutor for his son at school. Amusements in the form of the cinema or football matches, drinking and eating snacks in the shop, card and domino playing, all require cash.

The opportunities for earning cash are limited, especially in the villages. The sale of his labour is the chief method by which the villager can obtain a cash income. But the demand for his labour fluctuates with the season. Economically the year is divided into a crop season of five months when work is plentiful and wages are relatively high, and an inter-crop season of seven months when work is scarcer and wages low. In general, however, labour is always available, and from the villager's point of view labour-time has a relatively low value. Money, on the other hand, is difficult to obtain and therefore valued relatively highly. When the choice is open to him, the villager seeks to increase his money income by activities which require little or no money outlays and bring quick money returns. Wherever possible he will substitute 'unpaid' labour—his own and his family's—for factors of production which have to be bought with money.

OWNERSHIP AND MANAGEMENT OF CANE LAND

Sugar-cane land is the most important form of fixed capital an Indo-Mauritian can possess. In the villages informants always listed wealth as a defining characteristic (though not the only one) of an important man; and wealth in this context meant the possession of about 30 *arpents* of cane land.[1] The possession of even a small amount of cane land is a considerable economic advantage. A small planter can expect a profit of between Rs. 350 and 600 per *arpent* per year.[2] This

[1] An *arpent* is an archaic French measurement still used in Mauritius; 1 *arpent*=1·04 acres.

[2] The rupee is divided into 100 cents. It is linked to sterling: Re. 1=1s 6d.

compares with the Rs. 1,368 which has been computed as the average annual income of an agricultural labourer (Luce, 1958, p. 21).

TABLE 1

DISTRIBUTION OF CANE LAND AMONG HOUSEHOLDS
IN FOUR SETTLEMENTS

	Northern Village	Southern Village	Estate Camp	Town*
Number of Households	389	399	154	600
Amount of Cane Land				
No cane land	70·7%	73·5%	94%	97·5%
Under 1 *arpent*	6·9%	12·0%	5%	·3%
1–2 *arpents*	8·2%	4·5%	1%	—
2–5 *arpents*	7·7%	4·0%	—	·3%
5–10 *arpents*	2·6%	2·0%	—	·2%
10–30 *arpents*	1·5%	2·2%	—	·2%
30–100 *arpents*	1·4%	·9%	—	·2%
100 *arpents* and more	·3%	—	—	·5%
Amount unknown	·7%	·9%	—	·8%

* This is not the complete town, but only a section which I studied.

In the two villages the percentages of households owning some cane land (over 25 per cent) are higher than in the estate camp and in the town (under 6 per cent). But the majority of village holdings are under 2 *arpents,* and a number of households possess ¼ *arpent* or less. At the other end of the scale there is one villager with over 100 *arpents* and a couple of dozen with holdings of over 10 *arpents.* Only ten households in the estate camp held cane land and the holdings were all very small. Estate camp dwellers are particularly poor. They live in cubicles provided by the estate and work for monthly wages on whatever jobs the estate management assigns to them. Upward social mobility lies in the direction of the village and a homestead of one's own. The possession of cane land is a means to this ndependence. The planter moves out of the estate camp into the vill·age. A further factor is that the planter and his family must wor k his own cane land, and estate demands upon his labour may leav e him little time for this. From the village, upward social mobility is tow ard the town. Although there are fewer plante rs in the town, their holdings tend to be larger, one being over 400 *arpents.* These planters are absentee land owners whose estates are usually managed by relatives and paid employees.

Some of the village planters have holdings in as many as five different places, some of which may be far from the village of residence. This situation arises because the inheritance law, based on the French Civil Code, provides for the eq ual division of land among heirs. Though heirs make efforts to amalg amate holdings or to trade a plot of land in a distant area for one nea rer home, this cannot

333

always be done and scattered holdings result. The scarcity of cane land may also tempt a planter to buy land as and where it becomes available, even if this raises the difficulty of working small plots in different areas.

For a man with a small plot, say ¼ to 2 *arpents*, on which he and his family can do all the work, the chief money expenditures are for fertilizer and for transport of the cane to the mill. The planter with a larger plot has to hire labour for weeding, spreading manure and fertilizer, stripping the canes of dead leaves and cutting them, and transporting them to the mill.

Small planters obtain money to bring in the crop either from co-operative credit societies or middlemen. The co-operatives are run under the supervision of Government. Planters in each village form a society, and members applying for loans furnish proof of title to their land and the signatures of two persons as surety. The loan is made on the basis of the previous year's crop from funds supplied by the Central Bank. Credit co-operatives have shown a steady growth in Mauritius. They offer loans at low interest and might be expected to attract customers readily; yet many small planters do not use them, but prefer the middleman as a source of credit. There are a number of reasons for this. One has to do with the recurring theme of the need for cash. Middlemen, who are usually wealthier Indian planters known to their clients, often advance money to the planters more quickly than the co-operatives are willing to do. Even though the planters may get a smaller loan, they prefer ready cash received sooner. Indeed, many of them must have cash, and it is a matter of getting it from a middleman or borrowing it from someone else at an even higher rate of interest. Rates of interest for cash loans run from 2 per cent to 25 per cent or higher, but 10 per cent seems to be usual. One device for concluding a loan at more than the legal maximum rate of interest is to double the amount of capital stated in the promissory note. Thus a man who borrows Rs. 100 signs a note for Rs. 200 and pays interest on Rs. 200 (*v.* Mauritius, Commission of Enquiry, 1959).

Another reason why co-operatives are avoided by some borrowers is that every loan from a co-operative is discussed by fellow members who are also fellow villagers. Many villagers are not eager for other villagers to know how much land they hold or how much money they need. This sort of information attracts creditors and tax-collectors. The title deeds create a further difficulty; they are often not in order, or one man may apply for loan on land owned jointly or about to be divided. The middleman does not require so many proofs of ownership to make a loan; he makes his loan on a personal basis in the light of his own knowledge.

The co-operative usually advances money only on cane pro-

duction and not on other enterprises which are riskier. The middleman will often lend money not only for the cane crop, but also for
building a house or some other need.

The middleman builds and maintains his clientele through personal influence. The son of one successful middleman spent much of
his time attending marriages, funerals and other ceremonies of his
client households. The personal tie counts for a great deal, and the
successful middleman is a kind of patron to his clients, a role which
no co-operative credit society can fufill.

LIVESTOCK

Livestock provides a source of income in all settlements, particularly
among Indians.

TABLE 2

DISTRIBUTION OF LIVESTOCK AMONG HOUSEHOLDS
IN FOUR SETTLEMENTS

	Northern Village	Southern Village	Estate Camp	Town
Number of Households	389	399	154	600
No livestock	23·4%	43·6%	34·4%	92·3%
1 cow	7·5%	3·5%	18·8%	1·0%
2 cows	7·5%	5·7%	9·1%	1·6%
3 or more cows	1·7%	1·0%	1·3%	·7%
Total percentage of households keeping cows	16·7%	10·2%	29·2%	3·3%
1 goat	1·6%	3·0%	3·2%	·5%
2 goats	·5%	4·8%	1·3%	·5%
3 or more goats	3·3%	7·0%	·5%	·9%
Total percentage of households keeping goats	5·4%	14·8%	5·0%	1·9%
Chickens	28·5%	43·1%	55·2%	4·2%
Ducks	3·3%	5·5%	15·6%	2·5%
Pigs	·3%	—	3·8%	—
Other	2·6%	2·0%	1·9%	·7%

Cultural factors affect the keeping of livestock. Pigs are well suited
to Mauritian village economy. They can be fed on leftovers and are
easily sold. Yet no Muslim will keep pigs and they seem to be nearly
as abhorrent to Hindus. All the pig keepers in the estate camp were
Creoles, but no Creole or Chinese household kept pigs in either of the
Indian-dominated villages. Many Hindu families regarded fowls
other than chickens as ritually unclean, and most of the keepers of
ducks were Muslims, Creoles, Chinese or low caste Hindus.

Traditional beliefs have also hampered the Government's efforts
to improve the strain of cows. The Department of Agriculture provides artificial insemination free of charge, using semen from

335

imported Friesan bulls which, it is established, will double milk yields in the second generation. Yet many Indian cow keepers prefer to have the cows serviced by a bull for a fee. They believe artificial insemination deprives cattle of the legitimate right of copulation, that the Friesan foetus formed is too large and will kill the cow, and that the service is too inconvenient. These examples illustrate how factors in the traditional belief system inhibit possibilities for increased earnings.

The ecology of settlements affects the keeping of livestock. The crowded conditions of urban dwelling are clearly drawbacks, and it is more difficult to procure fodder for cows and goats. The estates, on the other hand, provide special facilities for housing cattle and often encourage cow-keeping as one way of attaching labourers to the estate. Fodder is more readily procurable than in the village. The manure can be sold to the estate for fertilizer. No such facilities are provided for goats which are kept in small pens near the dwelling. Village houseplots are more favourable for this and there are more goats per household in the villages.

The care of livestock depends on unpaid family labour, particularly that of women and children. Cows are usually kept in sheds made of thatch from cane trash. They rarely see the light of day as all fodder and water is carried to them. Women and children often trudge daily for miles to collect sufficient fodder. Men, who are carried in lorries to distant estates for a day's work, sometimes bring back bundles of cane tops or other greenery. Disputes sometimes arise when an estate wishes to close an area against fodder collection, as villagers tend to regard fodder collecting as a right. Government has long been experimenting with improved fodders which have been offered for sale at subsidized prices, but cow-keepers will not buy. Unpaid family labour, no matter how extravagantly used in terms of time, is still more readily available than even a small amount of money.

A cow costs from Rs. 300 to Rs. 600 and represents a considerable investment for a labouring family. Nevertheless, a cow is cheaper than the usual unit of cane land, and it provides a money income through the sale of milk, calves and manure. Poor families often share the ownership of a cow. A cow may be bought by an entrepreneur and given to a poor family to care for in return for half the milk, or the entrepreneur may buy the milk at half the retail price. By another method, a calf is given to a poor family to rear in return for half the milk or, should the animal be sold, half the proceeds. Manure is carefully collected and sold to the estates, yielding about Rs. 50 per adult animal per year.

Goats are much cheaper to buy (a kid can be purchased for as little as Rs. 15) and require less labour than cows. Their care is often entrusted almost entirely to children. Unlike cows, which are kept only by the Indian population, goats are kept by Creoles and Chinese. Goat is probably the most commonly consumed meat in Mauritius. Among Hindus all but the strictest Brahmins will eat it, though many of the higher castes will not slaughter the animal. Goat milk is not drunk by any community, so that income can only be realized by selling the animal for slaughter.

Chickens are very widely kept in all settlements by all communities. They require the lowest money inputs as a pullet can be bought for as little as Rs. 2. Chickens are allowed to run loose about the yard even in the town, and pick up whatever scraps they can find. Remainders of a meal of rice are often thrown to them. At night they roost in trees to escape the depredations of the mongoose, which is common in the country districts. Income is realized chiefly through the sale of eggs, which have a ready market as all but the strictest Brahmins will eat them. Individual members of the household, usually women, own the chickens.

OTHER SOURCES OF INCOME

Nearly all agricultural land owned by Indians is planted in cane. Other crops are grown on rented or share-cropped land or, where there is room, on part of the houseplot. The small tomato known in Mauritius as *pomme d'amour* is a favoured crop, though maize, manioc, various types of squash or marrow, potatoes and a few other vegetables are grown. The object is to plant a crop which matures quickly and requires the smallest outlay of cash. Often the rented land is in a field already planted with cane. The vegetables are set out in the rows between the cane, and must be harvested before the cane grows so high that it cuts off the sunlight. The planting and harvesting of vegetables is usually a family enterprise, employing unpaid family labour; but if the area planted is large or the family labour insufficient, labourers are hired on a daily basis. The crop is usually sold to a middleman who transports it to the central market in Port Louis, where it is auctioned to retailers. The principal risk in planting vegetables is the uncertainty of the weather; but considerable profits can be made. One wealthy villager founded his fortune by harvesting his crop of tomatoes and storing them in a stone building just before three devastating cyclones struck the island in 1945, practically wiping out the supply of fresh vegetables.

Land for planting vegetables is usually rented from other Indian planters in the village and occasionally from an estate. Most estates, however, make a practice of providing the interlines between the canes, rent-free, to trusted employees. Pieces of land which are uneconomic for the cultivation of sugar cane by the estate because of

337

rockiness, difficulties of irrigation, inaccessibility, etc. may also be provided rent-free to employees. The labour costs to the estate of bringing such lands under cultivation are too high; but they are not too high for an Indo-Mauritian using his own and his family's labour. The free loan of land helps to keep labourers attached to the estate. Share-cropping is a common practice with vegetables.

Tobacco is a crop of importance in the north of Mauritius where conditions favour its growth. The crop, which is planted, tended and harvested by family labour with the occasional assistance of hired labourers, is cured in small stone barns owned by individual planters. Women and children in the family sort and grade the cured leaves. The planting and marketing of tobacco is controlled by a tobacco marketing board. A single factory uses the entire product for making cigarettes for local consumption.

Fruit such as mangoes, litchis, avocados, papayas, etc. may be sold piecemeal, but it is more usual to sell the entire produce of a tree to a middleman. Often this is done on a speculative basis before the tree has borne, with the middleman harvesting the fruit himself.

Other vegetables of importance are the 'bredes', leafy greens of several varieties which grow mostly near rivers or streams. Concessions to harvest bredes are given by the estates to middlemen for a small fee. One joint family household, for example, rents the right to collect bredes on a stretch of about 2 *arpents* on a river for Rs. 12 per month. The family gathers it, cleans it and hawks it on bicycles.

Other kinds of holdings include plots of forest land on which fast-growing eucalyptus and casuarina trees are planted. Such lands may be had from either estates or Government. The wood is used for building purposes or reduced to charcoal for fuel. Concessions to gather ravenal, a kind of palm leaf which is woven into sheets for housebuilding, are also given by estates. Even shoots from the bamboo hedges which surround many dwellings are sold at 2–3 cents each and used as support for thatching.

Many more examples could be cited to show this persistent conversion of agricultural and natural products into cash. There is no subsistence farming: from the cane field to the kitchen garden, from the tobacco plant to the bamboo hedge, all agricultural produce is turned into cash. The Mauritian is constantly in need of money for his requirements. Surpluses, if any, are converted into cane land or other capital assets.

An income-producing activity for women is sewing. Lengths of cloth are bought from hawkers. Work-clothes and undergarments for both men and women and virtually all children's clothing are made at home. In the Southern village more than one-quarter of all households had hand-operated sewing machines. Women with sewing machines can earn small sums making dresses and children's clothes

338

from cloth which is provided by the customer. The charge in the village for a dress or child's garment is two or three rupees. The woman retains this money herself. In the town nearly a third of the households had sewing machines.

The input of unpaid family labour has been frequently mentioned as an economic base for the household. This is particularly marked in some of the large joint family households whose members are engaged in a variety of occupations. Some of these become family 'corporations' in which labour is pooled; and there is a pool of cash to run the household, though individual members may keep part of their earnings for themselves. One such household consisted of fifty members. The family possessed three shops; several houses which were let; 30 *arpents* of cane land; 6 *arpents* of tobacco land; vegetable plantations between the rows of sugar cane on their land; two tobacco barns for curing the tobacco and a grading shed for sorting it; two lorries, two cars and a bus which was leased to a bus company; nine goats and much poultry. All these enterprises were run by household members. Even the leased bus had family members as driver and ticket collector. The senior women ran the kitchens which not only fed the family but also supplied cooked food (usually octopus stew) for sale in the shops. Younger women and children helped harvest, cure and sort the tobacco, fed the livestock and did the lighter work in the family fields. Though village exogamy with virilocal residence is the rule among Northern Hindus in Mauritius, this family incorporated daughters' husbands into the household to help with the family enterprises. This example, though unusually large, is not unique, nor is it confined to rural areas. A fraternal joint family household in the town had one member running a vegetable stall in the central market with two young boys of the family as assistants; a second member was a job contractor providing labour for construction work; a third was in the police; a fourth worked for the Public Assistance department; two were in secondary school; and another had an army pension. The women maintained the household and common kitchen. A usual arrangement for land-owning families is to assign one member to look after the plantations while the others seek other occupations. Examples could be multiplied; but it is evident that joint family living offers advantages even in families whose members have widely differing occupations. The possession of a family houseplot, the provision of an unpaid domestic labour force and the pooling of kitchen expenses are considerable economic advantages.

SOME SOURCES OF BORROWING

A major source of borrowing has already been discussed in the section on ownership and management of cane land. Other sources of borrowing open to villagers must now be considered before describing the system of credit from shopkeepers which operates in Mauritius.

Whether he needs money for ceremonial expenditures, for current consumption or for the purchase of assets, the villager may turn to his employer, his kinsman and his friends and neighbours.

The villager is a day labourer. He is usually employed through a job contractor who contracts with the estate to do a certain task for which he receives 10 per cent of the wages of the men he employs. The estate hands the wages to the contractor and he pays his men at the end of the week. During the crop season a man can easily get work, but during the inter-crop period it is more difficult. The job contractor spreads the work among his men during the inter-crop period to keep them bound to him for the crop season. He also lends them money. The loan is usually quite small and is often free of interest or at a very low rate of interest. A man who accepts a loan from a job contractor feels obliged to work for him, and their relations are personal. They are from the same village and know one another. A casual labourer would not get this kind of loan. The job contractor recovers his money by taking a deduction from the man's wages during the crop season. In the Agricultural and Public Works departments, overseers and their men have much the same relations of borrowing and lending. An overseer will be more interested in keeping employed a man to whom he has loaned money.

We have already considered the role of estates in making concessions to overseers, job contractors and trusted employees in the form of a loan of land which it is uneconomic for the estates to plant. The overseer may recommend some of his men for such concessions, so that a villager can acquire access to producer's capital through his working relationships. These relationships are personal and depend on the personal knowledge of the overseer, job contractor and estate manager.

Kinship relations provide another source of finance. For the Indo-Mauritian villager, kinship itself is a kind of economic resource. In the first place, there is joint living. This means not only the sharing of capital assets such as a common house, houseplot, kitchen or budget, but it also means the pooling of labour. In the second place, kinship provides lines of communications for the villager. The recognition of kinship ties extends bilaterally for a long way. It is continually re-enforced by weddings, funerals and other ceremonies which take villagers all over the island. Thus at the wedding of a labourer's daughter in one village invitations were sent to the heads of over 300 households living in twenty different places widely scattered over the island. These ties are exploited when a villager is

340

looking for a new job or for backing in some enterprise such as the purchase of a small plot of land.

For money loans a villager may apply through any kinship tie which leads him to a wealthy relative; but undoubtedly the favoured relative is the wife's father. A man receives a cash dowry at his betrothal ceremony (*teeluck*) before the wedding; but if the father-in-law has means, further demands are often made upon him. Here the security is the wife herself, and the motive her father's desire to see her well treated. A father who is stingy about giving his daughter's husband a loan may find his daughter back on his hands. Most Indo-Mauritian marriages are religious ceremonies only. They are not legally recognized until a civil ceremony has been performed. This may not occur for years, if ever. Thus a man can send back his wife without incurring legal sanctions. In one case a man borrowed Rs. 1,000 from his father-in-law. Several years later he went to him for another loan. The old man refused, saying the boy already owed him Rs. 1,000. The boy was furious, as he considered the Rs. 1,000 as only a form of dowry. He sent back his wife, and it took the concerted efforts of both families to persuade him to take her again.

Lending and borrowing on a small scale is often effected by means of a pool, or 'cycle' or 'cheet' as it is known in Mauritius. A man or woman calls together a group of friends and neighbours. Suppose there are ten of them, and each puts in Rs. 10. They then draw lots and the winner takes the Rs. 100. (Sometimes the organizer automatically takes the first 'pool'.) The following month each again puts in Rs. 10, and another member takes the resulting Rs. 100; and so it continues for ten months until each member has had his Rs. 100. As so described, it is simply a kind of co-operative savings scheme, and those who draw last receive nothing by way of interest. This is the usual way it operates among Indians in both the villages I lived in. If the cycle continues for another round, the member who drew tenth on the first cycle draws first on the second, and so on. The Chinese on the island—as elsewhere—operate a variant of the cycle in which the 'lenders' (late drawers) in effect receive interest payments from the 'borrowers' (early drawers). The participants bid for turns; a man in need of quick cash may bid to take Rs. 90 instead of Rs. 100, if permitted to draw first, or he may agree to put in a total of Rs. 110 over the cycle if he can have Rs. 100 immediately. Thus the other members of the cycle receive in due course more than their contributions; the difference is a form of interest paid to them by those with more urgent need of money. If the second and third drawings are bid for as well, the total interest payments to the more patient members increase (cf. Freedman, 1959). The cycle is dependent on the mutual confidence of the participants. If a man takes his Rs. 100

and refuses to continue, there is no legal recourse available to other members of the cycle.

THE 'ROULEMENT' SYSTEM IN THE VILLAGES

Sociologically there is a great difference between cash and credit relations. The former are impersonal. It matters little who one's customer is or how one feels about him. One does not have to take into account his job or how he does it or the kinds of relations he has with other people or other jobs. The relation is specific in that it concerns a single cash transaction. Subsequent transactions are equally specific and discrete. The money is paid; the goods are handed over; the transaction is terminated. It has a very limited time span. Credit relations, at least of the kind described here, are very different. They are personal. It matters very much who one's debtor is. His job, his relations with others, even his personality and how one feels about him and how others feel about him must be considered. The relationship is diffuse and extends over many transactions. Indeed creditor-debtor relations may become almost permanent. Credit relations are firmly embedded in the social structure of Mauritius, and a case might even be made for analysing the society in terms of credit structure in much the same way that simpler societies have been analysed in terms of kinship structure.

The principal credit link is that between the villager and the shop. All villagers obtain their basic requirements from a shop. There is no village in the island without a shop, and most have several. The villager acquires the goods he needs from the shop, and promises to pay at the end of the week, more usually at the end of the month, or sometimes at the end of the year. He does not usually keep a record of his purchases, but leaves this to the shopkeeper who marks them down in a book in his customer's presence. Goods are bought daily in very small quantities. At the end of the month the shopkeeper asks for payment; but the full amount is not usually paid, and the debt is carried over to the next month. So it continues. The debt increases during the month and is reduced at the end of the month, but is never fully paid off. Villagers themselves refer to the system as *roulement*, and indeed it is a rolling debt going on from month to month.

A simplified example will clarify the way in which the system works. Suppose a client has a rolling debt of Rs. 50; that is, at the end of each month he owes the shopkeeper 50 rupees. In addition, he buys, say, 50 rupees' worth of goods per month. Thus he starts the month with a debt of Rs. 50. This grows until at the end of the month he owes Rs. 100. He pays Rs. 50 and begins the next month with Rs. 50 still owing. In other words, the *roulement* can be looked at as a kind of capital investment which the shopkeeper makes in his customer, in return for which he secures his custom.

This, of course, is a very simplified example of the way in which the system actually operates. The shopkeeper does not allow a new client to run up a big debt in his first month. The amount grows slowly. A client of long standing may be permitted to increase his debt. The amount of debt also varies with the season. During the inter-crop period the amount of debt becomes greater. During the crop season it is reduced. One shopkeeper estimated he was owed Rs. 500-600 per month during the inter-crop period, but only Rs. 100-200 during the crop season.

The shopkeeper makes allowance in his prices for a return on his investment in customers, and for the inevitable bad debts. He also tries to minimize his losses from bad debts, and the amount invested in each customer. Sharp practices apart, such as falsifying the account and giving short measure, this means both keeping the custom of his clients and keeping their debts at the lowest level compatible with it. The shopkeeper tries to keep down the debt and to get the maximum of it paid off by his client. Yet he cannot push his client too far for fear of losing him, in which case he might recover nothing of the debt. The promise to pay is verbal, *la parole* as the villagers say; there are no written agreements or signed receipts. An Indian shopkeeper tried to collect a debt of Rs. 142 owed him for two years by a neighbour now dealing at another shop. He retained a lawyer and went to court, but his case was dismissed because there was no signed acknowledgment of the debt; and he had to pay Rs. 50 costs. The only sanction a shopkeeper has is the cutting off of credit. A man can then go to another shop; but his reputation will follow him and the new shopkeeper will be chary of advancing him much credit. Should a man continue to default, he will find himself unable to get credit anywhere in the village. Without credit the villager will find it very difficult to live. Public Assistance Officers regard the cutting off of credit by a shopkeeper as one of the most serious disabilities a poor villager can sustain.

There are strong ties of mutual dependence binding together the shopkeeper and his clientele. From the point of view of the shopkeeper, it is a personal kind of relationship. It matters very much to the shopkeeper who his client is. He must be able to assess his client's ability to pay, to judge the amount of credit he can be given, and to estimate his character, position in the village and also his mobility. A man who is tied to the village by a large family and the ownership of a houseplot is, generally speaking, a better risk than a man without ties and living alone in rented premises. Such considerations may tend to limit the clientele of any one shopkeeper, and so help to account for the number of shops to be found in each village (cf. Ward, 1960). I found the average clientele of a village shop to number 150.

343

The *roulement* credit link between shopkeeper and villager is really the last link in a series of *roulement* credit relationships which extend from overseas exporters to importers and wholesalers in Mauritius, and from the wholesalers to the shopkeepers. The shopkeeper takes his goods from the wholesaler on one or two weeks' or a month's credit. He returns at the end of the period, pays part of his debt and takes more goods, leaving a balance of his debt outstanding. One large wholesaler estimates he sells between 75,000 and 100,000 bags of rice annually on a monthly *roulement* basis. He told me that payments on rice were three to six months in arrears, and he reckons that between 25 per cent and 30 per cent of the debts owing to him are uncollectable. (The village shopkeepers are probably in much the same position.)

Most village shopkeepers in Mauritius are Chinese. They are thus of a different ethnic group from their clients, most of whom are Indians. The Chinese, by remaining apart from village life, are better able to give and withhold credit than are the Indian shopkeepers with kinship, political and other social ties binding them to other villagers. Close relations, such as kinship ties, inhibit the creditor-debtor relationship. A Chinese, who took part in village politics in one village, soon found he had to withdraw when an opposing faction threatened to boycott his shop (*v.* Benedict, 1957). In a second village, two Indian shopkeepers are very careful to remain aloof from village politics.

The Chinese shopkeeper's kinship, social and economic ties reach out of the village towards the town. He rents his premises from an Indian landlord. If he should fail, he can withdraw and begin again in another village or in town. The Indian shopkeeper's ties are within the village. Many more sanctions can be brought to bear against him. He owns his premises. He cannot easily move; if he fails, he is out of business altogether. It is no accident that most shopkeepers are Chinese and that Indians, who own shop buildings, prefer to rent them to Chinese than to run them themselves. Wholesalers, most of whom are Indians, prefer to do business with Chinese. One large Muslim wholesaler told me he would not give credit to Hindu or Muslim shopkeepers because he felt they did not handle credit well and were encumbered with large families. Chinese families are just as large if not larger. The wholesaler was referring to the network of obligations which keep the Indian village shopkeeper from being an impersonal creditor.

'ROULEMENT' IN THE TOWNS

In town *roulement* has moved from the shopkeeper-client relationship to the employer-employee relationship. The villager is characterized by permanent residence and irregular day labour which fluctuates with the season, and he may find employment with many different employers. The townsman, by and large, has less permanent residence and a less marked feeling of belonging to a community; but his employment is regular with little seasonal variation, and his employment is with the same employer.

In an Indian area of the capital where I lived there were many Chinese and a few Indian shops. In contrast to the village where every shopkeeper had a large regular clientele, the town shopkeeper had much smaller regular clientele; few village shops had less than 100 regular clients, while few town shops had more than fifteen. While most of the village shopkeepers' business was credit, only a very small part of the town shopkeepers' business was credit, and nearly all their customers pay cash. Except with very well-known customers, credit is given only for a day or two, and no additional credit is given until the debt is paid off. There is little *roulement* here. Nor is the townsman so dependent on the shop. The most common item sold in village shops is rice; in town it is cigarettes. Foodstuffs can be bought at the central market in town at competitive prices and for cash. There are few bonds linking vendor and customer. This relationship is much more impersonal.

Where does a townsman, who is short of money, obtain cash in order to buy so widely without using trade credit? As is true for the villager, he could apply to his kindred, to a moneylender, or organize a 'cycle' giving him first drawing rights. But predominantly he will seek financial accommodation from his employer. His regular job gives him some basis on which to borrow both from his employer, and also from others. A few examples taken from the books of a large company show the debts of its employees. A *peon* earned a monthly wage of Rs. 100; on the fifteenth of each month he took an advance of from Rs. 75 to 80; he had a rolling debt of between Rs. 140 and 170. A clerk earned Rs. 425 per month; he was advanced between Rs. 75 and 125 on the fifteenth of each month; and had an outstanding debt of Rs. 700. A labourer borrowed Rs. 60 in six loans of Rs. 10 each during a single month. At the end of the month he still owed Rs. 10. It is apparent that we are once again dealing with *roulement*. Most employees owe their employers a month's salary, a debt which is carried over from month to month. The company's policy is to write off the debt when an employee retires or is discharged. In one year the company wrote off Rs. 1,200 in bad debts to clerks and Rs. 280 to regularly-employed day labourers. Though labourers are daily employees, there are regulars who are entitled to loans and free medical care for themselves and their wives and children. Casual daily employees do not receive these benefits.

In addition to borrowing from their employers, many employees

345

borrow from moneylenders or buy goods on hire purchase. This is true of Government employees. The amount that they can borrow from Government is limited; but their regular employment makes it easy for them to secure loans from other sources.

16

Capital Formation, Saving and Credit in Indian Agricultural Society

BY BERT F. HOSELITZ

The main objective of this essay is to present some empirical data on savings, capital formation and credit collected in a peasant society, and to show how these data may be employed in support of propositions of interest to economists. Economists have often been charged with being concerned mainly with purely abstract relationships, with developing generalizations from axiomatic assumptions and with analysing situations which have only slight relation to the real world. In the course of this argument it has especially been pointed out that economics, as it was developed in the context of a market economy with emphasis on capitalistic forms of exchange and capital accumulation, has no relevance to simpler peasant economies and that, therefore, a new and distinct set of propositions about the productive and allocative activities of peasant societies must be developed.

In this essay the attempt will be made to show that a 'new economics' for peasant societies is not necessary; that productive activity and the process of capital accumulation and saving in these societies can be described in terms familiar to Western economics; that it may even be possible to exhibit these relationships in a quantitative fashion; and that, from all this, we may gain a reasonably accurate picture of the degree of productive efficiency and growth capacity of peasant societies. But the main purpose of the essay is not the vindication of economic concepts or economic theories, but rather the attempt to show how the collection of certain sets of empirical data relating to productive activity may enhance our insight into the functioning of an economy based partially or fully on subsistence production. By implication, this paper, therefore, may be considered as an exercise in trying to determine the utility which may be assigned to the categories of modern economics in the study of societies with

347

relatively simple methods of production and to ascertain what valid and significant propositions can be made about the economic affairs of peasant societies on the basis of empirical data collected in the field.

India has been chosen as the area singled out for special study. The main reason for this is the availability of a larger amount of probably better and more detailed quantitative data on the productive and related activities among the Indian peasantry than are available for any other country in a similar level of economic performance. The data which we will use do not come from the intensive field work of one man in one locality. They were collected by large numbers of workers in the field, and they were obtained as the result of often far-flung surveys. These surveys could be carried out only on a large scale because they had the support of Government; and what the data gain in comprehensiveness and geographical coverage, they lose because the Government workers who collected them had to obey a set of rigid prescribed procedures, often had only scant information of the precise cultural framework of the localities they surveyed, and probably also were met in some places with some suspicion by their informants. Moreover, the field personnel did not have the specialized and highly sophisticated training of the cultural anthropologist. All these factors make it likely that the nature and quality of responses obtained in these surveys differ greatly from what would have been obtained by a trained field anthropologist.

An account of some of the procedures employed in these surveys and, above all, a brief presentation and discussion of their results, will be helpful to show how far one may go in obtaining useful data on the economic activity of peasant populations, and how well these results may be interpreted in terms of economic categories ultimately derived from the cultural context of the economically more highly advanced societies in Western countries.

I

One of the chief problems of concern in contemporary India is the question of the magnitude of rural investment, i.e. the net addition to the total stock of capital employed in agriculture. The reason for this concern is easy to see. More than four-fifths of the population of India live in villages, and rather more than two-thirds depend directly upon agriculture (mainly the production of field crops) for their livelihood. Clearly, the amount of resources available to this population and the amount of annual additions to this stock of resources are of great interest in determining the general level of well-being of this population and the conditions under which its well-being changes for the better or worse. It is not surprising, therefore, that several attempts have been made to estimate the overall magnitude of rural capital formation in India. Public expenditure on investment in agriculture and associated facilities (e.g., irrigation and the like) is not difficult to ascertain. But the matter is different with investment undertaken by private persons, i.e. the peasants themselves. Much of the effort expended in surveys and field studies, therefore, has been devoted to the study of the economic behaviour of the peasant, especially the small- and medium-sized owner-cultivator.

Village surveys have been done in India since before World War I. Pioneering studies at that time, especially on economic relations, were undertaken by Harold H. Mann in the Bombay Deccan, and a really thorough-going set of economic inquiries in agricultural villages was begun after the end of World War I by the Punjab Board of Economic Enquiry.[1] Since the attainment of independence, numerous state Governments, universities and other research groups have undertaken such surveys in increasing number, and a full enumeration of these studies would occupy several pages. We will concentrate, in this study, primarily on all-India surveys, but will have occasion at various points to make reference to special case studies.

The first all-India estimates of capital formation in agriculture by private individuals may be derived from the inquiries made by the National Sample Survey in its first three rounds during 1950 and 1951. The findings have been conveniently summarized by V. M. Dandekar. On the basis of Dandekar's summary tables, we may estimate that gross investment per rural family in the form of land improvements, new construction, other improvements to real estate, and net purchase of land, buildings, farm implements and other machinery, amounted to Rs. 143.50 per family.[2] To this amount should be added the increase in the stock of cattle, which came to Rs. 76.20 per rural family. But much of the 'addition' to the stock of cattle consists in transfers between different persons in the farm sector and hence cannot be regarded as a net addition on a country-wide basis. There was, of course, an increase in the numbers of livestock in India during the past few years, but whether this growth in numbers should be regarded as an increase in economic value is uncertain. Hence the annual increase in livestock certainly did not amount to an investment per rural family of Rs. 76 per year, and

---

[1] A brief list of the surveys in the Bombay Deccan is presented in Diskalkar, 1960, pp. 4–5. The Punjab studies have appeared since 1932–33 in an annual series under the title *Family Budget Studies*.

[2] This estimate is computed from data presented in Dandekar, 1954, Tables 28, 51 and 53. See also an estimate coming very close to the one made here by Panikar, 1961, Table 5.

should be reckoned at not more than perhaps one-tenth this amount. Hence, on the basis of the data of the National Sample Survey, we may not go far wrong if we assume a gross investment by each rural family of the order of Rs. 150. Since annual gross income of each rural family in 1950–51 amounted to Rs. 1,309 (computed by Panikar, 1961, Appendix), the rate of gross savings was in the neighbourhood of almost 12 per cent.

A second estimate was made by the Central Statistical Organization for the years 1948–49 to 1953–54. These figures are not quite inde-pendent of the findings of the National Sample Survey, i.e. the same raw data have partly been used to arrive at the estimates. In other words, the actual field data on which the estimates are based are to a large extent the same as those with which the National Sample Survey estimates have been constructed, and the two estimates, therefore, may be expected to be similar. The estimates of the Central Statistical Organization cover only a portion of the total private investment in Indian agriculture, namely, improvement of land, the construction of irrigation works, the procurement of agricultural equipment and the construction of rural dwellings, cattle sheds and other farm build-ings. The figures also include some investment in implements and machinery for small industry and a substantial portion of this industry is not located in rural areas. Moreover, although some small-scale 'industrial' production is carried on by peasant families during those parts of the year when field work does not occupy all available labour fully, the total investment in other than agricul-tural implements and machinery by peasants is very small.

As in the case of the National Sample Survey estimates, investment in cash and near-cash assets is not available. Hence, in spite of the inclusion of cottage industry, the investment estimates of the Central Statistical Organization must be regarded as falling short of actual total investment in rural India. The actual figures reported by the Central Statistical Organization show non-Governmental gross invest-ment in the rural sector to come to Rs. 326 crores, depreciation to amount to Rs. 126 crores, and net investment to Rs. 200 crores (Central Statistical Organization, 1955, p. 157). Comparing the gross figure with the one we derived from the National Sample Survey, we find that the estimate by the Central Statistical Organization is less than half that presented earlier. For if we assume that there were fifty-eight million rural families, gross investment per family comes not to Rs. 150, but only Rs. 65.20. How much of this difference is accounted for by omission of items which should have been included and how much is accounted for by bias is impossible to say.

Fortunately, we have still a third estimate on an all-India basis that was done probably more carefully and is based on more exhaustive investigations than the two estimates already cited. From November,

1951, to July, 1952, the Reserve Bank of India carried out the All-India Rural Credit Survey. This survey, which led to field studies in randomly selected villages in seventy-five districts of India, constitutes perhaps the largest and, from the viewpoint of survey methodology, most careful, far-flung field survey ever undertaken in India's countryside. Though the investigators were concerned primarily with establishing the degree of indebtedness of the Indian peasant, the reasons for which he borrowed, the persons or institutions from whom he borrowed, and the rates of interest to which he was subjected, it was clear that in the course of investigation considerable attention should also have been paid to the investment activities of the Indian cultivator.[1]

Some of the capital expenditures made by Indian peasants appear in the form of savings, e.g. expenditures for shares in co-operative societies, deposits in the postal savings scheme or in banks, and money lent out to other peasants. Also, there were quite a few farm families who reported expenditures on capital formation on 'non-farm business', i.e. expenditures on implements and machinery employed in subsidiary operations. For example, it was found that 54 per cent of the farm families in Palamau district of Bihar reported expenditures on capital formation in non-farm business. In this district, a large proportion of farm families are engaged in the collection of lac from the nearby forest, and the collection, storage and processing of lac involve a certain amount of expenditure in various materials and equipment. Similarly, in Quilon district, Kerala, where the coir industry and fishing are widely practised, a large proportion of cultivating families made capital expenditures on items employed in these businesses. However, in the few districts in which it was found that a sizeable proportion of farm families made capital expenditures for other than agricultural capital, these associated occupations were closely related to the exploitation either of forest or of water resources, or the simple processing of farm products (e.g. butter making, sugar cane crushing, rice hulling, etc.). Taking all seventy-five districts together, only 4 per cent of all farm families surveyed made capital expenditures in other than agricultural production.

If we turn now to capital formation in agriculture as such, we find the following picture. The Rural Credit Survey presents in one table an estimate of the constituent items of capital expenditure for purposes other than the purchase of land and livestock. These estimates

---

[1] See the Reserve Bank of India, *All-India Rural Credit Survey*, Volume I, The *Survey Report* in two parts, one dealing with 'Rural Families', the other with 'Credit Agencies', Bombay, 1956 and 1957; Volume II, *General Report*, Bombay, 1954; Volume III, *Technical Report*, Bombay, 1956. All subsequent references will be to Volume I, hereafter cited '*Survey Report*'.

Capital, Saving and Credit in Peasant Societies

are reproduced in the following table (*Survey Report*, p. 727):

	Rs. crores
Reclamation of land	24
Bunding and other land improvements	42
Digging and repairing of wells	56
Development of other irrigation sources	17
Laying of new orchards and plantations	26
Purchase of implements, machinery, etc.	57
Construction of farm houses, cattle sheds, etc.	26
Miscellaneous	50
Total	298

These are gross expenditures and include maintenance and repair costs estimated at Rs. 50 crores. If this amount is deducted, the net investment in these types of capital amounts to about Rs. 250 crores. To these expenditures must be added the expenditure on the net purchase (i.e. purchase minus sale) of land and livestock, which amounted to Rs. 7 and Rs. 26 respectively per rural household. Hence, for the sixty million rural household expenditures on these two items came to Rs. 42 and 156 crores. In brief, investment in productive capital in agriculture net of maintenance costs amounted to a total of Rs. 448 crores. To this should be added gross expenditure on rural housing, which was estimated by the Rural Credit Survey to amount to Rs. 250 crores and from which Rs. 80 crores are to be deducted for maintenance and repair costs, giving a total of Rs. 170 crores. Hence the total expenditure for the construction, maintenance and expansion of capital and durable consumers goods in agriculture net of maintenance and repairs amounted to almost Rs. 620 crores (*Survey Report*, pp. 586, 609, 728). According to the National Income Committee, the total net output of agriculture, animal husbandry and rural housing amounted to Rs. 4,971 crores in 1950–51.[1] We will not go far wrong if we assume it to have been approximately Rs. 5,000 crores in 1951–52 (the year to which our capital investment figures refer). On the basis of this assumption, gross capital formation in Indian agriculture amounted to 12.5 per cent. Even if we deduct depreciation costs, as proposed by the National Income Committee, of about Rs. 80 crores on agricultural capital and Rs. 120 crores on rural housing and other buildings, we obtain a figure of net capital formation of about Rs. 420 crores, or almost 8.5 per cent of total net output. Finally, if we deduct the investment in rural housing and confine our estimate only to productive capital employed in farming, we obtain a net capital amount of Rs. 368 crores (Rs. 448 crores minus Rs. 80 crores), or a net

[1] See Government of India, Ministry of Finance, Department of Economic Affairs, 1954, pp. 45, 51, 101.

352

investment of slightly over 7 per cent. This may not be sufficient for what W. W. Rostow has called a take-off, but it appears to be a fair performance for a system of farming in which only simple tools and technologically relatively backward methods of production are applied.[1]

Whichever of these figures is considered most relevant—and from the standpoint of farm production, the rate of net investment in productive facilities of agriculture should be considered most seriously—they have not been so widely discussed by students of Indian farm economics as they deserve. I know of only three discussions in which they have been commented upon (though with slightly different emphasis than in the present paper); two of these treatments accept them as substantially accurate, and the third rejects them as false (Krishna, 1961; Lackdawala, *et al.* 1958; Thorner, 1960). It should be noted that, on first view, these data might appear suspicious, especially if we consider that, during the First Five Year Plan, total outlay for agriculture on public account amounted to Rs. 284 crores for the five years; and if outlay on agriculture and combined power and irrigation schemes is added, the total for five years amounted to Rs. 716 crores, or an annual average of Rs. 143 crores (Government of India, Planning Commission, 1957, p. 19). Since a sizeable portion of this outlay must be charged to the development of power facilities rather than irrigation installations, it is probably not wrong to assume that net private capital formation for productive purposes in agriculture was at least three times net public capital formation for the same end. The importance of these data is that they show that, even in so development-conscious a country as India, about two-thirds of total investment in productive capital applied to agriculture is provided

---

[1] The presentation in this paragraph follows very closely a similar computation of net investment in Indian agriculture made by Raj Krishna, 'Some Aspects of Land Reform and Economic Development in India', 1961.

Any analysis of rural savings and investment in India can, at best, only provide approximate data, since part of the investment consists in the direct transformation of labour and other productive factors into real capital. One of the problems that arise in this context is the question of how to value these factors which are supplied, not through the intermediary of the market, but in kind. Even in instances of which certain services or goods are supplied by means of an exchange, the 'prices' at which they are obtained are based on customary or traditional valuations, rather than on current 'market' valuations. Hence whatever system of valuing these inputs is employed, an element of uncertainty cannot be eliminated. It becomes quite clear, from the discussion in the text above, that we have throughout employed such approximations; but since the estimates have been, on the whole, conservative, or have made use of proportions established with a fair degree of accuracy by such authorities as the National Income Committee, it is contended that the final figures reported in the text may be accepted as coming fairly close to the 'truth'. But it is granted that the question of valuation imposes a series of difficulties, some of which will be dealt with more explicitly in the last section of this essay.

M

for by private individuals and only about one-third by public sources.

To some, these relations have appeared unbelievable and they have disputed the accuracy of the findings of the Rural Credit Survey. To a large extent, this criticism is based upon alleged methodological flaws in the survey, a point we will take up later in this paper, but in part it is based on the absence of any confirming evidence of these rates of capital formation. Clearly, the data published by the Central Statistical Organization cannot be regarded as confirming evidence, since they include only a portion of investment in agriculture, and, above all, omit such important items as investment in livestock, tree crops and the like.

Although the findings of the National Sample Survey could be considered confirming evidence of the Rural Credit Survey findings, no one, with the exception of Panikar, has so far considered it worth while to retabulate these data so as to find a figure for savings or investment in the rural sector as a whole. But the confirmation of an approximate savings rate in Indian agriculture depends not only upon the rather high degree of coincidence between the gross savings rate yielded by the Rural Credit Survey and the National Sample Survey. Further confirmation is provided by additional local, regional, or village-wide studies which have been undertaken. The more important of these surveys have been reported by Panikar, who summarizes related findings from the Punjab, Hyderabad and the eastern Indian jute region, and discovers that agricultural gross investment in these regions varied from 8 to 14 per cent in recent years (Panikar, pp. 64–84). Additional evidence is provided further by P. D. Diskalkar in his study of Pimple Saudagar, a village near Poona. Diskalkar does not publish adequate data to estimate total rural savings, but from his account a minimum figure for savings may be deduced, for he shows that the annual gross income of the village he surveyed was almost Rs. 163,000 and that yearly expenditure on a lift irrigation scheme (in the form of direct expenditures for the scheme, as well as the repayment of loans made by the Government of Bombay State for the original establishment of the scheme) amounted to a little over Rs. 27,000 (Diskalkar, 1960, p. 155). Hence the rate of investment in Pimple Saudagar for the year under review may be assumed to exceed 16.5 per cent.

In the recent past, still another far-flung survey of agricultural production has been undertaken in India, the first results of which have been published in five volumes under the title *Studies in Economics of Farm Management.*[1] These studies, which were all carried out by employing similar methods of investigation in several regions of the coun-

[1] Government of India, Ministry of Food and Agriculture, 1957–58. The volumes deal with selected farms in two districts of each of the following States: Bombay, Madras, Punjab, Uttar Pradesh and West Bengal.

try, produced some very interesting results which will be discussed in greater detail in this paper. Unfortunately, the published results are not identical in the five volumes: though field procedures were, on the whole, the same, the volumes on Madras, Punjab, West Bengal and Uttar Pradesh do not contain useable data on investment in agriculture. Fortunately, the group working on the report for Bombay State considered this question of sufficient importance to include data on agricultural investment in its report.

The Bombay Farm Management study was carried out as follows: Two districts, Ahmednagar and Nasik, were selected, and, in each, several villages were chosen by a process of random sampling. Then careful examinations of the productive activity of randomly selected 421 farm holdings distributed among a total of twenty-three villages were carried out. The unit of investigation was not the village, but the farm holding. The farms were divided into two sub-samples, and in the case of each sub-sample a somewhat different method of recording economic data was undertaken. We have thus data for four sub-samples and can combine them if we wish to get more highly aggregated data.

The data in which we are interested in this context relate to investment in agriculture. Fortunately, the field workers in this study were instructed to ask questions, both as to the creation of new capital structures and the acquisition of new capital goods by farmers, as well as their liquidation. The following forms of capital investment were registered: (1) purchase of and repairs to implements; (2) purchase of land; (3) purchase of livestock; (4) digging of wells; (5) repairs to bunds; and (6) repairs to buildings. Since the buildings are farm buildings, other than houses, the total of this would constitute an approximate amount of gross investment. From this there was deducted liquidation of livestock by sale or death of the animals, liquidation of land through sale, depreciation of implements, etc. The resulting data may thus be regarded as being half-way between gross and net investment. To be sure, in a study expressly concerned with investment, somewhat different data would have been collected; but it is believed that the totals for net investment are not far off from what would have been arrived at by alternative procedures, provided the interpretations of instructions given to field workers were clear and proper valuations were applied to the various capital items acquired and liquidated. We present the relevant data for the four sub-samples in Table 1.

This table raises a number of problems, among them the obvious discrepancies between the amounts involved in Method (1) and Method (2), and the even more startling discrepancy in the rate of net new investment in the villages of Nasik district depending upon which method is chosen.

TABLE 1

RATE OF CAPITAL FORMATION IN BOMBAY STATE, 1954–55

District	New investment (Rs.)	Total acreage (acres)	Total product (Rs.)	New investment as % of total product
Method 1				
Ahmednagar	2,078	1,599	30,205	6·88
Nasik	804	953	16,789	4·79
Both districts	2,882	2,552	47,003	6·13
Method 2				
Ahmednagar	15,073	4,238	169,490	8·89
Nasik	24,997	1,799	108,638	23·00
Both districts	40,070	6,038	278,128	14·41

Source: Government of India, Ministry of Food and Agriculture, *Studies in Economics of Farm Management in Bombay* (Delhi, 1958), pp. 202, 231, 232, 233.

A comparison of the upper and lower panels of Table 1 shows that the two samples are of very different size. The total acreage covered by Method (2) is more than double that by Method (1); the total net investment ascertained by Method (2) in Ahmednagar is more than seven times, and in Nasik more than thirty times, that ascertained by Method (1); and as a result, the rates of net investment differ greatly. Differences are observed not only in acreage and the absolute amount of net investment, but also in total product, which, according to Method (2), was almost six times that found by Method (1). These differences are explained chiefly by the fact that Method (1) lists only activities (investment, production, etc.) for part of the year. Whereas the collection of data according to Method (2) covered a full calendar year, that according to Method (1) covered only a few months of the *rabi* season. But apart from this, the interpretation of net investment and perhaps also the valuation by the field workers charged with the collection of data according to Method (2) may have differed from those of field workers charged with the collection of data according to Method (1). From the published data, it is impossible to ascertain where the differences stem from, but the figure of 23 per cent of net new investment in Nasik district, which results from the investigation according to Method (2), makes us suspect that a special investment effort may have taken place in the villages studied during 1954–56. We would, of course, like to know more about it, since this knowledge might give us a clue to what long-sustained rate of investment is possible in rural India. Here is a blatant case, showing how important it may be for large-scale economic surveys to be supported by careful studies in depth.

However, one result appears quite clearly from Table 1. Invest-

356

ment in productive agricultural capital as a proportion of total output may easily reach a magnitude of 8 per cent, and the data presented in this table should, on the whole, be regarded as constituting full confirmatory evidence of the findings of the Rural Credit Survey and the National Sample Survey. The two districts in which this investigation has been carried out do not appear to be unusual. Nasik, to be sure, is commonly regarded as the more prosperous area, but even there many farm enterprises earned little more than their actual cash outlays, and neither in Ahmednagar nor in Nasik was the total 'profitability' of farming very different from other parts of India, as can be ascertained from the companion volumes to the Bombay State study.

II

The question must now be asked as to how this rate of investment is financed. We must not forget that the investment data presented in Table 1 refer only to productive investment in agriculture. Peasants also invest in other assets, e.g. dwelling houses, financial assets such as shares in co-operative societies or deposits in banks or the postal savings system, objects made of precious metals, and last but not least, productive capital in fields other than farming. If we find that additions to productive capital invested in agriculture amount to more than 8 per cent of total income, total investment in the formation of durable assets of all kinds doubtless is larger than this amount and may be assumed to reach a magnitude of 10 or even 12 per cent of total income. It becomes, therefore, important to ask whether and to what extent this formation of assets is financed out of savings or through credit, and what forms of credit are supplied and under what conditions.

There exist few adequate empirical studies of the rate and amount of total savings in India. The best published data that I have seen are contained in an essay by Bhatt and a publication of the Reserve Bank of India (Bhatt, 1958; Reserve Bank of India, 1960). But these publications do not contain detailed data on rural savings, and the rough published data are based on an assumed savings rate of approximately 5 per cent, rather than on actual findings as to what proportion of rural incomes are actually saved. Hence, since many of the expenditures on productive capital or durable consumers' goods which we found are apparently made in rural India and must be financed out of some accumulations of previous savings or out of borrowings, an analysis of how these expenditures are financed would provide us with an indication, not of the magnitude or proportion of savings, but of the importance which cash savings have in the expenditure patterns of Indian cultivators. The Rural Credit

Survey has collected some data (on an all-India-wide scale) of sources for different expenditures, and these data have been assembled in Table 2.

TABLE 2

SOURCES OF EXPENDITURE FOR DIFFERENT ITEMS BY INDIAN CULTIVATORS

Item of expenditure	Total amount spent by average family (Rs.)	Current income	Past savings	Sale of assets	Borrow-ing	Other sources
		\multicolumn{5}{c}{*Source of expenditure in per cent*}				
1. Family Expenditures:						
Construction and repair of houses	61	46·8	23·9	2·1	25·6	1·6
Household utensils and furniture	9	71·4	8·1	1·7	8·1	10·7
Clothing and bedding	132	84·8	4·0	0·7	9·3	1·2
Death ceremonies	13	47·6	10·5	2·6	37·5	1·8
Marriage ceremonies	86	31·9	21·1	2·7	42·3	2·0
Medical expenses	26	63·0	5·4	2·7	27·8	1·1
Educational expenses	18	86·9	5·8	0·6	5·5	1·2
Litigation expenses	16	43·3	8·5	2·8	42·5	2·9
2. Expenditures on Pro- ductive Capital Assets:						
Purchase of land	31	24·3	21·6	13·1	37·9	3·1
Purchase of livestock	68	29·3	13·2	12·4	44·0	1·1
Other capital expenditures	82	54·4	12·1	1·3	31·0	1·2

Source: Reserve Bank of India, *All-India Rural Credit Survey*, Volume I, Part 1 (Bombay, 1956), pp. 402–697 *passim.*

The items listed in this table comprise only categories of non-regularly occurring expenditures, which imply a rather sizeable out-lay of cash. This is even true of expenditures for clothing and bedding, and this category has been included, because in some parts of India these items are purchased at certain times of the year in rather sizeable quantity rather than on a more regular basis throughout the year. Now, if we observe the column headed 'past savings', we find that their importance as a source of funds is particularly great in the cases of construction and repair of houses, the purchase of land and expenditures associated with marriage ceremonies. They are of lesser significance in the case of purchase of livestock, of other capital assets used in agriculture, and in providing for the expenses of death ceremonies. A conclusion which can be drawn from this allocation of sources of expenditures is that past savings are used apparently mainly in those cases in which a particular expenditure (and its magnitude) is associated to some extent with considerations of status preservation or enhancement. This is most clearly true of expenditures for marriage ceremonies; but the size and elaborateness of a house, and the total amount of land held, are also important prestige-supporting features in an Indian village. In other words, past savings are used primarily for expenditures which will enhance a person's or his family's status, and only secondarily for expenses which will add to the productive capital of the peasant holding. Savings are used with least frequency for expenditures which add to the general level of comfort of a peasant family.

As can be seen from Table 2, the main alternative sources for non-recurring expenditures are current income and borrowings. We will examine borrowings somewhat more in detail further on, but it may be useful to take a brief look at the role which current income plays as a source of financing these expenditures, since this may reveal also—even though indirectly—some of the prevailing attitudes with regard to saving. First we find that, among all the expenditure items, the purchase of clothing, educational expenses, the purchase of household equipment and furniture, medical expenses, and, to a somewhat smaller degree, the purchase of various forms of capital equipment for agricultural production, are financed to the largest extent out of current earnings. All these expenditures may be considered as more regularly occurring expenses than the others listed in Table 2. Land and livestock are normally bought only once every few years; though the repair of houses is a more or less regular expense in India, since the monsoon rains do severe damage to most houses each year, the actual construction of a house cannot be regarded as a regular expense. And litigation, death and marriages occur only at substantial intervals in most peasant families, Hence, the table confirms a general principle, i.e. that current earnings are used primarily for current expenditures, and that the more regular an expenditure is the more common will be the practice of financing it out of the regular income of the family. Thus the chief alternative for the use of past savings as a source for financing family or capital expenses is not current income but borrowing.

But before we turn to borrowing, we must look at another item in Table 2, which, though small, is precisely of interest because it constitutes one form savings take. I refer to the role played by the sale of assets as a source of financing certain major non-recurring expenditures. As Table 2 shows, the sale of assets is of importance only in the case of purchase of land and cattle. In all family expenditures, it plays a negligible role. This gives the impression that assets are used almost solely in transactions in which other productive assets are acquired. But, in part, this interpretation depends upon what is meant by the term 'sale of assets'. Unfortunately, the Rural Credit Survey does not define this concept explicitly; but the clear implication may be drawn that only the sale of productive assets, mainly land

and livestock, were considered under this head. This would also explain why the item 'sale of assets' appears more prominently in the case of purchase of land and livestock than in that of family expenditures. In the former case it constitutes primarily an exchange of one piece of productively useable capital for another.

But Indian peasant families have assets other than land, livestock and implements. First among them are houses—which, admittedly, would only rarely be sold—and next to houses, they have a certain amount of financial assets, cash and ornaments made of precious metals. The Rural Credit Survey nowhere seems to have been concerned with the amount and value of these ornaments which are owned by Indian peasant families. Neither is expenditure for them singled out, nor are their sales recorded separately. I presume that the acquisition of ornaments is subsumed under either 'clothing and bedding' or under 'household furniture and fixtures'. Perhaps they were left entirely out of consideration, even though they represent an asset which plays a decided role in peasant economics. Clearly, their acquisition forms a part of the expenditures incurred at marriage and other ceremonies, and they are widely used as security for loans.[1] We have no estimate of the value of ornaments in the possession of Indian agricultural families. According to the findings of the National Sample Survey (Third Round), annual expenditures on ornaments ranged from Rs. 5.34 per rural household (cultivators and non-cultivators included) in East India to Rs.39.67 in North India, or an average of Rs. 19.62 for all India. Since, according to the same report, the annual average total gross consumers' expenditures of rural households amounted to Rs. 1,493 per family, expenditure for ornaments constituted 1.31 per cent of this total.[2]

It would clearly be appropriate to add this figure to the savings of households, especially since, as we have seen, ornaments perform a widespread function as security in the case of small borrowings, and since there is evidence that they are sold if special financial demands are made on a family—for example, in the case of marriage or litigation. Some further evidence that ornaments constitute properly a part of a family's savings becomes clear when we examine some of the answers solicited by the Rural Credit Survey in the investigation of financial assets held by Indian cultivators. Only 4.5 per cent of all cultivating families surveyed by the Rural Credit Survey held some financial assets, such as shares in co-operative societies, bank or

[1] Substantial evidence on this point could be provided from various studies on the economics of Indian villages undertaken by official and private sources. See, e.g. Punjab, Board of Economic Enquiry, 1931, p. 106; Mukhtyar, 1930, p. 154.

[2] See Government of India, Ministry of Finance, National Sample Survey, 1954, pp. 54, 26.

postal savings deposits or National Savings Certificates. The outlay for these instruments of savings was small, and most farm families, when questioned on this point, replied that they did not acquire them because they had no margin for savings. But in thirty-two districts of the seventy-five which were surveyed, varying numbers of cultivators said that they preferred to purchase gold or jewellery to acquiring securities or similar assets, and in eighteen districts some cultivators answered that it was their customary practice to purchase gold every year.

There is no question that the habit of acquiring financial assets is spreading slowly through the countryside. In some exceptional instances, it has even been reported that 'barren' ornaments were sold in order to convert the savings into Government bonds which would yield a cash return. Yet a certain amount of the cultivator's savings are still held in the form of gold, jewellery and ornaments, since here again the particular form in which the asset is held contributes to the status demands of the peasant family. Though gold and silver bangles are not worn generally, they do come out of their chests and other places of storage on the occasion of weddings and other cermonies. In addition to securities and ornaments, some families of cultivators hold their savings in the form of cash, a fact which was also revealed in the Rural Credit Survey. In fifty-eight of seventy-five districts, varying numbers of peasant families reported that they preferred to hold their liquid assets in cash rather than in various forms of savings certificates or bank deposits (*Survey Report*, Pt. 1, pp. 533, 542).

Apart from securities or deposits, cash or ornaments, a number of peasant families' assets are held in the form of loans to other peasant families. This fact is also made clear from the Rural Credit Survey in its report on the kinds of lenders to indebted peasant families. In its discussion of credit agencies, the Rural Credit Survey reports that, of the total outstanding debt, 25.2 per cent was owed to agriculturalist moneylenders, and 11.4 per cent to relatives. It is granted that both these concepts, which are not precisely defined in the survey, are somewhat vague and that, under both headings, other than peasant households may be included. But we are here not interested in the precise shares which each lending agency provided, and it is not of importance to us whether all relatives and all so-called agriculturalist moneylenders actually were cultivators themselves. There is scarcely any doubt that, even if some of them were traders, professional people, or otherwise not engaged in agriculture, the bulk of them were cultivators. The amount of outstanding debt to these two classes of lenders by all rural families (cultivators and non-cultivators combined) amounted to Rs. 103.7 per rural household. However, the total of this debt was distributed among the different lending agencies; it shows that some cultivating families apparently invested a sizeable amount of their savings in loans to other cultivators.[1]

It is impossible, on the basis of available data, to estimate the proportion of savings in the form of cash, precious metals, securities, deposits and outstanding loans; but they doubtless form only a small portion of the total assets of peasant cultivators. The bulk of their assets are in the form of houses, land, livestock and other kinds of productive capital. As concerns these assets, we have a number of interesting, and on the whole consistent, sets of data from two independent investigations, i.e. the Rural Credit Survey and the Studies of the Economics of Farm Management. These data are presented in Table 3.

A few words in explanation of the data presented in Table 3 may be in order. Both panels show the heavy preponderance of land among all the assets listed. This preponderance appears to be even more pronounced in Panel B than in Panel A. The explanation for this is that the Farm Management Studies include all land cultivated by a household, whether owned by the cultivator or not, whereas the Rural Credit Survey included only owned land. Next in importance are buildings; and among these, again, the value of dwellings appears to be outstanding. The proportion of productive investment in sheds and other buildings used for productive purposes, and even in irrigation facilities, is relatively minor. For example, in the Punjab (according to the Farm Management Study) investment in wells owned by the cultivators individually does not exceed more than 1 per cent of the total value of all assets, and in Bombay the proportion of investment in individually owned irrigation facilities is similarly of very small magnitude. Yet in both areas, irrigation plays a very important role, since in the Punjab, for example, output on irrigated land is valued at between Rs. 130 and 140, whereas on unirrigated land it is valued only at Rs. 54 to 69 (Ministry of Food and Agriculture, 1957–58, *Punjab*, pp. 45, 65–6).

The item of irrigation facilities, probably more than any other, shows how distorted may become our estimates of rural savings and investment if private and public (or community) facilities are held strictly separate. Irrigation technology demands that installations employed for this purpose be owned and operated by some public body, co-operative, or other organization representing a large number of cultivators. Though a good part of the irrigation facilities

---

[1] *Survey Report*, Part 2, p. 3. The fact that the bulk of the credit available to cultivators comes from the savings made in the rural sector in India is stressed also by Panikar, 1961, p. 66. This fact is important not only because it shows the relatively sharp cleavage in the economic sphere between town and country in India; but also because it exhibits a significant socio-structural feature of Indian society in emphasizing again the relative social and cultural separateness of rural as against urban population.

Capital Formation in Indian Agricultural Society

TABLE 3

PERCENTAGE DISTRIBUTION OF CULTIVATION ASSETS IN SELECTED REGIONS OF INDIA

	Total assets of average household (Rs.)	Land	Buildings (including irrigation work)	Livestock	Implements and machinery	Other Assets (loans and securities)
(A) Rural Credit Survey						
1. Upper Strata*						
Bihar-Bengal	9,728	74·4	17·0	6·2	1·0	1·4
Eastern U.P.	3,081	45·5	33·1	14·5	3·1	3·8
Western U.P.	6,903	49·7	30·8	14·7	3·7	1·1
Punjab	19,733	75·8	14·9	6·1	1·3	1·9
Central India	5,008	40·1	27·1	28·2	3·2	1·4
North Deccan	10,509	67·5	18·3	10·0	2·9	1·3
South Deccan	12,970	74·2	12·4	6·7	3·1	3·6
All-India	8,376	67·3	18·9	9·7	2·3	1·8
2. Lower Strata*						
Bihar-Bengal	2,401	68·4	21·9	9·2	0·3	0·3
Eastern U.P.	780	20·7	51·3	24·1	2·5	1·4
Western U.P.	2,229	33·6	38·0	21·4	4·4	2·6
Punjab	7,144	65·6	23·0	7·9	1·7	1·8
Central India	1,284	29·4	26·6	38·6	4·6	0·8
North Deccan	2,824	63·8	21·9	12·2	1·9	0·3
South Deccan	2,026	64·0	21·7	8·6	1·1	4·6
All-India	2,376	58·6	24·4	13·4	2·2	1·4
(B) Economics of Farm Management Studies	Average size of Farm (acres)					
Bombay	21·70	81·79	2·14†	11·37	4·58	0·12
Madras	6·9	70·0	22·0	7·0	1·0	0·0
Punjab	17·82	70·45	14·35	12·21	2·99	0·0
Uttar Pradesh	10·27	80·81	6·47†	9·96	2·76	0·0
West Bengal	2·87	55·3	26·3	6·5	1·0	11·0‡

Notes:

* The concepts 'upper strata' and 'lower strata' are used by the Rural Credit Survey to designate the wealthier and poorer halves of the cultivators surveyed.

† Data for Bombay and Uttar Pradesh include only buildings used productively and exclude the value of dwellings.

‡ This figure for 'other assets' in West Bengal appears to relate to irrigation works, but since it is not explained in the report one cannot be certain. Hence it has been listed separately.

Sources: For Panel A: Reserve Bank of India, *All-India Rural Credit Survey*, Vol. I, Part I, pp. 117–25.

For Panel B: Government of India, Ministry of Food and Agriculture, *Studies in Economics of Farm Management*, 5 vols., Delhi, 1957–58, *passim.*

available to cultivators are produced and owned by a state or the central Government, a substantial number of these facilities are owned by some association of peasants or tend to become acquired by the peasants in some form of sharing agreement. An example of this process is provided, for instance, in Diskalkar's description of the lift irrigation scheme in Pimple Saudagar. Irrigation is dependent upon a pump, the installation of which was financed in part by the peasants and in part by the Government of the state of Bombay. But the peasants are acquring full ownership of the pump by gradually repaying the Government, whose contribution is classified as a so-called *tagavi* loan. As we have seen before, current annual expenses for new irrigation installations (wells) plus payment of interest and repayment of the *tagavi* loans come to more than 16 per cent of the gross annual income of the community.[1]

A further feature which may be observed, especially in Panel A of Table 3, is the great variation of the share of land among assets between different regions. Among the upper- and lower-strata cultivators, land constitutes more than half the total assets, except in Uttar Pradesh and Central India. This may be explained by the fact that, in these two regions, tenancy is more widespread than in the rest of India. Finally, we find that the proportion of assets held in the form of livestock varies greatly in different regions, though it is understandably larger on the farms of smaller and poorer peasants than on those of larger and wealthier cultivators. The general picture which emerges from the Table indicates one of the main reasons for the backwardness and relatively low productivity of Indian agriculture: the under-investment in assets other than land.[2] It is not surprising that—as can be seen from the last three rows in Table 2—expenditures on productive assets other than land are very high. Moreover,

[1] See Ministry of Food and Agriculture, 1957–58, Punjab, p. 65, and Diskalkar, 1960, pp. 33–4. A case study like that of Pimple Saudagar makes one suspect that, in spite of their apparent height, the data on gross investment reported by the Farm Management Studies in Bombay State from Nasik District (which were presented in our Table 1) are accurate, especially if much of the investment in the district consisted in the expansion or construction of new irrigation facilities.

[2] In part, the high preponderance of land may be a result of over-valuation. Land is only rarely sold and, as is admitted, for example, in the Farm Management Study of Uttar Pradesh, 'the price of land varies according to its grade, location and availability of irrigation. In the enquiry it was found to vary from Rs. 500 to Rs. 3,000 per acre. There are very few cases of actual sales of land, therefore, the prices reported are based on personal enquiries from the farmers. As such the element of personal judgment has entered very largely in the estimates of land prices which are not very reliable individually but are fairly reliable as an average' (p. 34). It is difficult to see how individually unreliable valuations can give a reliable average, and one may suspect that the farmers questioned were more likely to overvalue than to undervalue their land. But even if this bias is taken into account, it still remains true that land makes up a very large proportion of total capital in production.

the data presented there refer to gross expenditures on land and livestock, i.e. only purchases of land and livestock were considered, but sales of these two items were not. As already mentioned earlier, the net purchases (i.e. purchase minus sales) of land per rural household amounted to Rs. 7 and the net purchases of livestock to Rs. 42. Hence even these two (net) expenditures together remain below the average expenditures on other forms of productive agricultural capital.

Innovation in Indian agriculture may, of course, be purely an outflow of application of new knowledge, i.e. changes in productive activity caused by better methods, without any significant change in the structure of productive assets. This is unlikely, since it is difficult to conceive that the development of new methods would not call for new forms of capital investment. Some evidence on this point is provided in a study by C. H. Shah of economically progressing and declining farm families in Maharashtra. I reproduce here one of Shah's tables which relates, in particular, to investment issues.

TABLE 4

INVESTMENT AND RELATED EXPENDITURE OF THIRTY-SIX
FAMILIES IN KODINAR TALUKA, BOMBAY STATE

	Progressing families		Declining families	
Items of expenditure	Amount in Rs.	Per cent	Amount in Rs.	Per cent
Housing (major repair and construction)	22,350	30·9	2,540	36·7
Purchase of bullocks	3,010	4·2	750	10·8
Construction of wells and purchase of oil engines	18,325	25·3	—	—
Land purchase and sale	14,135	19·5	—2,950	—42·6
Purchase of implements	1,230	1·7	—	—
Social expense (marriage, etc.)	10,050	13·9	6,050	87·3
Others (purchase of gold, etc., and litigation expense)	260	0·4	540	7·8
Cash	3,000	4·1	—	—
Total	72,360	100·0	6,930	100·0

Source: C. H. Shah, *Conditions of Economic Progress of Farmers* (Bombay: Indian Society of Agricultural Economics, n.d. [*ca.* 1960]), p. 22.

As can be seen from Table 4, the progressive farm families have allocated 25.3 per cent of their investment expenditures to the purchase of wells and oil engines for driving pumps and 1.7 per cent for the purchase of implements, whereas the non-progressive families have not allocated any funds for this. In fact, the only expense which may be regarded as falling in the class of productive investment that

365

non-progressive families made is the purchase of bullocks; and this is so basic a need for farming in India that refraining from such expenditure would have meant their relinquishing independent farming altogether. Moreover, when we read the case studies which Shah appends to his summary, we find that progressive farmers are distinct from their non-progressive brethren in that they use iron ploughs, tend to replace the old-fashioned Persian wheels by machine-driven pumps, use larger quantities of commercial fertilizers instead of farmyard manure, and have installed elaborate facilities for irrigation (Shah, 1960, p. 42). Hence it is quite clear that progress in the agriculture of India requires not merely more knowledge on the part of the peasant, but also a restructuring of the capital equipment which he uses, and, in many instances, increased investment in new forms of capital, i.e. new machinery and equipment.

III

We shall now turn briefly to the third topic under consideration, the role of credit in Indian peasant society. Not very much need be said in this place on this topic, because an exhaustive analysis of this problem is available in the voluminous reports of the Rural Credit Survey.[1] Rather than digest this work of several thousand pages, we will confine our attention to three problems: the role of borrowing for non-recurring expenditures, as presented in Table 2; the role of borrowing in the picture of total expenditure of rural households in India; and the analysis of credit agencies operating in the Indian villages.

From Table 2, it appears that borrowing is resorted to primarily in the cases of death and marriage ceremonies, the incurring of litigation expenses, and expenditures made on land, livestock and other productive capital assets in agriculture. If we leave out of consideration expenses for death ceremonies and litigation, because neither of these items is very large, we find that the main occasion for borrowing is either the acquisition of productive assets or a marriage.

Let us now look more closely at the borrowings of Indian rural inhabitants themselves. Unfortunately, the available data refer only to all persons in rural regions (cultivators and non-cultivators combined), though we do have some breakdown as to the rate of overall borrowings among the two groups. The total amount borrowed per family per year amounted to Rs. 159.9 during 1951–52; among cultivating families the average borrowed was Rs. 209.5, among non-cultivating families the average was 66.1. The much higher figure for cultivators does not stem from their greater credit needs, but

[1] The findings of the Rural Credit Survey on borrowing and indebtedness have, moreover, been admirably summarized in an essay by Jakhade, 1958, pp. 249–99.

Capital Formation in Indian Agricultural Society

rather from the lesser credit-worthiness of the non-cultivators. Land is an important asset to have when it comes to borrowing; and debts can, on the whole, be incurred most easily by those peasants who have land to offer as security for their borrowing. These are all-India averages, but there is a wide spread regionally. For example, the lowest borrowings are found in Orissa among non-cultivating rural families, where they amounted to Rs. 23.7, and the largest borrowing was encountered among cultivators on the south-east coast of India (Madras State), where they came to Rs. 305. These figures relate to regional averages per family, not to single families (Jakhade, 1958, p. 259). The variations show that borrowing patterns vary a great deal, that they are not strictly related to the level of wealth or income in a given region, and that undoubtedly many factors, which in a predominantly quantitive survey were not investigated, played a considerable role in both the motivations and readiness to borrow on the part of the debtors and the willingness to lend on the part of creditors. In other words, however satisfactory it may be to have nationwide averages and regional variations of the rate of borrowing, the explanation for both the overall level and, especially, the variations, requires much more careful studies in depth than could be afforded in the Rural Credit Survey.

If we now break down the all-India average of Rs. 159.9 and examine all the purposes for which rural people borrowed, we find the result presented in Table 5.

TABLE 5

PURPOSES OF BORROWING OF RURAL FAMILIES IN INDIA, 1951-52

| | Percentage of total borrowings | | | |
| | Non- | All | Amount in |
Purpose of borrowing	Cultivators	Cultivators	families	Rupees
Total borrowings	100·0	100·0	100·0	159·9
Capital expenditure on farm	31·5	6·0	27·8	44·4
Current expenditures on farm	10·6	1·1	9·3	14·9
Non-farm business expenditures	4·5	18·5	6·6	10·5
Family expenditures	53·4	74·4	56·3	90·1
Construction and repair of houses			8·1	13·0
Purchase of clothing, etc.			6·7	10·7
Marriage and death ceremonies			20·7	33·1
Medical and educational expenditures			4·6	7·3
Litigation charges			3·0	4·8
Repayment of debt			2·7	4·3
Other family expenditures			10·5	16·9

Source: Survey Report, Part 1, pp. 264–5, 502.

This table confirms, on the whole, the previously presented information, notably the data on borrowings in Table 2. Capital expenditures for farming expenses and expenses for marriage and death

367

Capital, Saving and Credit in Peasant Societies

ceremonies stand as the principal purposes for which loans are raised. Together, almost half of all the borrowings are for these two purposes. What is interesting in Table 5 (and does not appear from Table 2) is the high proportion of borrowings for 'other family expenditures'. Apparently most of these loans were made to finance ordinary current expenditures, many of them on food and similar necessities. The Rural Credit Survey reports that 'among the nine districts showing the highest average levels of borrowings for this purpose—Rs. 40 or above per family—those affected by adverse seasonal conditions number seven' (*Survey Report*, Part 1, p. 517).

We have confined ourselves so far to a discussion of borrowings during a particular year. Since the data which were presented have been averaged out over all of India or a particular region, they may be accepted as a fairly representative description of common practices—though, as we have just seen, the actual magnitude and distribution (by purpose) of borrowing may be affected by special conditions, such as crop failures or substantial changes in the socio-economic environment. It would be interesting to examine, in addition, the general state of indebtedness of peasant families instead of discussing this point in greater detail. We will merely present a few facts, which in themselves are of interest.

We have seen earlier that the average total amount borrowed during one year per cultivating family comes to almost Rs. 210. This should be compared with the average outstanding total debt per cultivating family of Rs. 364. In other words, the total debt is roughly equal to one and three-quarters times the annual borrowing. This means that a rather large part of the cultivators' debts have a fairly fast turnover, i.e. that many debts are repaid in less than a year's time. Considering the rather high rates of interest, and hence the high cost of borrowing, the borrowers would normally have every incentive to repay their debts as fast as possible. Though it is difficult to indicate the average cost of borrowing, some idea of this can be gained from the fact that, although Government loans were available at interest rates normally at not more than 6.25 per cent and loans from co-operative credit societies and land mortgage banks between 5.25 to 12.5 per cent, these sources supplied only a small portion of the total loans to rural debtors. Rates of interest charged by agricultural moneylenders, on the other hand, exceeded 18 per cent on 50 per cent or more of the total borrowings in thirty-three districts, and on 25 to 50 per cent of total borrowings in six additional districts. Since low-interest sources supplied at most 10 per cent of the loans incurred during 1951–52, high-interest sources at least 80 per cent of the loans (the other 10 per cent coming from sources where interest rates fluctuated widely—e.g. relatives), the conclusion may be fairly drawn that the cost of borrowing is high. Yet on an all-India basis, 63.3 per cent of all rural families are indebted, and among cultivating families this proportion rises to 69.2 per cent (Jakhade, 1958, pp. 272, 273, 281).

The fact of the Indian cultivator's indebtedness is well established. It was this concern, and also the high cost of borrowing, that led to the Rural Credit Survey. But indebtedness in itself is not a matter of concern, for almost all peasants have at all times been in debt, and the fact of indebtedness may almost be regarded as a normal fact of life of small peasant proprietors. What is a matter of concern is the relationship between the cost of borrowing and the return on the asset for which loans are made. Even high costs of borrowing need not disturb us if they are in line with the return at the margin in the peasant economy. In this context, the question of how Indian agriculture can be made more 'progressive'—i.e. how assets can be allocated to yield a higher net product—is of paramount importance. For the fixing of low interest rates by Government does not necessarily lead to improved forms of agricultural investment. It may, on the contrary, have the effect of leading to inefficiencies, favouritism, less productivity and inflation. Since, as we may confirm from the data presented in Table 5, a large portion of the borrowings are applied for consumption rather than productive purposes, low interest rates and easy conditions of borrowing are almost certain to have this result.

These conditions have, of course, also been recognized by the investigators of the Rural Credit Survey; and, in summarizing their findings, they have pointed to the 'social and economic' conditions and to certain 'basic weaknesses in the rural structure' as the fundamental factors in the unsatisfactory conditions of rural credit (Jakhade, 1958, p. 287). It is clearly impossible to identify these social and economic factors and these basic weaknesses by the kind of investigations carried out by the Rural Credit Survey, and much more intensive methods of field investigation are required. But this raises, in full force, the question of the method of investigation used in the several surveys and field studies to which we have referred and brings us back to the interrelationships between economic and anthropological studies and the role that anthropological research can play to supplement the economic surveys on which most of this paper is based.

IV

Most of the data which have been presented in the preceding sections of this paper were collected in three sets of field surveys. The first, which is an ongoing enterprise, is the National Sample Survey; the second, a one-shot, large-scale inquiry, is the Rural Credit Survey;

N

and the third, which is also an ongoing study, is the Survey of Farm Management. All these surveys employ basically the same set of procedures. The studies might be called 'questionnaire studies'—i.e. a large number of informants are asked a set of predetermined questions. The informants are selected by a random sample, and the sample—which is often stratified according to various characteristics which are assumed to be relevant—is sufficiently large to give results which stand up under most statistical tests of reliability. The charge has been made that, in the Rural Credit Survey, the sampling was insufficiently random; but it seems to me that this charge, even if true, is irrelevant, since the sample was so large that, unless a strong conscious bias were present, the results obtained would not be very dissimilar from a genuinely random sample. In the Farm Management Surveys, the sampling was not random as concerns the selection of districts. Hence we admittedly do not obtain data which are valid for any of the five states as a whole within which the districts were chosen; but we do have, for each pair of districts, a sample sufficiently large to produce results which can stand the normal tests of reliability.

More important is the charge that these surveys are of limited significance because, in all of them, the operation of an agricultural holding in India is regarded as a 'farm business', and the related charge that, for this reason, many questions asked are unintelligible to the Indian peasant and that the answers received are therefore of little validity.[1]

I should like to deal with these two arguments in order. There is no question that the Indian economists who inaugurated these various surveys were influenced in their theoretical outlook by economic concepts and ideas which originally stem from the West. There is also no doubt that the theoretical background which gave rise to these surveys was developed in conformance with similar surveys of farming in Britain, the United States and other Western countries, where farming is clearly a business. In India, on the other hand, it is argued, farming is mainly a productive activity directed toward a peasant's subsistence; and, though many Indian peasants are admittedly influenced by considerations of marketing parts of their crops, they do not attempt to maximize profits and they do not behave as the ideal

---

[1] These charges have primarily been levied by Daniel Thorner, 1960, *passim*. A similar argument is also raised by Harold H. Mann, for example, in a review of P. K. Mukherjee's *Economic Surveys in Under-Developed Countries*. Mann says that 'the collection of economic and social data in a peasant economy such as occurs in India is, except for the very simplest items, not only difficult, but very liable to very large errors. Even in such a matter as the total agricultural production of a village the results obtained . . . may be very wide of the mark . . . Any estimate of debts and other similar liabilities, however carefully checked, may have little relation to the facts.' See Mann, 1961.

'economic man' of Western political economy. This distinction is similar to that made by Werner Sombart in distinguishing between the principle of subsistence and the principle of gain as underlying motivations for economic action. Clearly, the determination of what will be produced will differ if the peasant is concerned primarily with his and his family's subsistence rather than with selling his crop under the best possible conditions. What we witness in Indian agriculture is a spectrum of motivations which range all the way from complete concern with subsistence to complete concern with profitability of the sale of crop. Most Indian cultivators probably produce in part for their own consumption and in part for sale. It is not likely that this motivational structure can be readily ascertained in the kind of general economic surveys which have been used in this paper, and on this point studies in depth would need to be undertaken.

But although it must be granted that the Indian cultivator is not engaged in the business of farming in the sense in which the British or American farmer is so engaged, the particular motivations and objectives of his productive activity are irrelevant for a determination of the efficiency with which he operates and for measuring his overall productive performance. It is granted that the notion of 'farm business' is an abstraction, originally derived from Western economics; but any alternative formula would also be an abstraction, and the concept of farm business has at least the advantage of providing some empirical data which may be used for comparative purposes. Moreover, even accepting the strong subsistence motivation in the Indian peasant's productive activity, we cannot deny that for most Indian peasants—indeed, for all but the most remote and miserable ones—production for subsistence and for the market are real substitutes: in other words, subsistence production has acquired a 'derived' commercial aspect. We do not have quantitative empirical data on the demand schedule for home-produced commodities by the Indian peasant; but it would be strange if this demand schedule were not closely comparable to that of the masses of Indians who buy their food in the market, and if we make this assumption, the distinction between production for home use and for the market becomes even less significant.

Hence the assumption that Indian peasants behave as if they were engaged in rational productive activity (which is merely another name for the more descriptive and narrow concept, 'farm business') is not an inaccurate one; and once this is granted, it is perfectly legitimate to expect that meaningful data on resource allocation and the efficacy of particular patterns of resource allocation can be studied by the methods of economic field surveys. Regardless of his motives, every peasant must make choices in allocating the resources he has at his disposal. It may be granted that often he has few degrees

371

of freedom, i.e. that his freedom of choice is severely limited. The main limitations are not his 'traditionalism', i.e. his lack of 'economic rationality', but his lack of knowledge, especially of technological alternatives, and the apparently high risk premium which he attaches to experimenting with new and untried methods. Given the severe scarcity of resources which he does have, this evaluation of the riskiness of innovation cannot be regarded as irrational. But here again is a problem which can be tackled only by research in depth.

But if it is granted that the Indian peasant does have a choice in his use of resources, the study of farming as carried out, for example, by the Farm Management Survey, is likely to yield information which does reflect these choices accurately, though it may still fall short as concerns valuation. For inputs and outputs are valued at market prices, or, where there are no adequate market prices—for example, in the case of land—on the basis of estimates. Yet these valuations become arbitrary for those inputs and outputs which are neither sold nor destined for sale, but are rather for consumption by the peasant and his family. For instance, in terms of 'commercial' standards, most holdings surveyed in the Farm Management Surveys are 'deficit' holdings; and the puzzle, which may need to be explained, of how alleged deficit holdings may nevertheless show a real positive net investment in productive capital, resolves itself if it is recognized that the particular pattern of valuation chosen may be responsible for it.[1]

Now, the question of valuation is troublesome not only in economies in which there is a large subsistence sector, but even in economies where virtually all transactions are mediated through the market. But the great margin of error which may be involved if the self-consumed output of a subsistence economy is valued at ordinary market prices has been plainly exhibited by Simon Kuznets in his comparative evaluation of Chinese national product according to alternative methods of valuation (Kuznets, 1953, pp. 152 ff.). The estimates in all the surveys cited are subject to similar errors of valuation, not only as concerns output prices but also input prices. But though these shortcomings are recognized, the data which have been assembled in these various surveys are the best and most comprehensive we have; and if we reject them as being subject to error, we have no data whatsoever. At the same time, however, these considerations again point to the fact that more knowledge in depth is required.

The problem of valuation and the uncertainties associated with it

---

[1] In the Farm Management Survey of Bombay State, for example, it was shown that, of the 278 farms in Ahmednagar and Nasik districts whose accounts were examined closely, 197 made losses and only 81 profits. Moreover, average losses outweighted average profits. In general, therefore, the picture presented is of a deficit agriculture.

is one aspect of the question of whether adequate communication between interviewers and informants is possible in the economic surveys on which this paper is based. Let us remind ourselves again that the questions asked have been drawn up by a group of economists, many of whom may be well acquainted with economic theory but may have little first-hand knowledge of Indian villages. The cultural gap between the Westernized Indian intelligentsia and the Indian peasantry has so often been commented upon as to be almost proverbial. The interviews are carried out in the vernacular languages, but the questionnaires are originally drawn up in English and translated, and the body of ideas on which they are based stems from modern Western agricultural economics and not from the conceptualizations and understandings of the Indian cultivator. Clearly, differences in the facility of communication may be expected if villagers are interviewed who live predominantly in a subsistence economy, as compared with those who not only are familiar with a money economy but even with a partly or even fully commercialized agriculture. And though the completely self-sufficient rural community is on its way out in India, monetization and, especially, commercialization have as yet taken very partial hold of many villages. To be sure, if a peasant is asked about rates of investment or imputed rent, he will not understand what he is asked, even if he participated in a fully monetized economy; but any peasant would be able to explain why he bought, sold or bartered a bullock, a piece of land, a tool or some other item of capital. And regardless of whether his objective is subsistence farming or making a maximum cash profit, he is concerned with efficiency, i.e. he is interested in employing the resources he controls to his best advantage. Thus, although the communication process in the questionnaire type surveys may sometimes be imperfect and lead to misunderstanding or even misinformation, it is certain to yield reliable information on some points; the degree of reliability of this method of inquiry could, again, be ascertained more adequately only by studies in depth.

Here, as several times in the preceding discussion, reference has been made to studies in depth. The most adequate type of study in depth is an intensive field study along anthropological lines. For ultimately the reasons for borrowing, the efficacy of the communication process, the role of valuation, the objectives of productive activity and other associated relationships in the village are outcomes of the village culture. Only a better understanding of village culture and, more particularly, of the role of production and its related processes within the village culture, can provide the insights by which a closer meaning of data collected in an economic survey can be evaluated.

But here another problem arises: intensive village studies cannot

373

be carried on on a mass scale. Our command of resources—both financial and, above all, qualified human resources—does not permit us to envisage parallel intensive studies in many villages as a practicable possibility, even if we confine our attention to India. We are thus again in the midst of a sampling problem; but this time randomness is definitely excluded because of the paucity of cases which make up the sample. Yet it appears that it is of the utmost importance to come to some closer determination of how intensive studies along anthropological lines can be combined with the necessarily somewhat superficial survey studies that are being conducted now so widely in India. The Farm Management studies have resolved this problem in one way. Six regions, each in a different State, were selected; and in each region, composed of two adjoining districts, a number of farms were studied rather intensively. Care was taken to select the regions in such a way 'that they represent the most important and typical soil crop complexes in the State concerned and these six regions taken together represent the major cropping patterns in the country'.[1] In other words, the selection was made with a view to differentiating along known or assumed distinctions in agricultural productive patterns.[2] It might be argued that a similar criterion of selection may be used for studies of village culture in its economic or productive dimension. Instead of differentiating regions in terms of patterns of agricultural production, a number of villages differentiated by the 'economic culture' should be studied. It is difficult to say what detailed criteria should be used in selecting typical regions or villages. Such aspects as the degree of market involvement, commercialization, the prevalence of a money economy, economic alternatives to agriculture—in brief, the basic dimension of economic organization—would doubtless be the dominant criteria. A number of basic studies in depth would provide perhaps some useful 'coefficients' by means of which the information collected in survey studies could be 'discounted' and at the same time provide one further important

[1] See the Introduction by D. R. Gadgil to each of the five volumes of *Studies in Economics of Farm Management*, par. 0.9.

[2] In spite of Professor Gadgil's statement, which gives the impression that the selection of districts took place in such a manner as to include only those which showed average characteristics of the State, the districts chosen in at least one state, Uttar Pradesh, are very unrepresentative of the agriculture of the State as a whole. I am not familiar enough with the districts in the other states to indicate whether and to what extent a similar bias has been used in the selection. The districts of Meerut and Muzzaffarnagar in Uttar Pradesh belong to the most prosperous districts of the State; and farm yields, average incomes of farmers and levels of living are substantially higher in these two districts than in most other parts of Uttar Pradesh. Hence it is inadmissible to regard the data which are contained in the *Studies in Economics of Farm Management* as representative of an entire state; at best, they may be considered as representative of the pair of districts actually selected for field study.

guide line along which stratification of survey samples should be made. Such studies in economic anthropology would not only provide a surer basis for the economic analysis of the rural economy of India, but would also have important implications for rural planning.

17

The Study of Peasant Economic Systems: Some Concluding Comments and Questions

BY B. S. YAMEY

Interest among economists in the studies of anthropologists is a fairly recent phenomenon, and it is by no means widespread. Alfred Marshall, writing in 1890, was able to dispose summarily of the economics of 'savage' societies in the following terms (Marshall, 1936, pp. 723–4):

> Scanty and untrustworthy as is our information about the habits of savage tribes, we know enough of them to be sure that they show a strange uniformity of general character, amid great variety of detail. Whatever be their climate and whatever their ancestry, we find savages living under the dominion of custom and impulse; scarcely ever striking out new lines for themselves; never forecasting the distant future, and seldom making provision even for the near future; fitful in spite of their servitude to custom, governed by the fancy of the moment; ready at times for the most arduous exertions, but incapable of keeping themselves long to steady work. Laborious and tedious tasks are avoided as far as possible; those which are inevitable are done by the compulsory labour of women.

No doubt few anthropological studies were available when he wrote, and most of them were devoted to the more exotic of 'savage' peoples. In recent decades many more of these studies have become available. An increasing number of them relate to peoples in economies which are now in closer political and economic contact with the more developed countries of Europe and North America. Meanwhile there has been an uninhibited burgeoning of interest among economists in the economic performance, problems and prospects of under-developed countries, including countries in which

376

large parts of the population live in the kind of communities and groupings which for long have provided a major part of the subject-matter of anthropological enquiries.

In the circumstances one might have thought that economists would have become more closely acquainted with the work of anthropologists. This could have been expected especially because many of those who are professionally interested in the economics of under-developed countries are well aware that different social arrangements, value systems and personal motivations and aspirations may have a pervasive influence on economic performance generally, as well as more narrowly on the prospects of success of particular economic policy measures. (It may be noted in passing that this awareness should not blind us to the fact that in the context of some problems—for example, some of those concerned with price formation—the influences of these differences may be so small as to be disregarded.)

Economists writing on the general problems of under-developed countries have, of course, used illustrative material taken from the monographs of anthropologists. But by and large in their work on particular under-developed countries, economists have not been much influenced by the work of anthropologists in the countries in question.

It is not difficult to suggest possible reasons for this neglect. There are obvious difficulties of inter-disciplinary communication and the fact that anthropologists quite naturally write primarily for themselves. Then, too, anthropologists have tended to concentrate on studies of small-scale societies, while economists usually are interested (or are required to interest themselves) in large-scale problems of an entire economy or of major sectors of it. Moreover, economists working on the problems of under-developed countries are often under such pressure of time to produce reports, recommendations, programmes or solutions that it may not be possible for them to steep themselves in the data already made available by other investigators, let alone to make detailed first-hand observations themselves. Perhaps, also, there has been some impatience with what may seem to be minutiae, when the call seems to be for boldness both in diagnosis and also in prescription. (This call for boldness seems, fortunately, to be on the wane.)

But perhaps the most important explanation of the self-imposed isolation of the economists in their work in the study of under-developed economies has been their tendency to concentrate on aspects of economic organization and on sectors of activity where it might seem that little is to be learnt from the work of anthropologists. The heavy concentration of interest on problems of external trade, public finance and industrialization may serve as examples of this tendency. As Miss Polly Hill has suggested (Hill, 1962), the interests of economists—and of the Governments who have employed them—have rarely drawn them into the study of indigenous types of economic activity, modes of economic behaviour and varieties of economic organization. And it is here more than anywhere else where one would expect the economist to have most to learn from the anthropologist (although anthropological findings and analysis are undoubtedly relevant for the understanding of problems in the 'non-indigenous' sector also, such as problems arising with attempts to establish an urban labour force for new industrial undertakings). Thus, for example, there has been much concern with the export marketing of crops and the control of their prices. But by contrast it has been rare for economists to probe very far into the organization of the pro-duction of the crops and the earliest stages of their marketing and related activities. With rare exceptions, it is as though they have allowed themselves to become interested in local indigenous economic activities at the point where their output has moved out of the local and into the international economic sphere, and that they have declined to pursue this output back to its source along a route which to them would be progressively less familiar and without the accus-tomed landmarks.

II

The limited preoccupations of economists have, I have suggested, limited their contacts with the work of anthropologists and other social scientists. One may go further and suggest that this has been harmful to their work even in their chosen fields, because the indigenous and non-indigenous sectors are not rigidly separated but inter-penetrate each other: the same individual may be partly engaged in each of the two sectors and may be making decisions concerning his commitment in each of them. A simple example may be helpful. Subsistence economic activity (in the indigenous sector) is relatively more important in under-developed largely agricultural economies than in developed largely industrial economies, where even farming tends to be highly specialized to the production of a narrow range of products for the market and is heavily dependent on the services of other specialist intermediaries and producers. Subsistence activity provides a measure of protection from market forces which is absent in a more highly specialized exchange economy based on more intensive division of labour. Up to a point subsistence production in under-developed countries provides a feasible alternative to production for the market. This has important consequences for at least two types of policy problem which are of much interest to economists concerned with under-developed countries: the stabiliza-tion of the producer prices (or proceeds) of export produce, and the raising of Government revenues. In connection with the first of these two problems, it is commonly assumed that instability of prices is seriously detrimental to the interests of small-scale peasant producers. This may indeed be so. But one suspects that the proposition is less firmly based for part-subsistence producers in an under-developed country than for highly-specialized commercial farmers in an advanced economy. In the former, it is far easier for producers to switch to activities not affected by market prices, and hence they are less exposed to price fluctuations. Furthermore, a proper economic assessment of the desirability of measures of price stabilization (which inevitably are attended by the risk that they may destabilize prices and also may have economic and possibly political side-effects) would call for some knowledge of whether fluctuations in money incomes are more or less conducive to capital formation in peasant economies, a matter which cannot be settled either by *a priori* reasoning or by reference to the experience of specialized producers in advanced economies. Questions of taxation—to turn to the second type of problem—are also affected by the presence of the real possibility of subsistence activity as an alternative to production for the market. The imposition of certain kinds of taxes may well in some circumstances induce a partial retreat from the exchange sector (where taxes are more easily levied) to the subsistence sector, or delay the extension of the former sector.

The economist who does not penetrate into the indigenous sector of an under-developed economy, or who does not take advantage of the guidance he could have from anthropologists who have been there before him, inevitably is at a disadvantage. If he fails to consult the anthropologist, he himself fails to take advantage of the benefits of the division of labour. He may more easily fall into the error of believing that he need not make any special allowance for the particular characteristics of indigenous societies, the social constraints operating on individuals and the opportunities open to them. According to Marshall (Marshall, 1936, p. 762), Ricardo and some of his followers let their desire for simplicity lead them 'sometimes to argue as though all mankind had the same habits as city men' whom they knew intimately. The economist may fall into a similar error of simplification in his studies of under-developed countries. Alternatively, he may fall into the opposite error, and regard the habits, attitudes and arrangements of the rural population as being so peculiar and so different from those familiar to him that he cannot conceive that they may be (or soon become) highly responsive to ordinary market inducements and economic stimuli.

The foregoing may be summarized as a plea that economists concerned with the study of under-developed countries should know more about the indigenous rural sector, not only because of its own interest and importance, but also because there is necessarily some measure of inter-action between that sector and the more familiar parts of the exchange sector, including those parts contiguous with the international economy. The importance of the indigenous sector for the economist, in particular, should be apparent from the fact that in under-developed countries a high proportion of the population is engaged in peasant agriculture or in pursuits closely connected with it, that a large part of the exports of such countries is agricultural, and that, as it is often loosely expressed, an agricultural 'revolution' is a necessary prior condition of industrialization or a necessary complement to it. It has been argued, also, that in improving his understanding of the indigenous sector and its external relationships, the economist is fortunate in often being able to draw on the accumulated results of anthropological investigation and the insights furnished by anthropological analysis of diverse societies.

III

Let us suppose that economists will increasingly turn to anthropologists for help in their contemporary enquiries into the economics of under-developed countries and in their endeavours to formulate policy measures designed to achieve specific limited objectives, or, both more ambitiously and more ambiguously, to promote 'economic growth'. What sort of help would they most like to have? In trying to answer this question, the temptation must be resisted to write generally about the causes of the feelings of inadequacy which many economists often experience when they are asked to pronounce on the 'causes' of the wealth of nations, or (to be more specific) when they are asked to explain, for example, why in recent years the rate of growth in Western Germany has been higher than that in the United Kingdom, or why a particular development programme has failed in some particular under-developed country. The importance of 'non-economic' variables and constraints is increasingly apparent, whether one is concerned with the economic prospects of the United Kingdom or those of some African state. The economist knows he is out of his depth here and is eager for help (though he may suspect that other social scientists may be in much the same situation as he is). In the construction of an economic model of a society or an economy, for example, it is necessary both to specify these non-economic constraints and forces and also to postulate the patterns of their interrelationships with the economic variables incorporated in the model. If such a model is to be used for planning purposes, it is necessary, further, to express quantitatively these forces, constraints and interrelationships. The general problems are much the same whether one is concerned with a highly industrialized economy or with one of the under-developed countries.

A consideration of these major problems would take us much too far afield. It must suffice to suggest that there is obvious scope for inter-disciplinary collaboration and enquiry in this range of problems, again whether one is concerned with the economy of the United Kingdom or with that of an African state. Instead, a more modest answer to the original question (what help economists would like from anthropologists) will be essayed here. Some specific but circumscribed points of interest to economists are selected and discussed briefly so as to suggest where economists might be helped in their work by the contributions of anthropology. To limit the discussion in another direction, the selection is confined to topics which fall within the subject-matter of the present collection of essays. As far as possible attention is focused on the sort of information and analysis an economist might like to find for his purposes in the specialist studies of anthropologists if he were trying vicariously to deepen his understanding of the selected aspects of the economic workings of peasant societies. The topics discussed here may seem a far cry from economic models or the grand issue of the causes of the wealth of nations. But perhaps this modesty of aim may have some merit of its own. In the study of economies consisting largely of peasant societies, there may be some wisdom in trying to gain a better understanding of economic activities as they are, and of their powers of adaptation or of resistance to change, before embarking on aggregative studies of entire economies on the move.

The four topics selected for discussion are the following: (1) the 'demonstration effect' and its implications for capital formation and investment; (2) the supposed inflexibility of interest rates in certain classes of transaction; (3) the rate of interest and investment decisions; and (4) arrangements for economizing in the use of capital assets. The first topic concerns saving and investment decisions; the second, an aspect of the working of the market for capital; the third, economic calculation; and the fourth, the management and control of capital assets. They therefore together touch upon several of the themes which appear in the essays in this book. And it should be apparent from these essays that anthropologists can contribute significantly to the elucidation of the various topics I have selected by way of illustrating some of the specific points of interest to economists. In particular, in many places the essays bear directly especially on the first and last of the four selected topics, and these may well be the most important of them. Yet the researches on which these essays are based were originally not directed to answering these (or other) economic questions. Deliberate attempts to find answers to these (or similar) questions are likely to be even more helpful to economists. Perhaps, moreover, the attempt to answer the economist's questions may prompt the anthropologist to pose further questions for himself within his own field of study. It may be that this is for him the most interesting and most fruitful result of this form of inter-disciplinary collaboration.

IV

(1) Economists interested in the economics of under-developed countries have been concerned with the economic effects of the discovery of new and desirable objects of consumption expenditure by members of a society, for example by contact with the people and products of other wealthier societies. The question is whether this has stimulated consumption at the expense of saving and capital accumulation, and thus has retarded economic growth: that is, whether the demonstration and subsequent adoption of new wants have acted as a barrier to economic growth. Or, on the contrary, does aspiration to the enjoyment of new satisfactions stimulate new enterprise and effort, including activity calling for additional investment, and thus promote economic growth?

The view that there is a 'demonstration effect' which inhibits economic advance by stimulating consumption has been made popular in recent years through the writings of the late Professor Nurkse. (Nurkse, 1953, pp. 68 *et seq.*) It has a long history. It rests on the self-evident proposition that, at any given time, what is spent on consumption cannot be saved for addition to the capital stock—a proposition effectively illustrated when the capital consists of assets such as livestock which can be consumed literally. The opposite view of the 'aspiration effect' also has a respectable ancestry, and has been espoused in more recent years by Bauer and myself, among others. (Bauer and Yamey, 1956, pp. 137–52.) This view rests, essentially, on the proposition that knowledge of new goods and services and the stimulation of new wants increase the desire for the necessary money income, a desire which can be made effective only by increased effort and enterprise, including activity calling for capital formation. This view is strengthened by the fact that in under-developed economies there is generally considerable scope for the transfer of effort and activity from the subsistence to the exchange sector, a transfer likely to be encouraged when more is known about the things that money can buy.

One might expect that developments would not be the same in all societies. And here one might hope that anthropological investigations would be enlightening, both in providing detailed examples of the working of the demonstration and aspiration effects and also in suggesting the characteristics of societies in which one or other of the two effects is likely to be dominant, and the speed of their operation.

(2) There are references or observations in the literature on peasant

382

economies suggesting that there is long-term stability in the values of such economic variables as the prices of particular goods or services, or the rate of interest in particular classes of transaction. It seems as if for long periods particular prices, wage-rates or rates of interest remain unchanged, despite other changes in the peasant economy at large. The economist, with his firmly entrenched idea that changes in prices both reflect changes in economic conditions and also bring about adaptation to the changes, is perhaps somewhat suspicious of the reality of such inflexibilities, just as he may be suspicious of the apparent long-term inflexibility of published or quoted prices in industrial markets in the West.[1] If a price—be it a rate of interest, a product price or a wage rate—in fact does not change even when conditions of supply and demand do change, the economist would expect to find evidence at some times of excess supply, and at other times of excess demand. When the price is 'too high', he would expect to find evidence of secret or indirect price reductions, probably on a discriminatory basis. When it is 'too low', he would expect to find evidence of additional collateral benefits to the suppliers (sellers, lenders), of more-or-less deliberate rationing of the available supplies by the suppliers, or of re-selling (re-lending) by some fortunate buyers (borrowers). How does all this work out in the 'capital markets' of peasant societies, where the majority of loans probably are on a largely unorganized personal basis between lender and borrower? If the capital market is highly fragmented, how does the observer ascertain the effective rate of interest on particular classes of loans, especially if, as is likely, other explicit or implied terms can be varied from transaction to transaction? It is difficult if not impossible to attach a precise meaning to 'the rate of interest' in an advanced economy such as ours, where numerous different rates of interest prevail, and where the assessment of the individual borrower's credit-worthiness is often an important consideration in the terms of a particular transaction. One would expect these difficulties to be greater where the 'capital market' is less organized. Moreover, if the rate of interest in particular classes of transaction were indeed effectively fixed, it would be of interest to know the criteria accord-

[1] The following quotation from a paper by Alfred Marshall is of interest in the present context:

'Things which are not sold by measure, but by name, are altered quickly in quantity; and since selling by name is the rule in backward districts, retail prices in them are often astonishingly sensitive. For instance, in 1878, when the taxes on salt were readjusted throughout India, being raised in the southern half and lowered in the northern, it was expected by many that the rule of custom and the smallness of retail purchases would prevent the raiyat from feeling the change for a long time to come. But the result was opposite. Salt was retailed by the pinch. And from the day when the new rule came into operation, the pinch was increased in size in the northern, and diminished in the southern half.' (Pigou, 1925, p. 456.)

ing to which lenders selected borrowers (and *vice versa*), especially at times when there is marked excess demand for funds (or marked excess supply of them). Skilled probing into these matters may help to throw some light on inter-personal relationships in both commercial and non-commercial activities.

The set of questions under this heading might best be investigated by considering the conditions in an economy in two different years, one a good year and the other a poor one. One would expect that funds for loans would be more limited in the second year, and the demand for loans greater. If rates of interest do not rise to clear the market, how is it cleared? Who are the disappointed would-be borrowers, and what do they do about their difficulties? It might be the case that the (postulated) smaller flow of loanable funds (including the flow of loans *in natura*) is 'rationed' by lenders by giving priority to those borrowers with closer social ties with, or claims on, the lenders, or to those who are better commercial risks. If this were so, it would imply that the favoured categories—favoured, respectively, for social and business reasons—are not favoured except in bad times, which might seem to be an odd state of affairs, especially in societies in which kinship and social ties, *inter alia*, are thought to be important in economic affairs.

A further topic of considerable practical importance is the response in a peasant economy to a new source of finance, say, loans offered by an official agency. Much may be learnt of the working of capital markets in peasant societies—and perhaps even of the structure of such societies—by a study of the process of adaptation to such a new 'impersonal' source of funds. It should also throw much-needed light on the real burden (as distinct from the apparent burden as indicated by the contract terms) of private loans. The fact—if it is such—that some borrowers prefer to borrow on apparently more onerous terms from private lenders than from an available official source on apparently easier terms would suggest that the real terms, as seen by the borrowers in question, were lighter for the private loans (though it may of course reflect no more than fear of contacts with authority).

(3) Other things being equal, a lower rate of interest might be expected to encourage borrowing for investment purposes. Capital is cheaper. An investment project which involves a present outlay of £100 and which promises total returns of £106 a year hence, is worthwhile when money can be borrowed at less than 6 per cent, but not when the relevant rate of interest exceeds 6 per cent. Moreover, a lower rate of interest might be expected to encourage investment projects involving a longer period or unremunerative waiting, or promising returns over a longer period. (From compound interest tables we learn that £100 accruing in five years' time is the equivalent of £91 today when the relevant rate of interest is 2 per cent p.a.;

it is worth only £40 when the rate is 20 per cent, or £27 when it is 30 per cent. The same amount accruing three years earlier is worth £96, £69 and £59 at 2 per cent, 20 per cent and 30 per cent, respectively.) Thus both the volume of borrowing for investment, and also the types of investment projects (differing, *inter alia*, in respect of capital-intensity and the time-pattern of expected returns) might be expected to be influenced by the level of interest rates (or, if interest rates are in fact stable despite changes in supply and demand, by the availability of loanable funds).

To what extent, and in what ways, do such considerations enter into investment decisions in peasant societies? How articulate are peasant investors about such matters as comparative levels of return in alternative activities, time-patterns of returns, risk, etc.? More generally, what sort of calculations do investors make? Economists know how difficult it is to study investment decisions in an advanced economy, or to determine the influence, say, of changes in the rate of interest. The detailed experience of anthropologists working in peasant societies would be of much interest, as would be their observations on the more general question of 'economic calculation'.

In so far as investment does not involve money expenditures but the use of the peasant's labour, e.g. in clearing land or erecting buildings, the rate of interest for loans is not directly relevant. But it may be relevant indirectly, where the labour could be used, alternatively, to produce an immediate income in money on which the rate of interest could be earned by making loans (or by avoiding borrowing). Again, it would perhaps be most helpful if observations on these matters could be contrasted as between good years and lean years.

(4) Anthropological studies and other material demonstrate both that certain features of some societies may be 'wasteful' of capital (e.g. the fragmentation of land holdings), and also that there is a strong propensity in poor societies to economize in the use of resources. A further question concerns the presence and strength in peasant societies of features which affect the establishment and operation of co-operative arrangements for economizing in the acquisition and the use of capital goods. Broadly, two types of arrangements are possible. First, assets can be acquired by groups of people collectively. Provided the members of the group do not all require the use of the assets simultaneously, the economies of pooling can be achieved. The working of such pooling arrangements calls for a high degree of mutual trust and for some skill in organization. Second, in the same circumstances one person can acquire the asset and hire out its services to non-owning users; that is to say, a market in the services is created. Does the existence of social groupings within a society facilitate pooling arrangements? Can anthropologists tell us what types of social arrangements or institutions are best

suited for such business purposes, especially when new economic opportunities emerge? Are these arrangements more or less common for traditional or 'indigenous' assets than for other assets, and for producer assets than for consumer assets? What happens when the social groupings become weaker with social or economic change? On the question of markets for the services of assets, how do they originate and who takes the initiative? This clearly brings us to the wider issue of entrepreneurship in under-developed economies, the importance of which is acknowledged by economists as well as other social scientists, but on which economists have had regrettably little to contribute.

BIBLIOGRAPHY

ARENSBERG, C., 1937: *The Irish Countryman; An Anthropological Study*, London.

ARMSTRONG, W. E., 1921–22: 'Anthropology of the South-Eastern Division', *Annual Report*, Papua, Port Moresby.

—1924a: 'Shell Money from Rossel Island, Papua', *Man*, No. 119.

—1924b: 'Rossel Island Money: a Unique Monetary System', *Economic Journal*, vol. 34, pp. 423–9.

—1928: *Rossel Island: An Ethnological Study*, Cambridge.

AYABE, T., 1961: *The Village of Ban Pha Khao, Vientiane Province*; a preliminary report, Laos Project Paper No. 14 (mim.).

BAILEY, F. G., 1957: *Caste and the Economic Frontier*, Manchester.

—1960: *Tribe, Caste and Nation*, Manchester.

BANFIELD, E. C., 1957: *Moral Basis of a Backward Society*, Glencoe, Ill.

BARNETT, K. M. A., 1962: *Hong Kong Report on the 1961 Census*, 3 vols., Hong Kong.

BARTH, F., 1960: 'The Land use pattern of migratory tribes of South Persia', *Norsk Geografisk Tidsskrift*, vol. 17.

—1961: *Nomads of South Persia*, Oslo.

BASCOM, W. R., 1952: 'The Esusu: A Credit Institution of the Yoruba', *Journal Royal Anthrop. Inst.*, vol. 82, pp. 63–9.

BASTIEN, R., 1951: *La Familia Rural Haitiana*, Mexico.

—1961: 'Haitian rural family organization', *Social and Economic Studies* vol. 10, No. 4, pp. 478–510.

BAUER, P. T., 1954: *West African Trade*, Cambridge.

BAUER, P. T., and YAMEY, B. S., 1951: 'Economic progress and occupational distribution', *Economic Journal*, vol. 61, pp. 739–55.

—1957: *The Economics of Underdeveloped Countries*, London.

BAUMOL, W. J., 1959: *Business Behaviour, Value and Growth*, New York.

BELSHAW, C. S., 1955a: *In Search of Wealth: A Study of the Emergence of Commercial Operations in the Melanesian Society of South-eastern Papua*, Amer. Anthrop. Ass., vol. 57, No. 1, Part 2, Memoir No. 80.

—1955b: 'The Cultural Milieu of the Entrepreneur: A Critical Essay', *Explorations in Entrepreneurial History*, vol. vii, No. 3, pp. 146–63, Cambridge, Mass.

BENEDICT, B., 1957: 'Factionalism in Mauritian Villages', *British Journal of Sociology*, vol. VIII, No. 4, pp. 328–42.

—1961: *Indians in a Plural Society*, London.

BHATT, V. V., 1959: 'Savings and Capital Formation', *Economic Development and Cultural Change*, VII, No. 3, pp. 318–42.

BHATTACHARJEE, J. P. (ed.), 1958: *Studies in Indian Agricultural Economics*, Bombay.

BOHANNAN, P., 1955: 'Some Principles of Exchange and Investment among the Tiv', *American Anthropologist*, vol. 57, pp. 60–70.

BOOKER, H. S., 1949: 'Debit in Africa', *African Affairs*, vol. 48, pp. 141–9.

387

BRITISH GUIANA, DEPARTMENT OF LABOUR, 1957: *Survey of family expenditure 1956*, Undertaken by the Department of Labour, under the guidance of Pauline B. Paro, ILO Consultant, Georgetown.

BUNZEL, Ruth, 1938: 'Economic Organization of Primitive Peoples' in Boas, F. (ed.), *General Anthropology*, Boston.

BURCHETT, W. T., 1957: *Mekong Upstream*, Hanoi.

CENTRAL STATISTICAL ORGANIZATION, 1955: 'Capital Formation in the Indian Union', in Government of India, Planning Commission, *Papers Relating to the Formation of the Second Five Year Plan*, Delhi.

CODERE, Helen, 1950: *Fighting with Property: A Study of Kwakiutl Potlatching and Warfare 1792–1930*, Mon. Amer. Ethnol. Soc. XVIII, New York.

COMHAIRE-SYLVAIN, Suzanne, 1958: 'Courtship, marriage and plasaj at Kenscoff, Haiti', *Social and Economic Studies*, vol. 7, No. 4, pp. 210–33.

DANDEKAR, V. M., 1954: *Second Report on the Poona Schedule of the National Sample Survey*, Poona.

DAVENPORT, W., 1961: 'When a Primitive and Civilized Money Meet', *Proc. Amer. Ethnol. Soc. Spring Meeting Symposium*, pp. 64–8, Seattle.

DEACON, B., 1934: *Malekula: A Vanishing People in the New Hebrides* (ed. Camilla H. Wedgwood), London.

DEWEY, Alice, 1962: *Peasant Marketing in Java*, New York.

DISKALKAR, P. D., 1960: *Resurvey of a Deccan Village: Pimple Saudagar*, Bombay.

EINZIG, P., 1949: *Primitive Money*, London.

FEI HSIAO-TUNG, 1943: *Peasant Life in China*, London.

FIJI, LEGISLATIVE COUNCIL, 1960: Report of the Commission of Enquiry into the Natural Resources and Population Trends of the Colony of Fiji, 1959. Paper No. 1, London and Suva.

FIRTH, R., 1936: *We, The Tikopia: A Sociological Study of Kinship in Primitive Polynesia*, London.

—1938: *Human Types*, London. (1958, revised ed. Edinburgh, New York.)

—1939: *Primitive Polynesian Economy*, London.

—1946: *Malay Fishermen: Their Peasant Economy*, London.

—1951a: 'Some Social Aspects of the Colombo Plan', *Westminster Bank Review*, May, London, pp. 1–7.

—1951b: *Elements of Social Organization*, London.

—(ed.) 1957: 'The Place of Malinowski in the History of Economic Anthropology', *Man and Culture: An Evaluation of the Work of Malinowski*, London.

—1959a: *Social Change in Tikopia*, London.

—1959b: *Economics of the New Zealand Maori*, Wellington.

FIRTH, Rosemary, 1943: *Housekeeping Among Malay Peasants*, London School of Economics Monographs on Social Anthropology, No. 7, London.

FORDE, D., and SCOTT, Richenda, 1946: *The Native Economies of Nigeria*, London.

FRASER, T. F. Jr., 1960: *Rusembilan*, Ithaca, N.Y.

388

Bibliography

FREEDMAN, M., 1958: *Lineage Organization of South-eastern China*, London School of Economics Monographs on Social Anthropology, No. 18, London.
—1959: 'The Handling of Money: A Note on the Background to the Economic Sophistication of Overseas Chinese', *Man*, vol. LIX, No. 89.

FURNIVALL, J. S., 1948: *Colonial Policy and Practice*, Cambridge.

GOVERNMENT OF INDIA: Ministry of Finance, Department of Economic Affairs, 1954a: *Final Report of the National Income Committee*, Delhi.
—Ministry of Finance, National Sample Survey, 1954b: *Tables with Notes on the Third Round, August-November 1951*, Delhi.
—Planning Commission, 1957: *Review of the First Five Year Plan*, Delhi.
—Ministry of Food and Agriculture, 1957–58: *Studies in Economics of Farm Management*, 5 vols., Delhi.

GUIART, J., 1952: 'L'Organisation Sociale et Politique du Nord Malekula', *Journal de la Société des Océanistes*, vol. VIII, pp. 149–259. Paris.

HALL, R. A. Jr., 1953: *Haitian Creole*, Amer. Anthrop. Ass. Memoir No. 74, Menasha, Wis.

HALPERN, J. M. (ed.), 1961: Laos Project Papers series, Department of Anthropology, University of California at Los Angeles (mim.): *Laotian Agricultural Statistics* (Laos Project Paper No. 9); *The Natural Economy of Laos* (Paper No. 17); *The Rural and Urban Economies* (Paper No. 19); *Government, Politics and Social Structure of Laos: A Study in Tradition and Innovation* (Paper No. 21).

HALPERN, J. M., 1961: 'The Role of the Chinese in Lao Society', *Journal of the Siam Society*, vol. XLIX, part 1, Bangkok.

HAVERS, C. R., 1945: *The Report of a Commission of Enquiry into Expenses Incurred by Litigants in the Courts of the Gold Coast and Indebtedness Incurred Thereby*, Gold Coast.

HEILBRONER, R. L., 1958: *The Quest for Wealth*, London.

HICKS, J., 1939: *Value and Capital*, Oxford.

HILL, Polly, 1962: 'Some Characteristics of Indigenous West African Enterprise', *Economic Bulletin of the Economic Society of Ghana*, vol. VI, pp. 3–14.

HOGBIN, H. I., and WEDGWOOD, Camilla H., 1953: 'Local Grouping in Melanesia', *Oceania*, vol. XXIII, pp. 241–76; vol. XXIV, pp. 58–76.

HONG KONG GOVERNMENT, 1953: *Chinese Law and Custom in Hong Kong: Report of a Committee appointed by the Governor in October, 1948*, Hong Kong.
—1962: *Hong Kong: Report for the year 1961*, Hong Kong.

IZIKOWITZ, K. G., 1951: *Lamet, Hill Peasants in French Indochina*, Etnografiska Museet, Göteborg.

JAKHADE, V. M., 1958: 'Rural Credit in India' in J. P. Bhattacharjee (ed.), *Studies in Indian Agricultural Economics*, Bombay, pp. 249–99.

JAY, R. R., 1963: *Javanese Villagers: Society and Politics in Rural Modjokuto*, New York.

JAYAWARDENA, C., 1962: 'Family organisation in plantations in British Guiana', *International Journal of Comparative Sociology*, vol. III, No. 1.
—1963: *Conflict and Solidarity in a Guianese Plantation*, London.

389

Capital, Saving and Credit in Peasant Societies

JIN-BEE, A., 1958: 'The Distribution of Present-Day Man in the Tropics: Historical and Ecological Perspective', *Proceedings Ninth Pacific Science Congress*, vol. 20, Bangkok.

KAUFMAN, H. K., 1961: *Village Life in Vientiane Province (1956–57)*, Laos Project Paper No. 12 (mim.).

KRISHNA, R., 1961: 'Some Aspects of Land Reform and Economic Development in India', in W. Froehlich (ed.), *Land Tenure, Industrialization and Social Stability*, pp. 214–56, Milwaukee.

KUNDU, A., 1962: *The economy of British Guiana: 1960–75*, Institute of Social and Economic Research, University of the West Indies, Jamaica (mim.).

KUZNETS, S., 1953: *Economic Change*, New York.

LACKDAWALA, D. T., *et al.*, 1958: in J. P. Bhattacharjee (ed.), *Studies in Indian Agricultural Economics*, Bombay.

LAMBTON, A. K. S., 1953: *Landlord and Peasant in Persia*, London.

LANCASTER, L., 1962: 'Crédit, épargne et investissement dans une économie "non-monetaire" ', *Archives Européennes de Sociologie*, vol. III, pp. 149–64.

LAYARD, J., 1942: *Stone Men of Malekula*, London.

LEGERMAN, Caroline J., 1962: 'Kin Groups in a Haitian Market', *Man*, vol. 62, No. 233.

LEWIS, W. A., 1955: *The Theory of Economic Growth*, London.

LIN, D. Y., 1957: *Report of a trial survey of the economic conditions of sixty families in the New Territories of Hong Kong* (mim.), unpublished.

LOWENTHAL, D., 1960: 'Population contrasts in the Guianas', *The Geographical Review*, vol. L, No. 1, pp. 41–58.

LUCE, R. W., 1958: *Report to the Government of Mauritius on Employment, Unemployment and Underemployment in the Colony in 1958 together with Report on an Investigation into the Wages and Conditions of Employment of Labourers and Artisans in the Sugar Industry*, Port Louis.

MALINOWSKI, B., 1922: *Argonauts of the Western Pacific*, London.

MANN, H. H., 1961: 'The Investigation of Economic Conditions in Underdeveloped Countries', *Economic Development and Cultural Change*, X, No. 1, pp. 102–4.

MARSHALL, A., 1936: *Principles of Economics*, 8th ed., London.

MAURITIUS, COMMISSION OF ENQUIRY, 1959: *Report of the Commission appointed to enquire into the Purchasing Power of the Rupee in Mauritius*, Port Louis.

MAUSS, M., 1954: *The Gift*, London (translation by Ian Cunnison of 'Essai sur le don, forme archaique de l'échange', *L'Année Sociologique*, 1925).

MEADE, J. E., 1960: *The Economic and Social Structure of Mauritius*, London.

MÉTAIS, P., 1949–50: 'Une monnaie archaique: la cordelette de coquillages', *L'Année Sociologique*, 3me ser., pp. 33–142.

MÉTRAUX, A., *et al.*, 1951: *Making a Living in the Marbial Valley (Haiti)*, UNESCO Occasional Papers in Education No. 10, Paris.

MINTZ, S. W., 1959: 'Internal market systems as mechanisms of social articulation', *Proceedings of the Annual Spring Meetings, American Ethnological Society*, pp. 20–30.

390

Bibliography

—1960a: 'The house and the yard in three Caribbean peasant societies', *Proceedings 6e Congrés International des Sciences Anthropologiques et Ethnologiques*. (In press.)

—1960b: 'Le système du marché rural dans l'économie haitienne', *Bulletin du Bureau d'Ethnologie*, série 3, Nos. 23, 24, 25, pp. 3–14.

—1960c: 'A tentative typology of eight Haitian market places', *Revista de Ciencias Sociales*, vol. 4, No. 1, pp. 15–58.

—1960d: 'Peasant markets', *Scientific American*, vol. 203, No. 2, pp. 112–18.

—1961a: 'The question of Caribbean peasantries: a comment', *Caribbean Studies* vol. 1, No. 3, pp. 31–4.

—1961b: 'Pratik: Haitian personal economic relationships', *Proceedings of the Annual Spring Meetings, American Ethnological Society*, pp. 54–63.

—1961c: 'Standards of value and units of measure in the Fond-des-Nègres market place, Haiti', *Journal of the Royal Anthropological Institute*, vol. 91, pp. 23–38.

—1962: 'Living fences in the Fond-des-Nègres region, Haiti', *Economic Botany*, vol. 16, No. 2, pp. 101–5.

MONROE, Elizabeth, 1954: 'The Shaikhdom of Kuwait', *International Affairs*, vol. XXX, pp. 271–84.

MORAL, P., 1959: *L'Economie Haitienne*, Haiti.

—1961: *Le Paysan Haitien*, Paris.

MOREAU DE ST MÉRY, L. E., 1797: *Description Topographique, Physique, Civile et Historique de la Partie Française de l'Isle Saint Domingue*, vol. I, Philadelphia.

MUKHTYAR, G. C., 1930: *Life and Labour in a South Gujarat Village*, Calcutta.

MYINT, H., 1960: 'The Demand Approach to Economic Development', *The Review of Economic Studies*, vol. XXVII (2), No. 73, pp. 124–32.

MYRDAL, G., 1958: *Rich Lands and Poor; The Road to World Prosperity*. New York.

NASH, June, 1960: *Social Relations in Amatenango: An Activity Analysis*. (Ph.D. thesis, unpub.), Chicago.

NASH, M., 1961: 'The Social Context of Economic Choice in a Small-Scale Society', *Man*, No. 219.

—1958: *Machine-Age Maya*, Mem. 87, American Anthrop. Assn., Glencoe, Ill.

NATH, D., 1950: *A History of Indians in British Guiana*, London.

NEWMAN, P., 1960: 'The economic future of British Guiana', *Social and Economic Studies*, vol. 9, No. 3, pp. 263–96.

NGUYEN, VAN VINH, 1949: 'Savings and Mutual Lending Societies (*Ho*), (Trans. Yale South East Asia Studies), New Haven.

NURKSE, R., 1953: *Problems of Capital Formation in Under-Developed Countries*, Oxford.

O'LOUGHLIN, C., 1958: 'The rice sector in the economy of British Guiana', *Social and Economic Studies*, vol. 7, No. 2, pp. 115–43.

—1959: 'The economy of British Guiana, 1952–56: A National Accounts Study', *Social and Economic Studies*, vol. 8, No. 1 (Special Number).

PANIKAR, P. G. K., 1961: 'Rural Savings in India', *Economic Development and Cultural Change*, X, No. 1, pp. 64–84.

391

PARKINSON, R., 1887: *Im Bismarck Archipel*, Leipzig.

PIGOU, A. C. (ed.), 1925: *Memorials of Alfred Marshall*, London.

POLANYI, K., ARENSBERG, C. M., and PEARSON, H. W., 1957: *Trade and Market in the Early Empires*, Glencoe, Ill.

POSTAN, M. M., 1939: *The Historical Method in Social Science*, Cambridge

PRATT, Jean, 1960: 'Emigration and Unilineal Descent Groups—Study of Marriage', *Eastern Anthropologist*, vol. XIII, No. 4, pp. 147–58, Lucknow.

PUNJAB BOARD OF ECONOMIC ENQUIRY, 1931: *An Economic Survey of Tehong*, Lahore.

—1932–33 *et seq.*: *Family Budget* (Pub. No. 40), Lahore.

QURESHI, A. I., 1945: *Islam and the Rate of Interest*, Lahore.

REAY, Marie, 1959: *The Kuma*, London.

REDFIELD, R., 1956: *Peasant Society and Culture*, Ithaca.

RESERVE BANK OF INDIA, 1954: *All-India Rural Credit Survey, Vol. II, General Report*, Bombay.

—1956a: *All-India Rural Credit Survey, Vol. I, The Survey Report*, Part 1, 'Rural Families', Bombay.

—1956b: *All-India Rural Credit Survey, Vol. III, Technical Report*, Bombay.

—1957: *All-India Rural Credit Survey, Vol. I, The Survey Report*, Part 2, 'Credit Agencies', Bombay.

—1960: 'Estimates of Saving in the Indian Economy', *Reserve Bank of India Bulletin*, XIV, No. 3, pp. 296–327, esp. pp. 320–2.

RICOT, E. P., 1961: 'Contribution a l'étude des marchés haitiens', *Bulletin du Bureau d'Ethnologie*, série 3, No. 27, pp. 46–64.

ROMAIN, J-B., 1955: *Quelques moeurs et coutumes des paysans haitiens*, Thèse de Doctorat (typescript), Paris.

SADIE, J. L., 1960: 'The Social Anthropology of Economic Development', *The Economic Journal*, vol. LXX, pp. 294–303.

SALISBURY, R. F., 1962: *From Stone to Steel*, London.

SAMUELSON, P. A., 1948: *Economics, An Introductory Analysis*, New York, Toronto, London.

SCHNEIDER, O., 1905: *Muschelgeldstudien*, Verein für Erdkunde, Dresden.

SHAH, C. H., 1960: *Conditions of Economic Progress of Farmers*, Bombay.

SHARP, L., *et al.*, 1953: *Siamese Rice Village, a Preliminary Study of Bang Chan*, Bangkok.

SMITH, A. H., 1899: *Village Life in China: a Study in Sociology*, New York.

SMITH, R. T., 1955: 'Land tenure in three Negro villages in British Guiana', *Social and Economic Studies*, vol. 4, No. 1, pp. 70–8.

—1956: *The Negro Family in British Guiana*, London.

—1957: 'Economic aspects of rice production in an East Indian community in British Guiana', *Social and Economic Studies*, vol. 6, No. 4, pp. 502–22.

—1962: *British Guiana*, Oxford.

SMITH, R. T., and JAYAWARDENA, C., 1958: 'Hindu marriage customs in British Guiana', *Social and Economic Studies*, vol. 7, No. 2, pp. 178–94.

—1959: 'Marriage and the Family Amongst East Indians in British Guiana', *Social and Economic Studies*, vol. 8, No. 4, pp. 321–4.

392

Bibliography

SPATE, O. H. K., 1959: *The Fijian People—Economic Problems and Prospects*, Legislative Council of Fiji, Paper No. 13, Suva.

STANNER, W. E. H., 1933-34: 'Ceremonial Economics of the Mulluk Mulluk and Madngella Tribes of the Daly River, North Australia', *Oceania*, IV, pp. 156-75, 458-71.

SWIFT, M. G., 1958: 'A Note on the Durability of Malay Marriages', *Man*, No. 58.

TAX, S., 1937: 'The Municipios of the Midwestern Highlands of Guatemala', *American Anthropologist*, vol. 39, pp. 423-44.

—1953: *Penny Capitalism: A Guatemalan Indian Economy*, Washington.

TITMUSS, R. M., and ABEL-SMITH, B., 1960: *Social Policies and Population Growth in Mauritius*, London.

THORNER, D., 1960: 'The All-India Rural Credit Survey Viewed as a Scientific Enquiry', *The Economic Weekly*, XII, Nos. 23-5, pp. 941-55.

UNDERWOOD, F. W., 1960: *The Marketing system in peasant Haiti*, Yale University Publs. in Anthropology, No. 57, New Haven.

WARD, B. E., 1960: 'Cash or Credit Crops? An Examination of Some Implications of Peasant Commercial Production with Special Reference to the Multiplicity of Traders and Middlemen', *Economic Development and Cultural Change*, vol. VIII, pp. 148-63.

WELLS, A. F., 1953: *Report on Friendly Societies in the West Indies*, London.

WHITE, L., 1959: *The Evolution of Culture*, New York.

WILMINGTON, M. W., 1955: 'Aspects of Moneylending in Northern Sudan', *Middle East Journal*, vol. 9, Washington, D.C., pp. 139-46.

WITTFOGEL, K., 1957: *Oriental Despotism*, Yale.

WOLF, E. R., 1955: 'Types of Latin American Peasantry: A Preliminary Discussion', *American Anthropologist*, vol. 57, pp. 452-71.

YOUNG, A., 1958: *The Approaches to Local Self-government in British Guiana*, London.

INDEX

Australian aborigines, 22
Accountings, 166, 200, 229
Administration, see Government
Aid, foreign or external, 84, 98, 322
Ancestors, 162, 188
Arabs, 231, 246, 247
Arensberg, C., 50
Armstrong, W. E., 16, 26, 38, 39, 41, 42, 43, 44, 45, 46, 47, 48, 49, 51
Associations, see Partnership and Saving, associations
Attitudes (and Beliefs, Values), 21, 22, 35–8, 79–80, 83–4, 90, 97, 98–101, 114–15, 135–7, 144, 150–1, 171–2, 174–5, 185, 210, 227, 260–5, 300–1, 312, 325, 335–6, 377
Ayabe, T., 82n
Aziz, Ungku A., 133n

Bailey, F. G., 106n, 108, 109, 118, 120, 121, 129
Banfield, E. C., 295
Banks and Banking, 65, 66, 77, 135, 136, 175–6, 202, 209, 235, 247, 249–51, 315–16, 321–2, 351, 360–1, 368
Barter, 92
Barth, F., 69, 75
Bascom, W. R., 32
Basseri tribe, chap. 4 passim
Bastien, R., 259n
Bauer, P. T., 269n
Bauer, P. T., and Yamey, B. S., 260n, 382
Baumol, W. J., 36
Belshaw, C. S., 28, 34, 51
Benedict, B., 330n, 331
Bhatt, V. V., 357
Bicycles, 139, 165, 291, 314
Boats (and Canoes), 21 et seq., 40, 43, 49, 193
Bohannan, P., 25, 27
Booker, H. S., 32
Borrowing, see Lending and Loans
Brokers, 128–31, 169, 180
Buddhism, 83–4, 90, 99, 178–9
Buffalo, 88–9, 100, 165–6
Bunzel, Ruth, 41n
Burchett, W. T., 91

Camps, 69–70

Capital: accumulation, 20–3, 60–8, 75–9, 108–12, 114–15, 154, 165–71, 182–6, 190–1, 194–206, 237, 268–71, 293–6, 323, 348 et seq.; forms, 19–20, 24, 40, 70–3, 84, 142, 165, 293; level, 20–1, 43, 48, 157, 194, 209, 210, 293, 299, 312; liquidity, 20, 24–5, 40, 57, 67, 73, 111, 136, 138, 174, 235, 248–9, 251–2, 274; management, 20–3, 27–8, 60–8, 71, 79–80, 174–5, 190–1, 194–5, 252, chap. 12 passim, 290, 299; social, 29, 115–16, 125, 153–4, 193–4, 204–5; substitution between labour and, 62, 86, 111–12, 123–4, 173, 233–4, 238–9, 243, 265–6, 269, 318
Cash crops, 21, 23, 52, 53, 54, 56, 62–3, 66, 67, 89, 105, 118–22, 133, 134, 140–4, 154–5, 190, 257, 272–3, 280, 309, 310, 331
Castes, 107–10, 114–17, 122–4
Cattle, 138–9, 146, 299, 313, 318, 335–6.
Ceremony (see also Feasts, Funerals), 28, 41, 49, 112, 183, 196–7, 205–6, 294, 361
Chang, Roy, 158n
Chiefs, 41–3, 49, 75, 153, 187–8, 189, 195
Chinese (and Cantonese), 59, 60–2, 66, 90, 101–3, 137, 149, 152, 154, chap. 8 passim, chap. 11 passim, 315, 331, 344–5
Choice (and Decision), 23–4, 26–8, 48, 65, 73, 79, 263–4, 371–2, 385
Christianity, 308, 309, 325–6
Churches, 162, 169, 194, 204–5, 325
Cloth (and Clothing), 24, 25, 94, 97, 247, 252, 315, 319–20, 338–9, 358
Cocoa, 21, 53, 54, 62–3, 66, 67
Coconuts (and Copra), 23, 52, 53, 54, 56, 62–3, 66, 67, 133, 190
Codere, Helen, 24
Coffee, 257, 272
Collective bargaining, 114
Comhaire-Sylvain, Suzanne, 259n
Communications (and Roads, Transport), 53, 70, 78, 82–3, 85, 89–91, 104–5, 125, 153, 159, 181, 193–4, 196, 200–1, 205, 232–4, 238, 270, 277–80, 296, 303, 313–14, 334

394

Index

395

Index

Vehicles, 53, 60–1, 63, 64, 67–8, 150, 209, 266–7, 294–5, 319
Voluntary Organizations, 294, 323

Ward, Barbara, 158*n*, 343
Wedgewood, Camilla H., 54*n*
Wells, A. F., 316
Western Society, 28, 32–3, 36, 39, 48, 50, 51, 97, 231
White, L., 41*n*
Wilmington, M. W., 31, 50*n*

Witchcraft (and Magic, Sorcery), 42, 115, 302
Wittfogel, K., 307
Wolf, E. R., 257*n*
Women, economic activities of, 64, 76, 90–1, 112, 137–8, 147–8, 166, 169, 176–7, 212–3, 215–16, chap. 12 *passim*, 297 *et seq.*

Yoruba, 31
Young, A., 308, 310

399

For Product Safety Concerns and Information please contact our
EU representative GPSR@taylorandfrancis.com Taylor & Francis
Verlag GmbH, Kaufingerstraße 24, 80331 München, Germany.